Latin America 1976

Latin America 1976

Edited by Lester A. Sobel

Writer: Christopher Hunt
Indexer: Grace M. Ferrara

FACTS ON FILE, INC.   NEW YORK, N.Y.

Latin America 1976

© Copyright, 1977, by Facts on File, Inc.

All rights reserved. No part of this book may be reproduced in any form without the permission of the publisher except for reasonably brief extracts used in reviews or scholarly works. Published by Facts on File, Inc., 119 West 57th Street, New York, N.Y. 10019.

Library of Congress Catalog Card No. 73-83047
ISBN 0-87196-256-X

9 8 7 6 5 4 3 2 1
PRINTED IN
THE UNITED STATES OF AMERICA

Contents

	Page
FOREWORD	1
REGIONAL DEVELOPMENTS	3
International Relations & Human Rights	3
Economic & Other Developments	16
ARGENTINA	23
Coup Ousts Peron's Widow as President	23
Events Preceding the Coup	24
Military Junta in Command	32
Violence & Violations of Human Rights	37
Other Developments	46
BOLIVIA	49
Violence	49
Earlier Developments	51
Economic Developments	52
BRAZIL	55
Opposition Under Pressure	55
Political Prisoners & Human Rights Abuses	56
Government & Politics	60
Economic Developments	62
Foreign & Other Developments	63
CHILE	65
Torture, Political Imprisonment & Other Human Rights Violations	65

Other Domestic Developments	81
Foreign Relations	83
COLOMBIA	87
Violence & Politics	87
Other Developments	93
CUBA	97
Domestic & Economic Developments	97
Cuban Forces in Angola Assure Victory by MPLA	99
Other Foreign Policy Developments	104
Terrorism	108
Abuses of Political Prisoners	111
ECUADOR	113
Bloodless Military Coup	113
Oil Industry	115
Labor & Other Unrest	116
GUATEMALA	119
Quake Devastates Nation	119
Other Developments	121
MEXICO	123
Lopez Portillo Succeeds Echeverria as President	123
Press Control	125
Leftist Activity & Terrorism	128
Economic Developments	131
Foreign Affairs & Other Developments	134
PANAMA	141
Domestic Affairs & Foreign Involvement	141
Canal Controversy	145
PARAGUAY	149
Abuses of Human Rights	149
Other Developments	152
PERU	155
Domestic Developments	155
Foreign Military Aid	158
PUERTO RICO	161
Controversy Over Status	161
Other Developments	165

URUGUAY	167
Military Depose Bordaberry, Mendez Appointed President	167
Abuses of Human Rights	169
Economic Developments	173
VENEZUELA	175
Foreign Affairs	175
Economic Developments	177
Unrest & Violence	180
OTHER AREAS	185
Bahamas	185
Barbados	185
Belize	186
Costa Rica	187
Dominican Republic	187
El Salvador	188
Grenada	190
Guyana	191
Haiti	193
Honduras	194
Jamaica	195
Nicaragua	197
Trinidad & Tobago	198
INDEX	201

Foreword

THIS IS THE FIFTH VOLUME of the FACTS ON FILE annual on Latin America. It records the history of Latin America and the Caribbean area during 1976.

The purpose of this series if to give researchers, students, educators, librarians and others a convenient, reliable, unbiased and inexpensive source of information on the many events that take place each year in this important part of the world. The 1976 volume, therefore, records the essential details of such events as the deposition of Juan D. Peron's widow as president of Argentina, the increase of violence in Brazil, the earthquake in Guatemala and the dispute between the U.S. and Panama over the future of the Panama Canal and Canal Zone. But it also covers more than just the most important occurrences. It provides facts on economic developments, guerrilla operations, labor action, diplomatic relations, government corruption, political maneuverings, student activism, military affairs and the many other events that make up the history of Latin America and the Caribbean area during 1976.

The material of the book consists largely of the Latin American record compiled by FACTS ON FILE in its weekly reports on world events. Such changes as were made in producing this book were largely for the purpose of eliminating needless repetition, supplying necessary amplification or correcting error. Yet some useful repetition was provided deliberately: for example, when two countries are involved in a single event, the report, or at least part of it, is often carried in the chapter for each of the two countries; this means more complete coverage of each country in the place the reader is most likely to look, makes is less likely that these items will be overlooked and reduces some of the need to consult the index and other chapters to locate a specific fact.

As in all FACTS ON FILE works, a conscientious effort was made to record all events without bias and to produce a reliable and useful reference tool.

Regional Developments

International Relations & Human Rights

SELA meets. The Latin American Economic System (SELA) held its first ministerial meeting at its headquarters in Caracas, Venezuela Jan. 12–15 to discuss broad policy issues and internal organization.

Delegates approved a statement calling for "a new world economic order" and condemning "any form of economic coercion" directed against developing countries by industrial nations, notably the U.S. Trade Reform Act of 1974, which many Latin nations found discriminatory.

The declaration also proclaimed the right of Latin American countries to "regulate the operations of transnational corporations" within their borders. The establishment of Latin American multinational companies was a major goal of SELA; Mexico and Venezuela had presented 60 specific plans for such enterprises.

SELA's members were Argentina, Bolivia, Brazil, Colombia, Costa Rica, Cuba, Chile, Ecuador, El Salvador, Honduras, Guatemala, Guyana, Haiti, Mexico, Jamaica, Paraguay, Nicaragua, the Dominican Republic, Panama, Peru, Trinidad and Tobago, Uruguay and Venezuela. Venezuela would contribute 17% of the organization's budget, while Argentina, Brazil and Mexico would each contribute 12.5%.

Opening the SELA meeting Jan. 12, Venezuelan President Carlos Andres Perez said: "For the first time Latin America has its own permanent forum for the defense of common interests, the adoption of actions for joint economic cooperation and dialogue with the U.S. and other industrial nations."

Russell court scores U.S., 11 regimes. The second Bertrand Russell Tribunal held its third and last session in Rome Jan. 10–17 to study militarism and abuse of human rights in Latin America.

The "court" issued a verdict Jan. 17 condemning the governments of the U.S. and 11 Latin American countries. The Latin regimes were "convicted" of "grave, systematic and repeated violations of the rights of man and of peoples," and the U.S. was found guilty of aiding in these violations, maintaining "colonial domination" over Puerto Rico, committing "military aggressions" against Cuba in 1961 and the Dominican Republic in 1965, and organizing the overthrow of the governments of Guatemala in 1954 and Chile in 1973.

The condemned Latin governments were those of Argentina, Bolivia, Brazil, Chile, Colombia, Guatemala, Haiti, Nicaragua, Paraguay, the Dominican Republic and Uruguay. Brazil's military regime was accused of "genocide," presumably for its mistreatment of Indian tribes in the Amazon region.

The Russell Tribunal was a 26-member international panel headed by Lelio Basso, the Italian Socialist senator, and including ex-President Juan Bosch of the Dominican Republic and the writers Gabriel Garcia Marquez of Colombia and Julio Cortazar of Argentina.

The second Tribunal, which held its first session in Brussels in 1973, disbanded Jan. 17 to make way for a foundation and the Association for the Rights and the Defense of Peoples, which were described as similar to the Tribunal but more universalist in scope. Basso said the new organizations would go beyond the Tribunal's "mechanism of denunciations" to "fight the origins of the diverse forms of oppression which are necessary to the survival of the capitalist system."

In a related development reported Jan. 9, a "systematic increase of human rights violations" in Latin America was protested by the World Council of Churches at its fifth general assembly in Nairobi, Kenya in November and December 1975. "Despite the fact that the majority of the countries in the Latin American community have subscribed to the Universal Declaration of Human Rights, the fundamental rights to health, education, work and a living wage have been either ignored completely or not sufficiently implemented by the majority of the governments," the Council declared.

Kissinger on tour. U.S. Secretary of State Henry Kissinger visited Venezuela, Peru, Brazil, Colombia, Costa Rica and Guatemala Feb. 16-24, conferring with their presidents on trade and other bilateral and international issues.

Kissinger also met in Costa Rica Feb. 24 with the foreign ministers of Honduras, El Salvador, Panama, Nicaragua and Guatemala. He had planned to hold a summit conference there with all Central American presidents, but the meeting had been canceled Feb. 17 after the leaders of Guatemala, El Salvador and Honduras declined to attend because of what they described as pressing domestic matters.

The tour was evidently designed to reaffirm U.S. interest in good relations with Latin America and to smooth over bilateral problems, notably those caused by what Latin American nations charged were discriminatory U.S. trade practices. However, the tour was criticized as merely symbolic in much of the Latin press, and Kissinger was received coolly in Venezuela, Peru and Colombia. Students in those countries and Costa Rica rioted to protest Kissinger's visit.

The highlight of the tour was Kissinger's stop Feb. 19-22 in Brazil, where he met with President Ernesto Geisel and other top officials and signed a consultative agreement Feb. 21 by which the U.S. effectively recognized Brazil as the major power in Latin America. The pact was denounced Feb. 23 in the Mexican, Colombian and Venezuelan press. In the U.S. it was criticized Feb. 26 by Sen. Edward M. Kennedy (D, Mass.), who chided Kissinger for favoring Brazil's repressive military government over more democratic regimes in Latin America.

Under the agreement, the U.S. and Brazil would "normally hold consultations semiannually, on the full range of foreign policy matters, including any specific issue that may be raised by either side." The U.S. secretary of state would travel to Brazil at least once a year to meet with its foreign minister, the pact stipulated.

Kissinger warmly praised his Brazilian hosts, asserting at a dinner in Brasilia that "Brazil's diplomats speak for a nation of greatness—a people taking their place in the front rank of nations, a country of continental proportions with a heart as massive as its geography, a nation now playing a role in the world commensurate with its great history and its even greater promise." Nevertheless, the secretary reportedly promised Brazil little in terms of improved trade relations, telling officials there as in the other Latin nations that the U.S. Congress was blocking the Ford Administration's attempts to change the U.S. Trade Reform Act of 1974 so it no longer discriminated against certain Latin American imports.

Security during Kissinger's visit was tight in Brazil as it was in the other nations on the tour. The building in which Kissinger met President Geisel Feb. 20 was described in press reports as besieged by soldiers. Kissinger was accompanied on the tour by 60 U.S. security agents, and he took along his own bullet-proof limousine for ground transportation.

The tour began Feb. 16 in Caracas, Venezuela. More than 20,000 police and national guardsmen were on hand for Kissinger's arrival, having dispersed hundreds of anti-Kissinger student demonstrators in the city only hours before. Kissinger met Feb. 16 and 17 with President Carlos Andres Perez and his foreign minister, Ramon Escovar Salom, and he made a major address Feb. 17 offering a six-point plan for U.S. cooperation in solving economic and other problems in the Western Hemisphere.

The plan, which offered no major new U.S. initiatives, committed the Ford Administration to: recognize that the more industrial nations in Latin America needed support and capital in their efforts to participate in the world economy; continue foreign aid to the neediest countries still "oppressed by poverty and natural disaster"; support regional and subregional organizations such as the Andean Group, the Central American Common Market and the Caribbean Common Market; negotiate all disputes on the basis of equality; support hemispheric collective security arrangements; and modernize the Organization of American States.

"It is time for all of us in the hemisphere to put aside slogans and turn from rhetoric to resolve," Kissinger told a group of businessmen, legislators and others in announcing the plan. The U.S. felt that it continued to have a "special relationship" with Latin America, he said, though in the past Washington had not "taken sufficiently into account that Latin America had experienced years of frustration in which lofty promises by the United States had been undone by the gradualism of the American political system, which responds less to abstract commitments than to concrete problems."

President Perez said Feb. 17 that he and Kissinger had discussed trade, oil and Cuban intervention in Angola, among other issues. The talks were reportedly cordial but cool. Perez said Kissinger had agreed to press for changes in the U.S. Trade Reform Act and to support the Latin American Economic System (SELA), and Kissinger said Venezuela and the U.S. generally agreed on the Angola issue.

The U.S. and Venezuela Feb. 17 issued a joint communique envisioning closer cooperation in energy research, educational development and narcotics control.

A student was killed in Caracas Feb. 17 as demonstrations continued against Kissinger's visit and protesters clashed with national guardsmen. Students and police clashed again the next day, leading authorities to close the major university campus and most high schools.

Kissinger continued to Lima, Peru Feb. 18, where he conferred with President Francisco Morales Bermudez and Foreign Minister Miguel Angel de la Flor. The talks were notably cool, according to the Mexican newspaper Excelsior Feb. 20; Morales forced Kissinger to wait outside his office for 10 minutes before their 55-minute meeting.

(In the days preceding Kissinger's arrival Peruvian officials had privately expressed doubts that the secretary could aid them in obtaining more loans and credits from the U.S. and other Western financial sources, according to the New York Times Feb. 19. Peru was short of foreign exchange, with reserves listed at $150 million in December 1975.)

Kissinger declared on arrival in Peru that the U.S. "understands and respects the objectives of the Peruvian revolution." He said "Peru has played a responsible role in its policy of nonalignment but at the same time we are part of the Western Hemisphere and we meet together frequently to discuss issues of common concern."

Kissinger and his hosts reportedly discussed Peru's nationalization of U.S. businesses and Cuba's intervention in Angola. Peru Feb. 20 recognized the Cuban-backed Popular Movement for the Liberation of Angola (MPLA), which the U.S. had opposed throughout the Angolan civil war.

Police in Lima had used tear gas to disperse anti-Kissinger student demonstrators Feb. 17. During Kissinger's visit Feb. 18 a group of students stoned the U.S. embassy before they were routed by authorities.

After the conclusion of his visit to Brazil, Kissinger flew Feb. 22 to Colombia, where students in Bogota and Medellin were rioting for the third day against his visit. He met Feb. 22 and 23 with President Alfonso Lopez Michelsen and Foreign Minister Indalecio Lievano

Aguirre. Lopez said at a press conference with Kissinger Feb. 23 that Colombia supported Panama's efforts to gain control over the Panama Canal and Zone, and that it would recognize the MPLA in Angola. In response to a question, Lopez refused to condemn Cuban intervention in Angola and he made a veiled reference to U.S. intervention in Vietnam in the 1960s and early 1970s.

Kissinger continued Feb. 23 to Costa Rica, where Foreign Minister Gonzalo Facio hailed him as "one of the greatest architects of world peace" and some 30,000 student demonstrators denounced him as "the principal architect" of the military coup in Chile in 1973. Facio praised the U.S. policy of detente with the Soviet Union and said Costa Rica proudly counted itself as a U.S. ally.

Kissinger stopped in Guatemala briefly on his return flight to the U.S. Feb. 24. He viewed some areas of Guatemala City that were badly damaged by an earthquake Feb. 4, and he pledged more U.S. reconstruction aid to Guatemala in a conference with President Kjell Laugerud Garcia. Back in Washington Kissinger briefed President Ford on his trip Feb. 25.

Kissinger reports on U.S.-Latin American relations—Kissinger reported at a hearing of the House Committee on International Relations March 4 about his February trip to Latin America and about U.S.-Latin American relations in general. He said in his prepared statement:

"... Latin America is changing. The nations of Latin America are experiencing, each in its own particular way, the stress of transition, internally from the rigid to the dynamic, internationally from dependence to interdependence.

"The quality of their ties to our country is changing in the process. The United States is experiencing a more open relationship with the nations of Latin America, a relationship which now turns, not on the memories of an earlier age of tutelage, on pretensions by us to hegemony or on national inequality, but on mutual respect, common interests and cooperative problem-solving.

"Yet, though our ties with them may be changing, the nations of Latin America have a new meaning and importance for us, for they are emerging in their own right on the global scene. This is so because:

"They are increasingly important factors in world commodity, mineral and energy markets;

"They hold the potential to become a region for increased agricultural output, to feed the world's hungry;

"And, perhaps most noteworthy, they are playing a more significant role in the political councils of the world, not merely because of their enhanced economic strength, but also because of their growing solidarity with the other developing countries of Africa and Asia and their juridical traditions of personal respect, national dignity and international collaboration which counts for so much in the arenas of world politics.

"Our policy in the Americas in the years ahead must recognize these new realities—of change in Latin America, and of the fundamental importance of Latin America to the world interests of the United States. We cannot take the nations of this hemisphere for granted. We should put aside earlier temptations to crusade. We must create a new, healthier relationship. We can accept and indeed welcome the emergence of the nations of Latin America into global importance. And we must preserve our special hemispheric ties, without slogans. . . .

"The inter-American experience of the recent past has helped illuminate these imperatives of our future relationships with Latin America. In the 1960s, the Alliance for Progress rallied by the energies and enthusiasms of people throughout the Americas. By 1969, its promises had begun to fade, and the nations of Latin America gathered together at Vina del Mar to stake out a new agenda of issues between us. In 1973, I called for a new dialogue between the United States and Latin America. At the meetings in Mexico City and Washington, the Foreign Ministers of the Americas met to discuss the Vina del Mar issues. Those meetings, however, were interrupted almost exactly a year ago, by the enactment of the Trade Act and the exclusion of Venezuela and Ecuador from the generalized system of preferences.

"Yet, if the new dialogue did not yield final results, it did teach some lessons about our future efforts to perfect the undeniable community which exists in this part of the world. For it demonstrated:

"On the one hand, the difficulties which await both the United States and Latin

America when the two sides attempt to reduce the complexity of their relationships to a series of demands for quick and categorical response and,

"On the other, that the regular, recurring non-rhetorical examination of our common problems together is a constructive mode of dealing with them.

"My trip to Latin America was an effort to do just that....

"In Venezuela, I saw a country not content to husband its own affluence but determined to promote the common destiny of Latin America. I made clear that we welcomed this and that we were confident that as long as they served higher purposes than confrontation we were prepared to cooperate with regional organizations and institutions which expressed the increased sense of solidarity and common purpose with Latin America.

"Brazil is an emerging world power, with broadened international interests and responsibilities, not by virtue of our granting them that rank, but by the reality of what Brazil has accomplished.... [A] memorandum of agreement which I signed with the Brazilian foreign minister, establishing procedures for consultation between our two governments on issues of common substantive concern, was a recognition of that plain fact.

"The bilateral relationship between the United States and Brazil is becoming more important and more complex all the time; at the same time Brazil's voice and influence in world councils is also growing. It was in recognition of Brazil's new world role that we institutionalized ... increased consultations which will be required, just as we have with the nations of Western Europe, Canada, and Japan. The Brazilian consultative agreement is bilateral. It touches only our relations with Brazil. While it reflects the reality of Brazil's international status, it does not affect our relations with any other country or represent an attempt to manage Latin America by proxy. I explained to the Presidents of the other countries which I visited that we are prepared to enter into similar arrangements with other nations in the Western Hemisphere, if they so desire....

"Peru's unique experiment of internal development and social change demonstrates the creative worth of the diversity in this Hemisphere. We accept the sovereignty of each Latin American state. Our policy, I said, is to support the aspirations and objectives of their program of social change, to conciliate differences before they become conflicts and to cooperate with the authentic development efforts of each of the nations of the Hemisphere.

"In Colombia, I saw at first hand another of the Hemisphere's practicing democracies, a nation with whom we have the warmest of relations and with whom we can discuss world political and security issues without complexes and with considerable profit. The single serious matter on our mutual agenda is trade, for improved access to our markets and to those of the other developed countries is vital to the success of that democracy....

"Throughout my trip, I emphasized that the United States regards our Hemispheric ties and responsibilities with a special seriousness and special hope. In a spirit of solidarity, I pledge that we should:

"Respond to the development needs of the more industrialized nations of the Hemisphere, and to the region as a whole; in the areas of trade and international finance;

"Assist on concessional terms the efforts of the neediest nations to advance themselves;

"Support and work with Latin American regional efforts to organize for cooperation and integration;

"Negotiate our differences with any nation or nations on the basis of mutual respect and sovereign equality;

"Maintain our firm commitment to mutual security against any who would undermine our common effort, threaten independence or export violence and terror; and

"Modernize and strengthen the inter-American system, by working with the other member states to develop new structures and processes in the OAS itself and with other organizations, to meet the new realities of our Hemisphere.

"These six points met with a positive response throughout my visit....

"The [U.S.] legislative threat of political retaliation, by cutting off the United States market or stopping multilateral aid projects, directed to states which do not follow our principles in nationalizing property within their borders, are still matters of concern in Latin America. I have suggested that if Latin America and the United States could develop a multinational code regulating both national and corporate behavior in investments and investment disputes, this would enhance the confidence in the [U.S.] Congress that compensation issues, at least, could be settled without the need for automatic statutory retaliation.

"As to trade policy, the system of generalized preferences in the Trade Act was an important advance in our relationship with Latin America, for their development aspirations depend on improved access to world markets, including our own. The exclusion of Venezuela and Ecuador from GSP did serious damage to the United States in the eyes of Latin America. We hope that Congress can give early and sympathetic consideration to repealing this legislation.

"I found considerable fear that our trade policies are becoming generally more protectionist, as reflected by new countervailing duty actions, escape clause cases and other restrictive measures taken with regard to imports from Latin America in the past year under the Trade Act. I also found new evidence of a willingness to conciliate and compromise some of the outstanding trade disputes, if the United States is in a position to respond reciprocally in a spirit of mutual accommodation....

"Latin America is still intensely interested in solving the problem of fluctuating commodity export earnings.

"The fact that the Administration will be requesting that the Congress approve United States participation in the new International Coffee Agreement and the International Tin Agreement has been widely applauded in the Hemisphere.... [T]hese agreements are of vital importance to Colombia, Brazil and Central America in the case of the Coffee Agreement and to Bolivia in the case of the tin accord and will be seen throughout the Hemisphere as earnest of our sincere desire to cooperate in their development efforts.

"Beyond that, I pointed out that the United States is prepared to work with other countries on a case-by-case approach to other commodities, and that in selecting commodities for such consideration, we would pay particular attention to those items of interest to the nations of Latin America.

"Exports take time. Meanwhile, the nations of Latin America continue to need considerable development assistance, on non-concessional terms in the case of most, to finance essential imports and capital investments. This session, Congress has before it the legislation to authorize and appropriate funds for our development assistance efforts through the Inter-American Development Bank, the World Bank complex and the Agency for International Development. The legislation providing for replenishment of the ordinary capital and the Fund for Special Operations of the Inter-American Development Bank is of particular importance to our Latin American policy, for that Bank is now the single most important source of official development capital for the nations of the Hemisphere...."

OAS meets in Chile. The Organization of American States approved a series of mild resolutions on regional economic, political and social issues at its sixth General Assembly in Santiago, Chile June 4–18.

The human rights issue dominated the meeting, primarily because Chile's military rulers had been accused repeatedly of violating individual liberties since they seized power in 1973. Mexico boycotted the assembly to protest the selection of Chile as host country. Its foreign minister said May 20 that Mexico would not contribute to the "legitimization" of a government that was "built on the death of Chilean democracy and the tomb of [President] Salvador Allende."

The assembly June 18 passed a compromise resolution that urged Chile "to continue adopting measures to assure the observance of human rights and to give the [OAS'] Inter-American Commission on Human Rights the cooperation it needs to carry out its work." The measure passed 19–1, with Jamaica voting against it and Chile and Brazil abstaining.

Jamaican delegate Patricia Durrant denounced the OAS for passing such a mild resolution after its human rights commission reported widespread torture and other abuse of human rights in Chile. According to Durrant, Jamaica would not join in the "conspiracy of silence" regarding the "absence of justice" in Chile.

Venezuela and Costa Rica had joined Jamaica in calling for a stronger denunciation of rights-abuse in Chile based on the commission's report.

A compromise was also reached on the most controversial economic issue before the assembly, the allegedly discriminatory clauses of the U.S. Trade Reform Act of 1974. The resolution adopted June 18 expressed "concern and dismay" over a clause that excluded Venezuela and Ecuador from preferential U.S. trade benefits because they belonged to the Organization of Petroleum Exporting Countries. It asked the U.S. to amend the act so it responded to "the interests and needs of the development of the Latin American countries."

A stronger condemnation of the act had been proposed by Ecuador, Venezuela, Colombia and Peru.

Among other resolutions passed June 18, the assembly:

- Expressed "hope" that by the end of 1976 the U.S. and Panama would conclude a new Panama Canal treaty that would eliminate "the causes of conflict between the two countries."
- Asked the Permanent Council of the OAS to inform all member nations of any proposals to reform the OAS charter that would be presented to an extraordinary OAS session in Lima, Peru. The session had not yet been scheduled.
- Pledged financial aid to Paraguay and Bolivia, Latin America's only land-locked nations.

The human rights issue dominated the assembly from the opening speech June 4 by Chilean President Augusto Pinochet Ugarte. Pinochet denied that human rights were violated in Chile and proposed that the OAS create a new human rights unit whose "right of action" and access to Latin nations would be "precisely defined." The proposal, which would apparently undercut the Inter-American Commission on Human Rights, was later rejected by the assembly.

Pinochet denounced the "armed expansionism" of the Soviet Union and called on all Latin American nations to join the U.S. in an "ideological war" against communism. "Peaceful coexistence" and "comfortable neutralisms" contained the "seeds of suicide," he asserted.

Pinochet said Chile had "freed itself from the imminent establishment of a Marxist-Leninist tyranny and had begun to build a new democracy through the creation of a new juridical institutionality." Soon the Chilean government would enact a series of constitutional reforms regarding human rights that would make the Chilean constitution "one of the most advanced and complete documents in the world," he declared.

Chile had announced the release of 305 political prisoners in May in an attempt to show the U.S. and other OAS members that it was concerned about human rights. However, lawyers and Roman Catholic priests in Chile claimed that month that political arrests were continuing.

The first 49 political prisoners were freed May 6, one day before U.S. Treasury Secretary William Simon arrived in Santiago for two days of economic talks. Simon said May 7 that U.S. aid to Chile was dependent on the military government's respect for human rights. He also praised the government for "clearly establishing the bases for economic development." In Washington May 16, Simon said he would ask Congress to continue economic aid to Chile without any further cuts.

Simon and the Chilean government announced May 19 that 49 more Chilean prisoners were being freed. Another 207 were released May 26. Nevertheless, a group of exiled Chilean ex-congressmen reported in New York May 20 that hundreds of Chileans had been arrested in the previous few weeks in a new wave of political repression.

Pinochet announced during the OAS assembly June 7 that another 60 political prisoners were being released. He allowed OAS Secretary General Alejandro Orfila to visit the Tres Alamos detention camp and he permitted the Santiago newspaper El Mercurio to print the text of a heretofore secret report by the Inter-American Commission on Human Rights that denounced widespread rights abuse by Chilean authorities.

The report's text, published June 9, had been circulating among delegates to the assembly. It detailed cases of arbitrary arrest, torture and summary execution by Chilean security forces, particularly the National Intelligence Directory (DINA), the political police force that answered only to Pinochet.

El Mercurio also printed the text of a long refutation of the report by the Chilean government. The regime said the report was based on "declarations of persons without scruples or badly informed," and argued that it was necessary to "maintain legal and administrative measures that limit the freedoms and rights of man in order to protect precisely the most important right of all, the right to a secure life."

Orfila said June 18 that at Tres Alamos he had spoken with imprisoned former government officials and with representatives of women prisoners, and that none had complained of torture. Visitors to the camp said later that women prisoners became angry when they learned of Orfila's statement, the New York Times reported June 21. A report by lawyers on the treatment of 85 women held in the camp until May said that 62 of the women had been raped and more than half had been subjected to electric shocks during interrogation after their arrest, the Times noted.

Five Chilean lawyers gave delegates to OAS assembly another report on extensive rights abuse by DINA agents, it was reported June 12. With at least 12,000 military and civilian employes, and a secret budget, DINA had become Pinochet's most powerful base of support, the lawyers said. Its personnel were forbidden to appear in court, forcing the Supreme Court and appeals courts "to close the cases involving homicide, kidnapping, disappearances and violations resulting from arrests" because of a lack of witnesses.

The lawyers' report provoked angry retorts from official Chilean spokesmen and from Jaime Eyzaguirre, president of the Supreme Court. Eyzaguirre said there should be no control over DINA under Chile's current state of siege. A government spokesman called the report "an unspeakable act of treason" by the lawyers, who included Jaime Castillo Velasco, a former justice minister and Christian Democrat.

(Before the OAS assembly began, another report denouncing DINA's "uncontrolled power" had been issued by the Roman Catholic "Vicariate of Solidarity" in Santiago, it was reported June 3. The report, which detailed widespread rights abuse by DINA since 1974, was signed by Bishop Enrique Alvear, whose religious office made him virtually immune from arrest. Hernan Montealegre, a lawyer for the vicariate, was arrested May 12.)

Chile was not the only nation criticized at the assembly for violating human rights. The Inter-American Commission on Human Rights appealed to Cuba to take immediate steps to end what the commission called "cruel, inhuman and degrading" treatment of Cuban political prisoners, it was reported June 11. A report by the commission, which did not visit Cuba, said individuals and organizations had given it information that provided a "solid basis" for the belief that Cuba treated its political prisoners with "complete disdain."

Amnesty International charges widespread atrocities—The U.S. affiliate of Amnesty International (A.I.U.S.A.) called on the OAS June 4 to take more effective action to curb what it described as "increasing violations of human rights in Latin America, including systematic use of torture, disappearance, the recent murders of parliamentarians in Argentina and uncontrolled activities of military intelligence services." In a cable to the secretary general of the OAS, A.I.U.S.A. Chairman Ivan Morris said:

Amnesty International, USA most respectfully submits the following recommendations upon the occasion of the 6th general assembly meeting of the OAS.
1. The Inter-American Commission on Human Rights of the OAS be allowed free access to investigate all reports of violations of human rights in any member state.
2. The U.N. Human Rights Commission visit Chile within the next 30 days as announced following U.S. Secretary of the Treasury William E. Simon's visit to Chile in mid-May.
3. The Inter-American Commission on Human Rights Report on Chile be thoroughly discussed at this General Assembly.
4. The rights of refugees and exiles in all member nations be guaranteed according to international legal norms.

I.A.U.S.A. said in the accompanying statement:

Amnesty International urges the OAS to fully discuss the agenda item of the report of the Inter-American Commission on Human Rights in Chile. This report which accuses the military junta of "very grave violations of human rights" is dated November 21, 1974. At last year's meeting, following a private agreement among member nations, the OAS General Assembly refused to discuss the report, giving as a reason the impending visit to Chile of the U.N. Human Rights Commission which was then denied entrance by the Chilean government.
As pointed out in a recent article in the New York Times by Jose Zalaquett, a lead-

REGIONAL DEVELOPMENTS

ing Chilean human rights lawyer arrested and deported to France after having spoken to three visiting U.S. Congressmen about human rights violations, "Although the junta is carrying out fewer arrests, it has recently undertaken new measures to increase fear and silence critics. They are directed primarily against the churches, universities, labor unions and some elements of the news media."

Amnesty International has recently learned of new arrests of at least 185 people in Antofagasta May 18th, and of further arrests of trade union leaders and members of the Communist party in the Santiago region on the 17th and 18th of May. Those arrested in Antofagasta have been taken to prison in Santiago.

This recent wave of arrests only underlines another point by Zalaquett, "A sophisticated totalitarian government is more dangerous than a crude one and the recent Chilean developments show the increased sophistication of the junta. But there is no evidence of any real progress for human rights."

The situation of "disappeared persons" is extreme in Chile and becoming so in Argentina. In his testimony before the U.S. House of Representatives subcommittee on International Organizations on May 5, 1976 Jose Zalaquett testified that the files of the Chilean ecumenical Committee for Peace included approximately 1,040 prisoners who have disappeared after being arrested whom the government does not acknowledge as even being placed under arrest....

If the OAS does not produce a clear statement on the issue of human rights, then the Chilean government will have succeeded in its tactic of making small temporary concessions with human lives during periods of increased international pressure, while continuing to silence all internal protest.

A.I.U.S.A. notes with deep regret the recent deaths of Uruguayan exiles arrested in Buenos Aires. Their bodies, most bearing marks of torture, were found in the outskirts of Buenos Aires on May 20th. These included two former Uruguayan parliamentarians, Senator Zelmar Michelini and Hector Gutierrez Ruiz, former President of the Uruguayan Chamber of Representatives. Another Uruguayan, Dr. Manuel Liberoff, disappeared at the same time and is still missing.

A.I.U.S.A. is alarmed at the recent tendency toward the abandonment of the traditional right to asylum and lack of tolerance toward political exiles and refugees.

In his inaugural address as President of Argentina in March, General Jorge Rafael Videla promised to respect human rights. Foreign Minister Cesar Augusto Guzetti assured the United Nations High Commissioner for Refugees April 5th that the thousands of political refugees from other countries living in Argentina will not be persecuted or returned to their countries of origin. There is overwhelming evidence to the contrary....

In spite of statements made by the new Argentine authorities that international law would be respected and the rights of refugees protected, reports from Argentina prove otherwise. There are approximately 9,000 defacto refugees who have been declared eligible for U.N. High Commission for Refugees protection but who have not been granted asylum. There are reports of "black lists" that have been circulated to embassies in Argentina naming people who must not be granted asylum.

It is alarming to us that the Argentine government has banned the press to report on arrests, disappearances or killings. Reports received by Amnesty International range from between nine and 30,000 arrests since the military takeover, but there are no reliable estimates as lists of detainees have not been issued even in the face of increasing international pressure. This lack of information is clearly disturbing to the population and to the relatives of arrested or disappeared persons who have no access to information about the fate of their family members....

A.I.U.S.A. also is concerned at reports that members of the Argentinian police and military are involved in the parapolice organization, Argentinian Anticommunist Alliance (AAA) responsible for over 2,000 killings before the March 1976 military coup and for at least 300 further assassinations after. It questions what steps have been taken to curb the activities of the AAA.

Just as in Chile after the September 1973 coup, Latin American exiles in Argentina are subject to persecution, torture and assassination because, in the eyes of the security forces, exiles are seen as potential "subversive" elements....

Amnesty International mounted a worldwide campaign this spring to exercise pressure on the Uruguayan authorities and to create mode awareness about the human rights situation in Uruguay. There are further reports that torture has not stopped—further reports brings the total to 28 known cases of death under torture. Amnesty International estimates there are 4000 political prisoners in Uruguay, a county of 2.5 million people.

Reports from Brazil indicate that many journalists (including Vladimir Herzog, who died in custody in October, 1975), trade unionists, lawyers and workers have been arrested during the past year for alleged connections with the Partido Comunista Brasilero (PCB), and there has been a consistent pattern of torture used to extract confessions, aimed at substantiation of the government's claims that the Movimiento Democratico Brasileiro (MDB) has links with the illegal communist party. Many of the accused have consistently denied the charges or retracted confessions extracted through torture. The estimated number of persons detained over the period of January to November 1975 has been put at 1500. Almost all reports of detention received by Amnesty

International over the past 12 months have been accompanied by allegations of maltreatment which range from psychological intimidation to the most brutal forms of torture.

Another wave of repression was launched by the Paraguayan authorities in early April, 1976, after the alleged discovery of a new guerrilla network, called the Organizacion Politico-Militar (OPM). Similar waves of violent repression in Paraguay have been carried out in the past. A conservative estimate says that about 350 people were arrested during April 1976. The Police Investigation Department—a place noted for the continuing use of barbaric torture was still crowded with many of the 200 people reportedly arrested or disappeared in late November and throughout December 1975. ...

Kissinger backs human rights, close trade ties—U.S. Secretary of State Henry Kissinger attended the OAS assembly June 7-10. He expressed U.S. support for observance of human rights, for close trade ties with Latin America and for a reduction of the OAS bureaucracy.

Addressing the assembly June 8, Kissinger noted reports of human rights abuse in Chile but stopped short of condemning the military government. "The condition of human rights as assessed by the Organization of American States' Human Rights Commission has impaired [the U.S.'] relationship with Chile and will continue to do so," he said. "We wish this relationship to be close, and all friends of Chile hope that obstacles raised by conditions alleged in the report will soon be removed."

Kissinger pledged June 9 that the U.S. would take a number of unilateral steps to improve trade relations with Latin American nations, including efforts by President Ford to add Latin American products to the list of goods accorded special preferences by the U.S. He urged Latin nations to take steps of their own to improve trade ties with the U.S.

Kissinger proposed June 10 that the OAS make drastic changes in its structure and financing to prevent it from becoming what U.S. officials had called "increasingly irrelevant." The OAS bureaucracy should be cut back and the U.S.' share of the OAS budget should be reduced from the current two-thirds, Kissinger said.

Kissinger visited Santiago during a four-nation Latin American tour that included stops in the Dominican Republic June 6-7, Bolivia June 7 and Mexico June 10-13. In Mexico Kissinger pledged to work to improve U.S.-Mexican trade relations and to study "with care" proposals for an exchange of prisoners held in Mexico and the U.S. American prisoners claimed they had been mistreated by Mexican authorities.

Excerpts from Kissinger's statement on human rights before the OAS assembly:

One of the most compelling issues of our time, and one which calls for the concerted action of all responsible peoples and nations, is the necessity to protect and extend the fundamental rights of humanity.

The precious common heritage of our Western Hemisphere is the conviction that human beings are the subjects, not the objects of public policy; that citizens must not become mere instruments of the state.

This is the conviction that brought millions to the Americas. It inspired our peoples to fight for their independence. It is the commitment that has made political freedom and individual dignity the constant and cherished ideal of the Americas and the envy of nations elsewhere. It is the ultimate proof that our countries are linked by more than geography and the impersonal forces of history.

Respect for the rights of man is written into the founding documents of every nation of our Hemisphere. It has long been part of the common speech and daily lives of our citizens. And today, more than ever, the successful advance of our societies requires the full and free dedication of the talent, energy, and creative thought of men and women who are free from fear of repression.

The modern age has brought undreamed-of benefits to mankind—in medicine, in technological advance, and in human communication. But it has spawned plagues as well, in the form of new tools of oppression, as well as of civil strife. In an era characterized by terrorism, by bitter ideological contention, by weakened bonds of social cohesion, and by the yearning of order even at the expense of liberty, the result all too often has been the violation of fundamental standards of humane conduct. ...

The shortcomings of our efforts in an age which continues to be scarred by forces of intimidation, terror, and brutality fostered sometimes from outside national territories and sometimes from inside, have made it dramatically clear that basic human rights must be preserved, cherished, and defended if peace and prosperity are to be more than hollow technical achievements. For technological progress without social justice mocks humanity; national unity without freedom is sterile; nationalism without a consciousness of human community—which means a shared concern for human rights—refines instruments of oppression.

We in the Americas must increase our international support for the principles of justice, freedom, and human dignity—for the organized concern of the community of nations remains one of the most potent weapons in the struggle against the degradation of human values.

The ultimate vitality and virtue of our societies spring from the instinctive sense of human dignity and respect for the rights of others that have long distinguished the immensely varied peoples and lands of this Hemisphere. The genius of our inter-American heritage is based on the fundamental democratic principles of human and national dignity, justice, popular participation, and free cooperation among different peoples and social systems. . . .

The central problem of government has always been to strike a just and effective balance between freedom and authority. When freedom degenerates into anarchy, the human personality becomes subject to arbitrary, brutal, and capricious forces. When the demand for order overrides all other considerations, man becomes a means and not an end, a tool of impersonal machinery. Clearly, some forms of human suffering are intolerable no matter what pressures nations may face or feel. Beyond that, all societies have an obligation to enable their people to fulfill their potentialities and live a life of dignity and self-respect.

As we address this challenge in practice, we must recognize that our efforts must engage the serious commitment of our societies. As a source of dynamism, strength, and inspiration, verbal posturings and self-righteous rhetoric are not enough. Human rights are the very essence of a meaningful life, and human dignity is the ultimate purpose of government. No government can ignore terrorism and survive, but it is equally true that a government that tramples on the rights of its citizens denies the purpose of its existence.

In recent years and even days, our newspapers have carried stories of kidnappings, ambushes, bombings, and assassinations. Terrorism and the denial of civility have become so widespread, political subversions so intertwined with official and unofficial abuse, and so confused with oppression and base criminality, that the protection of individual rights and the preservation of human dignity have become sources of deep concern and—worse—sometimes of demoralization and indifference.

No country, no people—for that matter no political system—can claim a perfect record in the field of human rights. But precisely because our societies in the Americas have been dedicated to freedom since they emerged from the colonial era, our shortcomings are more apparent and more significant. And let us face facts. Respect for the dignity of man is declining in too many countries of the Hemisphere. There are several states where fundamental standards of humane behavior are not observed. All of us have a responsibility in this regard, for the Americas cannot be true to themselves unless they rededicate themselves to belief in the worth of the individual and to the defense of those individual rights which that concept entails. . . .

Procedures alone cannot solve the problem, but they can keep it at the forefront of our consciousness and they can provide certain minimum protection for the human personality. International law and experience have enabled the development of specific procedures to distinguish reasonable from arbitrary government action on, for example, the question of detention. These involve access to courts, counsel, and families; prompt release or charge; and, if the latter, fair and public trial. Where such procedures are followed, the risk and incidence of unintentional government error, of officially sanctioned torture, of prolonged arbitrary deprivation of liberty, are drastically reduced. Other important procedures are habeas corpus or amparo, judicial appeal, and impartial review of administrative actions. And there are the procedures available at the international level—appeal to, and investigation and recommendations by established independent bodies such as the Inter-American Commission on Human Rights, an integral part of the OAS and a symbol of our dedication to the dignity of man. . . .

We have all read the two reports submitted to this General Assembly by the Commission. They are sobering documents, for they provide serious evidence of violations of elemental international standards of human rights.

In its annual report on human rights in the Hemisphere, the Commission cites the rise of violence and speaks of the need to maintain order and protect citizens against armed attack. But it also upholds the defense of individual rights as a primordial function of the law and describes case after case of serious governmental actions in derogation of such rights.

A second report is devoted exclusively to the situation in Chile. We note the Commission's statement that the Government of Chile has cooperated with the Commission, and the Commission's conclusion that the infringement of certain fundamental rights in Chile has undergone a quantitative reduction since the last report. We must also point out that Chile has filed a comprehensive and responsive answer that sets forth a number of hopeful prospects which we hope will soon be fully implemented.

Nevertheless the Commission has asserted that violations continue to occur, and this is a matter of bilateral as well as international attention. In the United States, concern is widespread in the Executive Branch, in the press, and in the Congress, which has taken the extraordinary step of enacting specific statutory limits on United States military and economic aid to Chile.

The condition of human rights as assessed by the OAS Human Rights Commission has impaired our relationship with Chile and will continue to do so. We wish this relationship to be close, and all friends of Chile hope that obstacles raised by conditions alleged in the report will soon be removed. . . .

The Commission has worked and reported widely. Its survey of human rights in Cuba

is ample evidence of that. Though the report was completed too late for formal consideration at this General Assembly, an initial review confirms our worst fears of Cuban behavior. We should commend the Commission for its efforts—in spite of the total lack of cooperation of the Cuban authorities—to unearth the truth that many Cuban political prisoners have been victims of inhuman treatment. We urge the Commission to continue its efforts to determine the truth about the state of human rights in Cuba....

We can use the occasion of this General Assembly to emphasize that the protection of human rights is an obligation not simply of particular countries whose practices have come to public attention. Rather, it is an obligation assumed by all the nations of the Americas as part of their participation in the Hemispheric system.

To this end, the United States proposes that the Assembly broaden the Commission's mandate so that instead of waiting for complaints it can report regularly on the status of human rights throughout the Hemisphere.

Through adopting this proposal, the nations of the Americas would make plain our common commitment to human rights, increase the reliable information available to us and offer more effective recommendations to governments about how best to improve human rights. In support of such a broadened effort, we propose that the budget and staff of the Commission be enlarged. By strengthening the contribution of this body, we can deepen our dedication to the special qualities of rich promise that make our Hemisphere a standard-bearer for freedom-loving people in every quarter of the globe.

At the same time, we should also consider ways to strengthen the inter-American system in terms of protection against terrorism, kidnapping and other forms of violent threats to the human personality, especially those inspired from the outside.

It is a tragedy that the forces of change in our century—a time of unparalleled human achievement—have also visited upon many individuals around the world a new dimension of intimidation and suffering....

Orfila on 'challenges.' OAS Secretary General Alejandro Orfila, speaking before the National Press Club in September, described three of the "pressing challenges which, I believe, require critical examination." He listed them as "the challenge of the new development agenda before the Americas; the strengthening of the OAS' role as the principal multilateral forum of the Americas; the resurgence of hemispheric concerns for the protection of human rights." Among excerpts from Orfila's remarks:

The foremost challenge ahead is that beyond long-standing security issues a new agenda is at hand in the Americas—not just the traditional one of the past but the agenda of integral human development: political, cultural, economic and social, for the millions of Americans who remain outside the mainstream of contemporary life and opportunity....

Throughout the post-war period Latin America has, of course, made economic and social progress. There has been a reasonable growth of production, economies and exports have been diversified, and non-traditional industries have appeared upon the scene. These advances have coincided with growing complexities in the social structure and with greater opportunities for individual advancement.

But this is only part of the picture. The more important part is evident from a comparison of the hemisphere's past with its future. Twenty-five years ago Latin America had the same population as the United States. Twenty-five years from now Latin America will have 600 million people—twice the number projected for the United States. In this situation the crucial test for Latin American countries will be to provide millions of new jobs, increased food production, further reduce severe poverty, educate millions of citizens and modernize their societies.

Not everyone is fully aware of the dimensions of this new agenda. However, I think it critical for us to grasp that hemispheric debate is centering around several major areas of concern which are closely linked to each other. Aside from pending bilateral matters such as the future of the Panama Canal, Latin America now believes that to confront this agenda it must discover newer and more adequate instruments so as to increase income from exports while stabilizing markets for primary products; rapidly accelerate the expansion of trade; transfer technology in ways adapted to national needs; provide a code of conduct for multinational corporations; promote joint venture investment; and re-channel foreign assistance so that debt financing becomes less burdensome and alternative financing opportunities are opened up.

We in this hemisphere especially recognize that the priority issue on the development agenda is for Latin America to generate more foreign exchange without going deeper and deeper into debt. It seems evident that Latin America must seek ways and means to expand export earnings to help finance the heavy international debt burden.

I lay bare no diplomatic secrets when I take note that during the past decade Latin America has generally found the United States wanting in confronting this newer, more complex and less tractable hemispheric development agenda....

It would be wrong not to observe that in some major ways the United States has supported Latin America's development initiatives and given them strong encouragement and support. It must be pointed out, however, that the great experiments in multi-

REGIONAL DEVELOPMENTS

lateral cooperation such as the Alliance for Progress, have withered away.

Newer attempts to lay different bases for collective effort, such as the Dialogue of Tlatelolco in 1974, have not achieved a level of organized endeavor comparable to that of the Alliance for Progress, nor have they helped institute a process for making significant response to urgent problems that await solutions.

Nonetheless, this year Secretary Kissinger has made a number of major policy overtures and important proposals to reverse that situation of drift and indecision. Congressional bodies have also been re-evaluating the U.S. "special relationship" with Latin America in the light of these changing conditions. We at the OAS welcome this renewed U.S. interest in Latin America and we agree that further U.S. neglect of our region could only imperil hemispheric peace and harmony.

While bilateral solutions to hemispheric problems are indeed necessary and useful from time to time, the long-lasting inter-American forum provided by the OAS should be the bulwark of hemispheric relationships. It is within this framework where the new development agenda of the Americas should be realistically thrashed out and dealt with.

Since 1960, critical leadership in protection of human rights in the Americas has been provided by the OAS Commission on Human Rights. The independence, thoroughness, and objectivity with which it goes about its business are widely acknowledged. This year, its work gained for it new recognition within the OAS General Assembly.

It is essential that the OAS provide such hemispheric leadership, giving real meaning to the words "human rights" and "human dignity." These must be perceived not as mere legal concepts or rhetorical expressions; they must be deeply felt, and honored in practice.

I think that a right whose violation finds no thorough redress in the administration of justice is a right with no real meaning or existence. Old civilizations have understood that full protection of human rights requires an international judicial instance.

So, true protection of human rights among us may involve the creation of a judicial body of an inter American nature which may be called upon to investigate and to judge alleged violations of human rights.

In this sense, an important precedent was established in November 1969 when twelve Latin American countries signed the Inter-American Convention on Human Rights.

Only two nations—Colombia and Costa Rica—have so far ratified this convention and it has therefore not entered into effect. The Convention authorizes the creation of an Inter American Court of Human Rights, an international juridical organism endowed with faculties for determining violations of rights or liberties protected by the Convention. The Court would be able to order measures for redressing violations of human rights.

I believe an important way for us to demonstrate respect for the protection of human rights in this hemisphere is not only to identify every alleged violation but also to encourage the implementation of an international judicial process to fully guarantee the respect of those rights.

I think we must do everything possible to expand our inter American standards and practices to defend human rights wherever they are threatened. No persons, group or movement, no matter what their motives, no matter what their objectives, no matter what their role in society, can justify themselves if their actions rely upon violence and destruction of human life. . . .

Press talks by developing states. Officials of dozens of developing nations met in July to formulate new policies toward local and international news media. Resolutions passed at the meetings were criticized by private news agencies and press groups.

Representatives of 21 Latin American and Caribbean nations held an "intergovernmental meeting on mass communications media" in San Jose, Costa Rica July 12–21 under the auspices of the United Nations' Educational, Scientific and Cultural Organization (UNESCO). The delegates passed 11 resolutions including one to establish "a news agency or consortium of news agencies that will represent the governments and the private interests of our region."

The resolution on the regional news agency, passed July 21, charged that most of the news circulated in Latin America was distributed by foreign agencies "not greatly concerned or interested in reflecting the real motivations, whole truth or background of regional events." The resolution added: "It is the duty of the countries of the region to equip themselves with systems of their own, capable of counterbalancing the serious imbalance existing in communication and giving the world a true, objective and complete image of their own realities."

Other resolutions passed by the delegates July 21 called for:

■ Elaboration of "a concerted policy with respect to the information content that should circulate via satellite between Latin American countries, and between our region and other parts of the world."

■ Creation of national communications policies, with emphasis on the establishment of regional centers to upgrade the training of "communicators" and radio and television journalists.

- Participation of the private sector in communications policymaking.
- Free access to information on a national and international level.
- A right-of-reply in the international communications media.

The UNESCO meeting and its resolutions were denounced July 23 by the Inter-American Press Association (IAPA). The group issued a statement in Miami describing the conference as an attempt to control and manipulate all news media in Latin America and the Caribbean. The UNESCO meeting confirmed "that the people's right to be fully and freely informed is threatened today more than ever before," the IAPA said.

The UNESCO nations had discarded traditional principles such as "freedom of the press" and "freedom of information" in favor of concepts "made to order for those governments that seek absolute power," the IAPA charged.

The IAPA's executive committee had met in San Jose July 12-13 to express concern over the UNESCO conference and speak with its participants. Amadou Mahtar M'bow, UNESCO director general, who organized the conference, July 18 denied IAPA charges that the meeting was aiding countries that tried to gag the free press. The IAPA's members were seeking "freedom of expression for themselves without allowing others to express themselves," M'bow charged. "The UNESCO position was always very clear," he said. "UNESCO is in favor of total freedom of information."

European, Latin social democrats meet. Leaders of European and Latin American social democratic parties held an unprecedented conference in Caracas, Venezuela May 23-25 to express solidarity and discuss social, economic and political issues.

Delegates to the meeting, including chiefs of government and political exiles, issued a declaration May 25 that called for "transatlantic cooperation" against dictatorships and in favor of a new international economic order.

The declaration condemned "inhuman repression and political persecution" under dictatorships, but it did not single out the Chilean military regime as some delegates had hoped. The statement called for a new economic order that recognized the rights of developing countries to own their natural resources, to receive "just and remunerative prices for their raw materials" and to gain access to the markets of industrial countries producing manufactured goods.

The conference was opened May 23 by Romulo Betancourt, founder of Venezuela's ruling Democratic Action Party and former president of the country. Betancourt said that Latin America would recover its social democratic character before long.

The opening session was also addressed by Venezuelan President Carlos Andres Perez and by Willy Brandt, chairman of West Germany's Social Democratic Party and former West German chancellor. Perez called on European premiers and social democratic leaders to promote fairer economic treatment for developing countries. Brandt said cooperation between the industrialized West and the developing nations would not succeed unless there was a more equitable internal order in the developing states.

Other conference delegates included Austrian Chancellor Bruno Kreisky; Danish Premier Anker Jorgensen; Felipe Gonzalez, leader of the Socialist Workers' Party of Spain; Victor Raul Haya de la Torre, founder of Peru's Popular Revolutionary Action Party; Ricardo Balbin, leader of Argentina's Radical Party, and two former Chilean senators, Anselmo Sule of the Radical Party and Aniceto Rodriguez of the Socialist Party. Sule and Rodriguez were political exiles.

After the conference issued its declaration, Sule and the Socialist parties of Portugal and Italy issued separate statements calling for intensified international support "for the Chilean people in their struggle against fascism."

Economic & Other Developments

Economic decline in 1975. Enrique V. Iglesias, executive secretary of the United Nations' Economic Commission for Latin America, said Jan. 13 that living conditions in Latin America had "worsened terribly" in 1975.

REGIONAL DEVELOPMENTS

The region's economic growth rate had fallen to 3.3% in 1975 from 7% the year before, while its trade deficit had risen to $10.3 billion from $9.2 billion in 1974, Iglesias reported. Export prices in 1975 had risen by 1% overall while import prices rose by 14%, he noted.

The decline of Latin American economies in 1975 weighed "frighteningly" on the poorest inhabitants, Iglesias continued. "There are currently more than 300 million Latin Americans," he noted, "about 100 million of whom live in conditions of extreme poverty."

'75 Latin payments deficit up. The International Monetary Fund reported May 10 that Latin America's global balance-of-payments deficit had increased from 628 million special drawing rights at the end of 1974 to SDR 1.93 billion at the end of 1975. One SDR was valued at $1.15.

Argentina experienced the most adverse change in its balance of payments, falling from a surplus of SDR 96 million at the end of 1974 to a deficit of SDR 878 million at the end of 1975. Mexico fell from a surplus of SDR 30 million to a deficit of SDR 87 million.

Among other regional economic developments:

U.S. exports to Latin America were worth $17 billion in 1975, the Latin America Economic Report said March 19. This was 11.1% more than in 1974. Mexico was the biggest U.S. customer with $5.4 billion in purchases, followed by Venezuela with $3.1 billion. U.S. sales to Peru increased to $1.5 billion, 50% more than in 1974. Sales to Brazil declined by 17%.

Latin America supplied 73% of the world's bananas, 60% of its coffee, 51% of its sugar, 23% of its meat, 18% of its cocoa, 17% of its tobacco and 15% of its maize, according to Enrique Iglesias, executive secretary of the United Nations' Economic Commission for Latin America, quoted in the May 7 Latin America Economic Report. Despite this, 100 million Latin Americans suffered from malnutrition, and Latin America's food production would have to be doubled in the next 15 years, Iglesias said.

Low regional defense spending reported. Latin America spent proportionally less on its defenses than any other region of the world, according to a study in Air Force magazine, reported by the Miami Herald Jan. 2.

Latin governments allocated an average of only 2% of their gross national product for defense budgets, compared with allocations in the double digits for several Middle Eastern countries, 10.6% for the Soviet Union and 6% for the U.S., the study noted. Latin America and the Caribbean reportedly spent about $4.5 billion annually on a total defense establishment of 1.5 million persons.

Brazil continued to lead other Latin nations with the largest armed force and defense budget. Next came Argentina, Cuba, Mexico, Chile, Colombia, Peru and Venezuela. (See table for figures on selected Latin countries.)

Latin American Defense Budgets and Military Establishments*

	Defense Budget	Armed Forces	Paramilitary Forces	Combat Aircraft
Argentina	$1 billion (1975)	133,500	21,000	132
Bolivia	$35 million ('74)	27,000	5,000	37
Brazil	$1.3 billion ('75)	254,500	200,000	160
Chile	$213 million ('74)	73,800	30,000	32
Colombia	$102 million ('74)	64,300	5,000	16
Cuba	$290 million ('71)	117,000	113,000	205
Dominican Rep.	$36 million ('74)	15,800	10,000	32
Ecuador	$52 million ('73)	22,300	5,800	24
Mexico	$423 million ('74)	82,500†	---	15
Paraguay	$19 million ('73)	14,500	5,000	13
Peru	$226 million ('74)	56,000	20,000	94
Uruguay	$68 million ('73)	22,000	22,000	6
Venezuela	$494 million ('75)	44,000	11,500	85

†Plus 250,000 reservists.
*Source: Air Force magazine, cited in Miami Herald.

U.S. bribe scandal spreads. Military and civilian officials in a number of Latin American countries were implicated in February in the growing scandal over bribery of foreign officials by U.S. corporations.

The Colombian government began an investigation Feb. 8 into reports that two air force generals had received illegal payments from Lockheed Aircraft Corp., which was alleged to have bribed officials in European and other countries as well. Venezuela's air force Feb. 10 began investigating reports that Lockheed had bribed some of its officers, and the Venezuelan government issued a report Feb. 14 naming seven persons who allegedly received illegal payments from Occidental Petroleum Corp.

In addition, Lockheed was said to have paid a $75,000 bribe to a Mexican air force colonel—Mexico's defense ministry denied it—and Northrop Corp. admitted making illegal payments in Brazil, according to the Feb. 23 issue of Newsweek magazine of the U.S.

(In an earlier scandal, Gulf Oil Corp. told the Bolivian government Jan. 14 that it had given the late Bolivian President Rene Barrientos Ortuno a helicopter and $1.8 million in cash in 1966. Bolivia responded that there were doubts that Barrientos took the money and "suspicions" that the alleged payments were "used by Gulf Oil's officials for their own benefit.")

The Colombian scandal broke Feb. 8 when newspapers in Bogota printed three letters released by the U.S. Senate's Subcommittee on Multinational Corporations, which was investigating illegal payments abroad by U.S. firms. The letters, addressed to Lockheed offices in Marietta, Ga. by two Lockheed officials in Colombia, Edwin Schwartz and Jose Gutierrez, discussed "sugar" (bribe payments) demanded by two Colombian air force generals and other officials in exchange for inducing the government to purchase Lockheed Hercules aircraft in 1968-69.

The generals—Jose Ramon Calderon and Armando Urrego, both former air force commanders in chief—allegedly exaggerated Colombia's defense needs to secure the purchases, for which they allegedly received some $200,000 from Lockheed. Both Calderon and Urrego denied the bribery charge and cooperated fully with the government investigation which began Feb. 8, according to press reports.

The Venezuelan air force began its investigation of alleged Lockheed bribes Feb. 10, after the Mexican newspaper Excelsior Feb. 7 printed an internal Lockheed letter noting that the company had paid for a visit to Disney World, Florida in 1974 by a Venezuelan lieutenant colonel, J. M. Laurentin, and his family.

Venezuelan President Carlos Andres Perez Feb. 14 gave his attorney general an official report on alleged bribes by Occidental Petroleum Corp., whose assets were nationalized by the Venezuelan government Jan. 1 along with those of all other foreign oil companies. The report said that in order to secure oil exploration contracts from the previous Venezuelan government, Occidental had paid $1.6 million in bribes to seven persons including Alberto Flores, then an official in the mines ministry and currently Venezuela's minister to the Organization of Petroleum Exporting Countries (OPEC).

(Venezuelan newspapers reported Feb. 17 that to secure oil contracts in 1971, Occidental had made payments to relatives of a number of officials, including $106,400 to Alberto Flores' father.)

IDB '75 loans set record. The Inter-American Development Bank provided 70 loans totaling a record $1.375 billion to foster Latin American economic and social development in 1975, according to the bank's annual report.

The report was submitted by IDB president Antonio Ortiz Mena to the 17th annual meeting of the bank's board of governors, held in Cancun, Mexico May 17-19. Representatives of the IDB's 24 member nations attended.

The 1975 loan total was 24% higher than the record $1.11 billion authorized by the bank in 1974.

Projects completed in 1975 with the aid of IDB financing included the improvement and bringing into production of 11.3 million acres of land; improvement or expansion of 77 industrial plants and 6,350 small firms, and improvement or construction of 28,962 miles of roads, 360,000 low-cost housing units and almost 70 learning centers.

REGIONAL DEVELOPMENTS

The report noted that Latin American economic growth had dropped sharply in 1975. The combined gross domestic product of the region rose slightly more than 3% in 1975. In 1974 it rose more than 7%. The fall was attributed partly to effects of the 1974–75 international recession.

In a May 18 address to the meeting, Ortiz Mena cited Latin America's heavy load of foreign private debt, attributing it to a "drastic cutback" in official foreign aid to the region. Private indebtedness accounted for 73% of Latin America's foreign debt in 1972-75, Ortiz said. The region's total debt was $70 billion.

Because of Latin America's dependence on loans and capital issues from private banks and lenders in the industrial nations, 80% of its debt matured in less than 10 years, Ortiz said. Payment of interest and amortization had increased from $2.5 billion in 1970 to $5.3 billion in 1974, he added.

The IDB planned to increase its capital from $12 billion to $18.3 billion, with $2.25 billion of the increase coming from the U.S. The U.S. was the bank's largest contributor and held one-third of its votes. Another $750 million would be contributed by 12 nations outside the Western Hemisphere. The 12 would become IDB members later in 1976.

Eight of the nations would be admitted to the bank in July, it was reported June 3. They were West Germany, Japan, Great Britain, Spain, Switzerland, Denmark, Israel and Yugoslavia. The countries to be admitted later were Belgium, the Netherlands, Italy and Austria. Their legislatures had not yet approved IDB membership although their executive branches had pledged contributions to the IDB in December 1974.

The IDB's lending policy was criticized during the meeting by three Andean countries—Peru, Bolivia and Ecuador. Peru charged May 18 that the bank had refused to support projects aimed at regional economic integration, had discriminated against Peru, Chile and Colombia because they were countries of "intermediate" development, had denied support to the Andean Group's Andean Development Corp., had neglected to finance exports adequately and had ignored urban development.

Bolivia charged May 19 that the IDB had increased regional economic imbalance by consistently favoring Brazil, Argentina, Mexico and Venezuela, Latin America's most developed nations. Ecuador charged the same day that it had received not only fewer loans than other countries but harsher repayment terms.

Venezuela called May 18 for a new world economic order that was fairer to developing nations. Venezuela called on Latin American governments to seek "new paths to integration" and expressed support for the new Latin American Economic System, a regional forum that excluded the U.S.

15-year IDB record—Sen. Hubert H. Humphrey (D, Minn.) inserted in the U.S. Congressional Record March 30 a report he had developed in the IDB's 15-year record:

IDB BENEFICIARIES

The Inter-American Development Bank completed a decade and a half of operations in 1975. During its 15-year existence, the Bank has lent $8.685 billion to help finance social and economic development projects involving a total investment of approximately $33.4 billion in Latin America. For each $1 of IDB resources, an additional $3 is provided by member countries.

Agriculture: The creation of new agricultural production to increase employment in rural areas and feed growing populations.

Amount: 202 loans amounting to $1.975 billion for projects totalling $5.384 billion.

Impact: As of December 31, 1975: 11.3 million acres brought into production; 1.1 million farm credits to individual farmers; 110 cooperative associations have received credit for seed, fertilizer, tools and equipment; new integrated rural agricultural programs providing sanitation, health facilities, extension schools as well as farm credit, attempt to create large-scale employment and to reach farmers whose average annual income is approximately $100.

SANITATION

Amount: 112 projects amounting to $752 million for projects valued at $1,752 billion.

Impact: Helping to build or improve 4,800 rural drinking water systems and 400 sewer systems benefiting 57,000,000 people.

ELECTRIC POWER

Amount: 81 loans for $1.856 billion for projects costing $9.083 billion.

Impact: To assist in making possible additional 16 million kilowatts of power; 95,484 miles of power lines to 2,637 communities.

TRANSPORTATION AND COMMUNICATIONS

Amount: As of December 31, 1975: 19,286 miles of roads of which 14,432 miles were farm to market; 1,664 miles of gas lines; 14 ports, 7 grain elevator facilities, one ship canal improved, 9 major telecommunications systems financed.

EDUCATION

Amount: 74 loans amounting to $375 million for projects costing $816 million.

Impact: Helping to modernize and improve 694 learning centers of which 504 are vocational or technical schools, 70 are universities, 80 are special schools or facilities of universities, 18 primary of secondary schools, 19 research centers.

URBAN DEVELOPMENT

Amount: 52 loans amounting to $454 million for projects costing $1.019 billion.

Impact: Helping to build 361,123 housing units along with community facilities and 10 municipal markets.

INDUSTRY AND MINING

Amount: 155 loans amounting to $1.254 million are helping finance projects costing $10.728 billion.

Impact: 50 industrial plants in production; 26 under construction; 6,353 small and medium sized firms assisted to build or expand facilities.

PREINVESTMENT

Amount: 76 loans amounting to $138 million is helping to finance preinvestment programs amounting to $254 million.

Impact: 1,281 preinvestment studies completed.

TOURISM

Amount: 6 loans amounting to $71 million finance projects costing $185 million.

Impact: These loans mobilize energies and provide basic skills to large numbers of unemployed who formerly lived below subsistence levels.

EXPORT FINANCING

Amount: 18 loans amounting to $132 million helping to finance capital goods exports with an invoice value of $190 million among Latin American countries.

Impact: To foster Latin American integration and intra-regional export trade.

As estimated, 2 million individuals will benefit directly from approximately one-fifth of the money lent in 1975. Each of these is a member of a producer or consumer cooperative, a credit union or some other form of association of small farmers, fishermen or industrial workers. Of the additional $1.1 billion, no ready estimates are yet available, but several million more individuals will benefit directly and indirectly whether they be members of new rural water associations, new customers for expanding rural electrification networks, or workers in mines or factories, where new investments made possible by Inter-American Development Bank loans are about to take place.

U.S. votes funds—Legislation authoring $2.25 billion for fiscal years 1977–79 for the U.S. contribution to the Inter-American Development Bank (IDB) cleared Congress May 20 when the House approved it 257–120.

Actual cash outlays under the bill were expected to come to less than $750 million.

The bill also would:

■ Authorize the U.S. delegate to the IDB to vote in favor of extending membership to countries outside Latin America, including Japan, Israel and 10 European countries.

■ Authorize the first U.S. contribution—of $25 million—to the African Development Fund (ADF).

■ Require the U.S. delegates to both the IDB and ADF to vote against loans to countries engaging in a "consistent pattern of gross violations of internationally recognized human rights unless such assistance will directly benefit needy people."

Sen. Jacob K. Javits (R, N.Y.) had told the Senate March 30 of the impact IDB operations had on the U.S. economy:

The importance in dealing with the financing mechanisms of the Inter-American Development Bank is to recognize what it means to us as a nation overall. We enjoy a trade surplus with Latin America of about $1 billion a year. Exports and imports run to about almost $30 billion a year, which is roughly 15 percent of all our foreign trade. Latin America is a critical source of raw materials for iron ore, copper, bauxite, sugar, coffee, and even in the field of petroleum. The fact is that Venezuela and Equador continued the supply of petroleum, notwithstanding the embargo by the OPEC nations during the time when we had such a grave oil stringency less than 2 years ago in this country. An estimate of the procurement, resulting from the activities of the Bank insofar as the United States is concerned, comes to about $1 billion a year, involving, in a very important way, thousands of U.S. employees who are engaged in supplying what the IDB facilitates.

We have been with the Bank for 15 years. Our experience with it has been a very good one.

Chile resigns from Andean Group. Chile left the Andean Group Oct. 6 after trying unsuccessfully to change the group's limits on foreign investment and its common external tariff.

Chile had argued for the past year that because it needed to attract capital, it could not accept the group's restrictions on foreign investment, particularly the investment code known as Decision 24, which put a 14% limit on annual remittable profits. Group members had offered to raise the limit to 20%, but Chile had argued for no limit.

Chile also had opposed the common external tariff scheduled to be adopted by the group in 1978 as a move toward establishing an Andean common market.

Chile's withdrawal left the group with five members—Bolivia, Colombia, Ecuador, Peru and Venezuela. The withdrawal meant that Chilean exports would lose preferential access to the five group countries, which had a combined population of 60 million.

Four nations vow antidrug effort. Mexico, Colombia, Panama and Costa Rica had agreed to establish joint commissions with the U.S. to combat the illegal narcotics traffic, according to a statement Jan. 20 by two New York congressmen, Lester L. Wolff (D) and Benjamin A. Gilman (R).

Wolff said he hoped the Ford Administration would "keep its pledge to the American people to do 'whatever it takes' to cut off [the] heroin" traffic, but he expressed concern over "the strong possibility of high-level political protection for individuals involved in the drug traffic in Latin America." He gave no further details, but said he knew of no such corruption among U.S. officials.

Wolff said he and Gilman had learned that the U.S. annually received $1 billion worth of Mexican heroin and cocaine and $500 million worth of Colombian narcotics. He noted that by March "17,000 opium fields in Mexico" would be in bloom.

Wolff commended Mexico for using herbicides in a new campaign against illegal opium poppy cultivation, but added that he was "very disappointed that to this point only 10%–15% of the Mexican poppy fields have been destroyed."

Mexico, which supplied an estimated 70%–90% of the heroin consumed in the U.S., had launched a broad campaign against the narcotics traffic in December 1975 in close collaboration with agents of the U.S. Drug Enforcement Administration, the New York Times reported Jan. 2. The results of the program's first month showed a sharp increase in the amount of pure heroin seized and poppy fields destroyed, according to the Times.

To carry out the program, 200 Mexican agents had been trained over the previous year by French, British, U.S. and Mexican specialists. Most of their equipment was donated by the U.S.—including 27 helicopters, nine fixed-wing aircraft and two aerial photographic systems—but the campaign was run exclusively by Mexico, with about 20 U.S. agents exchanging information with their Mexican counterparts, the Times reported.

U.S. Attorney General Edward Levi had visited Mexico secretly Dec. 29, 1975, conferring with Mexican Attorney General Pedro Ojeda Paullada on the narcotics traffic and delivering a message from President Ford to Mexican President Luis Encheverria Alvarez, the Mexican newspaper Excelsior reported Jan. 19. Ford had said a few days earlier that he had spoken personally with Echeverria about the drug problem, though he did not specify when

In New York, meanwhile, 12 Colombians were convicted Jan. 26 of conspiracy to distribute Colombian cocaine and marijuana in the U.S. in what U.S. prosecutors described as "the biggest Colombian narcotics organization ever uncovered." Prosecutors said the organization distributed more than 20 pounds of cocaine per week in New York in 1972–74, with a weekly wholesale value of $250,000 and a street value of $2.5 million. U.S. authorities had seized $3\frac{1}{2}$ tons of the organization's marijuana with a wholesale value of $2 million, the prosecutors added.

Argentina

Coup Ousts Peron's Widow as President

Armed forces depose Mrs. Peron. President Maria Estela Martinez de Peron was overthrown early March 24 in an apparently bloodless coup led by the commanders of the three armed forces. She had served as president of Argentina since the death of her husband, President Juan D. Peron, July 1, 1975.

The commanders—army Lt. Gen. Jorge Videla, navy Adm. Emilio Massera and air force Brig. Orlando Agosti—formed a ruling junta which pledged to "restore [Argentina's] essential values," eliminate left-wing subversion, promote economic development and "assure subsequently the establishment of a republican, representative and federal democracy."

Mrs. Peron was arrested and flown to a government-owned retreat in the Andean lake region of Neuquen Province. Also seized were Mrs. Peron's private secretary, Julio Gonzalez; her labor minister, Miguel Unamuno; many Peronist labor leaders, including Lorenzo Miguel of the powerful Metallurgical Workers' Union (UOM); and other Peronists and non-Peronists suspected of corruption or subversion. About 800 persons were arrested throughout the country, according to a military source March 25.

The armed forces imposed martial law, closed Congress and the labor unions, and took control of the federal and all provincial and local governments. Prior press censorship was imposed March 24, but it was lifted the next day. Schools were closed March 24–25 and banks and exchange houses were shut down until a new economy minister was named.

No armed or other resistance to the coup was reported, although there was a shooting incident as soldiers took over UOM headquarters. Buenos Aires and the other major cities were reported calm, with many residents of the capital reporting to work March 24 and business returning to partial normality the next day. Nevertheless, the army guarded major roads, public buildings, banks and transport services and warned that terrorists and saboteurs would be shot.

(There was only one report of brutality by the military. Soldiers reportedly fired unnecessarily into a Communist Party office in Buenos Aires and beat a man who emerged subsequently. The incident was filmed by a television crew but the film was confiscated by military authorities.)

Soldiers occupying government and labor union offices seized documents and records for apparent use in corruption investigations. Illegal arms caches reportedly were found at UOM headquarters and in the social welfare ministry, which was alleged to have supplied money and weapons to right-wing terrorists.

The coup had been meticulously planned and had been widely expected in recent months as economic problems, political indecision and terrorism reached the highest levels of Mrs. Peron's 20-month administration. Inflation for the year ending Feb. 29 was 423.6%, according to reports March 24. The political death toll reached 175 as right- and left-wing terrorism accelerated in the week before the coup.

Peron had been warned repeatedly by military, political and labor leaders to resign or at least change her cabinet, but she refused. The coup became inevitable after a move to impeach Mrs. Peron failed in the Chamber of Deputies Feb. 26 and Senate President Italo Luder refused March 4 to call a joint session of Congress to consider declaring the president unfit for office.

Mrs. Peron had dismissed Defense Minister Ricardo Guardo Feb. 23 after he reportedly told her that her policies were forcing a military coup.

(Demands for a cabinet change centered around hostility to associates in the cabinet of the exiled former social welfare minister, Jose Lopez Rega. Chief among the associates was Mrs. Peron's secretary, Gonzalez. Lopez Rega's extradition from Spain was asked March 8 by Alfredo Nocetti Fasolino, a judge investigating official corruption, who said Lopez Rega must face charges of "graft, fiscal fraud" and other violations during his tenure as social welfare minister.)

Events Preceding the Coup

Cabinet revised. Two months before her fall, Mrs. Peron Jan. 15 had dismissed four cabinet ministers in a move that was widely regarded as an attempt to strengthen the right-wing or "loyalist" forces in her government.

Mrs. Peron accepted the resignations of Interior Minister Angel Robledo, Defense Minister Thomas Vottero, Justice Minister Ernesto Corvalan Nanclares and Foreign Minister Manuel Arauz Castex. All but Corvalan had been appointed by Sen. Italo Luder when he served as interim president during Mrs. Peron's leave of absence in September–October 1975.

Robledo was replaced Jan. 15 by Roberto Ares, president of the National Bank, and Corvalan was succeeded by Jose Deheza, a former federal prosecutor. Arauz Castex was replaced Jan. 16 by Raul Quijano, Argentina's representative to the United Nations. The defense post vacated by Vottero was not immediately filled.

The changes were criticized by politicians, labor leaders and military officers, who considered them the work of two of Mrs. Peron's closest and most conservative advisers—Julio Gonzalez, the president's private secretary, and Raul Lastiri, the former Chamber of Deputies president and son-in-law of Jose Lopez Rega, the exiled former social welfare minister.

Labor union officials led by Casildo Herreras, head of the General Labor Confederation, complained that they had not been consulted on the cabinet changes and that the new ministers would follow Lopez Rega's conservative economic policies, it was reported Jan. 18. Herreras charged Jan. 21 that Mrs. Peron was surrounding herself with advisers who sought to separate her from the labor movement. However, the president retained the support of Lorenzo Miguel, head of the Metallurgical Workers' Union and of the 62 Organizations, the Peronist umbrella group, it was reported Jan. 23.

Labor leaders and politicians were critical of the dismissal of Robledo, who had been their intermediary in discussions with the president and was considered the most "flexible" of the cabinet officials, it was reported Jan. 16. The Radical Civic Union, the major opposition party, charged Jan. 25 that Mrs. Peron's increasing political isolation was encouraging "subversion" and a "military coup."

(One apparent cause of Robledo's dismissal was his opposition to the removal of the provincial governors of Buenos Aires and Santa Fe, sought by right-wing Peronists because of the governors' persistent criticism of the president, according to press reports. Buenos Aires Gov. Victorio Calabro charged Jan. 27 that Mrs. Peron's isolation would lead Argentina to "civil war or communism.")

Military officers saw the cabinet changes as an attempt to establish the supremacy of a small right-wing group of presidential advisers associated with the exiled Lopez Rega, the London Times reported Jan. 17.

Political and labor groups also objected to the removal of Foreign Minister Arauz Castex only two days after he had asked Great Britain to withdraw its ambassador because of the continuing conflict between Argentina and Great Britain over the Falkland Islands. The critics feared Arauz' dismissal would imply a weakening of Argentina's position, according to the London Times.

The cabinet changes coincided with the opening of an unofficial campaign by supporters of Mrs. Peron for her reelection in October. The president was reported in the foreign press to want to run for a full term, but Economy Minister Antonio Cafiero said Jan. 13 that she would retire after the election and the National Council of the Justicialista (Peronist) Party said Jan. 20 that it was not authorizing a campaign for her reelection.

(The government announced Jan. 26 that a new date would be set for the election because the date originally selected, Oct. 17, was "inappropriate." Peronists traditionally celebrated "loyalty day" Oct. 17, and opposition groups had complained that this might unfairly affect the outcome of the vote.)

Mrs. Peron then dismissed her economy and labor ministers Feb. 3 as workers struck for higher wages and businessmen announced plans for a lockout Feb. 16. Economy Minister Antonio Cafiero was replaced by Emilio Mondelli, former president of the Central Bank, and Labor Minister Carlos Ruckauf was succeeded by Miguel Unamuno, leader of the insurance workers' union and former president of the Buenos Aires City Council.

'75 inflation 334.8%. The cost of living in Argentina had risen by 334.8% in 1975, compared with an increase of 40% in 1974, the National Statistics Institute reported Jan. 5. Economists predicted an even higher inflation rate for 1976, according to press reports.

Labor pressures on the government increased after the inflation rate was announced. The powerful textile and commercial employes' unions threatened to strike unless wages were increased by 40%, and workers at a state-owned brewery struck for higher wages and other benefits, it was reported Jan. 8. The brewery's management refused to consider the demands and fired 70 strikers, according to union sources.

Wage hike scored. An 18% wage increase decreed by the government Jan. 22 was denounced by labor groups as too small and by management organizations as too large.

The raise, accompanied by a 40% increase in family allowances and a doubling of the minimum taxable income, was negotiated by Economy Minister Antonio Cafiero and the most powerful labor leaders—Casildo Herreras, head of the General Labor Confederation, and Lorenzo Miguel, chief of the Metallurgical Workers' Union and of the 62 Organizations, the Peronist umbrella group. Herreras said labor had sought a 30% increase.

The General Economic Confederation, the Peronist management group, was left out of the negotiations without explanation. Its second vice president, Juan Carlos Paz, said Jan. 23 that companies could not afford the wage hike and that it would resolve nothing "as long as there is no attack on the real causes of the present crisis." Other management groups opposing the increase were the Apege federation and the union of fuel company owners in Buenos Aires Province, it was reported Jan. 28.

State employes threatened to strike for still higher wages, forcing the government to grant a 40% raise to 1,600 of them Jan. 27. This increased the government's 1976 payroll by about $600 million, inflating a budget deficit previously estimated at $2 billion, according to the New York Times Jan. 28.

Bakery workers began a 48-hour strike Jan. 29 and mail, telecommunications and automotive transport workers threatened to strike within a week unless they received increased wages and benefits. The movie industry was paralyzed Jan. 30 when workers began an indefinite strike for similar demands.

Subway workers in Buenos Aires struck for higher wages Feb. 3, rejecting the 18% wage increase announced by the government Jan. 22 but not yet officially decreed by Mrs. Peron. Prices had risen by 14.6% in January, according to government statistics released Feb. 2.

Other economic developments. Among economic developments preceding the coup:

Argentina's relatively low prices were bringing more than 14,000 Brazilian tourists into Buenos Aires every month, it was reported Jan. 9. The visitors reportedly spent an average of $400 apiece, helping compensate for declining domestic demand; their money was virtually all changed on the black market.

The poor wheat harvest in Brazil and the low official price paid for Argentine wheat had led to smuggling on a vast scale, with Brazilian wheat buyers offering twice or three times as much as the official Argentine price, it was reported Jan. 9.

A drought in Santa Fe, Buenos Aires and Cordoba Provinces had damaged the corn and sorghum crops, with farmers predicting a 50% loss in potential corn production in 1976, it was reported Jan. 17.

The National Grain Board said a group of U.S. banks—Chemical Bank, First National Bank of Boston and Bank of America—would make available $100 million in rotating credits to finance Argentine corn, sorghum and wheat exports, it was reported Jan. 28.

Argentine beef exports to Europe had dropped 80% because of an embargo placed on beef imports by the European Common Market beginning in July 1974, it was reported Feb. 2. Before the embargo Argentina had exported more than 70% of its beef to Europe.

Argentina and Venezuela signed a multifaceted economic agreement Jan. 14 that included an exchange of Argentine grains for Venezuelan iron ore. The pact followed four days of negotiations in Caracas between Economy Minister Antonio Cafiero and his Venezuelan counterpart, Hector Hurtado.

Crude oil production in Argentina dropped by 4% in 1975, it was reported Jan. 9.

Automobile production in 1975 was 16.2% lower than in 1974, it was reported Feb. 11.

Peso devalued. The government devalued the peso by 3.7% Jan. 12. The currency had been devalued 13 times in 1975, with regular "mini-devaluations" in effect since August.

The peso was devalued Jan. 26 for the second time in 1975, by 3.65%.

Foreign tourists continued to pour into Argentina to take advantage of the peso's plummeting value, the newsletter Latin America reported Feb. 27. Many Argentine industries reportedly were surviving solely on the basis of tourism and contraband.

Argentina experienced the most adverse change in its balance of payments, falling from a surplus of SDR 96 million at the end of 1974 to a deficit of SDR 878 million at the end of 1975.

Peron testament published. The "National Project," the political testament of the late President Juan Peron, was published by the Buenos Aires newspaper Clarin Jan. 7. Peron's widow and successor as president, Maria Estela Martinez de Peron, had created a government council Jan. 5 to discuss and implement the ideas in the document.

The testament called for a "social democracy" embodied in "a system of social and political institutions that will guarantee the presence of the people in the elaboration and fulfillment of decisions." True democracy was "that in which the government does what the people want and defends only one interest: the people's," the document said.

Peron rejected capitalism and communism as lacking "substantial values" and he said Christianity, though "impregnated with spiritual richness," lacked "sufficient political content for the effective exercise of government." Peron had advocated a political course between capitalism and communism since his first term as president in the late 1940s.

Mrs. Peron suspends Congress, resists resignation demands. Mrs. Peron closed Congress' special session Feb. 16 as political, labor and management leaders urged her to resign to avert a military coup.

Mrs. Peron apparently acted to prevent the Chamber of Deputies from either impeaching her or declaring her unfit for office, and to cut off further congressional investigation of corruption in the executive branch. However, angry deputies including some Peronists asserted they would reconvene the Chamber Feb. 25 under a constitutional provision requiring approval by only 25% of the deputies.

Numerous calls for Mrs. Peron's resignation and reports of an impending military coup had preceded the closing of Congress. Three prominent politicians—former Economy Minister Alvaro Alsogaray, dissident Peronist Deputy Luis Sobrino Aranda and Radical Sen. Luis Leon—had urged Mrs. Peron to withdraw on a television program Feb. 10, prompting the president to ban the program from the air. Mrs. Peron ordered the Buenos Aires newspaper La Opinion closed for 10 days after the paper said Latin American embassies were making preparations to receive political refugees in anticipation of a military coup that would occur "very soon."

Commercial activities throughout most of Argentina were virtually paralyzed Feb. 16 by a management lockout called by the businessmen's organization Apede to protest the government's foundering economic policies. The strike, added to the deepening political crisis, reportedly increased pressure on the armed forces to seize power and restore order.

Army commander Gen. Jorge Videla met with his senior generals for 10 hours Feb. 20 for what was described as "an analysis of the national situation in relation to the campaign against subversion," it was reported Feb. 21. Various military factions supported a coup, but the generals were divided, many of them feeling that the left-wing guerrilla movements must be eliminated first and that meanwhile Congress should find a political alternative to Mrs. Peron, according to the London newsletter Latin America Feb. 20.

In an apparent effort to avert a coup without resigning, Mrs. Peron announced Feb. 18 that she would not run for a full term later in 1976 but she would complete her current term scheduled to end in May 1977. The government announced Feb. 20 that the elections would take place Dec. 12.

Calls for Mrs. Peron's resignation continued despite her rejection of a full term. Joining in the chorus for the first time was Tulio Jacovella, director of the moderate Peronist newspaper Mayoria, who said in an editorial Feb. 19 that Mrs. Peron should resign to "help save the movement and the government."

Peronist labor leaders demanded Feb. 20 that the president name a new cabinet excluding associates of the exiled former social welfare minister, Jose Lopez Rega, and including officials suggested by the labor movement, notably former Interior Minister Angel Robledo. The demand, led by Jose Baeza, second vice president of the Justicialista (Peronist) Party, severely split the Peronist movement. Six of the 16 members on the party's ruling council resigned, accusing Baeza and his followers of "treason."

The Baeza group again asked Mrs. Peron to revise her cabinet Feb. 23, but she apparently refused. Mayoria called again for her resignation, and published a full-page advertisement urging her withdrawal by Hector Villalon, one of the architects of the return to Argentina in 1972 of the late President Juan Peron, Mrs. Peron's husband and predecessor in office.

Political violence. At least 50 people were killed Jan. 3–Feb. 1 as political violence continued unabated. The 1975 death toll from such violence was 898, the Associated Press reported Jan. 3.

A policeman was murdered in Mendoza Jan. 3, presumably by leftist guerrillas, and a union leader was assassinated in Zarate, outside La Plata, Jan. 5. The army claimed Jan. 6 that soldiers in Tucuman Province had killed 14 leftist guerrillas in a skirmish two days before.

The bodies of eight metalworkers were found outside Rosario (Santa Fe Province) Jan. 8, one day after the workers were kidnapped by presumed right-wing terrorists, the Mexican newspaper Excelsior reported Jan. 9.

Unidentified rightists were also held responsible for a bomb explosion Jan. 2 which killed two persons at a Buenos Aires theater presenting a show which featured the prominent leftist actress Nacha Guevara. Guevara fled the country, resuming an exile she began in 1974 after receiving death threats from the Argentine Anticommunist Alliance, the right-wing assassination squad.

President Maria Estela Martinez de Peron urged Argentines Jan. 9 to join in fighting the "atheist, mercenary and delirious" guerrillas of the left "to ensure the survival of our country as a civilized community."

Right-wing terrorists posing as policemen murdered three metalworkers in Villa Constitucion and kidnapped 14 persons in Cordoba Jan. 9. Workers at a Cordoba car plant went on strike to protest the abduction of fellow employes, and municipal workers planned a protest against the kidnapping of two city council employes. Credit for at least one of the abductions was claimed by the rightist Liberators of America group.

Police and soldiers killed three persons in Buenos Aires Jan. 10 when the victims refused to stop their automobile and identify themselves.

Leftist guerrillas attacked a police academy and arms depot near La Plata Jan. 11 in an unsuccessful attempt to steal weapons. They were repulsed by police fire but no casualties were reported.

By Jan. 12, the number of kidnappings in Cordoba since Jan. 3 had mounted to at least 20. The city's archbishop, Raul Francisco Cardinal Primatesta, called on the local army commander to "take pertinent measures" against the abductions "according to law." The Cordoba provincial government claimed the kidnappings resulted from "quarrels between the [leftist] guerrilla factions," but Roman Catholic authorities and automobile workers' leaders blamed them on right-wing terrorists, according to press reports. The kidnap victims included students, workers and members of the Authentic Party, the left-wing Peronist group linked to the Montoneros guerrillas.

Montoneros guerrillas set fire to a commuter train outside Buenos Aires Jan. 13 to protest the recent abduction of Roberto Quieto, one of their leaders, by gunmen posing as police and military intelligence officers. The army and police said they knew nothing of the Quieto's seizure.

The AAA was held largely responsible for the kidnapping wave in Cordoba, which had claimed 25 victims by Jan. 16, the Mexican newspaper Excelsior reported Jan. 17. "The entire population of Cordoba lives under fear of a death threat," charged Sen. Jose Antonio Allende of the Popular Christian Party. "Things occur as if individual guarantees had ceased to exist. The authorities have been unable to stop the wave of violence and its authors operate with complete impunity."

The local branch of the General Labor Confederation had declared a state of "alert" and municipal workers had gone on strike to protest right-wing terrorism, which was generally attributed to off-duty policemen. Relatives of Norma and Gloria Waquim, two church social workers, charged the police had refused to intervene while members of the AAA searched their house and kidnapped the two women, Excelsior reported.

In other assassinations attributed to rightists, two persons were found killed in Buenos Aires and a third in La Plata Jan. 15, and Guillermo Savloff, an Argentine representative to the World Health Organization, was found dead in La Plata Jan. 21.

The Montoneros, meanwhile, claimed responsibility for the assassination Jan. 29 of two Argentine executives and a police guard at a plant belonging to Bendix Corp. of the U.S. in Munro, a Buenos Aires suburb. Montoneros were also presumed responsible for an armed attack on a police station near La Plata Feb. 1 in which at least three insurgents were reported killed and several more captured.

Leftists were also blamed for coordinated attacks on a police station, a steel plant and a petroleum installation in Villa Constitucion Jan. 29, and for the bombing of a bridge in southern Buenos Aires Province and a police station in Cordoba Jan. 26. The explosion of two bombs at the British Cultural Institute in Cordoba Jan. 15 was attributed to neither the right nor the left but was linked to Argentina's ongoing dispute with Great Britain over the Falkland Islands.

The AAA published a manifesto Jan. 26 vowing to step up its terrorist activities in collaboration with two other rightist groups, the Liberators of America and the Joint Forces Command.

ARGENTINA

"Within six months we will exterminate and annihilate all individuals, whatever their nationality, religious creed, race or investiture, who respond to the interests of foreign Marxists, Masons, anti-Christians or synarchic international Judaism," the manifesto said. "In particular we will execute economic delinquents, venal and corrupt functionaries, especially ministers of state, judges, senators, deputies, mayors and councilmen, as well as corrupt labor union leaders, priests of the "Third World" movement, representatives of synarchy and leftist infiltrators in our Catholic Church."

Also slated for execution were "members of the two guerrilla organizations, the Montoneros and the ERP (People's Revolutionary Army), and the Communist Party, the Authentic Party, the Revolutionary Workers' Party, the Revolutionary Youth of the Radical Civic Union and the Revolutionary Communist Party," the AAA asserted. Pablo Fernandez Long, a federal deputy who had recently left the Justicialista (official Peronist) Party and joined the breakaway leftist Authentic Party, would be executed by Feb. 12, the manifesto declared.

Montoneros Feb. 5 assassinated Jose Miguel Tarquini, public relations director of the social welfare ministry, charging in a communique to the press later that day that Tarquini was "one of the chiefs" of the AAA.

Maria Caride de Lanusse, daughter-in-law of Gen. Alejandro Lanusse, the former dictator, was killed Feb. 9 by a bomb presumably planted by leftist guerrillas.

Col. Rafael Reyes, director of the anti-subversive campaign in Mar del Plata, was assassinated Feb. 11 by leftist guerrillas. The Red Brigades of Workers' Power, a splinter group of the Marxist People's Revolutionary Army (ERP), claimed responsibility for the murder. However, police claimed March 10 that Reyes was killed by Federico Baez, a Montonero. The mutilated bodies of Baez' parents and sister were found by police March 7 in Dolores (Buenos Aires Province). The relatives were presumably killed by the AAA.

The army announced Feb. 25 that soldiers had killed 10 ERP guerrillas in Tucuman Province. The same day an army colonel was murdered by guerrillas in Cordoba, two policemen were assassinated in San Fernando (Buenos Aires Province) and a wealthy businessman was killed in Mar del Plata when he resisted being kidnapped.

Rev. Francisco Soares, chaplain of a church in Tigre (Buenos Aires Province) and a member of the leftist Third World Movement, was shot to death Feb. 13, presumably by the AAA. Another priest belonging to the movement was murdered the next day. The AAA sent a death threat to the archbishop of Cordoba, Most Rev. Raul Francisco Cardinal Primatesta, it was reported March 13. Primatesta had denounced the AAA's wave of kidnappings in January.

U.S. Sen. Jesse Helms (R, N.C.) inserted in the U.S. Congressional Record March 22 the following summary of political violence in Argentina during January:

MONTH OF JANUARY
Analysis of the subversive situation

The subversive situation for the period of January 1 to 31, 1976, registered a decline of 6.25 percent, in total occurances in comparison with previous period (December 1975). This decrease has been accentuated by 12.19 percent decline of the total acts of subversive organization that were evaluated as such.

The center of gravity of subversion was in the province of Buenos Aires with 39.5% of the total and following distribution in other provinces: Corboda—26.6%, Federal Capital—10.47%, Santa Fe—9.04%, Mendoza—6.66%, and insignificant percentages for Santiago Del Estero, Tucuman, Salta, San Juan, Formosa, Misiones, and Rio Negro.

Distribution by the type of subversive actions was as follows: Assaults—158, Assaults with logistical means—25, Psychological actions—25, Operations—2. Distribution by organizations was as follows: Montoneros—27, E.R.P.—8, E.R.P.-Montoneros—1, Unidentified groups—174.

Assassinations

Buenos Aires	21
Federal Capital	4
Misiones	1
Santa Fe	5
Total	**31**

Significant acts

January 11, 1976: Buenos Aires (La Plata), A group of extremists attacked different cars from the Police School and the Police Troops of the Buenos Aires Provinces. The guards retreated towards the school's armory to prevent the taking of the arms. Two hours after beginning the attempt of capture, the subversive elements intensified the attack of the Levene station throwing Bengal lights to facilitate their work. Towards the end other police groups assisted in repressing the attack. Two airplanes from the Naval base in Puinta Indio helped to supress the extremists.

January 12, 1976: Buenos Aires (Villa de Mayo), Incendiary attempt against the train from F.C. Gal Belgrano causing the destruction of the cars and part of the station. Montoneros.

January 15, 1976: Corboda, Explosion in front of the Naval delegation of Corboda.

January 16, 1976: Buenos Aires, Attacks against transportation means: Hurlingham—Incendiary of railroad lines, dissemination of explosive artifacts of which one caused the death of the Police Chief of Buenos Aires, Benedicto Aronda.

Ramos Mejia, Robbing and incendation of the collective.

Castelar, Explosion of an artifact on the railroad lines in Sarmiento. Montoneros.

January 17, 1976: Buenos Aires (Lomas de Zamora), Assault with explosive and guns against the Capitan of Fragata, Alberto Padilla, Montoneros.

Buenos Aires (La Plata)—Bombings, barricades, fires, assaults with guns, propaganda in certain points of the city—"Enumeration follows."

Cordoba—Assaults with arms at the following places: Police Infantry, Military District, Police Chief, The Red Brigade of the Power Worker.

January 20, 1976: Buenos Aires (La Plata y Ensenada), Interception of passenger vehicles making them vacuate. Incendation of a bus from the National Highway Department.

January 21, 1976: Cordoba (Ciudad Capital), Numerous assaults with arms against public bases.

Capital Federal, Occupants of a private auto shot at the sentries of the Air Base "Aeroparque."

Capital Federal, Assassination from an auto of a Federal Agente, Juan Carlos Piaz, who was assigned to the house of a Police Chief.

January 25, 1976: Cordoba, Capture of the local commissary, with the taking of arms and uniforms, following with blowing up the building.

January 26, 1976: Rio Negro, Explosive attempt of the railroad bridge that connects the cities of Viedma and Carmen de Patagones.

January 27, 1976: Buenos Aires (San Isadro), Armed assault from a private auto against Rear Admiral Juan Martin Poggi's home.

January 27, 1976: Buenos Aires (Olivos), Armed assault against the capitan of the Frigate, Roberto Domingo di Bella.

January 28, 1976: Buenos Aires (San Fernando), An extremist group attacked uniformed policemen which resulted in the death of one and the critical wounding of another.

January 29, 1976: Buenos Aires (Munro), Assassination of the Manager of Industrial Relations, Alberto Olabarrieta, and the Supervisor of Personnel, Dr. Jorge Zarlenca, of the Bendix Corporation. Also assassinated was Juan Carlos Garabaglia, who intervened.

January 29, 1976: Santa Fe (Villa Constitucion), Armed assaults: 6th Regional Union, The E.N.T.E.L. guards, Factory in Chapuy, Home of a local politician, Grain elevators of the National Junta.

CONCLUSIONS

Quantitatively, not only did subversive actions diminish numerically as to the number of acts, but also with those that had correspondent authority.

The focal point for the extremist activity centered around major industrial provinces, like Buenos Aires, Cordoba, and Santa Fe, regions considered by armed clandestine organizations as vital to infiltrate and agitate.

From the analysis of the acts of major significance, emerges as the purpose of these groups to intimidate in a systematic manner unities and agencies of the FF.AA and security, also committing assassinations and intimidations of the people.

Numerous assaults were made against public transportation, some by the subversive organization and others by non-identified groups whose motives were as follows:

Stirring up public attention about acts that affect the organizations.

Help guild recoveries.

The activities initiated by the "Red Brigade" of the "Workers Power" and their radical methods stand out during this period.

Army blocks provincial takeovers—Top military leaders blocked an attempt by the federal government to "intervene," or replace, the provincial governments of Buenos Aires and Santa Fe, where recent political violence had been centered, it was reported Jan. 8. It was the second time in a month that the military had vetoed the planned ouster of Buenos Aires Gov. Victorio Calabro, a harsh critic of President Maria Estela Martinez de Peron.

Pre-coup violence—The military coup followed more political violence throughout Argentina in February and March. The unrest accelerated in the third week of March with widespread bombings, kidnappings and killings, bringing the 1976 political death toll to 175, according to press reports.

Nine policemen were shot to death and at least 30 civilians were kidnapped and murdered March 13-20, and a wave of bombings swept Buenos Aires and other major cities. The policemen were presumed killed by leftist guerrillas, notably the Montoneros, while the civilians were presumed to be victims of the AAA and other rightist groups.

ARGENTINA

(The AAA had been organized by ex-Social Welfare Minister Jose Lopez Rega, and its members, mostly off-duty federal policemen, had used social welfare ministry funds to buy arms smuggled in from Paraguay, according to testimony given to a congressional investigative panel by Salvador Horacio Paino, an imprisoned former army lieutenant and AAA recruiter, it was reported Feb. 4. Paino said two other former social welfare ministers, Carlos Villone and Rodolfo Roballos, were also involved in organizing and funding the commando group.)

The most serious of the bombings occurred March 15 in the parking lot of the army's general command building in Buenos Aires, killing one person and seriously wounding 29. Military sources said March 16 that the bomb was aimed at Lt. Gen. George Videla (who later led the coup that overthrew Mrs. Peron). Videla, however, escaped any injury. A second bomb apparently aimed at President Peron was dismantled by police March 18 after officers found two unidentified persons placing it near her office. Bombs set off by the Montoneros destroyed two restaurants in Cordoba March 13, killing two private guards and a kitchen employe.

Economic plan protested. The military coup was also preceded by strikes and protests by political, labor and management groups against the Peronist government's faltering economic policies.

The protests were directed mainly against an "emergency" plan announced March 5 by Economy Minister Emilio Mondelli. The plan, designed to control inflation, cut imports and promote exports, was approved by the International Monetary Fund (IMF), from which the government had hoped to obtain credits worth $304 million to meet its severe balance of payments problems. The plan's provisions included:

A 12% wage increase effective March 1 (against price rises of 40% since the last wage hike Jan. 1); a subsequent six-month wage freeze accompanied by controls on the prices of essential consumer goods; immediate price increases of more than 80% for fuel, 100% for electricity and postal rates, 70% for telephone service, 80%–150% for transportation, 50% for milk and 90% for wine; and a 70%–80% devaluation of the peso (which had already been devalued five times in 1976, the last time by 4.6% Feb. 23).

Mondelli admitted that the plan would be hardest on "the working man," but he said the worker "should know that if it is not put into effect by his government it will be imposed by others, and not precisely with his welfare in mind." The statement was taken as a warning that the armed forces would enact a similar plan if they seized power, according to press reports.

The plan was rejected March 6 by political, labor and management groups, newspapers and much of the public, according to reports. The Buenos Aires newspaper La Opinion asserted: "A way of life died last night in Argentina."

Thousands of metallurgical workers and automobile mechanics in Cordoba went on strike to protest the plan March 8 despite endorsement of the plan by Lorenzo Miguel, head of the Metallurgical Workers' Union. They were joined by auto workers in Buenos Aires, who remained on strike March 9 while the Cordoba strikers returned to their jobs. Shopkeepers in Buenos Aires struck against the plan's price controls March 9, and the two leading management groups, the General Economic Confederation (CGE) and Apede, issued statements denouncing the plan. (CGE head Julio Broner resigned March 8 after denouncing the government's policies and the labor unions' wage demands.)

President Peron modified the plan March 10 to mollify the protesters, raising the wage increase to 20% and creating a Remunerations Institute to protect real wages. However, more than 100,000 industrial workers struck in Buenos Aires, Cordoba and Santa Fe March 11–12 to demand a bigger increase. The strikes subsided March 13 after labor leaders warned that they might bring on a military coup.

The plan was also protested by congressional leaders, who were reportedly outraged when the government urged them to approve the plan because it had IMF backing. The congressmen demanded to know why the IMF had been apprised of the plan before they had been consulted, according to the Latin America Economic Report March 12.

Military Junta in Command

New government sworn. A new president and cabinet formally assumed power March 29, five days after the armed forces overthrew the government of President Maria Estela Martinez de Peron.

Lt. Gen. Jorge Videla, the army commander, took the oath of office as president and swore in a cabinet of two civilians and six military officers. The key civilian official was the new economy minister, Jose Martinez de Hoz, a leading industrialist who had held the economy post under a previous military government in the 1960s.

The other cabinet ministers were Ricardo Bruera, education; army Gen. Albano Harguindeguy, interior; Gen. Horacio Liendo, labor; Rear Adm. Cesar Guzzetti, foreign affairs; Rear Adm. Julio Pardi, social welfare; air force Brig. Julio Gomez, justice, and Brig. Jose Maria Klix, defense. Most of the military officers in the cabinet were relatively young and had no previous experience in public administration, according to press reports.

Final executive power was entrusted to the military junta composed of Videla, Adm. Emilio Massera and Brig. Orlando Agosti, according to a decree issued March 25. The junta members would serve three-year terms (regarded by observers as statutory limits only, and not an indication of how long the armed forces intended to rule). Legislation would be developed by a nine-man committee of top-ranking military officers headed by Gen. Carlos Dalla Tea, secretary of the army high command.

(Dalla Tea, like Videla, was regarded as a moderate opposed to a long and harsh period of military government. He had co-ordinated negotiations between Videla and civilian political and labor groups before the coup, according to press reports.)

Videla pledged March 30 to protect human rights and combat "subversive delinquency in all its forms," and he called for "sacrifice, work and austerity" to resolve the nation's acute economic crisis. The coup, he asserted, was "not directed against any social group or political party," and was undertaken only after the Peronist government ignored "repeated warnings" from the armed forces.

The new military government would carry out a "national reorganization" aimed at creating a strong state which exercised "control over the vital areas of security and development," Videla said. A new economic program would be instituted which would "assure private enterprise, and national and foreign capital, all the necessary conditions to participate with their maximum potential and creative force in the rational exploitation of our resources," he declared.

Brig. Jesus Orlando Capellini was appointed commander of the air force wing and academy in Cordoba April 10. Capellini had been arrested in December 1975 after he had led an unsuccessful attempt by air force officers to overthrow the Peronist government.

Economic plan made public—The military junta's economic plan had been drawn up by Martinez de Hoz and approved by military leaders before the coup, and it was leaked after the coup to the Buenos Aires newspaper La Prensa, which printed its essential points March 31. The plan declared "sanitation of the currency" to be its "principal objective" and it forecast unemployment and a fall in the buying power of wages.

Among the plan's provisions:

■ The foreign investment law would be replaced by one which restricted to the "indispensable minimum" the areas forbidden to foreign investment. Companies would be required to have only 51% local ownership—instead of the current 80%—to be categorized as "national" firms, and the confused category of "mixed" companies—part national and part foreign—would be eliminated. Representatives of foreign firms would no longer have to be registered, and problems created "artificially" to harass foreign companies would be "resolved soon and with all possible justice."

■ Controls on prices, exchange and importation would be removed, along with export subsidies, to halt the deterioration of the purchasing power of the peso.

■ Fiscal expenditure would gradually be reduced, money received for budgetary purposes would be increased and productive investment would be substantially raised.

ARGENTINA

■ Some state-owned companies, such as the railways, would remain in state hands but with new officials named for their ability and not their "political merits." Companies in which the state had partially intervened, especially industries, would have their state-owned shares gradually sold to "private capital." Firms taken over completely by the state to create sources of employment not provided by privately-owned firms would be offered for sale to private investors.

■ The black market would be eliminated along with the "overvalued" official exchange rate, with the aim of creating a single and free kind of exchange.

■ The state petroleum firm YPF would offer contracts to foreign companies to help halt the decline in oil production.

Martinez de Hoz, chairman of the board of Acindar, Argentina's largest steel firm, was well-known in international banking circles, according to press reports. Upon assuming office March 29 he swore in a nine-man team of economic assistants headed by Guillermo Walter Klein Jr. as secretary of economic coordination and programming.

(The military coup was followed by a rise in industrial productivity and worker attendance despite the occupation of the labor unions by soldiers. Labor sources confirmed that military officers and anti-Peronist labor leaders had reached a fairly detailed understanding before the coup, according to the Washington Post April 2. The labor leaders reportedly were told who would be arrested, which unions would be taken over and what economic policies would be instituted, in exchange for which they promised to offer only token resistance to the coup.)

Leftist groups outlawed. The military junta issued a decree March 25 outlawing five extreme leftist groups including the leading guerrilla organization, the People's Revolutionary Army (ERP).

The decree did not outlaw the Justicialista (Peronist) or Communist Parties, but it declared them in indefinite recess. The Communists expressed their "critical support" for the junta March 27 and said March 29 that it was "auspicious" that the junta had not pursued "a Pinochetist solution." The reference was to Gen. Augusto Pinochet, the Chilean military dictator who outlawed all leftist parties and instituted severe repression after seizing power in 1973.

(Nevertheless, Communists continued to clash with military soldiers seizing their offices. Two persons were killed March 25 in a 20-minute gunfight at Communist headquarters in Buenos Aires when marines went there to confiscate party documents.)

In other decrees March 25, the junta dismissed justices of the supreme court and other tribunals and ordered the removal of all state employes "connected in whatever form to subversive and allied activities." It also confirmed the temporary suspension of labor union activities and the right to strike.

In a further decree March 30, the junta froze the bank accounts of 74 political figures and 84 officials of eight major trade unions. The politicians included ex-President Peron, former President Hector Campora and 18 former cabinet ministers.

Security regulations tightened. Argentina's military junta issued a new security law March 26 providing stiff prison sentences and even the death penalty for a wide variety of offenses.

Under the law, attacks on military personnel, security police or prison officials would be punished with up to 15 years' imprisonment. If the attacks caused serious injury or death, they would be punished with indefinite jail terms or execution. The same penalties applied to attacks on military, police or prison installations or property.

Persons who resisted or refused to obey the orders of police, military or prison personnel would be sentenced to up to four years in jail, and those who threatened or "offended the dignity" of such personnel would face up to 10 years' imprisonment.

An earlier security decree that took effect March 24, the day the armed forces overthrew the Peronist government, provided 10-year prison terms for persons who "encouraged violence or disturbances." It provided for longer terms or death for persons who endangered the lives of others by damaging factories, gas or water supplies, public transport or other services, by poisoning or contaminating food or medical supplies or by detonating explosives.

Anyone shielding such criminals faced punishment as secondary participants in their crimes, with sentences of 15-25 years in prison in the case of crimes punishable by death. Special military courts throughout the country were to try offenders and death for those so sentenced would be by firing squad, according to the March 24 decree.

Other early junta actions. Among other actions taken during the military junta's early days in power:

■ A decree March 26 imposed strict controls on newspapers, radio and television stations. The media were ordered to defend "Christian morality" and "the institution of the family," and were forbidden to carry "sensationalist, violent or erotic" material or to quote "persons unqualified or lacking specific authorization to express themselves on matters of public interest."

(At least three newspapers had been closed since the coup, it was reported April 8. The newspaper Cronica of Comodoro Rivadavia had been shut down for 48 hours for interviewing the mother of a labor leader who was on trial there, and the Peronist daily La Manana of Victoria [Entre Rios Province] had been closed indefinitely for undisclosed reasons. Some 30 journalists had been arrested since the coup, it was reported March 30.)

■ A new Supreme Court of five conservative civilian lawyers was sworn in April 1 with the task of reorganizing the civil justice system. Twenty-four judges were officially dismissed April 5. The Buenos Aires courts resumed activities the next day after being closed since the coup March 24.

In the first trial since the military coup, an army court in the Patagonian port of Comodoro Rivadavia April 8 sentenced six Peronist labor leaders and a former Labor Ministry inspector convicted of illegal possession of arms and explosives to 3-10 years in prison. In a decision April 9, a military court in Mendoza sentenced a man to eight years' in prison for attacking police officers.

The nine-man Legal Advisory Commission that would assist the junta would be headed by Rear Adm. Antonio Vannek, and not by Gen. Carlos Dalla Tea, as announced earlier, it was reported April 2.

■ A decree April 1 provided for imprisonment of persons who promoted strikes. (Seventeen metalworkers in Cordoba were arrested April 17 for allegedly inciting other laborers to strike.)

■ Another decree April 1 barred political activities and associations in the universities. Teachers, students and university employes lost their say in university policymaking, which was left strictly to rectors, deans and Education Ministry officials.

■ The government April 2 ordered all foreign political refugees to report to authorities immediately to confirm their documents and addresses, and to report to the police monthly thereafter.

■ The government assured the United Nations' High Commissioner for Refugees that the 12,000 Chilean and other foreign political refugees in Argentina would not be returned to their native countries, it was reported April 9. At least 35 Chilean refugees were arrested April 3 at U.N.-financed residences in Buenos Aires, but about 20 were freed after questioning.

■ The death penalty was restored to the Argentine penal code by government decree June 26. It could be applied to persons convicted of killing a government official or any member of the armed forces or police, or persons convicted of other terrorist acts which resulted in death or serious injury. The death penalty had been abolished in Argentina in 1921, restored in 1970 and abolished again in 1972.

Political activities banned. The military junta issued a set of decrees June 4 that dissolved 48 political, labor and student organizations and established prison sentences for persons who engaged in political activities.

Twenty-two of the dissolved groups were declared illegal. The 22 included left-wing Peronist groups such as the Peronist Youth and the Peronist Working Youth, and extremist movements such as the Revolutionary Workers' Party and its armed wing, the People's Revolutionary Army. Among the dissolved groups that were not declared illegal were small Trotskyite, Maoist and orthodox Communist parties.

Persons who engaged directly in political activities would receive prison sentences of one month to three years. Possession, production or distribution of political literature was punishable by one month to two years in jail, and reporting of political activities or propaganda in the news media was punishable by one month to one year in prison.

(President Jorge Videla told a Brazilian newspaper July 11 that political parties and labor unions would be allowed to reorganize "at an opportune moment." There would be popular elections, he added, but only after the "complete annihilation" of political terrorism and the recovery of Argentina's economy.)

Action vs. Mrs. Peron & supporters. The junta June 23 revoked the political rights of ex-President Maria Estela Martinez de Peron and 35 former Peronist government officials and labor leaders. All were ordered arrested, although most were already in custody. Some others were living safely abroad.

Losing their rights along with Peron were Hector Campora and Raul Lastiri, both former presidents; Oscar Bidegain, Jorge Cepernic and Alberto Martinez Baca, former provincial governors; Jose Lopez Rega, Carlos Villone, Antonio Benitez, Anibal Demarco, Carlos Ruckauf and Jorge Taiana, all former Cabinet ministers, and Casildo Herreras, Lorenzo Miguel and Rogelio Papagno, former labor leaders.

Jose Gelbard, economy minister under both Campora and the late President Juan Domingo Peron, lost not only his political rights but also his Argentine citizenship. Gelbard, a naturalized Argentine of Polish birth, was living in the U.S.

The junta charged that the former politicians and labor leaders had "harmed the superior interests of the nation," neglecting their "public duties," tolerating "administrative corruption" and "facilitating subversion."

Mrs. Peron was formally charged with embezzling public funds. The charge was made in a report submitted to President Videla by Sadi Conrado Massue, a special government prosecutor. The report was leaked to the press June 4.

The fiscal mismanagement of Peron's administration had "no precedent in the annals of the handling of public finance," Massue reported. "It seems that deliberately, nothing was omitted to lead the country to the abysmal limits of a chaotic state, near the complete breakdown of the moral and material values that always . . . had filled the people with justified pride," he declared.

Massue's investigation was said to have concerned the disappearance of about $750,000 in presidential funds, much of which apparently was changed into foreign currency, the London Times reported June 18.

Mrs. Peron faced a second unspecified charge of embezzlement brought against her by Federal Judge Rafael Sarmiento, the Times reported. He brought the charge after reading Massue's report, the newspaper said.

Sarmiento issued an order July 1 that froze the goods of Peron and four of her former aides—Jose Lopez Rega, Carlos Villone, Julio Gonzalez and Luis Caballero. The four were also under investigation for misuse of public funds.

Lanusse arrested, freed. Ex-President Alejandro Lanusse was detained at an army base Aug. 6–11 as punishment for releasing an open letter in which he denounced the arrest of a number of university professors.

The letter, released Aug. 4, was addressed to Gen. Abdel Vilas, deputy commander of the Fifth Army Corps, who had announced at a press conference that 19 professors in Bahia Blanca had been arrested as "leftist infiltrators" and that 31 other persons were being sought as "conspirators." The 31 included Gustavo Malek, who had served as Lanusse's education minister in 1971–73.

In the letter, Lanusse had defended Malek and assailed the arrest of the professors. He said the professors were improperly charged and were denied any opportunity to defend themselves.

Malek, who was living in Uruguay as an official of the United Nations Educational, Scientific and Cultural Organization, denied Vilas' charge against him and made himself available to Argentine authorities at the Argentine Embassy in Montevideo, it was reported Aug. 5.

Rights curbs approved. The military government approved a series of curbs on individual rights as part of its campaign to root out "generalized corruption," it was reported Aug. 19.

The regime's anti-corruption unit, the National Administrative Investigations Court, was given unrestricted authority to conduct searches and to intercept mail and telephone conversations. The court would be assisted by all government information, security and police agencies.

Economic plan set. The military government April 2 announced a conservative economic recovery program designed to strengthen the role of the private sector and attract foreign investment.

The plan, described in a nationwide radio and television address by Economy Minister Jose Martinez de Hoz, reversed the nationalist and populist policies of the ousted Peronist regime. Martinez said the measures were necessary to curb rising prices, which he said had gone up 560% since March 1975, and to avoid what he called the "proletarianization" of Argentina's middle class.

Domestically, the program would remove price controls but place wage increases under strict government supervision. Collective bargaining would be prohibited, and the labor laws would be revised to make it easier for employers to dismiss workers. Nonessential state jobs would be eliminated to help cut the $2.38 billion budget deficit.

Tax laws would be strictly enforced for the first time, and new taxes would be introduced to cover individual and corporate property exceeding $20,000, transfers of real estate and stocks and bonds, and windfall profits. The official prices of farm products would be raised to stimulate exports, and the state monopoly on agricultural exports would be abolished.

Externally, foreign investors would be encouraged through tax breaks and other measures to invest in Argentina, particularly in areas such as the oil industry which could not be developed by local capital or required foreign technology. The exchange market would be liberalized as a first step toward a free, unified exchange system with a single rate for Argentine pesos. Initially the peso would be devalued by 30% in the effective rate for imports and exports.

A report in the Washington Post April 4 said that the program would insure continued unemployment, rising costs and falling purchasing power. The Post report said that these burdens would fall hardest on the middle- and lower-middle-class laborers who had supported the Peronist government. Observers likened the program to the economic policy of the reactionary military regime in Chile, although Martinez de Hoz denied that it entailed the "shock measures" imposed in Chile.

Martinez asserted it was not the state but the private sector that "drives the whole economic process. The state must not try to nullify the mechanism of the market as the basic orienting principle for economic activity and replace the market by complicated official regulations."

IMF approves standby credit. The International Monetary Fund announced Aug. 6 that it had approved a standby arrangement authorizing the Argentine government to purchase currencies up to the equivalent of 260 million special drawing rights ($300 million) over the next 12 months.

The credit was to support the financial program adopted by the military government in April. It was the largest loan granted by the IMF to a Latin American government.

The IMF had confirmed a $127 million loan to help alleviate Argentina's foreign exchange shortage, it was reported April 2.

Another loan, worth $87 million, was granted to Argentina by the Inter-American Development Bank for the construction of a 125-mile gas pipeline from Tierra del Fuego, in the extreme south, to Buenos Aires, it was reported Aug. 27.

Other economic developments. Among economic developments during the junta's early months in power:

The European Economic Community's ban on beef imports had cost Argentina

ARGENTINA

about $700 million per year since 1974, it was reported April 9. Sales to the Soviet Union of 100,000 tons of beef had helped ease the situation but stocks of live cattle had risen to 56 million head, according to the Latin America Economic Report.

Economy Minister Jose Martinez de Hoz announced that the 1976 budget provided for a deficit of 480 million pesos, equivalent to 5.6% of the gross national product, it was reported July 9. The 1975 deficit was equivalent to 12% of the GNP.

Argentina recorded a $400-million trade surplus in the first half of 1976, compared with a $700-million deficit in the same period of 1975, it was reported Aug. 2. Exports totaled $1.7 billion and imports, $1.3 billion. The European Economic Community was expected to become a major purchaser of Argentine agricultural and livestock exports because of the drought in Europe, according to the Aug. 20 Latin America Economic Report.

The real value of wages in Argentina had fallen by 43.2% between December 1975 and July 1976, according to Central Bank figures quoted by the Aug. 13 Latin America Economic Report. The fall in income was actually greater, the report said, because there was no overtime work and many companies were operating on three- or four-day weeks. The auto industry, which employed more than 100,000 workers, was nearly closed down, the Wall Street Journal reported Aug. 30.

Nevertheless, the stock exchange in Buenos Aires was booming, the New York Times reported Aug. 16. The average price of shares had risen to nearly 50¢ from the equivalent of 3¢ before the March military coup. Investors were profiting from a favorable tax climate, with no capital-gains tax and only a 5% tax on stock transfers, the Times said.

The government Aug. 14 issued a liberal new foreign investment law, reversing a restrictive law enacted three years before by the ousted Peronist regime. The new measure gave foreign investors the same rights and obligations as local investors, with access to local sources of credit. It placed no limit on the repatriation of profits or capital, so long as foreign exchange was available, but it imposed a special tax on profit remittances of more than 12% of the registered capital. The register of foreign investments would be controlled by the Central Bank, while the law would be administered by a new dependency of the Economy Ministry.

The government had fired 7,228 of the 1.7 million public employes from March 31 to June 30, but there had been a net gain of 646 public jobs in the period, the Wall Street Journal reported Aug. 30. The regime had pledged, when it took power in March, that it would drastically cut the top-heavy bureaucracy.

Hard-line generals retired. The army Dec. 3 announced the retirement of eight generals, including three prominent hard-liners, in an apparent move by President Jorge Videla to concentrate power among moderate officers.

None of the regional commanders, including Gen. Benjamin Menendez, the reputed leader of the rightists, was removed. But all of their deputies were replaced with officers considered to be moderates. The most prominent retiree was Gen. Acdel Vilas, deputy commander of the Fifth Army Corps in Bahia Blanca.

Debate reportedly continued in the army between the moderate faction, led by Videla and Gen. Roberto Viola, and the hard-liners, led by Menendez and Gen. Ramon Diaz Bessone. Military sources said the moderates wanted to return power to civilians in the near future while hard-liners wanted the armed forces to remain in control, the Associated Press reported.

Videla had tried to weaken Diaz Bessone by moving him to the newly created planning ministry, but Diaz and his allies had turned the agency into a superministry responsible for short, medium and long-term planning and supervision of policy in all areas, the London newsletter Latin America reported Oct. 29.

Diaz was allied with Adm. Emilio Massera, the navy commander who had presidential ambitions, Latin America said.

Violence & Violations of Human Rights

The political violence that had shaken Argentina for years continued unabated under the ruling military junta. It was charged that Argentinian opponents of the regime and leftwing refugees from Chile, Uruguay and Brazil were being subjected in Argentina to fresh repression—ranging from threats, arrests and kidnappings to torture and assassination. The Argentinian government was accused of complicity in, connivance at or at least tolerance of such acts.

Amnesty International's charges. An increase in violations of human rights in Argentina was reported by Amnesty International (AI) June 2. In what it described as a "brief summary of the human rights situation in Argentina," AI said:

Since the military coup of 24 March 1976, there has been a steady deterioration in the human rights' situation in Argentina. There are an estimated 20,000 people in detention at present, accurate figures are not available as yet, although the Argentinian government has promised to issue a complete list of prisoners. The majority of those detained have not been charged or tried and are being held under the State of Siege provision which has been in force since November 1974 (despite the fact that in January 1976 the now defunct Supreme Court declared the continuation of the State of Siege illegal).

The situation has been aggravated by the withdrawal after the coup of the right to opt for exile, this provision is contained in Article 23 of the constitution. Prison conditions are extremely poor: inadequate diet has caused malnutrition among the prisoners (families are not allowed to supplement the prison diet); inadequate medical attention; almost total censorship of all reading matter; families and friends visiting prisoners are intimidated and humiliated.

Whereas the Argentinian authorities have mounted an anti-guerrilla offensive, there have been remarkably few attempts to curb the activities of rightwing terrorists such as the Argentinian Anti-Communist Alliance (or AAA), and abductions and assassinations attributed to these groups have reached the alarming proportions of 15 political assassinations a day. One of the groups most vulnerable to this kind of attack is the Latin American refugee community who are regarded by the military as potentially subversive. Even those refugees who are under the protection of the United Nations High Commissioner for Refugees have been arbitrarily arrested or abducted. Although all refugees have been ordered to officially register as such, most are afraid to do so.

There have been various allegations received by Amnesty International that the huge military barracks of Campo de Mayo in Buenos Aires is used as a torture center and that many missing people are in fact being held there (e.g. Oscar Luis Montenegro, missing since October 1975 was recently seen there).

Whilst the Argentinian authorities insist that certain restrictive measures are necessary to combat leftwing subversion, many of the victims of the repression cannot be classified as guerrillas....

The U.S. affiliate of Amnesty International (A.I.U.S.A.) urged the Organization of American States (OAS) June 4 to take action against the violation of human rights in Argentina. Its statement said:

A.I.U.S.A. notes with deep regret the recent deaths of Uruguayan exiles arrested in Buenos Aires. Their bodies, most bearing marks of torture, were found in the outskirts of Buenos Aires on May 20th. These included two former Uruguayan parliamentarians, Senator Zelmar Michelini and Hector Gutierrez Ruiz, former President of the Uruguayan Chamber of Representatives. Another Uruguayan, Dr. Manuel Liberoff, disappeared at the same time and is still missing.

A.I.U.S.A. is alarmed at the recent tendency toward the abandonment of the traditional right to asylum and lack of tolerance toward political exiles and refugees.

In his inaugural address as President of Argentina in March, General Jorge Rafael Videla promised to respect human rights. Foreign Minister Cesar Augusto Guzetti assured the United Nations High Commissioner for Refugees April 5th that the thousands of political refugees from other countries living in Argentina will not be persecuted or returned to their countries of origin. There is overwhelming evidence to the contrary.

On April 10, Chilean refugee Edgardo Enriquez Espinosa was abducted from his home in Buenos Aires together with a Brazilian woman, Regina Macondes. In early May it was reported that he had been repatriated and was held in a torture center in Chile. The Argentinian authorities are reported to have denied the repatriation, but they continue missing.

In spite of statements made by the new Argentine authorities that international law would be respected and the rights of refugees protected, reports from Argentina prove otherwise. There are approximately 9,000 defacto refugees who have been declared eligible for U.N. High Commission for Refugees protection but who have not been granted asylum. There are reports of "black lists" that have been circulated to embassies in Argentina naming people who must not be granted asylum.

It is alarming to us that the Argentine government has banned the press to report on arrests, disappearances or killings. Reports received by Amnesty International range from between nine and 30,000 arrests since the military takeover, but there are no reliable estimates as lists of detainees have

ARGENTINA

not been issued even in the face of increasing international pressure. This lack of information is clearly disturbing to the population and to the relatives of arrested or disappeared persons who have no access to information about the fate of their family members.

A.I.U.S.A. questions what measures have been taken to investigate allegations that foreign political police agents (Chilean, Paraguayan and Uruguayan) operate inside Argentinian territory with impunity. There is evidence of collaboration between the political and military police of neighboring countries throughout the Southern Cone.

A.I.U.S.A. also is concerned at reports that members of the Argentinian police and military are involved in the parapolice organization, Argentinian Anticommunist Alliance (AAA) responsible for over 2,000 killings before the March 1976 military coup and for at least 300 further assassinations after. It questions what steps have been taken to curb the activities of the AAA.

Just as in Chile after the September 1973 coup, Latin American exiles in Argentina are subject to persecution, torture and assassination because, in the eyes of the security forces, exiles are seen as potential "subversive" elements. Some of the exiles have been politically active in their countries; others have been persecuted simply because they were relatives of alleged subversives, intellectuals or officials of a former government, or sometimes for no apparent reason whatsoever.

Kennedy on repressions. U.S. Sen. Edward M. Kennedy (D, Mass.) told the U.S. Senate June 15 of his "great concern, sadness and horror at the daily barrage of human rights violations now reported from Argentina." Kennedy said, according to his statement printed in the Congressional Record:

Despite the pledge of the new Junta in Argentina that it would not follow the course of the Chile or Uruguayan military in their political repression and violation of human rights, the events in Argentina raise deep questions of its will and its capacity to rein in the extremists.

What is worse, the recent burglary in the refugee center under the supervision of the United Nations High Commissioner, a center barely a block from a local police precinct, raise serious fears that there are some in the new military government who are quietly looking away or even encouraging the paramilitary squads terrorizing the refugee community.

We heard of the forced return of Edgardo Enriquez, a Chilean leader of an extremist group to Chile, and of his disappearance.

Then came the abduction and murders of two former Uruguayan legislators, neither of whom had any record of extremist activity.

Daily reports continue as well of refugees and Argentine citizens disappearing one day, their bodies found along riverbeds or on city streets the next.

Last week, the same submachine gun toting groups broke into the Catholic refugee center offices and stole the list of refugees in Argentina who were under UN protection.

A day later, 25 refugees, men and women who had fled political repression from Chile, Uruguay and Paraguay, were abducted at gunpoint from a hotel under U.N. responsibility.

A day later they were turned loose, in some cases, simply pushed from cars into the street. They had been tortured. They had been beaten. And they had been warned to leave the country.

One had hoped that the change in government in Argentina might lead to a restoration of stability, and a restoration of a democratic political system, surely one which respected basic human rights.

The failure to put a halt to the paramilitary terrorist activities has changed those hopes into grave concerns. The current government in Argentina, whether fairly or unfairly, is going to be held to account for its failure to control these brutal paramilitary groups within the country.

The Argentina Government must recognize that not only individual suffering, violence and death are being sown by these paramilitary groups but the undermining of any possible cooperation by international agencies and organizations, and or by other friendly governments in the economic restoration needed in Argentina today.

Regime aids Uruguayan squads? Amnesty International's Committee to Abolish Torture charged that Uruguayan government kidnap, torture and murder squads operated against Uruguayan refugees in Argentina with impunity and with apparent support of the Argentine regime. According to a committee statement:

Convincing evidence that the campaign of terror against refugees in Argentina has increased dramatically since the March 1976 coup there comes from 12 Uruguayan refugees, including three children, who arrived in Paris in mid-July.

Three of the refugees, one woman and two men, had been kidnapped and severely tortured during captivity by unknown assailants, whom the victims believe to have included both Uruguayans and Argentinians. The three torture victims were abducted in Buenos Aires on 6 July by about 30 armed men, who hooded them and bundled them into a car and took them to what they believe to be a private house in the countryside.

The three were released on 13 July, the same day that 23 other Uruguayan refugees, including 11 women and two children, were abducted in Buenos Aires. Amnesty International believes that it is unlikely that many of these 23 are still alive.

The three torture victims now in Paris were photographed and fingerprinted while in captivity in Argentina. They were also shown lists of names of other Uruguayan refugees who were being sought. Some of the names were marked with a cross. They were told this meant that these persons were marked for death.

Prior to a news conference in Paris, sponsored by Amnesty International's French section, the torture victims were examined by two members of the Amnesty International Danish doctors' team. The doctors confirmed that the marks and symptoms on the victims are consistent with their allegations. They were also consistent with marks and symptoms shown by other victims of torture examined in the past by this team in Greece and among Latin American refugees in Scandinavia.

The woman victim, aged about 22, has marks of electrical shock over her breasts and thighs and a very bad bruise on her spine. She has cigarette burns on her wrists, breasts, arms and legs.

She stated that she had also had buckets of freezing cold water thrown over her (it is now winter in Argentina). She is currently undergoing tests for tuberculosis and bronchitis. She further alleges that she was raped in front of her two companions.

One of the male victims, aged about 25, has electric shock marks on his chest, navel, and the top of his legs, as well as bruises on his legs, severe cigarette burns on his arms and legs and 40 cigarette burns on one hand. Besides similar marks, the second man, aged about 24, shows symptoms of psychological stress from a former two-year period of solitary confinement in prison in Uruguay before his kidnapping in Argentina.

The refugees confirmed the substance of the following excerpt from a letter received in August by Amnesty International from other Uruguayan exile sources in Buenos Aires: the Uruguayan security forces, with the tacit support of the Argentinian authorities, are those directly responsible for all that has happened to Uruguayan residents in Buenos Aires. At this moment it would be impossible for their families to negotiate for the life or liberty of these victims because their disappearance forms part of the so-called *Plan Mercurio* destined to eliminate all Uruguayans of leftwing tendencies in both countries. This plan relies on the official support of the police authorities in both countries.

To this information the refugees who arrived in Paris adds that there is a specially selected force of 600 Uruguayan army personnel operating in Argentina under the direction of a certain Colonel RAMIREZ, who, according to the refugees, recently arrived from the United States to direct the campaign. With his second-in-command, Campos HERMIDAS, he operates from private houses without any set headquarters in Argentina.

The particular targets for these semi-clandestine activities are Uruguayan trade unionists in Argentina, who have accounted for a relatively high percentage of the kidnap and murder victims in the last several months.

Rep. Koch describes situation. U.S. Rep. Edward I. Koch (D, N.Y.) told the U.S. House of Representatives Aug. 26 that "what at present is happening in Argentina ... is a haunting specter of rampant anticlericalism and anti-Semitism, of rightwing thugs murdering Catholic priests and terrorizing those whose policies are simply democratic, while the Argentine government tacitly approves these actions." Koch said (as recorded in the Congressional Record):

Eleven Roman Catholic priests have been arrested in Argentina in the last few months, apparently because their nonviolent work for social justice is considered "subversive" by the government. Tragically, at least three other priests have been murdered by right-wing gunmen. It was particularly outrageous to Americans when an American Roman Catholic priest, Rev. James Martin Weeks of the La Salette Novitiate was arrested, beaten, and held for 10 days along with five seminarians in Argentina. Thanks to the efforts of the State Department and my good friend and colleague, JOE EARLY, Father Weeks was released and flown to the United States, but many have been left behind who are in danger of death.

Nazi publications are flourishing in Argentina. There is widespread distribution of "Mein Kampf" and the fraudulent anti-Semitic tract, Protocols of the Elders of Zion. Rightist magazines are characterizing Hitler as the "Savior of the West." Such material has been distributed in the schools. The Argentine Government piously says that it is not condoning this practice, but it has taken

ARGENTINA

no steps to prevent its distribution. All of this is happening at a time when all democratically oriented literature—always denounced as leftist—has been banned. There is no freedom of expression in Argentina, and by its silence in the face of Neo-Nazi propaganda, the Government of Argentina has legitimized that virulent philosophy.

Perhaps most threatened are the thousands of South American refugees who have fled political persecution in Chile, Brazil, Uruguay, and elsewhere. The Argentine Government has already determined that these refugees are not compatible with the nation's security. The U.N. High Commissioner on Refugees has appealed to member nations to take 1,000 refugees from Argentina, terming the situation as "grave." Some have already been killed, and many more have been terrorized. The level of violence has not yet reached its crescendo and continues to escalate. The world was shocked by the discovery of 47 more people slaughtered by right-wing groups and Argentine security forces only last weekend.

Koch Sept. 8 described a spate of anti-Semitic literature recently appearing in Argentina and "even ... distributed in the schools." He added:

But the situation has gone beyond proliferation of hate literature. Last week, a new group calling itself the Argentine National Socialist Front emerged to proclaim an all out war against "a Jewish-Bolshevik plutocracy." This group, the FNSA, is seeking to blame Argentina's 500,000-member Jewish community for the country's growing economic problems and has taken credit for the bombing of two synagogues and a drug store in Buenos Aires August 27. In a letter from the FNSA publicly circulated after the bombings, the neo-Nazi group said that the bombings marked the opening of a campaign of "diverse punitive operations against important elements of international Judaism."

AI team probes abuses. A three-member team representing Amnesty International gathered extensive evidence of human-rights abuse during a visit to Argentina Nov. 5–15.

U.S. Rep. Robert Drinan (D, Mass.), a Catholic priest who was on the team, said Nov. 15 that the team had heard "incredible tales of torture being used" by the Argentine government. "There's no reason to deny or question the veracity of witnesses," Drinan said. "It's just an unbelievable situation."

Drinan said that the team's report would include comments on political violence, on conditions in Argentine prisons, on claims by prisoners of mistreatment, on the problems of political refugees, on kidnappings and on emergency legislation enacted by the military government.

With Drinan on the team were Lord Avebury of Britain and Patricia Feeney, a British citizen who was a special representative of Amnesty International.

Rights abuses damage U.S. relations. The abuse of human rights in Argentina had damaged the country's relations with the U.S. Washington had quietly warned Buenos Aires that it should exercise more restraint in its campaign against leftists, the Miami Herald reported Oct. 5. Argentine Foreign Minister Cesar Guzzetti charged Oct. 6 that U.S. congressional hearings on human-rights abuse in Argentina constituted "interference" in his nation's internal affairs.

Guzzetti charged that witnesses at recent hearings by a subcommittee of the House International Relations Committee included known subversives. He cited as an example the Rev. James M. Weeks, an American priest who had been expelled from Argentina in August after being held for two weeks on subversion charges.

(The U.S. Embassy in Buenos Aires had compiled a classified report on rights abuse in Argentina. The report was compiled at the request of Rep. Donald M. Fraser [D, Minn.], the subcommittee's chairman. A suit to force release of the document had been filed by the recently formed Council on Hemispheric Affairs, it was reported Dec. 19. Laurence R. Birns, the council's director, said that those who had read the report said it strongly condemned the human-rights record of the Argentine government and appeared to establish government complicity in right-wing death squads.)

The Argentine government announced in the last week of December that it had freed 559 political prisoners since the beginning of November and 1,537 since April. Security sources told AP that 3,000 political prisoners still were being held, including ex-President Maria Estela Martinez de Peron and many of her key aides.

British couple freed. A British university lecturer and his Argentine wife, Richard and Cristina Whitecross, were released from prison in Buenos Aires April 8 after being held without charge for more than four months. They flew April 11 to England, where Richard Whitecross called the Argentine police "torturers, murderers, inhuman people."

Whitecross said he and his wife had been tormented in custody but not tortured physically. Whitecross claimed to have been threatened with death and forced to watch police severely beat a fellow prisoner.

Argentine magazines close. Two independent Argentine periodicals, Crisis and Cuestionario, ceased publication in June because their staff members lacked adequate protection from attacks by right-wing terrorists, the London newsletter Latin America reported July 23.

Both magazines had been founded in May 1973, after the installment of the Peronist government of ex-President Hector Campora. Crisis had been considered one of the leading cultural and political journals in Latin America, effectively replacing the left-wing Uruguayan journal Marcha, which was banned by the Uruguayan government in November 1974.

Right-wing Argentine terrorists, widely presumed to be off-duty policemen and soldiers, had threatened and attacked many journalists with whom they disagreed politically. "It seemed stupid to wait until they actually killed somebody," an editor of one of the closing magazines told Latin America.

Political murders, abductions continue. Assassinations and political kidnappings continued throughout Argentina in the last quarter of 1976. The political death toll for the year passed 1,400, according to press reports Dec. 19.

The majority of victims were known or suspected leftists who were killed by security forces or by death squads composed of policemen and soldiers. Army officers admitted that violence by police death squads had become as big a problem as guerrilla violence, the Washington Post reported Sept. 11.

The suspected leftists included Roman Catholic priests who were arrested and tortured by plainclothed policemen. Patrick Rice, an Irish priest working with the poor in Buenos Aires, was arrested Oct. 11 and subjected to electric shock and immersion before he was released and deported Dec. 3. Pope Paul VI had demanded Sept. 27 that the Argentine government provide an "adequate explanation" for the killing of several priests earlier in 1976.

Other victims included security officers and business executives who were killed by members of the People's Revolutionary Army (ERP) and the Montoneros, the two leftist guerrilla forces. However, the ERP suffered severe reverses. Gen. Antonio Bussi, governor and military commander of Tucuman Province, said Nov. 24 that the last ERP guerrillas operating in the Tucuman mountains had been killed.

The many guerrilla movements had lost 4,000 members in 1976 through deaths, arrests and desertions, according to military and press reports cited by the Mexican newspaper Excelsior Jan. 3, 1977. The hardest hit was the ERP, which reportedly lost 1,800 persons, or 90% of its members. The group also lost almost all of its weapons to security forces, including large quantities of rifles, machine guns, pistols and explosives used in the ERP's raids in rural Tucuman Province.

The Montoneros were said to have lost 1,600 persons, or about 80% of their members. This estimate might be too high, Excelsior said, noting, however, that the Montonero leadership definitely was in disarray. Roberto Quieto, the guerrillas' second-in-command, had been arrested at the beginning of 1976, and Norma Arrostito, another top leader, had been killed in November.

Other small guerrilla organizations such as "ERP-August 22" and "Workers' Power" reportedly had lost 750 persons, or nearly all their members, Excelsior said.

In addition to losing most of their members, the guerrilla groups were having little success getting new recruits, Excelsior reported. Practically no new guerrillas were coming out of the factories and the universities, the old strongholds of Montonero support, the newspaper noted.

Consequently the Montoneros and the ERP were talking of forming political parties to conquer power by peaceful means, Excelsior reported. The ERP had decided to give up armed struggle, but the Montoneros had not yet taken that step, the newspaper said.

Victims of violence following the coup included Chief Police Inspector Guillermo Pavon, assassinated March 29, and guerrilla leader Eduardo Castelo Soto, a Peruvian who had headed the Cordoba branch of the Revolutionary Workers' Party, the political arm of the ERP. Castelo was killed in a shootout with Cordoba security officers April 3.

(In a related development, Olga Talamante, a U.S. citizen jailed in 1974 for allegedly aiding Peronist guerrillas, was freed and deported March 27. On arrival in the U.S. the next day she repeated her earlier charges that she had been tortured in custody.)

The worst bloodshed occurred during the first five days of July, when at least 76 persons were killed. This was only the number of confirmed deaths, the London Times noted July 6. There were indications that as many as 120 persons might have been killed during the period, the newspaper said.

Soldiers killed 17 leftist guerrillas July 2 when the insurgents attacked the Campo de Mayo army installation north of Buenos Aires. Later that day presumed leftists detonated a bomb in the dining room of a Buenos Aires building housing the security department of the federal police. The police said that 18 persons were killed and 66 injured in the blast, but unofficial sources told the London Times July 5 that 43 had died.

In apparent reprisal for the bombing, right-wing terrorists killed at least 20 persons in Buenos Aires July 3-4. The bullet-riddled bodies of 15 unidentified persons were found in the streets of the capital July 3. The next day three Roman Catholic priests and two seminarians of an Irish-Argentine order were shot to death in the parish residence of St. Patrick's Church in Buenos Aires.

The priests' killers wrote a message in chalk on the wall of the residence, but police rubbed it out. A priest who saw the message said it read, "For the police that died," an apparent reference to the July 2 bombing. However, the priest said the victims "never had any political activity."

Murders by right-wing terrorists had escalated after the assassination June 18 of the federal police chief, Gen. Cesareo Cardozo. He was killed by a time-bomb placed under his bed by a friend of his daughter. The friend was later identified by police as Ana Maria Gonzalez, a member of the ERP.

The bullet-riddled bodies of seven unidentified persons were found in Buenos Aires June 19, next to a placard signed by the "Gen. Cardozo Commandos." One of the bodies bore a sign saying, "I am Ana Maria Gonzalez," but the body was too badly burned to be identified positively.

Earlier in June, right-wing terrorists had kidnapped and then released 25 foreign political refugees in Buenos Aires. The exiles—23 Chileans, a Paraguayan and a Uruguayan—were taken from their hotels June 11. They were released June 12 after strong protests were made to the Argentine government by the office of the United Nations' High Commissioner for Refugees, which looked after thousands of political exiles in Argentina.

All 25 refugees had been beaten and some had been tortured with electric prods. They said that their abductors had given them 48 hours to leave Argentina and had threatened to kill them if they spoke to the press about the kidnapping. Police guards were assigned June 12 to 18 residences of refugees in Buenos Aires. The residences were financed partly or wholly by the U.N.

The quick release of the kidnapped refugees was one of several indications that their captors were off-duty policemen. The kidnappers had used unmarked Ford Falcon automobiles to take away the refugees. These cars were normally used by members of the Argentine Anticommunist Alliance and other terrorist groups consisting of police and military intelligence agents. Nevertheless, the government deplored the kidnapping and told the U.N. June 12 that no security officers had been involved in it.

Officials of the U.N. High Commissioner's office in Geneva said June 14 that they were asking other countries to take Latin American refugees who felt that their lives were endangered in Argentina. Priority was given to the 25 kidnap victims. Refugees in Buenos Aires were particularly worried by the theft June 10 of a list of names and addresses of 2,000 political refugees from offices of the Roman Catholic International Migrations Committee. The list was taken by armed men who fled in an unmarked Ford Falcon.

Senior military officers were elated by the successes against the guerrillas in July and early August, notably the killing of Mario Roberto Santucho, ERP founder and leader, the London Times reported Aug. 9. A combat general told the Times that 80% of the ERP leadership and 50% of its guerrillas had been eliminated. Other officers spoke of a "total war" against Argentine guerrillas in which authorities used interrogation techniques similar to those used by the French army in Algeria in the late 1950s and early 1960s.

"When the French army captured a guerrilla, they had the name of his whole cell within half an hour," an officer told the Times. "Let's not talk about what happened in that half hour, but the same is happening in Argentina," he said, alluding to widespread reports that jailed guerrillas were being tortured.

Acknowledging their recent losses, the Montoneros and the ERP went into what they called a period of "strategic withdrawal," concentrating on political organization and only occasional kidnappings, bombings and assassinations, the London newsletter Latin America reported Aug. 20. The two groups and a third, new guerrilla organization, the Red Brigades of People's Power, were forming a united Argentine Liberation Organization, Latin America had reported Aug. 6.

Two major incidents occurred before dawn Aug. 20, when presumed rightists killed 47 persons in two Buenos Aires suburbs. Thirty of the victims were shot and then mutilated with explosives in an isolated area of Pilar. Beside their bodies were signs reading, "Montonero Cemetery" and "Executed for being enemies of the fatherland." The bodies of the other 17 victims were found along a main highway in Banfield.

The government vigorously condemned the killings and promised to find and punish the culprits. A government source said later that a military officer was responsible for the Pilar murders, the New York Times reported Aug. 28. The victims, the source said, included Montoneros who had been arrested for trying to assassinate President Jorge Videla in March.

Nine other Montoneros were killed by security forces in Cordoba Aug. 14–15, and four more died in a shootout with police in a Buenos Aires suburb Sept. 4. Many ERP guerrillas also were killed by authorities, including at least four in Rosario Aug. 2 and two in Cordoba Aug. 29. Security forces broke up an ERP arms-manufacturing operation Sept. 1, confiscating 300 weapons at nine metallurgical plants.

Incidents reported—Among incidents reported in 1976's final seven months:

—Soldiers killed eight leftist guerrillas June 1 in a raid on a guerrilla camp in the mountains outside Cordoba. Security officers June 18 killed 10 guerrillas in Bahia Blanca, 11 on June 20 in Buenos Aires, a total of 10 on June 24 in Bahia Blanca and La Plata, 12 on June 29 in La Plata and seven in Cordoba July 5.

—The Spanish magazine Cambio 16 reported June 19 that Argentine political dissidents were being thrown to their deaths from navy airplanes flying at heights of 2,000 meters. The dissidents were first abducted by plainclothes security officers who stole the victims' furniture and other possessions, the magazine said.

—The Rev. James M. Weeks, an American Roman Catholic priest who had taught in Argentina since 1967, was arrested in Cordoba Aug. 3 with one Chilean and four Argentine seminarians. Police ransacked Weeks' home, claiming to have found "abundant Marxist-Leninist literature and a record of subversive songs." Weeks was held incommunicado for more than a week before he was allowed to see a U.S. consular official. After the U.S. State Department made an official protest, Weeks was released Aug. 17 and expelled from Argentina Aug. 19.

Weeks said Sept. 2, after returning to the U.S., that clergymen and others who worked for the poor in Argentina lived in fear of being kidnapped, tortured and murdered by rightist groups allied to the police and armed forces. He said that at least nine priests and seminarians had been killed in Argentina recently and that he suspected foul play in the Aug. 4 death of Enrique Angelelli, the bishop of La Rioja. Angelelli, who had spoken out for the rights of political prisoners, died when the pickup truck he was driving went out of control and crashed. The Buenos Aires newspaper La Opinion had voiced the same suspicion Aug. 6.

—Jesus Cejas and Crescencio Galanena, administrative employes of the Cuban Embassy in Buenos Aires, disappeared Aug. 9. The Cuban government told Argentina the next day that it was "deeply worried" about the incident, fearing the two aides had been kidnapped by rightists. The Associated Press in Buenos Aires received a purported message from the Cubans Aug. 16 saying they had "deserted the embassy to enjoy the freedom of the western world."

—Hipolito Solari Yrigoyen and Mario Abel Amaya, ex-federal legislators of the left-wing faction of the Radical Civic Union, were kidnapped by rightists in Chubut Province Aug. 18. They were rescued Aug. 30 when police intercepted an automobile in which they were being transported by the abductors.

—Presumed left-wing guerrillas Aug. 19 assassinated Carlos Antonio Bergonetti, an executive of the Fiat automobile company in Cordoba, and retired Gen. Omar Actis, president of the government organizing committee for the 1978 World Cup soccer championship in Buenos Aires. The assassinations were the first major guerrilla operations since the killing of ERP leader Santucho the previous month.

—Presumed rightists set off bombs Aug. 27 in front of two synagogues and in front of shops and a newspaper (La Opinion) that were owned by Jews. The next day a bomb ripped through a drugstore in a predominantly Jewish area of the city. The explosions followed other attacks on businesses owned by Jews. The incidents coincided with a proliferation of anti-Semitic and pro-Nazi literature in Buenos Aires. The literature, produced mostly by the company Editorial Milicia, included Spanish translations of "The Protocols of the Elders of Zion," an anti-Semitic tract, and Adolf Hitler's "Mein Kampf."

Criterio, the leading Roman Catholic magazine, urged the government Aug. 15 to prohibit the circulation of Nazi publications. Two Jewish groups, the Israelite Cultural, Educational and Recreational Association and the Delegation of Argentine Jewish Associations, denounced the Nazi literature Aug. 28. The government had decided to ban the distribution and export of the literature, but President Jorge Videla had not yet signed the decree, the New York Times reported Aug. 30.

—Carlos M. Baldovinos, chief inspector of the federal police bureau in Bahia Blanca, was killed Sept. 12 by presumed guerrillas. He had gained prominence by investigating charges that professors at the local university were involved in subversive activities. Gustavo Malek, a former education minister who had been implicated in the probe, was acquitted by a local court.

—Patricia Erb, an American student living in Buenos Aires, was kidnapped Sept. 15. She turned up Oct. 2 in a Buenos Aires jail, where she was allowed a brief visit with her father, John D. Erb, a Mennonite missionary. She presumably was arrested for left-wing activities at the National University.

—Domingo Lozano, manager of the Renault auto plant in Cordoba, was killed by presumed guerrillas Oct. 10.

—The naked bodies of nine youths were found Oct. 14 floating in a river north of Buenos Aires. They had been in the water for 45 days, according to the police. The youths were presumed to be death-squad victims.

—A bomb exploded Oct. 16 in the movie theater of the Buenos Aires army officers' club, wounding more than 50 persons. The Montoneros claimed responsibility for the blast, according to press reports.

—Mario Abel Amaya, an imprisoned former legislator belonging to the Radical Civic Union, died Oct. 19. The French newspaper Le Monde reported Oct. 22 that his death was the result of poor treatment in jail.

—The army announced Oct. 20 that Chris Ana Olson de Oliva, a 30-year-old American citizen, had been killed in a shoot-out with soldiers. The army claimed that Mrs. Oliva, the daughter of Carl Olson, a vice president of Kaiser Industries, was a leftist guerrilla.

—The Associated Press reported Nov. 21 that authorities had killed more than 120 guerrillas during November, 45 of them in the previous week.

—The army announced Dec. 3 that it had killed Norma Arrostito, a Montonero leader who had participated in the 1970 assassination of ex-President Pedro Aramburu.

—In retaliation for Arrostito's slaying, the Montoneros set off a bomb Dec. 15 in an auditorium in the Defense Ministry building in Buenos Aires, killing nine persons and seriously injuring 19.

—At least 17 guerrillas were killed by security forces in Buenos Aires Dec. 16–18.

Torres of Bolivia slain—Retired Gen. Juan Jose Torres, who led a leftist Bolivian government in 1970–71, was kidnapped in Argentina June 1 and slain.

Torres' blindfolded and bullet-riddled body was found June 2 on a rural road about 60 miles from Buenos Aires. No one claimed credit for the assassination, the third of a foreign political leader in Argentina in two weeks.

Torres had lived in Buenos Aires since 1973, when he fled Chile after the right-wing military coup. He had been living in Chile since the 1971 fall of his government in a bloody revolt led by Gen. Hugo Banzer Suarez. At the time of Torres' slaying, Bolivia's rightist regime was led by Banzer.

The slaying also was condemned by the Bolivian and Argentine governments. They blamed it on "international extremists," presumably referring to allies of a leftist group that claimed credit for the May 11 assassination in Paris of Gen. Joaquin Zenteno Anaya, Bolivian ambassador to France.

European socialists protest violence—A group of Western European socialist and social democratic leaders took a paid advertisement in the New York Times Aug. 26 to express their concern over the rising tide of violence in Argentina.

The statement, signed by Swedish Premier Olof Palme and Austrian Chancellor Bruno Kreisky, among others, asserted that "the measures adopted until now by the military junta ... place new obstacles in the way to a peaceful and democratic solution to the problems of the country, and they promote new acts of violence."

Other leaders signing the statement included Anker Jorgensen, premier of Denmark; Mario Soares, leader of the Portuguese Socialist Party, and Francois Mitterrand, the French Socialist leader.

Press unit asks arrest probes. Adepa, the national press association, asked the government Dec. 30 to investigate the cases of journalists who had been arrested or had disappeared.

Arturo Keolliker Frers, editor of the German community magazine La Plata Ruf, and Luis Fossatti, a contributor to the magazines La Semana and Panorama, were among the missing journalists, according to an Adepa statement published in local newspapers.

Roberto Vacca, a television commentator, was recently released by armed men who had kidnapped him and held him blindfolded for two weeks, it was reported Dec. 30. Ricardo Bach Cano, director of the newspaper Prensa Libre, was believed being held by security forces.

In earlier developments:

—David Kraiselburd, two-year-old son of Raul Kraiselburd, editor of the La Plata newspaper El Dia, was kidnapped by unidentified persons Sept. 1. The boy's grandfather, David Kraiselburd, had been kidnapped and killed by left-wing Peronists in 1974.

—The government banned 12 anti-Semitic publications, it was reported Sept. 14.

—The government closed the Cordoba newspaper Los Principios Sept. 13–18.

Other Developments

Falkland Islands dispute. British Ambassador Derick Ashe returned to London "for consultations" Jan. 19, six days after the Argentine government asked him to leave Buenos Aires because of the

ARGENTINA

renewed conflict between Britain and Argentina over the Falkland (Malvinas) Islands.

Argentina's ambassador in London, Manuel de Anchorena, had returned to Buenos Aires in December 1975 after a British mission headed by Lord Shackleton arrived in the Falklands to study ways of diversifying the islands' economy, particularly by developing petroleum and fishing industries. De Anchorena would remain in Argentina indefinitely, the government announced Jan. 14.

Argentine Foreign Minister Manuel Arauz Castex had then asked the British government Jan. 13 to withdraw its ambassador (Ashe) because of Britain's refusal to discuss Argentina's claim to sovereignty over the islands.

Arauz Castex rejected as "unacceptable" a note from British Foreign Secretary James Callaghan calling the dispute over the islands a "sterile" argument. Argentina had renewed its request for negotiations over the Falklands following public protests in December 1975 against the Shackleton mission.

(Argentina strenuously objected to British exploitation of the Falklands' potential oil reserves, the London Times reported Jan. 20. A U.S. consortium involving Ashland Oil Inc. had been pressing the British government for permission to explore for offshore deposits in the area, according to the Times.)

In a related development Jan. 15, the Inter-American Juridical Committee of the Organization of American States declared its support for Argentina's "unassailable right to sovereignty" over the Falklands.

An Argentine destroyer fired two warning shots at a British research ship near the Falkland Islands Feb. 4, provoking stern protests from Britain.

The shots were fired after the British ship, the Shackleton, ignored orders from the Argentine destroyer to stop and be escorted to an Argentine port in Tierra del Fuego. The Shackleton proceeded to Port Stanley in the Falklands, pursued by the Argentine destroyer until it came within six miles of the port.

Argentine Foreign Minister Raul Quijano charged Feb. 4 that the Shackleton had been conducting unauthorized geological and geophysical research in Argentine waters. Great Britain reaffirmed its sovereignty over the Falklands and the Shackleton resumed its research off the islands Feb. 21.

'76 inflation sets record. Economy Ministry figures showed that the Argentine cost of living rose by a record 347.5% in 1976, up slightly from 335% in 1975, according to press reports Jan. 7, 1977.

The biggest increase was in rents, which rose by 453.7% in 1976. Food was next with a 365.6% increase.

Bolivia

Violence

Police, guerrillas clash. A policeman and a student were killed April 2 during a gun battle between police and suspected leftist guerrillas in La Paz.

The government said the dead student was an insurgent who belonged to the Workers' Revolutionary Party, political arm of the National Liberation Army (ELN), Bolivia's major guerrilla group. The ELN's leader, Ruben Sanchez, reportedly escaped during the gunfight.

(Sanchez, a former army major, had led one of the army columns which tracked down the ELN's founder, the late Ernesto "Che" Guevara, in 1967. Sanchez had joined the guerrillas in 1971, after the leftist regime of Gen. Juan Jose Torres was overthrown in a right-wing military revolt.)

The gun battle followed police raids on three ELN "safe-houses" in La Paz, the government said April 4. Eight guerrillas had been arrested in the raids and authorities had confiscated arms, bombs and literature belonging to the ELN and its political party.

Interior Minister Juan Pereda Asbun said April 8 that 18 more subversives, including an undisclosed number of foreigners, had been arrested in raids in La Paz, Cochabamba and Oruro. Bolivian guerrillas were supported by Chile's Revolutionary Left Movement, Argentina's People's Revolutionary Army, and "Peruvian seditionaries," Pereda asserted.

Zenteno slain in Paris. Joaquin Zenteno Anaya, 53, the Bolivian ambassador to France, was shot and killed by terrorists May 11 on a Paris street. Following the assassination, a group calling itself the "International 'Che' Guevara Brigade" claimed responsibility for the killing in a phone communique to Agence France-Presse, a French news service.

In 1967 Zenteno had commanded the expedition that captured and killed Ernesto "Che" Guevara, the Latin American revolutionary, in Bolivia.

The spokesman for the terrorists accused Zenteno of being "the architect of Che Guevara's assassination" and said this was one motive for the slaying. Another motive given was Zenteno's alleged role in attempting to stop the French government from seeking the extradition from Bolivia of a German war criminal, Klaus Barbie.

Torres slain in Argentina. Retired Gen. Juan Jose Torres, who led a leftist Bolivian government in 1970–71, was kidnapped in Argentina June 1 and slain.

Torres' blindfolded and bullet-riddled body was found June 2 on a rural road about 60 miles from Buenos Aires.

Torres had lived in Buenos Aires since 1973, when he fled Chile after the right-wing military coup. He had been living in Chile since the 1971 fall of his government in a bloody revolt led by Gen. Hugo Banzer Suarez. At the time of Torres' slaying, Bolivia's rightist regime was led by Banzer.

The slaying caused widespread protests in Bolivia June 3. Mineworkers held a nationwide strike, blaming Torres' death on "international fascists." Leftist students and workers in La Paz, Cochabamba and Oruro joined the protests.

Banzer offered to hold a state funeral in Bolivia for Torres, but withdrew the offer June 6 after Torres' widow demanded that the service be held at headquarters of the mineworkers' union. Torres' body was flown to Mexico for burial June 7.

(Banzer also offered an amnesty June 3 to Bolivian political exiles who feared assassination abroad. Several opponents of Banzer, including former Cabinet ministers Ciro Humboldt, Jorge Gallardo and Samuel Gallardo, took advantage of the offer, returned to Bolivia and were promptly arrested, the Associated Press reported June 6. Interior Minister Juan Pereda Asbun later explained that the amnesty did not apply to persons whom the government considered "extremists.")

Meanwhile, a controversy grew in Bolivia over the roles played by Zenteno and Torres in the 1967 execution of Ernesto "Che" Guevara, the Argentine-born Cuban revolutionary who was captured by Bolivian forces while trying to organize a peasant revolt in the Bolivian mountains. Zenteno's assassins had claimed he was the "architect of Che Guevara's assassination."

Gen. Luis Reque Teran, who had commanded the army division which tracked down Guevara's guerrilla band, was quoted by the Ecuadorean magazine Vistazo April 14 as saying Guevara was executed on orders of Torres and Gen. Alfredo Ovando Candia. Ovando later became Bolivia's president. Guevara was executed by Sgt. Mario Teran Ortuno, Reque asserted.

Ovando was quoted in the Spanish newspaper Arriba May 9 as saying the execution was ordered by the late Gen. Rene Barrientos Ortuno, then Bolivia's president. Ted Cordova-Claure, a former aide to Torres, agreed with Ovando in an article in the Venezuelan newspaper El Nacional May 13.

Gen. Raul Alvarez Penaranda, Bolivia's current army commander, denounced Reque May 15 for revealing "military secrets." Alvarez, who said that Reque would be dismissed from the army for "treason," charged that Reque's revelations had led to the assassination of Zenteno in Paris.

Reque charged in Buenos Aires May 17 that Zenteno's murder had been ordered by Banzer. Reque accused Banzer and Alvarez of "genocide" in the slaying of hundreds of Bolivian peasants and political prisoners.

Banzer threatened to impose sanctions against the Bolivian press May 20 after newspapers published accounts of Reque's charges. Newspapers and radio stations went on strike across Bolivia May 22 to protest Banzer's threat, and Banzer withdrew the warning May 23.

Cordova-Claure reported May 13 that Teran, the man who Reque said actually executed Guevara, had become a "drunk vagabond" who wandered the streets of Santa Cruz, Bolivia trying to "sell" his version of Guevara's death to journalists.

State of siege imposed; miners strike. The government imposed a nationwide state of siege June 9 following widespread student and mineworker protests of the assassination of Torres.

The arrest of mineworkers' leaders under the siege led mineworkers to begin an indefinite general strike June 14.

The protests had begun June 3, when news of Torres' death reached Bolivia. They accelerated after June 6, when the Bolivian government retracted an offer to have Torres' body repatriated and buried in La Paz. Torres was buried in Mexico June 9.

High school students rioted June 8 in Oruro, La Paz, Cochabamba and Sucre, protesting both Torres' death and a recent government order that increased the mandatory military service of students from four months to a year. One student was killed when soldiers opened fire on demonstrators in Oruro, and another student was fatally wounded when soldiers fired on marchers in La Paz. (The La Paz student died June 12.) The Education Ministry ordered the immediate start of high school vacations, which had not been scheduled until July 1.

Five thousand mineworkers in the Huanuni district (Oruro Department) struck for 24 hours June 8 to demand the repatriation of Torres' body. Other mineworkers had struck sporadically since June 3, demanding not only the body's repatriation but a 100% wage increase.

When the siege was imposed June 9, most leaders of the leftist Bolivian Mineworkers' Federation (FSTMB) were arrested. Troops occupied all state-owned mines and closed down the mines' radio stations, which had been urging mineworkers to stay calm. Student leaders were also arrested throughout the country.

Interior Minister Col. Juan Pereda Asbun claimed the siege was necessary in view of "the obvious climate of subversion existing in the country." A huge subversive plot had been hatched, placing Bolivia "in danger of a civil war," he said.

(President Hugo Banzer Suarez had said June 7 that leftists had planned to revolt upon the arrival in Bolivia of Torres' body.)

The state of siege suspended constituional guarantees for 90 days. It allowed preventive detention and arrests without trial, and prohibited public meetings, demonstrations and strikes. Trips by individuals to the interior of Bolivia required government permission.

Seven thousand miners in the Catavi and Siglo XX districts (Potosi Department) went on strike June 10 to protest the occupation of the mines, the arrest of mineworkers, the closing of mine radio stations and the denial of a Bolivian burial for Torres. At Huanuni, soldiers ended their occupation of the mine but remained on alert at an outpost nearby.

Banzer visited the occupied mines June 11 and vowed to raise mineworkers' wages. In La Paz, students at the metropolitan university went on strike in solidarity with the miners.

The miners' strike spread to the Unificada and Colquiri districts June 12, and grew into a general strike June 14. Estimates of how many miners were on strike varied from 20,000 to 50,000. Students struck at the major universities in Cochabamba, La Paz and Oruro, and were joined by workers at the Manaco shoe factory in Quillacollo, outside Cochabamba.

The government offered the mineworkers wage increases of 15%–30% June 15, but it placed the mining departments of Oruro and Potosi under martial law. Strike leaders June 17 rejected the wage offer and continued to direct the stoppage from their mineshaft hideouts. Interior Minister Pereda said June 19 that the government would not negotiate with the strikers because the stoppage was "essentially a political problem." The strike was costing Bolivia an estimated $800,000 per day.

Meanwhile, Torres' body arrived in Mexico June 7. His widow, Emma Obleas de Torres, and her children were met at the Mexico City airport by prominent Latin American political exiles, including Marcelo Quiroga Santa Cruz, a former Bolivian Cabinet minister; Clodomiro Almeyda, former Chilean foreign minister, and Hortensia Bussi de Allende, widow of Chile's President Salvador Allende Gossens. Torres was buried in Mexico City June 9 before more than 200 exiles who shouted slogans against Banzer.

Mrs. Torres charged at a press conference June 8 that the Argentine and Bolivian governments were responsible for her husband's death. She said her husband had been threatened "directly" by Col. Raul Tejerina, Bolivian military attache in Buenos Aires. Argentina had denied Torres "the guarantees and personal security which it was obligated morally and juridically to provide for a political refugee in its territory," she added.

Earlier Developments

Military chiefs replaced. President Banzer had dismissed his three military commanders Jan. 6, replacing them with their immediate subordinates. He gave no reason for the action, but there had been discontent in the armed forces over Bolivia's plan to cede some national territory to Chile in exchange for a corridor to the Pacific Ocean, the London newsletter Latin America reported Jan. 9.

It was the first time in Bolivian history that the military chiefs had been replaced without a coup d'etat, press reports noted.

"They are leaving by the front door," Banzer said.

The new commanders were army Gen. Raul Alvarez Penaranda, replacing Gen. Carlos Alcoreza Melgarejo; air force Col. Luis Garcia Pereira, replacing Gen. Oscar Adriazola, and Rear Adm. Gutemberg Barroso Hurtado, replacing Adm. Javier Pinto.

Banzer changed his finance and housing ministers Jan. 12. Gen. Victor Castillo handed over the finance post to Carlos Calvo, an economist and the first civilian to serve in the cabinet in more than a year, and Capt. Walter Nunez Rivero left the housing portfolio to Capt. Santiago Ameser. Castillo became army chief of staff and Nunez, navy chief of staff.

Sea outlet study panel named. President Hugo Banzer Jan. 7 created the National Maritime Council, a top-level commission which would study "in the most complete secrecy" Chile's proposal to grant Bolivia an outlet to the Pacific Ocean.

Banzer would preside over the council, which would also include the foreign, defense, planning and interior ministers, the three military commanders and "citizens of recognized prestige and honesty." The civilians would be drafted under the government's compulsory service law, which required citizens over 21 to perform any duty ordered by the regime under penalty of a jail sentence.

The Peruvian government also appointed a commission to study Chile's proposal, headed by former President Jose Luis Bustamante, it was reported Jan. 7. Peruvian approval was required before Chile could grant Bolivia any land taken from Peru by Chile in the War of the Pacific in the late 19th century.

Appointment of the study panels followed reports, cited by the London newsletter Latin America Jan. 2, that, in exchange for the corridor, Chile was demanding not only an equal piece of Bolivian territory (including compensation in land for the loss of 200 miles of territorial waters in the Pacific), but exclusive use of the waters of the River Lauca, compensation in cash for the cession of the La Paz-Arica railway, demilitarization of the Bolivian corridor, and cessation of all claims by Bolivia to land it had lost to Chile in the War of the Pacific.

Demilitarization of the corridor was opposed by Bolivian military officers, Latin America reported, and the land exchange was opposed by mineworkers and executives. The National Federation of Bolivian Mining Cooperatives objected Jan. 3 to the transfer to Chile of Bolivian land rich in minerals and petroleum, and the Bolivian Mineworkers' Federation said consultation between the government and the people on the issue was "indispensable."

The proposed exchange was also denounced by four Bolivian ex-presidents, it was reported Jan. 1. They were Victor Paz Estenssoro, Hernan Siles Zuazo, Luis Adolfo Siles Salinas and retired Gen. Juan Jose Torres. All but Siles Salinas lived in exile. Torres called for the overthrow of President Banzer in a speech broadcast by a mineworkers' radio station in the Catavi district, it was reported Jan. 5.

Economic Developments

'75 economic growth reported. The planning ministry reported Jan. 9 that Bolivia's gross domestic product had grown 7.3% in 1975, for its highest growth rate in 20 years. The inflation rate for the year had fallen to less than 12%, the ministry added.

Gulf Oil bribe scandal. Gulf Oil Co. told the Bolivian government Jan. 14 that it had given the late Bolivian President Rene Barrientos Ortuno a helicopter and $1.8 million in cash in 1966. Bolivia responded that there were doubts that Barrientos took the money and "suspicions" that the alleged payments were "used by Gulf Oil's officials for their own benefit."

Foreign loans obtained. Bolivia received loans of $9.5 million from the World Bank and $45 million from the Inter-American Development Bank (IDB) for domestic development projects, the Miami Herald reported April 13.

The World Bank loan would aid an integrated community development project in one of the watersheds of the Altiplano,

BOLIVIA

Bolivia's high plateau. The IDB loan would help build and pave a road from La Paz to Trinidad, capital of the northeastern department of Beni, where cattle, tropical crops and timber were produced.

In a related development, the Bolivian state oil company YPFB arranged a $14-million loan from Lloyds Bank of London to finance the purchase of British equipment and services for a planned refinery in Santa Cruz Department and a lubricating oil plant in Cochabamba, the Financial Times of London reported April 14.

YPFB had signed March 12 for a $30 million Eurodollar loan from Grindlays Bank Ltd. and the Euro-Latinamerican Bank Ltd. of London, and the Bank of Montreal. Among the projects for which the money was earmarked was a 300-mile gas pipeline through the Andes mountains from Cochabamba to Oruro and La Paz.

A foreign syndicate headed by the Bank of America agreed June 18 to lend Bolivia $50 million for domestic development projects.

The other banks in the syndicate were the Banque Canadienne Nationale (Canada) and the European Brazilian Bank Ltd. Part of the loan would help finance expansion of existing Bolivian oil fields and purchase of exploration equipment by the government's mining company, COMIBOL.

The Inter-American Development Bank agreed to lend Bolivia $24.5 million to expand the country's electric-power system, it was reported June 21.

Bolivia signs international tin pact. Bolivia signed the fifth International Tin Agreement April 30 after forcing the International Tin Council to raise the floor and ceiling prices it had set for tin sales.

The agreement, to come into force July 1, was reached by tin-producing and -consuming countries to prevent excessive fluctuations in tin prices and to raise the export earnings of producing nations.

Bolivia had forced the rise in prices by threatening April 26 not to sign the agreement. The council originally had set the floor price at 950 Malaysian dollars per picul (about 60 kilograms) and the ceiling at M$1,100 per picul. After the Bolivian threat the floor was raised by M$50 and the ceiling by M$100.

Cargo jet crashes in Bolivia. More than 100 persons, most of them children, were killed Oct. 13 when an American-owned 707 cargo plane plowed through a schoolyard shortly after take-off from El Trompillo Airport in Santa Cruz, Bolivia, 350 miles southeast of La Paz. The three-man American crew was killed. There were no passengers aboard.

The four-engine jet, owned by Jet Power Inc. of Miami, Fla. and chartered to Lloyd Aereo Boliviano, had just delivered oil-drilling machinery and was scheduled to return to Miami when it crashed. The accident was called the worst aviation disaster in Bolivian history.

Brazil

Opposition Under Pressure

5 opposition deputies ousted. President Ernesto Geisel removed two opposition legislators and suspended their political rights for 10 years after the government accused them of having won election with aid from the outlawed Brazilian Communist Party, it was reported Jan. 6.

Those ousted, both members of the Brazilian Democratic Movement (MDB), the only legal opposition party, were Alberto Marcelo Gatto, a Sao Paulo federal deputy, and Nelson Fabiano Sobrinho, a Sao Paulo state representative. They vehemently denied any links to the Communists.

Press reports noted that Gatto and Fabiano Sobrinho had made public references to allegations that political prisoners and suspected leftists were tortured by authorities. When first indicted on charges of collaborating with Communists, Gatto had said: "The Brazilian people know how much suffering, torture and fear are behind that indictment."

Geisel did not give a reason for firing the two legislators, but political analysts in Rio de Janeiro believed he had bowed to pressure from extreme rightist military officers who felt Brazil was in danger of Communist infiltration and who opposed Geisel's professed desire to return Brazil to democratic rule, the Washington Post reported Jan. 7.

Geisel dismissed the legislators under Institutional Act. No. 5, which gave the president dictatorial powers. He had used the Act in 1975 to fire a senator of the ruling Arena party who had been accused of corruption.

Geisel ousted three more MDB federal deputies and suspended their political rights for 10 years after each publicly criticized the government.

The ousted legislators were Nadyr Rossetti, Amaury Muller and Lysaneas Maciel. Rossetti and Muller were dismissed March 29 and Maciel, April 1.

Rossetti and Muller had made "violent speeches" against the government at a rally March 20 in their home state of Rio Grande do Sul, according to a Justice Ministry statement March 29. Rossetti had told the rally that the regime did not "have the people's support." Muller had said Brazil was "dominated by a uniformed aristocracy."

Maciel, who represented a district in Rio de Janeiro, was dismissed for denouncing the firing of Rossetti and Muller in the Chamber of Deputies and accusing the government of "repression, torture and killing." "This Congress is aware that it plays the counterpoint to a farcical dictatorship," Maciel charged before his microphone was cut off and he was removed.

MDB arrests reported. Scores of MDB members were arrested in February and March. The arrests followed assertions by the exiled Communist leader, Luis Carlos Prestes, that the MDB had links to the outlawed Brazilian Communist Party (PCB). The government had charged the connection existed.

Prestes told a French Communist Party Congress in Paris Feb. 8 that the MDB had won Brazil's 1974 federal and state legislative elections because the PCB had "told the people to use their vote as a weapon against dictatorship" and had persuaded the MDB "to present a program of popular demands." The MDB denied Prestes' claim, it was reported Feb. 10.

MDB members were among 29 persons reported arrested in Curitiba Feb. 21 and 23 reported in custody in Sergipe Feb. 27.

More than 100 party members were arrested in March, according to the London newsletter Latin America March 26. Other detainees included Ayrton de Albuquerque Queiroz and Alexandre Magalhaes da Silveira, both university professors, and Luiz Santana Machado, a photographer for the Rio de Janeiro newspaper O Globo. Their arrests on charges of pro-Communist activities was confirmed by security police March 9.

The MDB protested the arrests but the protests were cut from newspapers and radio broadcasts by government censors. MDB legislators walked out of the Chamber of Deputies March 31 during a ceremony commemorating the 12th anniversary of the armed forces' seizure of power.

Political Prisoners & Human Rights Abuses

Prisoner's 'suicide' brings D'Avila ouster. The alleged suicide of a political prisoner Jan. 17 at the army's Department of Internal Operations (DOI) resulted Jan. 19 in the removal of Gen. Ednardo D'Avila as commander of the 2d Army in Sao Paulo.

D'Avila, an opponent of President Ernesto Geisel's avowed policy of political relaxation, had carried out an independent campaign against alleged subversives in Sao Paulo, and had reportedly been reprimanded by Geisel in 1975 after the widely protested death of another political prisoner, the journalist Vladimir Herzog. He was recently reported to have conspired with other hard-line generals against the president.

D'Avila's removal was announced on the national radio minutes after it was announced that Manoel Fiel Filho, a metalworker jailed on suspicion of subversive activities, had been found dead Jan. 17 in his cell at the DOI, an apparent suicide. Geisel transferred D'Avila to the army's training and investigations department in an apparent attempt to avert protests such as those that followed Herzog's death, according to press reports.

D'Avila handed over his command to a temporary successor Jan. 20 and asked to be retired rather than moved to his new post. He would be replaced within a week by Gen. Dilermando Gomes Monteiro, a close associate of Geisel, according to the Rio de Janeiro newspaper Jornal do Brasil.

The army's claim that Fiel Filho had committed suicide was challenged by Roman Catholic priests at masses in Sao Paulo, it was reported Jan. 26. Rev. Antonio Haddad said he performed a mass "to remember a human being massacred by other men," and Auxiliary Bishop Angelico Bernardino asked: "Did Manoel Fiel Filho die of torture? Is there anyone who doubts that [the DOI] has been turned into a house of horrors, where prisoners are submitted to terrible confinements and violence that shame this country?"

At one mass, Rodolfo Konder, a magazine editor held in the DOI in 1975, said he had been tortured with electric shocks in custody and had overheard the screams of Vladimir Herzog while Herzog was tortured.

The Order of Brazilian Lawyers issued a statement in Sao Paulo Jan. 29 denouncing the deaths of Herzog and Fiel Filho and calling for a return to "a state of law." The lawyers condemned "arbitrarinesses" by authorities that "disgracefully have been practiced in inadmissible detriment to the dignity of human beings."

Most large-circulation newspapers in Brazil had printed a letter Jan. 13 from the Sao Paulo journalists' union criticizing alleged contradictions in the government's report of Herzog's alleged suicide. The letter, which called the report a whitewash, was signed by 467 journalists including prominent moderate supporters of President Geisel such as Carlos Castello Branco, the political columnist of Jornal do Brasil.

Castello Branco and others also protested Geisel's ouster of MDB legislators Alberto Marcelo Gatto and Nelson Fabiano Sobrinho, it was reported Jan. 23. O Estado de Sao Paulo said that the dismissals had not been forced on Geisel by hard-line officers (as widely reported) because Geisel's position in the armed forces was the most secure it had been during his presidency. "It is the government which initiates the hard line," O Estado asserted.

(Geisel had secured the full support of the military leadership at the end of 1975, the newsletter Latin America reported Jan. 9. The outcry which followed Herzog's death apparently pushed a number of uncommitted generals to Geisel's side against hard-line officers, and aborted a conspiracy headed by Gen. D'Avila, according to the newsletter.

(The London Times reported April 15 that the journalist Sergio Gomes da Silva had been "brutally tortured" since his arrest in October 1975. Gomes, who had worked for the newspaper O Estado de Sao Paulo, was held without charge but scheduled for a military trial.)

11 'death squad' victims found. Eleven maimed and bullet-riddled bodies had been found on deserted roads outside Rio de Janeiro within the past week, it was reported Jan. 29. The victims bore the traditional marks—signs of torture, multiple bullet wounds, strangulation—of execution by the "death squad" of off-duty policemen which killed petty criminals in the area.

AI charges torture. Amnesty International charged in a message to the Organization of American States (OAS) June 4 that political prisoners in Brazil were subjected to torture. The IA statement said:

Reports from Brazil indicate that many journalists (including Vladimir Herzog, who died in custody in October, 1975), trade unionists, lawyers and workers have been arrested during the past year for alleged connections with the Partido Comunista Brasilero (PCB), and there has been a consistent pattern of torture used to extract confessions, aimed at substantiation of the government's claims that the Movimiento Democratico Brasileiro (MDB) has links with the illegal communist party. Many of the accused have consistently denied the charges or retracted confessions extracted through torture. The estimated number of persons detained over the period of January to November 1975 has been put at 1500. Almost all reports of detention received by Amnesty International over the past 12 months have been accompanied by allegations of maltreatment which range from psychological intimidation to the most brutal forms of torture.

Communists charge torture—Seventy-six Communists, who were tried in Sao Paulo on charges of subversion, said they had been tortured by police and military officers, Latin America reported Sept. 10.

In the course of the trial, the public prosecutor asked for 48 acquittals, saying that there was inadequate proof for conviction. Nine of the defendants were found guilty and received sentences of six months to four years.

In most of the cases, the prosecutor's evidence rested on confessions extracted from the defendants under torture at headquarters of the army's Department of Internal Operations (DOI), Latin America reported. One of those who was eventually acquitted, Waldir Jose de Quadros, said that at DOI headquarters he was "brutally tortured, without interruption, for about three nights and two days."

Widespread violence reported. Bombings, murders, kidnappings and torture were reported in Rio de Janeiro and other cities in July–October. The growing violence, although not exclusively political, was linked by observers to the municipal elections planned for November and to efforts by hard-line military officers to stifle any attempt by President Ernesto Geisel to relax political repression.

Much of the violence was attributed to the Brazilian Anti-Communist Alliance (AAB), a terrorist group that had threatened the lives of opposition leaders in 1974. The AAB charged Aug. 19 that the government was "timidly backing down" before a "new attempt to communize Brazil."

Bombs planted by the AAB exploded at headquarters of the Brazilian Press

Association in Rio Aug. 19 and at a military court in Porto Alegre Aug. 20. The press group had campaigned for greater democracy in Brazil. Prudente de Moraes Neto, the group's president, recently had appeared as a character witness for a newsman on trial for alleged Communist subversion.

The AAB also claimed credit for attacks Sept. 23 on the Roman Catholic bishop of Nova Iguacu, a Rio suburb, and on the home of an owner of the Rio newspaper O Globo. Bishop Adriano Hipolito was kidnapped, stripped, painted red and then released on a city street, and his car was blown up in front of the Rio headquarters of the National Conference of Brazilian Bishops. The AAB told a radio station that Hipolito had been "punished" for being a "progressive priest."

Two servants were injured when an AAB bomb exploded on the roof of the home of Roberto Marinho, the O Globo owner. His newspaper had been reporting on the increasing number of murders in Nova Iguacu by members of a "death squad," presumed to be made up of off-duty policemen.

The AAB also threatened the lives of other bishops and journalists, opposition leaders and political prisoners, according to the Oct. 8 London newsletter Latin America. The terrorist group left leaflets outside a prison in Sao Paulo asserting: "Those who do not die in the cells will die when they regain freedom." The majority of prisoners were due for parole soon, Latin America said.

The AAB's actions constituted the first overt political terrorism in Brazil in at least five years, the Washington Post said Aug. 19. In another terrorist act, unnamed persons sent a letter bomb in September to Gen. Dilermando Gomes Monteiro, commander of the Second Army, based in Sao Paulo, the London Financial Times reported Oct. 14. Gomes Monteiro was close to President Geisel and had largely ended torture and police brutality in Sao Paulo in recent months. The attack on Gomes Monteiro was part of "a war of nerves against the Geisel administration," a government source told the Financial Times.

Meanwhile, there were reports of continuing murders, torture and other brutality by police in other regions of Brazil. The most widely reported incident was the fatal shooting of a Jesuit priest by police in Ribeirao Bonito (Mato Grosso State) Oct. 12.

Rev. Joao Bosco Penido Burnier was shot in the head when he went to a police station, accompanied by Bishop Pedro Casaldaliga, to ask clemency for two female prisoners who had been tortured. The women claimed that police officers had forced them to kneel on bottles, had whipped them with wire and had stuck nails under their fingernails. The local police chief said that a medical examination had confirmed their charges.

Geisel Oct. 13 ordered a thorough investigation of the incident and police announced Oct. 14 that four policemen had been arrested for Penido Burnier's murder. The Ribeirao Bonito police chief said the men who tortured the female prisoners also would be punished.

Jesuit priests in the district around Ribeirao Bonito issued a statement Oct. 16 asserting that Penido Burnier's murder was not "an isolated incident," as the government claimed.

"The deep causes are in a system that scorns the human person, performs torture and oppresses the Indians, the poor, the peasants and the workers, and all who support them," the priests declared.

Residents of Ribeirao Bonito destroyed the local police station after attending a memorial mass for Penido Burnier, the London newsletter Latin America reported Oct. 29.

Among other repercussions of Penido Burnier's slaying:

■ A bomb exploded Oct. 22 in the offices of a company owned by the priest's cousin, Brig. Gen. Joao Paulo Burnier, an extreme rightist. A group calling itself the Revolutionary People's Vanguard claimed responsibility for the blast, but pamphlets left behind by the culprits closely resembled pamphlets of the Brazilian Anti-Communist Alliance, a right-wing group responsible for several recent terrorist acts, Latin America reported Oct. 29.

■ Leaders of the Roman Catholic Church discussed Penido Burnier's slaying and other recent violence against the church at a six-day meeting of the National Conference of Brazilian Bishops, Latin America reported Nov. 5. However, the bishops decided to withhold until after the November municipal elections a pastoral letter describing and analyzing recent attacks on the church in Brazil and other Latin American nations.

■ President Ernesto Geisel discussed Penido Burnier's slaying with another of the priest's cousins, Archbishop Geraldo Maria de Morais Penido of Juiz de Fora (Minas Gerais State), Latin America reported Nov. 5. Geisel reportedly said: "I do not deny that torture continues to be used in this country, but there are strict orders to the army not to use torture." He and the archbishop also discussed slavery in the Amazon region. The archbishop said afterward that Geisel was "sincerely and deeply involved in improving the situation," Latin America reported.

Police violence. Among other allegations of police violence:

■ The Madrid newsmagazine Cambio 16 reported Sept. 20 that a prisoner had been hanged in his cell at the police station in Vitoria (Espirito Santo State) in August. The police said the prisoner had committed suicide, but it was learned later that his hands had been tied behind his back when his body was found. Newspapers reporting the prisoner's death charged that no Brazilian citizen was safe from being arrested, tortured and even killed by authorities, Cambio reported.

■ The London newsletter Latin America reported Oct. 22 that Manoel Santiago da Silva, a 16-year-old boy who had been trying to organize an association for abandoned minors in Espirito Santo, was arrested, beaten, raped and then released by police in Vitoria. Police reportedly warned him that if they found him in the streets again they would repeat the treatment.

■ The "death squads" had killed at least 34 persons in Nova Iguacu and surrounding areas since late May, the Miami Herald reported July 23. The last two victims, killed July 17, had been shot by mistake, the Herald reported. Many of the death squads' victims were said to have been killed by mistake when the assassins took them for petty criminals. Nevertheless, Gen. Oswaldo Ignacio Domingues, chief of security in Rio de Janeiro, insisted that "there is no Death Squad," Latin America reported July 9.

■ Lawyers in Rio de Janeiro charged that Evil Brandao, a bus driver, had died after 11 days of police torture for a crime he did not commit, Latin America reported July 9. Brandao reportedly had been forced to sign a false confession in the murder of a bank manager.

The police brutality and AAB terrorism coincided with denunciations of the opposition in the right-wing weekly O Expresso, which was strongly supported by the government of Sao Paulo State, Latin America reported Aug. 27. O Expresso had charged in July that the Communist Party had devised a plan to overthrow the government and had infiltrated the Brazilian Democratic Movement (MDB), the only legal opposition party.

Policemen held in Death Squad murders. Four policemen were under arrest in Rio de Janeiro in connection with a Death Squad execution in which one of the intended victims survived, the Washington Post reported Oct. 11.

The officers were jailed after Daniel Sousa, 23, said they had arrested him and two companions late Sept. 28, driven them to an isolated spot outside Rio and shot them early Sept. 29. Sousa's companions died but he survived despite being shot four times, once in the head.

Sousa reportedly described the incident to Helber Murtinho, chief of the homicide division of the Rio State Public Safety Department, who was in charge of Death Squad investigations. Murtinho visited Sousa in a Rio hospital where Sousa was convalescing under special guard.

Sousa said that the policemen had arrested him and his companions on suspicion of possessing marijuana. The Death Squad generally killed petty criminals or suspected criminals on the ground that Brazil's regular police and court system was not effective in fighting crime.

A book that became a best-seller in Brazil charged that the police "death squads" in Sao Paulo and Rio de Janeiro had protectors "at the highest levels" of the armed forces, it was reported Dec. 26. The book was by Helio Bicudo, who was named special prosecutor of death squad crimes in Sao Paulo but was dismissed when his investigation closed in on powerful figures. Bicudo said the death squads were "like the Mafia," with interests in "drug trafficking, prostitution and the strong-arm racket."

Bishops score violence. The National Conference of Brazilian Bishops issued a statement Nov. 16 denouncing what it called the climate of fear and violence in Brazil.

The strongly worded document did not mention the government but was clearly directed against it. The bishops deplored "the ideology of national security which is placed above personal security"; the protection given by higher authorities to policemen accused of corruption, torture and murder; the unequal distribution of wealth and land throughout Brazil, and the encroachments of white settlers on the dwindling Indian population of the Amazon region.

The statement was particularly critical of the military police, which it accused of "practicing violence and arbitrariness" against Catholic priests and the poor.

"It is the poor, the defenseless who fill the jails where torture is frequent...," the bishops said. "For the powerful the situation is completely different. There are criminals who are not punished because they are protected by the power of money, by prestige.

"Grave is the case of policemen who, though accused of death crimes, corruption, drug peddling and white slavery, are not brought before the tribunals of law because because higher officials claim that they are valuable elements in the repression of political crimes."

The bishops said that gross violations of human rights were linked to the spread throughout Latin America of "the ideology of national security," which held that national economic growth was impossible unless the armed forces provided strict security.

"Regimes of force, claiming to fight communism and carry out economic development, declare an antisubversive war against all those who do not agree with an authoritarian vision of society," the bishops' document declared. "Liberties of press and thought are sacrificed, individual guarantees are suppressed. This doctrine has led regimes of force to take on the same characteristics and practices of communist regimes: the abuse of power by the state, arbitrary imprisonment [and] torture..."

The bishops condemned "the bad distribution of land in Brazil," which had "grown acute... in the last years." Large companies had "surged, backed by juridical and financial resources, to finish off the small property owners, and to expel Indians and settlers from their lands," the document said.

"Indians, when they survive, go on to be exploited as cheap labor or move on to city outskirts, or wander sick and famished along the roads that lacerate their reservations," the bishops noted.

The bishops' document was prompted by a series of recent attacks on Catholic clergymen. The bishops had drafted the statement in October but withheld it until after the municipal elections Nov. 15.

In a related development, Rev. Florentino Maboni was arrested in Para State Oct. 31 when he went to a military police station to complain about poor treatment of local farmers and their families by local authorities. The priest was charged with inciting small farmers to armed insurrection. Roman Catholic Church sources who reported the arrest denied the charges against Maboni.

Government & Politics

Government corruption detailed. O Estado de Sao Paulo, Brazil's most respected newspaper, published three articles Aug. 3-5 detailing widespread corruption among current and former government officials.

The expose, unprecedented in Brazil's largely censored press, caused President Geisel to issue a decree Aug. 4 suspending for 10 years the political rights of five persons who were already under investigation for alleged corruption. The five were: Jose Cortez Pereira Araujo, who was governor of Rio Grande do Norte State in 1971-75; his brother, Benvenuto Pereira de Araujo Neto, and three former directors of the state's electric company including Ney Lopes de Souza, currently a federal deputy from the ruling Arena party.

Lopes de Souza was the fifth federal deputy to have been stripped of his political rights by Geisel in 1976. Geisel acted under Institutional Act No. 5, which gave the Brazilian president virtually dictatorial powers.

O Estado de Sao Paulo's revelations were highly embarrassing to the government, which had been recommending austerity to combat Brazil's economic problems. However, the government did not deny the newspaper's allegations, and it did not restore the prior censorship under which the paper once had been forced to operate.

Among O Estado's allegations:

■ Officials who had worked for the state oil company Petrobras when Geisel was its director, and had been transferred when he became Brazil's president in 1974, still received their full Petrobras salaries plus 20% of the salaries to which they were entitled in their new posts. Petrobras salaries were substantially higher than those of the public service. Included in this arrangement were Shigeaki Ueki, the mines and energy minister, and Humberto Barreto, Geisel's press officer.

■ Officials of government ministries and government-linked agencies could increase their already-high salaries by $70,000 a year thanks to government fringe benefits. The average Brazilian's annual income was less than $800.

■ Officials routinely used rented cars and planes, paid for by the government, for personal trips. They threw lavish parties at the government's expense, with entertainment that included movies, such as Bernardo Bertolucci's "Last Tango in Paris," that were not allowed to be seen by the Brazilian people.

■ Labor Minister Arnaldo Prieto had 28 maids, butlers and household servants at his official residence in Brasilia. For special parties he had beef flown in from 12,200 miles away at government expense.

MDB campaigning curbed. The Brazilian Democratic Movement was campaigning for the November municipal elections under severe restrictions from the government, which had decided to make the vote a referendum on its policies. Among other restrictions, the government majority in Congress had pushed through a bill that barred both the MDB and the government's Arena party from campaigning on radio or television, it was reported June 28. The government simultaneously forced radio and television stations and movie theaters to run programs extolling President Geisel's accomplishments.

The severity of the restrictions stemmed from the government's fear that the unequal distribution of income and the growing inflation rate—expected to reach 50% by the end of 1976—would work in favor of the MDB at the polls, the New York Times reported June 28. The MDB had defeated Arena in the 1974 elections, which were acclaimed for their fairness.

An estimated 60,000 persons in Brasilia had called for an end to the military dictatorship at a funeral march for former President Juscelino Kubitschek, who died in an automobile crash Aug. 23, it was reported Aug. 27. There were similar but smaller demonstrations in Rio de Janeiro. The government, which had canceled Kubitschek's political rights in 1964-74, reluctantly declared three days of national mourning for the late president after the demonstrations.

Government wins municipal vote. The ruling Arena party won control of about 70% of the nation's mayoralties and city councils in municipal elections Nov. 15.

The Brazilian Democratic Movement (MDB), the only legal opposition party, won the city council vote in the major cities—Sao Paulo, Rio de Janeiro, Belo Horizonte, Porto Alegre and Salvador. However, the cities remained under tight government control because, as state capitals, their mayors were appointed by state governors who in turn were appointed by the federal government. Mayors had full control of budgeting and patronage.

About 40 million persons voted in the elections. Many cast protest ballots. In Rio de Janeiro, at least 120,000 citizens cast write-in votes for "black beans," a staple that had been in short supply recently, according to the Rio newspaper O Globo.

Despite its comfortable margin, the government was not considered to have won a major victory. The MDB had been unable to field candidates in 1,339 of the 3,789 electoral districts, and the party's supporters had suffered some police harassment. In addition, the government had imposed campaign restrictions on both the MDB and Arena which hurt the MDB more than the government party.

Nevertheless, both parties expressed satisfaction with the election results. President Ernesto Geisel, who had campaigned actively for Arena, said Nov. 19 that "it looks as if Arena is winning a great victory." Rep. Ulysses Guimaraes, the MDB president, said the results were "positive in terms of Brazilian institutions," explaining: "One election leads to another."

Franco Montoro, the MDB leader in the Senate, Nov. 20 ascribed his party's defeat to "four boulders placed in our path" by the government. He said that they were:

■ A recently passed law that forbade political campaigning on radio and television. Under the law each candidate was allowed brief radio and television spots in which he could give only his name, party, number of the ballot and "personal qualifications" such as military service, educational degrees, church, samba club or soccer team.

■ A government radio and television campaign which, without mentioning the ruling party or the elections, extolled the accomplishments of the military regime.

■ Geisel's own vigorous campaigning, which turned the elections into tests of both his personal prestige and the popularity of his avowed plan to return Brazil slowly to democracy.

■ Welfare programs and other benefits instituted by the government shortly before the elections to enhance Arena's chances in the vote.

The campaign restrictions were imposed to prevent the MDB from repeating its victory over Arena in the 1974 congressional elections. Under the restrictions, the MDB could criticize the government only at old-style political rallies, where the participants were frequently harassed by police.

The government's radio and television advertisements praised the economic progress made by the military regimes of the last 12 years. The television spots concluded with a map of Brazil and the slogan "This is a country that is moving forward." The satirical weekly Pasquim, which had often been censored by the government, used the slogan as a caption for a cartoon showing Brazil fleeing its numerous international creditors.

Economic Developments

Oilfield found. Mines Minister Shigeaki Ueki said technicians had found a major new oilfield on the continental shelf off Rio de Janeiro, it was reported Jan. 6. The field was estimated to contain at least 240 million barrels of oil, and further testing would be conducted to determine whether the area could contain as many as 800 million barrels, as some early tests had indicated, Ueki said.

Foreign trade. Among foreign trade developments:

Finance Minister Mario Henrique Simonsen said Brazil's foreign trade deficit in 1975 was $3.5 billion, down from $4.6 billion in 1974, it was reported Jan. 6. The cost of servicing Brazil's $22 billion foreign debt had canceled out 44% of the 1975 export earnings, Simonsen added.

Brazil's income from coffee exports had dropped to $933 million in 1975, down from $980 million the year before, despite a rise in the volume of exports and a sharp rise in prices following the July 1975 frosts, it was reported Jan. 9.

A congressional investigation of the operations of transnational corporations in Brazil had ended with the issuance of rival reports by the investigating committee's majority (seven deputies of the ruling Arena party) and its minority (six of the opposition Brazilian Democratic Movement), it was reported Jan. 9. The majority report praised the companies' contributions to Brazilian economic development, while the minority report asserted the 11 most important transnationals had contributed little to the economy in terms of bringing in capital, and had generated huge surpluses in Brazil in comparison with their original investments. The committee heard testimony from businessmen on monopolistic practices, government backing for foreign takeovers of Brazilian businesses, and price fixing.

BRAZIL

The Sheraton and Inter-Continental hotels in Rio de Janeiro reported that Jews in the U.S. had canceled 1,000 reservations to protest Brazil's vote in favor of a United Nations resolution equating Zionism and racism, it was reported Jan. 15. In New York, The B'nai B'rith and Bnai Zion organizations said they had canceled vacation tours that stopped in Rio.

January price rises. The prices of bread, mineral water, cigarettes and bus fares rose by 9%–41% early in January and price increases were scheduled for school fees, electricity, automobiles, spare parts and other items, it was reported Jan. 16.

The rises followed an increase in the cost of living in 1975 estimated at 29.4% by Finance Minister Mario Henrique Simonsen and at higher figures by independent observers, according to the Miami Herald. The Rio de Janeiro newspaper Jornal do Brasil, cited by the Herald, reported that essential food items such as mandioc flour, beef and cheeses had increased in price by an average of more than 70% in the past year.

The government had devalued the cruzeiro by a total of 21.9% in 1975, following devaluations totaling 19.7% the previous year, it was reported Jan. 9.

Inflation rate highest since 1964. The inflation rate for 1976 would be 46%, the highest since the armed forces seized power in 1964, the government announced Dec. 31.

Other developments. Among other economic developments:

Thousands of unemployed farmworkers in Bahia State had joined municipal food lines as a drought in Bahia and three other northeastern states entered its second month, it was reported Jan. 16. The government had begun a food airlift to the region.

The auto industry had grown by only 2.7% in 1975, compared with growth of 18% the year before, it was reported Jan. 20.

Mineracao Rio Norte, a new bauxite company owned 51% by Cia. Vale do Rio Doce, the state-controlled steel firm, began operations in the Amazon area with a production goal of 3.3 million tons per year, it was reported Jan. 16. Cia. Brasileira de Aluminio owned 10% of the new firm's shares, while Alcan Aluminum of Canada owned 19%. Reynolds Metals Co. of the U.S. and companies from Norway, Spain, Great Britain and Holland each owned 5%.

Brazil-U.S. Business Council formed. A Brazil-U.S. Business Council was formed in Washington, D.C. Jan. 30 by the U.S. Chamber of Commerce and a Brazilian Joint Commission representing four Brazilian business organizations. The chamber said that the council would provide "a channel for direct dialogue between business leaders and key commercial decision-makers of the two countries." The statement added:

The Brazilian Joint Commission represents the Confederation of Industry of Brazil, the Confederation of Commerce of Brazil, the Brazilian Exporters' Association and the Confederation of Commercial Associations of Brazil.

The co-signers of the agreement were Marcus Vinicius Pratini de Moraes, chairman for the Brazilian Joint Commission and executive president of Grupo Peixoto de Castro, and Dr. Richard L. Lesher, president of the Chamber of Commerce United States.

Witnessing the signing were H. E. Joao Paulo dos Reis Velloso, Brazilian Minister of State and Secretary of Planning to the Presidency and U.S. Under Secretary of Commerce James A. Baker, III. Also on hand were over 150 guests including representatives of business, government and international organizations and 20 chief executives of Brazilian companies who traveled to Washington with Minister Reis Velloso for the occasion.

Dr. Lesher said the Council would "be a major step to strengthen trade and industrial cooperation between the two countries."

Total U. S.-Brazilian trade in 1975 amounted to approximately $4.5 billion. The United States is Brazil's largest trading partner while Brazil ranks as the seventh largest trading partner of the United States. Brazil has the single largest amount of U. S. investment in Latin America.

Foreign & Other Developments

Kissinger's visit. U.S. Secretary of State Henry Kissinger visited Brazil and other South American countries during a Latin American tour Feb. 16–24.

The tour was evidently designed to reaffirm U.S. interest in good relations with Latin America and to smooth over bilateral problems, notably those caused by what Latin American nations charged were discriminatory U.S. trade practices. However, the tour was criticized as merely symbolic in much of the Latin American press.

The highlight of the tour was Kissinger's stop Feb. 19–22 in Brazil, where he met with President Ernesto Geisel and other top officials and signed a consultative agreement Feb. 21 by which the U.S. effectively recognized Brazil as the major power in Latin America. The pact was denounced Feb. 23 in the Mexican, Colombian and Venezuelan press. In the U.S. it was criticized Feb. 26 by Sen. Edward M. Kennedy (D, Mass.), who chided Kissinger for favoring Brazil's repressive military government over more democratic regimes in Latin America.

Under the agreement, the U.S. and Brazil would "normally hold consultations semiannually, on the full range of foreign policy matters, including any specific issue that may be raised by either side." The U.S. secretary of state would travel to Brazil at least once a year to meet with its foreign minister, the pact stipulated.

Kissinger warmly praised his Brazilian hosts, asserting at a dinner in Brasilia that "Brazil's diplomats speak for a nation of greatness—a people taking their place in the front rank of nations, a country of continental proportions with a heart as massive as its geography, a nation now playing a role in the world commensurate with its great history and its even greater promise." Nevertheless, the secretary reportedly promised Brazil little in terms of improved trade relations, telling officials there as in the other Latin nations that the U.S. Congress was blocking the Ford Administration's attempts to change the U.S. Trade Reform Act of 1974 so it no longer discriminated against certain Latin American imports.

Security during Kissinger's visit was tight in Brazil as it was in the other nations on the tour. The building in which Kissinger met President Geisel Feb. 20 was described in press reports as besieged by soldiers. Kissinger was accompanied on the tour by 60 U.S. security agents, and he took along his own bullet-proof limousine for ground transportation.

After returning to the U.S., Kissinger reported March 4 to the House Committee on International Relations. He said of his visit to Brazil:

"Brazil is an emerging world power, with broadened international interests and responsibilities, not by virtue of our granting them that rank, but by the reality of what Brazil has accomplished. The memorandum of agreement which I signed with the Brazilian foreign minister, establishing procedures for consultation between our two governments on issues of common substantive concern, was a recognition of that plain fact. The bilateral relationship between the United States and Brazil is becoming more important and more complex all the time; at the same time Brazil's voice and influence in world councils is also growing. It was in recognition of Brazil's new world role that we institutionalized the increased consultations which will be required, just as we have with the nations of Western Europe, Canada and Japan. The Brazilian consultative agreement is bilateral, it touches only our relations with Brazil. While it reflects the reality of Brazil's international status, it does not affect our relationship with any other country or represent an attempt to manage Latin America by proxy."

Meningitis deaths totaled. The Sao Paulo Health Department disclosed that 1,629 persons had died of meningitis in the Sao Paulo area in 1975, following 2,575 deaths in the city's epidemic the year before, it was reported Jan. 8.

Chile

Torture, Political Imprisonment & Other Human Rights Violations

The military junta that seized control of Chile in September 1973 has acquired the reputation of running one of the most repressive regimes in the world. The number of persons arrested for political reasons has been estimated by some observers as up to 100,000. Political prisoners have been routinely tortured, according to numerous and apparently reliable reports. Some, it was said, were tortured to death. More than 1,000 political prisoners were reported to have disappeared. Many political foes of the regime avoided arrest by fleeing the country or taking refuge in foreign embassies.

Torture of British doctor denied. The government officially denied Jan. 5 that Sheila Cassidy, a British doctor imprisoned in Chile for two months in 1975, had been tortured in custody.

A note delivered to the British foreign office by Rear Adm. Kaare Olsen, Chile's ambassador in London, said the government had investigated Cassidy's charge that she was tortured with electric shocks and found it to be false.

Reginald Seconde, the British ambassador, recalled from Chile in protest against Cassidy's alleged mistreatment, on returning to London Jan. 1 had reiterated his "absolute belief" in Cassidy's story.

A U.N. Human Relations Commission panel in Geneva Jan. 19 received testimony from Cassidy on torture in Chilean prisons.

Cassidy submitted a 24-page written statement detailing her experiences in three Chilean jails—the Cuatro Alamos detention center, the Tres Alamos prison and the Casa Grimaldi "torture center"—and quoting accounts of torture she heard from other prisoners. Cassidy said she had been tortured with electric shock and forced to sign three confessions.

At Tres Alamos, Cassidy testified, some 90% of the 120 women prisoners had been tortured. "It's a sort of systematic thing," she said. "Everybody who doesn't break down at the first harsh word or slap across the face, get the electrical treatment—electric shocks on the most sensitive parts—usually once. If they then talk that's enough. But people can get it up to 15 times. I was lucky in that I only had it three.

"Then body blows to the blindfolded person," Cassidy continued, "resulting in quite a lot of kidney damage, people hung by the wrists for different periods of time. There's a Brazilian torture where they're suspended by their wrists and knees and given genital stimulation. There's a lot of introduction of foreign objects into the vagina and rectum, submersion in water, there's an endless series."

The food in Chilean prison camps was inadequate to maintain health or even life,

Cassidy added. The women prisoners at Tres Alamos, she said, were a "mixed bag" including some professional revolutionaries but also nurses, teachers, sociologists, journalists and others who had been arrested for helping persons opposed to the military government.

Cassidy reported that she had been arrested after treating Nelson Gutierrez, "a wounded leftist revolutionary" who was apparently connected with Andres Pascal Allende, "the head of the MIR (Movimiento Izquierdo Revolucionario), the revolutionary leftist movement in Chile." She had treated Gutierrez on the request of a "Chilean priest," she said, and she apparently had been working with other priests and nuns. Her torture, she reported, had started in a house that did not appear to be a regular prison:

> We entered the house and I was taken immediately to a room of interrogation. I was interrogated for what I think was only a few minutes and then told to remove my clothes. I declined to do so and my interrogator then began to tear my shirt off. Not wishing to be further manhandled, I removed all my clothes. I was then told to lie on the bed. In the room there was a double metal bunk. They removed the mattress from the bottom floor of the bunk and I was tied to the frame of the bunk. My wrists and ankles were secured to the side of the bunk and I was spreadeagled with my legs apart. I was further secured by a wide band across my abdomen and two straps were passed around my upper arms. I was very tightly blindfolded but before they tightened the bandage I was able to see that this was a small room in which there was a metal bunk, a chair and a large street map of Santiago hung from the wall. There was also a woman present amongst the group of some five men. They then began to interrogate me. They immediately gave me a violent electric shock which seemed to be a generalised shock. At that time I think the electrodes had been placed on my wrists but I couldn't be sure. They asked me where I had treated Gutiérrez. When I saw that they didn't know where I had treated him I realised that they must be ignorant of the involvement of the priests and nuns in the treatment and subsequent asylum of Nelson Gutiérrez. Not wishing to implicate the Church, and more especially not wishing to endanger the lives of the Chilean priests who had helped him, I invented a long and detailed story of how I had treated Gutiérrez in a private house at the request of a Chilean doctor and in a distant part of Santiago. It was not particularly difficult to invent this story as all their questions were direct and I just fabricated answers to each of the questions. When I realised that they were believing me and that I was diverting them completely from my friends it became easier still to lie in this way. Every time I faltered in my story they gave me another electric shock. These were extremely painful, but providing I kept talking it was possible to bear it....
>
> I was taken by car, once more blindfolded, back to the original place of detention. I was led immediately to the same room, ordered to remove my clothes and once more secured to the bed frame. This time they inserted an electrode in my vagina and began to stimulate me with a wandering electrode, by which I mean they had an electrode which had some kind of a pincer and they stimulated me in various parts of my body, largely over my lower abdomen and thighs and pubic regions. Whether because of the siting of the electrodes or because of the increase of current, this pain was greatly more severe, and I was very distressed. Their attitude was very much more aggressive and although they told me that when I was prepared to talk, I should raise my fingers; when I did so they gave me several more shocks, each time before they removed the gag from my mouth to allow me to talk. After what I would imagine was about 20 minutes of this repeated shock treatment, I disclosed that I had treated Gutiérrez in a Roman Catholic convent. They found this idea so fantastic and, because I had previously lied, did not believe me, so they continued with the interrogation and the shocks. After a total of about an hour they believed me and I was once more freed and taken from the bed, dressed and taken by car to show them the location of the convent. This I did and I was brought back to the detention site....
>
> After my second return to this house of interrogation, I was again returned to the bed, stripped and tied in a similar manner, electrodes were again placed in my vagina and I was again given electrical shocks over various parts of the lower part of my body. This time because of the known association between Nelson Gutiérrez and Pascal Allende and especially because Mary-Ann Beausire had been in the house when I treated Gutierrez they were convinced that I knew his whereabouts, but they did not believe me and continued with repeated shocks. They shouted at me many times that I was lying. In between the shock sessions I was left stripped, tied to the bed, while my interrogators went away to confer amongst themselves. While left in the hands of men who I presume are more junior members of the torture team, I was frequently stroked and fondled and asked if I enjoyed it. They repeatedly asked whether or not I was a virgin and I was very fearful that they would try to rape me.
>
> ... On Sunday 2 November I was interrogated many times during the day but received no further torture. I was, however, struck many times about the head and face, but not enough to leave any permanent damage apart from a slightly split lip. I was taken on one occasion to the room where I had been tortured and told that I would be

CHILE

making a statement. I was told that if I did not make his statement things would go very badly for me and that I was to say just what I was told to say. The statement began, "I, Sheila Cassidy in Santiago without any physical or mental duress declare". Then they dictated to me questions and answers. The information contained in the statement was true apart from the fact about it not being made under duress....

I should mention at this point that at the very beginning of the torture I told them that I was a British citizen and that their behaviour could lead to an international incident, and they replied "Our image abroad is so bad that it doesn't matter."

I was interrogated in all over a period of 12 hours, and judging by the voices and behavior of the interrogators at the office, it was by a group of very senior men. It was certainly not one or two junior torturers, and a man, who I believe to be a senior official, told me, "Doctor, you are a sensible woman, you must realise that you have now received three sessions of electrical treatment and that this can go on and on, up to ten or twelve or thirteen, and that after each session you will be in a progressively worse physical condition."

Eventually, I was returned on two further occasions to the torture room where I was stripped and tied to the bed, but on each of these last two occasions there was a long lapse of time and a discussion with the chief of the interrogation and I was released without further electrical current being passed. ...

Church 'solidarity' unit created. The Roman Catholic Church of Chile announced in Santiago Jan. 16 that it had created a "vicariate of solidarity" to help political prisoners and their families and give economic aid to the unemployed.

The vicariate would effectively replace the Committee of Cooperation for Peace in Chile, a similar organization founded in 1973 by Catholic, Protestant and Jewish leaders and dissolved toward the end of 1975 at the request of President Augusto Pinochet Ugarte, who charged the committee had been used by Marxists to "create problems disturbing the public order."

The vicariate, to be headed by Rev. Cristian Precht Banados, executive secretary of the defunct peace committee, would give legal assistance and set up soup kitchens, clinics and job referral services in an effort to "awaken and channel the capicity for service of the Christian community and men of good will," according to a statement released by the archbishopric of Santiago.

Bishops ask foreign priests to stay. Four Roman Catholic bishops including Raul Cardinal Silva Henriquez, archbishop of Santiago and primate of the Chilean church, published a letter Jan. 23 asking foreign priests and nuns to remain in Chile to face "the challenges of today, tomorrow and always."

The letter was a response to "the uncertainties" expressed by the 1,398 foreign priests and nuns in Chile regarding the government's "unjustified" and "shameful" action against several of them late in 1975, the bishops said.

The government had expelled three U.S. nuns Nov. 8, 1975 for allegedly aiding fugitive members of the Revolutionary Left Movement; it had deported two Italian priests Nov. 28 for allegedly carrying out subversive activities in the northern town of Copiapo; and it was denying permission to re-enter Chile to a Dutch priest who had left the country in December, the bishops' letter noted.

The leaders of the church hierarchy had held an "extraordinarily positive and interesting" meeting with President Augusto Pinochet Ugarte Jan. 20 to try to improve relations between the church and state, according to Bishop Francisco Fresno, quoted by the French news agency Agence France-Presse Jan. 21.

Rev. Cristian Precht, head of the Roman Catholic Church's "vicariate of solidarity" in Santiago, said Jan. 26 that torture of prisoners by security officers was continuing. "It is unfortunate, but it exists, and where it occurs we put the matter in the hands of the pertinent authorities," Precht said.

Prisoners' rights set. President Augusto Pinochet Ugarte signed a decree Jan. 28 establishing certain rights for prisoners under the state of siege and setting measures to prevent torture in custody.

Under the new law, an arrest could not be made without a warrant signed by a local chief of security; a prisoner's immediate family must be notified within 48 hours of his arrest; a prisoner must be charged or set free within 48 hours of arrest; a prisoner must be given a medical examination on entering and leaving jail to determine whether he was tortured in custody; and the Supreme Court president and the justice minister were empowered to make surprise visits to detention centers and order an immediate medical check on any prisoner showing signs of torture.

Where doctors found a prisoner had been mistreated, legal proceedings against his alleged torturers would be initiated within 48 hours, the decree stated. No penalties were prescribed for convicted torturers.

The decree was criticized Feb. 2 by the International Commission of Jurists in Geneva, which noted in a telegram to Pinochet that there already were doctors at detention centers in Chile and that prisoners were merely held until signs of their torture disappeared. A suspect "should be seen by a doctor of his or his family's choice on arrest and every 48 hours thereafter while in custody of security forces," the telegram said.

Text of the Jan. 28 decree:

Decree 187.—Whereas: The need to regulate adequately the norms designed to guarantee the rights of the persons arrested during the State of seige, as established in Article 1 of the Decree-Law 1009, of 1975, and keeping in mind what was established in Article 10, number 1, e) of the Decree-Law 527,

Be it decreed that:

Article 1. Every person arrested by any organization and in the situation referred to under Article 1 of the Decree-Law 1,009 of 1975, even before going into the offices, facilities or places of detention under each one, shall be examined by a physician. The same medical examination shall be given the arrested person before leaving these offices, facilities or places.

The Legal Medical Services and the National Health Service, jointly shall assign a physician to these offices, facilities or places previously mentioned to perform the physical examinations required by this article.

The above mentioned physicians shall file a written report in each case in which he shall describe the state of the person examined, and shall forward it immediately to the Ministry of Justice.

Article 2. If in the certificates mentioned in the last paragraph of the preceding article, it might be understood that the person arrested had been the object of brutality or undue pressure, the Ministry of Justice shall proceed to denounce the facts to the corresponding authorities, be it administrative, institutional or judicial, depending on the case.

Article 3. Arrests made in compliance with the regulations in force during the state of siege referred to in Article 1 on the Decree-Law 1009, of 1975, can only be applicable previous of written order issued by the Chiefs of the corresponding specialized security agency, and which shall contain a listing of the following items:

A. Identification of the arrested person;
B. Identification of the person making the arrest;
C. Place where the arrested person shall be taken;
D. Date, time and place where the person was arrested;
E. Name, position and signature of person who ordered the arrest, and
F. Seal and stamp which authorizes such order.

A copy of the arrest order shall be delivered to the next of kin of the person arrested, as chosen by himself, and who resides at the same address where the arrest was made, within the 48 hours established in Article 1 of the Decree-Law 1009 of 1975.

Article 4. If in order to comply with the order of arrest referred to in the previous article or as a consequence derived from it, it would seem necessary to break into a house, or a building or any other locked place—public or private—the Chief of the corresponding specialized agency shall issue a written order authorizing the officer to do so. Such order shall be previously down to the head of the household, or to the resident-manager or locked place, or in any case, to the person to whom a copy shall be handed once the search is completed.

Article 5. If in carrying out the arrests or break-ins mentioned in this Supreme Decree, resulted in the loss of freedom of an alien, the Ministry of the Interior shall proceed, in compliance with its legal functions, to deport him from the country.

Article 6. The President of the Republic, under the Supreme Decree which shall bear the signatures of the Ministers of the Interior and National Defense, shall identify the places and facilities destined for detention and referred to in Articles 1 and 3 letter c) of this Decree, and in which promises, a book—with pages duly numbered—shall be used to enter the arrival and departures of the arrested persons, indicating date and time in which they take place, as well as the order under which these were carried out.

Article 7. It shall be the function of the President of the Supreme Court and/or of the Minister of Justice, to appear, without previous warning, at any place of detention assigned for this purpose under the application of these regulations under the State of Siege, in order to inspect them and to verify the strict compliance with the legal norms and regulations in force regarding the rights of the arrested persons and to inform about irregularities which might have been found to the corresponding authorities, through written, confidential reports, which fact shall not prevent them from ordering the immediate physical examination of the arrested person who complained during the inspection visit about brutality or undue pressure during his stay at the place inspected.

Article 8. In the geographical sites not include in the metropolitan area, the Minister of Justice, in complete accord with the President of the Supreme Court, shall appoint an officer who shall perform all or part of the functions and activities mentioned in Article 7 of this Supreme Decree.

Article 9. The corresponding authority shall order, in the cases described in the preceeding Articles 2, 7, and 8, and within 48 hours, the initiation of the corresponding summary, which shall start with the denunciation of the President of the Supreme Court, of the Minister of Justice or of the officer appointed by the latter, in order to determine who are responsible for the facts denounced and to apply to them the penalties established by law. It shall be specially considered, within this summary, the investigation and the verification of those facts that are relevant to eventual violations of Articles 150, 253 and 255 of the Penal Code and of 328 and 330 of that of Military Justice.

Article 10. The Ministry of the Interior or that of National Defense in the metropolitan area, and the Quartermasters or Governors of the Provinces or the Commandants in their respective jurisdictions shall provide the President of the Supreme Court, the Minister of Justice or the officer appointed by the latter every means conducive to the performance of their functions.

The employees who deny or in any way fail to provide due assistance in the performance of the functions previously mentioned shall be responsible of serious offenses while in the performances of their duties.

The Justice Ministry Feb. 26 sent an official note to the Ministry of Health directing the National Health Service and the Legal-Medical Institute, in compliance with Decree 187, to designate physicians to ascertain the condition of persons detained.

"Surprise visits" were made by Justice Minister Miguel Schweitzer to the Cuatro Alamos Detention Center March 5 and by Supreme Court President Jose Maria Eyzaguirre to the Tres Alamos Detention Center March 8 in what were presumed to be actions in defense of prisoners' rights. Schweitzer was accompanied by Justice Sub-Secretary Mario Duvauchelle, Dr. Rene Merino, director of the National Health Service, and Dr. Alfredo Vargas, director of the Legal-Medical Institute.

Foreign embassies pressed on refugees. The foreign ministry announced Jan. 9 that it had asked the embassies of Austria, Venezuela and the Vatican to turn over to Chilean authorities several "common criminals" among the political refugees they were harboring in Santiago.

Venezuela replied that the 17 refugees in its embassy had received safe-conducts and would soon leave Chile, but Austria said the seven refugees in its mission would never receive safe-conducts, since Austria had no political asylum treaty with Chile and the refugees had forced their way into the embassy. The Vatican mission harbored two alleged extremists, Nelson Gutierrez and Maria Elena Bachman.

Two other refugees—Andres Pascal Allende, a top leader of the Revolutionary Left Movement, and his friend Marie Anne Beausire—were in the Costa Rican embassy. Costa Rica had granted them political asylum in 1975 but Chile had refused to grant them safe-conducts on grounds that they were "common delinquents."

In a related development Jan. 13, 33 refugees at a United Nations center in Santiago began a hunger strike to protest the poor food at the center and delays in their transfer from Chile to political havens abroad.

MIR leaders exiled. Andres Pascal Allende, leader of the Revolutionary Left Movement (MIR) and nephew of the late President Salvador Allende Gossens, flew to San Jose, Costa Rica Feb. 2 after being granted a safe-conduct to leave the Costa Rican embassy in Santiago, where he had taken political asylum in November 1975.

Chile immediately asked Costa Rica to extradite Pascal and his friend Marie Anne Beausire, who had taken refuge with him in the embassy and accompanied him to San Jose. Chile accused Pascal of "subversion, attacks on members of security (forces) and hold-ups," according to the French newspaper Le Monde Jan. 23. But a judge in San Jose refused April 9 to grant the extradition request.

Pascal's second-in-command in the MIR, Nelson Gutierrez, was one of nine refugees in the quarters of the Apostolic Nunciature (Vatican embassy) in Santiago who were given safe-conducts to leave the country Jan. 28.

Gutierrez arrived in Stockholm Feb. 22 with his companion Maria Elena Bachman and their infant daughter. He said that he would return to Chile secretly as soon as possible.

A judge in San Jose, Costa Rica refused

April 9 to grant Chile's request for the extradition of Andres Pascal Allende.

Twelve Chilean refugees were allowed to leave the Venezuelan embassy in Santiago Feb. 4 and fly to Caracas. The last political refugee in the embassy flew later to France, the Venezuelan ambassador said Feb. 16. Remaining in the embassy were two Chilean soldiers who were accused of deserting the army and thus were denied safe conduct from Chile.

Six more Chilean refugees flew to Europe March 6 after receiving safe conduct from their refuge in the Hungarian embassy in Santiago. Five were bound for Hungary and the sixth for Sweden, according to the news agency LATIN.

Rights abuse charges continue. Representatives of foreign governments and international organizations continued to charge in February, March and April that Chile's military government condoned torture and other abuses of human rights.

The report, prepared by a five-member group headed by Ghulam Ali Allana of Pakistan, charged that torture was "an integral part of the current [Chilean] regime" and that "the methods used are characterized by an extreme cruelty that surpasses all imagination." The report cited about 80 alleged torturers and 20 torture centers in Chile, and said that the torture activities were directed by a man named Oswaldo Romo. More than 3,000 political prisoners had been tortured to death or "executed without trial" since the Chilean armed forces seized power in 1973, the report alleged.

Those making the charges included members of the human rights units of the United Nations and the Organization of American States (OAS), and officials of the U.S. and Venezuelan governments.

The U.N. Human Rights Commission passed a resolution Feb. 19 asking Chile to "end the institutionalized torture" of political prisoners and other "flagrant violations of human rights." The resolution was based on a report submitted to the commission by an investigative panel Feb. 10 and denounced by Chile Feb. 18 as "neither objective nor serious."

A statement by the U.N. Information Service in Geneva said:

The Working Group states that it hoped to be able to report on facts and measures indicating an improvement in human rights in Chile. But the information freshly examined forces it to conclude that the situation of human rights in Chile, as reported at the end of August 1975, has not substantially changed.

The Group notes as a positive development the fact that a number of persons considered by the Government as opponents to the regime or dangerous to state security and order have been allowed to leave the country....

Concerning the new legislation reportedly intended to mitigate the harshness of the state of seige, the Group, after what it describes as a careful and genuine search for changes, declares itself unable to report any significant progress. In the Group's view, the state of siege, in force for over two years, prevents meaningful judicial review of military trials and affords the government junta powerful means to influence and intimidate judges of all ranks.

State security police agencies, the Group reports, have used methods characterized by extreme ruthlessness. The report speaks of the cold, methodical application of torture to adults as a means of extracting information, and to children to obtain information from their parents. It states that the punishment and destruction of political opponents have frequently been accompanied by manifestations of barbaric sadism on the part of individual operators. Statements made before the group in this connexion stagger the imagination, it adds.

Torture, the report says, is indeed institutionalized and has become part of the Government; the present rulers of Chile still act as if they were the military occupiers of a foreign hostile territory. The report quotes reliable witnesses as having attributed to high Chilean officials such statements as: "National security is more important than human rights" and "If they are not tortured they will not sing."

The group cites what it calls very disturbing information indicating that the Chilean authorities have turned their attention to the church and the clergy. It notes, in particular, the disbanding of a humanitarian organization establised by the co-operative efforts of various churches in Chile....

After the formal Chilean denial Feb. 18, President Augusto Pinochet Ugarte charged April 24 that the U.N. was afraid to investigate human-rights abuse in other countries. All allegations of rights violations in Chile were leftist propaganda, Pinochet said.

A refutation of the charges against Chile had been written by John Philip Sousa in the Times of the Americas Feb. 4. While "Chile is no paradise,... neither is it the bloody hell of fear and violence it is purported to be," Sousa said. He reported being allowed to travel throughout the country and to "talk with whomever I wanted to talk." "Most Chileans do not believe the charges made by British physician Sheila Cassidy," he reported. "Most everyone I talked with expressed dismay at the publicity given the doctor's allegations of mistreatment, particularly in light of both her reportedly known leftist leanings and her failure, so far, to prove that she was indeed tortured." Sousa asserted that most non-government officials he had questioned had "said that, yes, there might have been some torture and 'roughing up' of political prisoners when the present administration took over, but not now, 'or we would have known about it.'"

Three members of the OAS' Inter-American Commission on Human Rights denounced rights abuse in Chile. They said that they would not seek reelection to the commission because they doubted the OAS really sought to protect human rights, the Washington Post reported March 5. The members—Justino Jimenez de Arechaga of Uruguay, Genaro Carrio of Argentina and Robert F. Woodward of the U.S.—were dismayed over the OAS' refusal to act on a commission report alleging human-rights abuse in Chile, and over the OAS' decision to schedule its 1976 assembly in Chile in June.

(Alejandro Orfila, the OAS' secretary general, visited Chile March 14-17 to help organize the assembly. After meeting with Gen. Pinochet March 16, Orfila praised the dictator as a "magnificent" man of "great sensitivity, personality and simplicity." The statement was denounced March 18 by Excelsior, the leading Mexican newspaper. Pinochet "maintains the Chilean people buried in terror, ignominy and misery," Excelsior said. Orfila replied from Bolivia March 19 that his respect for a nation's leader did not mean agreement with his policies.)

Members of the U.S. Congress made several protests of human-rights abuse in Chile. A House-Senate conference voted March 31 to maintain the U.S. ban on military aid to Chile but to allow Chile to buy arms from the U.S. with cash. In an earlier protest of Chilean rights abuse the Senate had voted to cut off all military sales to Chile. The House later voted to allow them.

Three Democratic congressmen March 17 had supported the Senate ban. They said that they had found during a visit to Chile March 11-15 that people there were "still being detained, still disappearing and still being tortured." The representatives—Thomas Harkin (Iowa), Toby Moffett (Conn.) and George Miller (Calif.)—said that they had found "a silent and pervasive fear in all segments of Chilean society, the oldest of Latin American democracies. The [military] junta is now directing and increasing the wrath of its intelligence and torture apparatus against former members of the Christian Democratic Party, a party based in the Catholic Church, a party without any history of violence or revolution."

The congressmen later expressed fears that the junta would take reprisals against persons to whom the lawmakers had spoken in Chile. The U.S. State Department said March 25 that it had "absolutely no evidence" any reprisals were planned. However, one person interviewed by the congressmen—Jose Zalaquett, lawyer for the Roman Catholic Church's Vicariate of Solidarity in Santiago—was arrested April 5 and exiled to France April 12. The State Department formally protested the action April 19.

In another protest, U.S. Rep. Henry Reuss (D, Wis.) charged March 23 that documents of the World Bank showed that the bank had recently loaned $33 million to Chile for political reasons. Reuss was chairman of an international economics subcommittee of the Joint Economic Committee of Congress. In a March 19 letter to Robert McNamara, the World Bank's president, Reuss said that since Chile was "broke" and thus a poor credit risk, he must conclude that the bank had "succumbed to political pressure to shore up an inhuman right-wing dictatorship..."

McNamara defended the loan in a written reply to Reuss, claiming that the bank had "used the same economic and technical criteria in assessing the creditworthiness of Chile's present government as it used for its predecessor," it was reported April 12. The bank had denied loans to Chile while it was ruled by the late President Salvador Allende.

The Venezuelan Senate, meanwhile, passed resolutions April 23 denouncing "the fascist dictatorship that shames the people of Chile" and expressing "solidarity with exiled, persecuted, jailed and tortured" Chileans.

Censorship decree scored. Owners of newspapers and radio stations criticized a stringent censorship decree issued by the military junta in December 1975, it was reported Jan. 9.

The decree forbade the information media to "disseminate opinions, news reports or communications tending to create alarm or displeasure among the population; disfigure the true dimension of events; be manifestly false, or contravene instructions given [the media] for reasons of internal order."

The National Press Association asked President Augusto Pinochet Ugarte to rescind the decree, and the Association of Chilean Radio Broadcasters complained that the measure "implies self-censorship and limits the duty to inform." The College of Newspapermen, dominated by Christian Democrats, expressed "profound surprise" at the decree and noted that it did "not contribute to maintaining the climate of harmony and collaboration" existing between the press and the military junta.

Arrests, censorship continue—Political arrests and press censorship continued in Chile in March.

Belisario Velasco, manager of the Christian Democratic radio station Radio Presidente Balmaceda, was arrested March 24 and exiled to a remote northern community near the Peruvian border. Jose Weibel, former leader of Chile's Communist Youth, was seized March 29, according to the French newspaper Le Monde April 5.

Velasco was arrested immediately after he filed a court appeal against the closing of Radio Presidente Balmaceda March 22. The station was shut down for six days, apparently for reporting an alleged sugar shortage in Chile. It had reopened Feb. 6 after being closed since Jan. 20 for allegedly broadcasting "antipatriotic propaganda."

Ercilla, a news magazine also linked to the Christian Democrats, was shut down for an undisclosed period March 23. The government apparently had taken offense at a series of articles on Chile's universities.

OAS assembly discusses Chilean rights abuses. The Organization of American States (OAS) held its sixth General Assembly in Santiago, Chile June 4–18.

The human rights issue dominated the meeting, primarily because Chile's military rulers had been accused repeatedly of violating individual liberties since they seized power in 1973. Mexico boycotted the assembly to protest the selection of Chile as host country. Its foreign minister said May 20 that Mexico would not contribute to the "legitimization" of a government that was "built on the death of Chilean democracy and the tomb of [President] Salvador Allende."

The assembly June 18 passed a compromise resolution that urged Chile "to continue adopting measures to assure the observance of human rights and to give the [OAS'] Inter-American Commission on Human Rights the cooperation it needs to carry out its work." The measure passed 19–1, with Jamaica voting against it and Chile and Brazil abstaining.

Jamaican delegate Patricia Durrant denounced the OAS for passing such a mild resolution after its human rights commission reported widespread torture and other abuse of human rights in Chile. Durrant announced that Jamaica would not join in the "conspiracy of silence" regarding the "absence of justice" in Chile.

Venezuela and Costa Rica had joined Jamaica in calling for a stronger denunciation of rights-abuse in Chile based on the commission's report.

The human rights issue dominated the assembly from the opening speech June 4 by Chilean President Augusto Pinochet Ugarte. Pinochet denied that human rights were violated in Chile and proposed that the OAS create a new human rights unit whose "right of action" and access to Latin nations would be "precisely defined." The proposal, which would apparently undercut the Inter-American Commission on Human Rights, was later rejected by the assembly.

Pinochet denounced the "armed expansionism" of the Soviet Union and called on all Latin American nations to join the U.S. in an "ideological war" against communism. "Peaceful coexistence" and "comfortable neutralisms" contained the "seeds of suicide," he asserted.

Pinochet said Chile had "freed itself from the imminent establishment of a

CHILE

Marxist-Leninist tyranny and had begun to build a new democracy through the creation of a new juridical institutionality." Soon the Chilean government would enact a series of constitutional reforms regarding human rights that would make the Chilean constitution "one of the most advanced and complete documents in the world," he declared.

Chile had announced the release of 305 political prisoners in May in an attempt to show the U.S. and other OAS members that it was concerned about human rights. However, lawyers and Roman Catholic priests in Chile claimed that month that political arrests were continuing.

The first 49 political prisoners were freed May 6, one day before U.S. Treasury Secretary William Simon arrived in Santiago for two days of economic talks. Simon said May 7 that U.S. aid to Chile was dependent on the military government's respect for human rights. He also praised the government for "clearly establishing the bases for economic development." In Washington May 16, Simon said he would ask Congress to continue economic aid to Chile without any further cuts.

Simon and the Chilean government announced May 19 that 49 more Chilean prisoners were being freed. Another 207 were released May 26. Nevertheless, a group of exiled Chilean ex-congressmen reported in New York May 20 that hundreds of Chileans had been arrested in the previous few weeks in a new wave of political repression.

Pinochet announced during the OAS assembly June 7 that another 60 political prisoners were being released. He allowed OAS Secretary General Alejandro Orfila to visit the Tres Alamos detention camp and he permitted the Santiago newspaper El Mercurio to print the text of a heretofore secret report by the Inter-American Commission on Human Rights that denounced widespread rights abuse by Chilean authorities.

The report's text, published June 9, had been circulating among delegates to the assembly. It detailed cases of arbitrary arrest, torture and summary execution by Chilean security forces, particularly the National Intelligence Directory (DINA), the political police force that answered only to Pinochet.

El Mercurio also printed the text of a long refutation of the report by the Chilean government. The regime said the report was based on "declarations of persons without scruples or badly informed," and argued that it was necessary to "maintain legal and administrative measures that limit the freedoms and rights of man in order to protect precisely the most important right of all, the right to a secure life."

Orfila said June 18 that at Tres Alamos he had spoken with imprisoned former government officials and with representatives of women prisoners, and that none had complained of torture. Visitors to the camp said later that women prisoners became angry when they learned of Orfila's statement, the New York Times reported June 21. A report by lawyers on the treatment of 85 women held in the camp until May said that 62 of the women had been raped and more than half had been subjected to electric shocks during interrogation after their arrest, the Times noted.

Five Chilean lawyers gave delegates to OAS assembly another report on extensive rights abuse by DINA agents, it was reported June 12. With at least 12,000 military and civilian employes, and a secret budget, DINA had become Pinochet's most powerful base of support, the lawyers said. Its personnel were forbidden to appear in court, forcing the Supreme Court and appeals courts "to close the cases involving homicide, kidnapping, disappearances and violations resulting from arrests" because of a lack of witnesses.

The lawyers' report provoked angry retorts from official Chilean spokesmen and from Jaime Eyzaguirre, president of the Supreme Court. Eyzaguirre said there should be no control over DINA under Chile's current state of siege. A government spokesman called the report "an unspeakable act of treason" by the lawyers, who included Jaime Castillo Velasco, a former justice minister and Christian Democrat.

(Before the OAS assembly began, another report denouncing DINA's "uncontrolled power" had been issued by the Roman Catholic "Vicariate of Solidarity" in Santiago, it was reported June 3. The report, which detailed widespread rights abuse by DINA since 1974, was signed by Bishop Enrique Alvear, whose religious office made him virtually immune from arrest. Hernan Montealegre, a lawyer for the vicariate, was arrested May 12.)

U.S. Secretary of State Henry A. Kissinger attended the OAS assembly June 7-10.

Addressing the assembly June 8, Kissinger noted reports of human rights abuse in Chile but stopped short of condemning the military government. "The condition of human rights as assessed by the Organization of American States' Human Rights Commission has impaired [the U.S.'] relationship with Chile and will continue to do so," he said. "We wish this relationship to be close, and all friends of Chile hope that obstacles raised by conditions alleged in the report will soon be removed."

The U.S. chapter of Amnesty International June 4 had sent OAS Secretary General Orfila a cable urging thorough discussion by the assembly of the charges against Chile. An accompanying AI statement said:

Amnesty International urges the OAS to fully discuss the agenda item of the report of the Inter-American Commission on Human Rights in Chile. This report which accuses the military junta of "very grave violations of human rights" is dated November 21, 1974. At last year's meeting, following a private agreement among member nations, the OAS General Assembly refused to discuss the report, giving as a reason the impending visit to Chile of the U.N. Human Rights Commission which was then denied entrance by the Chilean government.

As pointed out in a recent article in the New York Times by Jose Zalaquett, a leading Chilean human rights lawyer arrested and deported to France after having spoken to three visiting U.S. Congressmen about human rights violations, "Although the junta is carrying out fewer arrests, it has recently undertaken new measures to increase fear and silence critics. They are directed primarily against the churches, universities, labor unions and some elements of the news media."

Amnesty International has recently learned of new arrests of at least 185 people in Antofagasta May 18th, and of further arrests of trade union leaders and members of the Communist party in the Santiago region on the 17th and 18th of May. Those arrested in Antofagasta have been taken to prison in Santiago.

This recent wave of arrests only underlines another point by Zalaquett, "A sophisticated totalitarian government is more dangerous than a crude one and the recent Chilean developments show the increased sophistication of the junta. But there is no evidence of any real progress for human rights."

The situation of "disappeared persons" is extreme in Chile and becoming so in Argentina. In his testimony before the U.S. House of Representatives subcommittee on International Organizations on May 5, 1976 Jose Zalaquett testified that the files of the Chilean ecumenical Committee for Peace included approximately 1,040 prisoners who have disappeared after being arrested whom the government does not acknowledge as even being placed under arrest. According to estimates of the Committee for Peace, about 95,000 people were arrested during the first 18 months of the military government for a period of at least 24 hours, a report accepted by the New York Times as recently as April 12, 1976. In Argentina, because of the news blackout, there are no reliable estimates.

If the OAS does not produce a clear statement on the issue of human rights, then the Chilean government will have succeeded in its tactic of making small temporary concessions with human lives during periods of increased international pressure, while continuing to silence all internal protest.

U.N. group relays charges. The U.N. Economic & Social Council's Human Rights Commission said in a paper made public June 4:

The World Council of Churches reported that since 11 September 1973 about 100,000 persons have been deprived of freedom, of whom 6,000 are still in detention, while 2,000 have disappeared or are missing in Santiago province alone and about 50,000 persons have left the country in order to avoid political persecution.

The evidence before the Group shows conclusively that, either in violation of their own laws or in disregard for generally accepted international human rights standards, the right to be free from arbitrary arrest and detention is not respected in Chile today.

The statements received by the Working Group show that, contrary to what has been repeatedly stated by the Chilean authorities, torture and cruel, inhuman or degrading treatment continue in Chile on a large scale. Reliable documents and written information indicate that they are still widely practiced.

The report names 77 Chileans accused of torture of political prisoners and recommends that Oswaldo Rom DINA's master torturer, be tried for crimes against humanity.

Bishop Helmut Frenz, of the Lutheran Church, stated that he himself had had conversations with General Pinochet four times, the last time in December, 1974. On that occasion he gave the President voluminous documentation on tortures and missing persons in Chile. According to this witness, President Pinochet said, "Of course we have to torture the members of the MIR because without torture they will not sing ... You are naive pastors, but you must know that

CHILE

national security is more important than human rights."

Kennedy accuses junta. Sen. Edward M. Kennedy (D, Mass.) indicated to the U.S. Senate June 14 that the Chilean junta might have deceived U.S. Treasury Secretary Simon about the state of human rights in Chile. Among charges made in Kennedy's statement, as printed in the Congressional Record:

In recent weeks, we have learned of the arrest of the daughter of a former Senator, two architects, the former vice president of a major labor union, two attorneys, an engineer and others. These individuals we have the names of because their relatives specifically have contacted either our Embassy, volunteer groups, or friends and relatives outside Chile and we have their names. But there are many more we still have no detailed knowledge of. We do know in Santiago alone, 133 men and women were imprisoned in May under the state of seige—and even that number only represents the ones reported to the Catholic Church.

The point is that the arrests continue, the repression continues.

For 10½ hours while the Secretary of Treasury was there it may have appeared different, but behind diplomatic curtains the repression was continuing.

While the junta was releasing some, it was arresting others to take their places in jails.

And they did not even have the courtesy to release all of those named on the release list, nor could they. Three of them were already in the United States. Another two had been released before he arrived. And another half dozen had been on a release list announced in February. And some 4,000 political prisoners remain, 700–1,000 of them without charge.

Where are the 1,000 men and women who have disappeared in the night, documented by the Chilean church committee, arrested by members of the DINA who never appear again?

Their families saw them being arrested but now file habeus corpus petitions fruitlessly; the church files petitions fruitlessly on their behalf and yet the government continues to deny knowledge of their whereabouts?

There are four questions one can ask to determine the situation in Chile:

First, can the junta order the arrest of anyone it wants without any cause? The answer is "Yes."

Second, can it keep him indefinitely imprisoned without charge, totally isolated? The answer is "Yes."

Third, can it abuse him and torture him without effective recourse? The answer is "Yes."

Fourth, can any public objection be raised to that conduct? The answer is "No."

That is the reality in Chile today.

The most recent events in Chile continue to demonstrate the pattern of gross violaions of human rights which exist in that country.

The most recent events have been the continued arrests of Chilean citizens, without charge, without reason, all for political motives.

The most shocking arrest was that of a distinguished lawyer, Hernan Montealegre, the attorney for the Catholic Church's human rights organizations, the vicariate of solidarity.

The effort to terrorize all who have any concern for human freedom and dignity is clear when within 5 weeks the two attorneys for this human rights organization are arrested. The church committee was created by the cardinal of Chile to provide some relief to the families of political prisoners and to try and provide them with some help when their husbands or wives or children are suddenly whisked off in the middle of the night by the DINA, the Chilean secret police.

Kennedy quoted from what he described as a report by a Chilean torture victim:

In Villa Grimaldi, the present general headquarters of the DINA, the agents of Pinochet are devising much more sophisticated torture. The hundreds of detained persons who arrive there each week are kept blindfolded or hooded so that they can not identify their torturers. Chains and balls are secured to their feet and their hands tied to prevent any resistance to the torture. The interrogations can last as much as 60 days.

The first step in the interrogation consists of a beating and kicking by a circle of five or six individuals armed with iron fists, handcuffs, blackjacks, and clubs. They beat without letup until the prisoner is in danger of dying. It is supervised by a doctor of the DINA who determines medically the resistance to the torture.

The prisoner might have a rest of two or three hours, or simply continue with the treatment in the following phases: electric shocks on a metal bed spring to which the interrogated person is tied by the hands and feet facing upward to facilitate the application of electric current . . .

The interrogated, with a rope secured to

his arms tied behind his back, is suspended from a high post and is left to hang there for three or four hours, loosing all sensation.

Time magazine report. In an article on "Torture as a Policy," the Aug. 16 issue of Time magazine cited Chile:

In the three years since the overthrow of the Marxist Allende government, according to respected church sources, an estimated 1,000 Chileans have been tortured to death by the ruthlessly efficient secret police, the DINA. In one wave of arrests 18 months ago 2,000 people were brought in; 370 have never been seen again. These gruesome statistics confirm the worst fears of many Chileans, that certain suspects are marked first to be tortured—generally for information about their political associations—and then executed.

The torture takes place in clandestine and ever changing places of imprisonment; one center is the Villa Grimaldi in Santiago, a former discothèque. Many suspects who live through their tortures are simply transferred to a detention camp, like Tres Alamos in Santiago. According to one report by reliable groups within the country, there were 85 female prisoners at Tres Alamos as of May; 72 of them insisted that they had been tortured. The most common methods: beating, rape (sometimes by trained dogs), electric shock and burnings with lighted cigarettes.

The DINA is fairly ecumenical in finding victims: former parliamentarians and army officers have been tortured, as well as suspect leftist terrorists. Recounts Carlos Pérez Tobar, once a lieutenant in the Chilean army arrested by the junta after he tried to resign his commission: "I was tortured with electric shock, forced to live in underground dungeons so small that in one I could only stand up and in the other only lie down. I was beaten incessantly, dragged before a mock firing squad, and regularly told that my wife and child and relatives were suffering the same fate."

Church-state conflict widens. Strained relations between the military government and the Roman Catholic Church were aggravated in July and August by the alleged continuation of human rights abuse and by alleged affronts to church leaders and their associates by government agents.

Bishop Carlos Camus, secretary of the Episcopal Conference (national bishops' council) told the newspaper La Tercera Aug. 22 that while Chile appeared to be calm, "many people are terrified." Camus said that in Chile there were three kinds of repression—unemployment and extreme poverty, fear of the police, and lack of political participation. Chileans felt "impotent before the law, before a police that can't be identified, that responds to no one," the bishop said.

The church hierarchy had been outraged Aug. 15 when a rock-throwing mob including government and police agents attacked three bishops at the Santiago airport. The bishops, who were not injured, had just returned from Ecuador after being expelled from that country for participating in an allegedly subversive church meeting.

The Chilean church Aug. 17 decreed the excommunication of four of the bishops' attackers. One was identified as Manuel Cabrera, a government employe, and the other three were said to be agents of DINA, the secret police. The excommunication order was signed by Raul Cardinal Silva Henriquez, archbishop of Santiago and primate of the Chilean church.

The government deplored the attack on the bishops. President Augusto Pinochet Ugarte invited the bishops and the members of the Episcopal Conference's Permanent Committee to lunch at the presidential palace Aug. 18. The government said afterward that the discussion at lunch had been "frank and cordial."

Nevertheless, the Episcopal Conference issued a statement Aug. 18 condemning the expulsion from Chile Aug. 6 of Jaime Castillo Velasco and Eugenio Velasco Letelier, two lawyers who had defended political prisoners and represented the Vicariate of Solidarity, the church's relief organization in Santiago. The government had charged Aug. 6 that the lawyers were "a danger to state security." Castillo, Velasco and three other lawyers had angered the government in June by presenting a report on human rights abuse in Chile to delegates of the Organization of American States' General Assembly, then meeting in Santiago.

In another development, the bishops' Permanent Committee issued a statement July 29 denouncing the treatment accorded to Cardinal Silva in early July when he had attempted to visit Hernan Montealegre, an imprisoned lawyer for the Vicariate of Solidarity. Silva had been warned that his life would be endangered if he attempted to see Montealegre, the bishops said. They also said that the prisoner had been switched to another jail to make him difficult to locate. Silva finally was allowed to see Montealegre after making strenuous protests.

The Santiago archdiocese July 16 denied the government's charges against Montealegre, which included keeping contact with Communists, participating in terrorist activities and possessing subversive propaganda.

Ex-minister freed. Fernando Flores Labra, who served as economy minister in the Cabinet of the late President Salvador Allende, was released from prison Aug. 5 and flown to the U.S., where he took a job as a computer technician with Stanford University. Flores, who had been arrested in the September 1973 military coup, was cleared of charges of misuse of public funds.

Foreign Ministry sources said Aug. 4 that 250 other prisoners whose jail terms had been commuted to banishment from Chile, were still being held because the countries they had chosen for exile had not granted them residents' visas. The prisoners included former leaders of the Allende government, the sources said.

Junta abuses reportedly continue. International organizations reported in August that torture and other abuses of human rights were continuing in Chile at an alarming rate.

The French section of Amnesty International declared in Paris Aug. 23 that "the wave of repression begun in Chile in May of 1976 does not seem to have declined in intensity." The statement named four journalists and two doctors who had been arrested for political reasons since the beginning of August, and a leftist leader who had been seized earlier.

The Geneva-based International Commission of Jurists charged Aug. 31 that torture and arbitrary arrests continued in Chile despite assurances by the military junta that human rights would be respected.

(Forty-seven persons who had been arrested in Chile in May and June had disappeared without a trace, the Washington Post reported Aug. 7. Chilean authorities denied holding them, and their relatives assumed that most or all of them had been killed. The missing persons included Bernardo Araya, a former member of the Chamber of Deputies, the Post reported.)

Chileans continued to seek asylum in foreign embassies in Santiago to avoid arrest. The Venezuelan Embassy confirmed that it had given asylum to the alleged leader of Red September, a new insurgent group said to consist of members of the Communist Party, the Revolutionary Left Movement (MIR) and the Christian Left, according to the Aug. 27 London newsletter Latin America. Diplomatic sources quoted Sept. 8 by the Associated Press said that the Venezuelan Embassy was harboring two MIR members.

The government had announced Aug. 15 that DINA had discovered a Red September arsenal in Santiago, confiscating arms, ammunition and false identification papers. Most members of the leftist group were said to have been arrested.

Letelier killed in U.S. Orlando Letelier, a former Cabinet minister and former Chilean ambassador to the U.S., was killed in Washington, D.C. Sept. 21 when a bomb exploded under his car as he drove to work.

Ronni Karpen Moffitt, an associate of Letelier at the Institute for Policy Studies, also was killed in the blast. Her husband, Michael Moffitt, was in the car but was not injured.

U.S. legislators and associates of Letelier charged that he was murdered by agents of Chile's military government, which Letelier had criticized recently for alleged violations of human rights. Friends and co-workers of Letelier said that he had told them of repeated threats against his life in recent months.

Sen. Edward M. Kennedy (D, Mass.) called Letelier's slaying "political terrorism," and Sen. James Abourezk (D, S.D.) said that the "tyranny" of the Chilean dictatorship had now been extended to the U.S. Kennedy, Abourezk and Sen. Hubert Humphrey (D, Minn.) introduced a Senate resolution calling for "thorough investigation of the circumstances surrounding the bombing." A parallel resolution was introduced in the House of Representatives by Rep. Toby Moffett (D, Conn.) and 47 other legislators.

The Chilean Embassy in Washington denied Chilean government complicity in the murder, calling it a "deplorable deed" and an "outrageous act of terrorism." About 75 persons, including some staff members of the Institute for Policy Studies, demonstrated outside the embassy Sept. 21 after the explosion. Several hundred persons staged a similar protest there the next day.

Richard Barnet and Marcus Raskin, co-directors of the institute, blamed Letelier's assassination on DINA, the Chilean secret police agency. Barnet said at a press conference Sept. 21 that there was "sufficient evidence, based on what has happened in Rome, in Buenos Aires, and now here in Washington, D.C., of a pattern of conduct by Chilean intelligence agencies."

Barnet referred to attacks against Chilean political exiles in the Italian and Argentine capitals. Bernardo Leighton, former leader of the left wing of Chile's Christian Democratic Party, was shot and wounded in Rome in 1975 by presumed agents of DINA. Carlos Prats Gonzalez, a former army general and Cabinet member, had been killed by a bomb that exploded under his car in Buenos Aires in 1974. Chilean exiles in Argentina had been harassed recently by Argentine security forces and right-wing terrorists presumably working in concert with DINA.

Letelier had been defense minister in the Cabinet of the late President Salvador Allende when Allende was overthrown by the Chilean armed forces in September 1973. Letelier was arrested in the military coup and held until September 1974, when he was released and sent into exile through the efforts of both the Venezuelan government and U.S. Secretary of State Henry Kissinger.

After some time in Venezuela, Letelier had moved to Washington, where he had been employed by the Institute for Policy Studies, a privately-funded research organization. He kept silent about Chilean affairs until recently, when he began denouncing the military junta's alleged use of torture and other rights violations. In retaliation, the junta Sept. 10 revoked Letelier's Chilean citizenship.

Letelier had told friends and co-workers that his life had been threatened repeatedly during the past year, the Washington Post reported Sept. 23. Anonymous telephone callers, some speaking in Spanish, had warned him that he would be killed unless he stopped criticizing the Chilean junta.

The week before his death, Letelier had received a letter from a well-placed Chilean who reported a high-level discussion in the military government over whether Letelier should be killed to silence his criticism. Existence of the letter was disclosed to the Washington Post by Eqbal Ahmed, an associate of Letelier at the Institute for Policy Studies.

Lillian Montecino, Letelier's assistant at the institute, said Sept. 22 that Letelier had told her that he had reported the death threats to the Federal Bureau of Investigation. However, a spokesman for the FBI's Washington field office, which was taking part in the investigation of Letelier's murder, denied that the threats had been reported.

The FBI said Sept. 22 that it had "a lot of leads" in the investigation but no suspects. Among the leads was a report from a Chilean that he saw a high-ranking official of DINA disembark from an airliner that arrived in New York Aug. 25 from Santiago.

Letelier had made his last address in New York Sept. 10, at a rally and concert in Madison Square Garden for the benefit of the Chile Human Rights Committee, which was headed by his wife, Isabel. Commenting on his loss of citizenship that day, Letelier said: "I was born a Chilean, I am a Chilean and I will die a Chilean. They (the fascists) were born traitors, live as traitors and will be remembered forever as fascist traitors."

Letelier was buried in Caracas Sept. 29. Before the burial ceremony Venezuelan President Perez and his Cabinet expressed personal condolences to Letelier's widow and "solidarity for Chileans who believe in freedom and democracy."

More than 2,000 persons had attended a memorial Mass for Letelier in Washington Sept. 26. They marched down the city's Embassy Row, where the Chilean leader was killed, then filled St. Matthew's Cathedral. The burial Mass was celebrated by Bishop James Rausch, general secretary of the U.S. National Conference of Catholic Bishops. "The senseless violence of terror has struck in our midst," Rausch said in his homily. Americans had been "brutally reminded of the cost that many have paid for our unjustified intrusion in another country's life," he declared.

The Mass was attended by Hortensia Bussi de Allende, widow of Salvador Allende, who blamed the Chilean military junta for the deaths of Letelier and Ronni Moffitt, who was fatally injured by the bomb that killed Letelier.

Cuban exiles deny involvement in slaying—Venezuelan police denied recent reports that Orlando Bosch had told them that two Cuban exiles, Guillermo and Ignacio Novo, had planted the bomb that killed Letelier, the Washington Post reported Oct. 21.

Guillermo Novo, who lived in Union City, N.J., denied Oct. 20 that he or his brother had been involved in Letelier's assassination.

A spokesman for the Institute for Policy Studies, which had employed Letelier at the time of his death, said Oct. 18 that the FBI was sending one or two agents to Venezuela to investigate possible links between Cuban exiles there and Letelier's murder. The FBI refused to confirm or deny the report, the Washington Post said Oct. 20.

The institute spokesman said that the Novo brothers, whom the institute suspected of having killed Letelier, had "worked directly with DINA, the Chilean secret police." DINA initially had been suspected by many observers of having carried out or arranged Letelier's assassination.

The Venezuelan newspaper El Nacional had reported Oct. 19 that after arresting Bosch, leader of the Cuban anti-Castro group CORU, Venezuelan police officials had learned that Bosch had told associates that the Novo brothers had placed the bomb.

U.S. intelligence sources also had received tips linking Bosch and CORU to Letelier's assassination, the New York Times reported Oct. 12. The sources said that the U.S. Federal Bureau of Investigation had learned that Cuban exile groups had carried a long-time grudge against Letelier for his role in improving relations between Cuba and Chile under the government of the late Chilean President Salvador Allende.

The U.S intelligence sources quoted by the Times Oct. 12 said that the FBI and the CIA apparently had ruled out the possibility that Letelier was killed by agents of DINA, Chile's secret police. The officials said they understood that killing Letelier could not have served the purposes of Chilean President Augusto Pinochet Ugarte, who had complete control over DINA, the Times reported.

(Top officials of the CIA and the U.S. Justice Department were participating in the FBI's investigation of Letelier's murder, the Washington Post reported Oct. 9. The CIA's role in the investigation posed sensitive ethical and legal questions, according to officials close to the probe. The CIA had been involved in efforts to overthrow the Chilean government in which Letelier served, and the investigation might turn up sensitive information that the CIA would rather keep secret, the officials said. Furthermore, the CIA operated under a charter and other federal regulations that restricted its domestic activities, the Post noted.)

U.S.S.R., Chile exchange prisoners. The Soviet Union and Chile Dec. 18 exchanged two widely known political prisoners, Vladimir Bukovsky and Luis Corvalan. Bukovsky, who had publicized the imprisonment of Soviet dissidents in mental institutions, and Corvalan, who had headed Chile's Communist Party, were exchanged at an airport in Zurich, Switzerland. The exchange was mediated by the U.S. since Moscow and Santiago had no diplomatic relations.

Bukovsky, who had been imprisoned intermittently for 15 years (continuously since 1972), was accompanied to Zurich by his mother, his sister and an ailing nephew. Corvalan, in jail since 1973, was accompanied by his wife. Bukovsky stayed in Switzerland for medical observation, while Corvalan traveled on to Moscow.

The exchange of political prisoners, thought to be unprecedented, was first proposed by Andrei Sakharov, the Soviet dissident physicist. The Chilean government agreed, but it took more than a month of secret negotiations to obtain Soviet approval, the Associated Press reported Dec. 18. Chile proposed a simultaneous exchange of Jorge Montes, another jailed Chilean Communist, for Huber Matos, a Cuban political prisoner, but Cuba ignored the offer, a Chilean official said Dec. 18. The official claimed the Montes was the sole remaining political prisoner in Chile.

The Bukovsky-Corvalan exchange was hailed by Chile, the Soviet Union and Eastern European countries, but criticized by Western European Communist parties.

The Chilean mission to the United Nations office in Geneva said Dec. 18 that the exchange was a success for "humanitarian principles." The Soviet and Eastern European press hailed Corvalan's release as a "victory of international solidarity" but did not mention Bukovsky's release. The Soviet and Eastern European press earlier had denounced the Chilean exchange proposal as "outright impudence."

Trucco: One political prisoner remains. Manuel Trucco, Chile's ambassador to the U.S., claimed Dec. 18 that the only political prisoner remaining in Chile was Jorge Montes, the former Communist senator whom Chile had proposed to exchange for a Cuban political prisoner.

Trucco said that there were 400 other prisoners who had been arrested since the military coup of September 1973, but only Montes was held under the state-of-siege law used against political opponents. The 400 had been sentenced by military tribunals for criminal offenses, including possession of weapons, Trucco said.

The Chilean government had released 304 political prisoners Nov. 17–18, and it began exiling another 18 prisoners considered dangerous to state security. Thirteen of the 18 had been exiled by Dec. 11, when former Economy Minister Jose Cademartori was released and flown to Venezuela.

The releases came amid a growing debate in the Chilean government on how to respond both to international pressures and to the election of Jimmy Carter as U.S. president, the Washington Post noted Nov. 16.

However, Adm. Jose Toribio Merino Castro, a member of the military junta, said Nov. 22 that the prisoners had not been freed "to ingratiate [Chile] with Jimmy Carter." Carter had criticized abuse of human rights in Chile during his presidential campaign.

Many prisoners disappear—There were other reasons for the dramatic decline in the number of Chilean political prisoners, the London newsletter Latin America said Nov. 5. Many prisoners with two- or three-year sentences had served them and been released. Several hundred others had left Chile under a 1975 law that allowed prisoners to choose exile over continued confinement. And more than 1,000 other prisoners had simply disappeared.

According to the Roman Catholic Church's Vicariate of Solidarity, cited Nov. 5 by Latin America, the percentage of disappearances among detainees in Chile had risen from 5% in January to 57% in August. The Vicariate presented a petition to the Chilean Supreme Court in August asking that a special investigator look into the cases of 383 disappeared prisoners. The court rejected the petition by a 7–5 vote, Latin America reported.

It was widely assumed that the missing prisoners had been killed by security forces to reduce the number of political detainees, Latin America said. Marta Ugarte Roman, who had been secretary to a Communist deputy before the 1973 military coup, was arrested in mid-August and found strangled on a beach Sept. 12. A court in Valparaiso ordered an investigation of her death, and the conservative magazine Que Pasa called for a full inquiry into other cases in which bodies, often mutilated, had been discovered.

The United Nations was pressing Chile for a full report on the death of Carmelo Soria, a leftist official of the U.N. Economic Commission for Latin America in Santiago. Soria, who had disappeared July 14, was found dead July 16 in an irrigation canal outside the city. His car had been found upside down in the canal July 15.

The Chilean police claimed that Soria had died of injuries suffered when he drove his car into the canal in a drunken stupor. However, Chile refused to give the autopsy report to the U.N., a U.N. spokesman said Dec. 14. Three doctors who read the coroner's findings said that Soria's injuries were more consistent with beating and torture than with an automobile accident, the Washington Post reported Dec. 14.

The coroner found that Soria had died 24 hours after his car plunged into the water, and that he had been dead when he entered the water. Moreover, an examination of the car showed that the doors were "hermetically closed," making it impossible for Soria to have been thrown out of the vehicle during or after the accident, the Post reported.

Friends of Soria said that he had spoken of being followed by agents of DINA, Chile's secret police. Enrique Pemjean, a former associate of Soria who had been arrested and expelled from Chile in May, said Chilean interrogators had told him, "Sooner or later we will get Soria," the New York Times reported Dec. 15.

In a related development, a panel of five U.N. diplomats reported Oct. 14 that the Chilean military government was systematically extending its abuse of human rights to the Catholic church, trade unions, universities, professional groups and other sectors of society. The panel, which reported to the U.N. General Assembly, urged governments to exercise economic pressure on Chile to abandon its practice of arbitrary arrests, torture, killings and deportations.

8 more leftists reported missing—Eight Chilean leftists had disappeared following a wave of recent political arrests by security forces, legal sources close to the Roman Catholic Church reported Dec. 22. Those missing included Edras Pinto, former secretary to Luis Corvalan, the exiled leader of Chile's Communist Party. Pinto was arrested Dec. 20 before witnesses in Santiago, the sources said. The seven other persons reportedly disappeared Dec. 15.

Other Domestic Developments

Military staff chief replaced. Gen. Sergio Arellano Stark, chief of the armed forces general staff, resigned unexpectedly Jan. 3 and was replaced by Rear Adm. Jorge Seburgo Silva Jan. 6.

The shift was followed by reports in the foreign press of military discontent with President Gen. Augusto Pinochet Ugarte. The reports, carried by the London Sunday Times Jan. 4, the French news agency Agence France-Presse Jan. 9 and the Economist of London Jan. 10, said dissident officers were led by Arellano and Gen. Gustavo Leigh Guzman, the air force commander and military junta member. Leigh denied the reports Jan. 7, asserting that to divide the Chilean armed forces was "the same as trying to separate the pyramids from Egypt."

According to the London Sunday Times, 10 generals had demanded at the end of 1975 that Pinochet change his economic policies, dissolve the secret police and resign from office by March. The officers were upset over Pinochet's increasing personal power, the growing conflict between the government and the Roman Catholic Church, Chile's sharp economic decline and its poor image abroad.

Agence France-Presse reported that Arellano and two other officers—Adm. Horacio Justiniano and Gen. Jose Berdichevsky—had tried unsuccessfully to unseat Pinochet in November 1975, and the Economist reported that the U.S. had been "privately urging Pinochet's removal over the past year."

Pinochet Jan. 28 denied recent reports of political divisions in the military, asserting at a public appearance with the three other military junta members that "the monolithic unity and ironclad discipline of our armed and security forces will never be broken." The junta members—Adm. Jose Toribio Merino, air force Gen. Gustavo Leigh Guzman and national police Gen. Cesar Mendoza—pledged their "absolute loyalty" to Pinochet.

Ex-presidents accept advisory roles. Former Presidents Gabriel Gonzalez Videla and Jorge Alessandri agreed to serve on the Council of State, an advisory panel created Dec. 31, 1975 by President Augusto Pinochet Ugarte. Gonzalez Videla's acceptance was reported Jan. 2 and Alessandri's, Jan. 4.

A third ex-president, Eduardo Frei, announced Jan. 2 that he would not serve on the council because it was only advisory and it was not the result of a plebiscite. "A council like this could only be useful . . . as part of an institutional framework, which can only originate in a political constitution chosen by the people, the only sovereign body which can sanction a fundamental charter," Frei declared.

Frei, who had supported the 1973 military coup, had called recently for a restoration of democracy in Chile, charging that the "most extremist" and "fascist" groups had attained "political preeminence" under Pinochet's regime, it was reported Jan. 3.

Publication of Frei book approved. The government Jan. 23 authorized publication in Chile of a book by ex-President Eduardo Frei which criticized the military regime's social and economic policies and called for a return to democratic rule.

The book, titled "The Mandate of History and the Demands of the Future," had been published in mimeograph form in Argentina and had been circulating informally in Chile. The government said it was authorizing Chilean publication as an "exception" that took into account Frei's status as a former president. However, the information ministry Jan. 31 banned further discussion of the book in the Chilean press, asserting the "sterile debate" over the volume was reviving partisan politics whose advocates "consciously or unconsciously have joined the international aggression against Chile."

Frei had been attacked indirectly Jan. 21 by President Augusto Pinochet Ugarte, who denounced "bad politicians" and "Kerenskys" who were allegedly trying to divide the armed forces and "drag us again into Marxism." Rightists in Chile had called Frei the "Chilean Kerensky" for handing over the government in 1970 to his elected successor, the Socialist Salvador Allende. The reference was to Alexander Kerensky, the liberal Russian prime minister ousted in the Bolshevik coup of 1917.

In a related development Jan. 20, the government closed Radio Presidente Balmaceda, the radio station of Frei's Christian Democratic Party, accusing the station of carrying out a "campaign of antipatriotic propaganda."

University purged. Three hundred teachers and administrators were dismissed from the University of Chile by its new rector, Col. Julio Tapia, it was reported Jan. 8.

Tapia took office Dec. 30, 1975 and immediately demanded the resignations of all vice rectors, deans and department chairmen, asserting he needed "absolute freedom of action" to reform the university. He declared that the school, Chile's largest with about half of the nation's university students, was "the place principally chosen by forces antagonistic to Chile to infiltrate action, since there is no better place to propagate Marxist doctrines against the principal national activities."

The purge was criticized in the Santiago newspaper El Mercurio in an article by Jorge Millas, a university professor, it was reported Jan. 8.

Cabinet shuffled. President Augusto Pinochet Ugarte replaced his labor, health and transportation ministers March 8 after the entire Cabinet had resigned March 5 to give him a "free hand" in developing new policies.

The new officials were Gen. Fernando Mattei, who replaced Gen. Francisco Herrera Latoja as health minister; Gen. Raul Vargas, who succeeded Gen. Enrique Garin as transport minister, and Sergio Fernandez, who replaced Gen. Nicanor Diaz Estrada as labor minister.

Mattei, Vargas and Diaz were air force generals, Herrera was a retired air force general and Garin was a retired army general. Fernandez became the eighth civilian in the 14-member Cabinet.

The replacement of Diaz Estrada was the most significant of the changes, according to the March 12 London newsletter Latin America. Diaz had "shown some signs of bending under the pressures put on him" by labor leaders dissatisfied with the government's economic policies, the newsletter reported.

Economic developments. The junta's ban on automobile imports was lifted at the beginning of January, it was reported Jan. 9. Imported vehicles would carry a tariff of 115% and value-added tax of 20% over the cost of freight and insurance.

Chile had lost $800 million in 1975 due to the fall in copper prices on the international market, while its bill for imported petroleum had risen by $300 million, according to a statement by Benjamin Mira, Chilean representative to the Inter-American Development Bank, printed by the Wall Street Journal Jan. 29.

The managers of the nation's four major nationalized copper mines resigned March 5. The government was preparing to reorganize the state copper firm Codelco as a mixed company to allow the entry of foreign—principally U.S.—capital, according to sources cited by the Cuban press agency Prensa Latina March 5.

The unemployment rate in the greater Santiago area was 19.1% in April–June, according to government statistics cited by the Latin America Economic Report Aug. 13. The jobless figure was 40.4% in the construction industry and up to 50% in some other sectors.

Nearly 500 of the companies that were under state control before the 1973 military coup had been sold to private owners since then, according to officials of the state development firm CORFO, quoted by the Miami Herald Oct. 16. Thirty-two companies remained to be sold, including two large paper-manufacturing complexes and the Santiago gas company. The government would retain control of 23 companies considered vital to the national interest.

Chile's Central Bank announced Nov. 4 that the Chilean peso would be devalued 6.09%, from 15.76 pesos to 16.72 pesos to the U.S. dollar, during the ensuing 30 days. Including the latest devaluation, the currency had lost 96.7% of its value in at least 19 separate actions since Jan. 1.

(The devaluations had been interrupted briefly June 30 when the government revalued the peso upward by 11.2%, from 13.90 to 12.50 to the dollar, following an increase in international copper prices. President Pinochet had claimed then that Chile had "regained international creditability.")

According to statistics (made public Jan. 4, 1977), the cost of living in Chile had risen by 174.3% in 1976. Inflation for 1975 had been 340.7%, according to government figures.

Foreign Relations

U.S. aid reportedly continued. The U.S. granted Chile $276 million in economic and military assistance in 1975 despite legislation passed by Congress in 1974 banning military aid to Santiago and placing a $25 million ceiling on economic assistance, according to Rep. Michael Harrington (D, Mass.). Harrington's statements were inserted in the Congressional Record Jan. 26.

Documents in the Library of Congress showed the Ford Administration had given Chile $91 million in bilateral economic aid, $90 million in military assistance and $95 million in additional aid through debt rescheduling in 1975. This aid was "in clear contradiction of the intent of Congressional aid limitations and recent human rights amendments," Harrington declared.

The Administration also planned to give Chile substantial aid in 1976, including an estimated $102 million in arms, Harrington asserted.

The Administration circumvented the $25 million economic assistance ceiling by funneling aid to Chile "through several bilateral aid programs not specifically subject to Congressional control," Harrington noted. "And as if all this were insufficient," he continued, "the Administration has also quietly offered to guarantee a $55 million housing loan to Chile for 1976 from the Federal Home Loan Bank of New York."

"One is led to the conclusion that present policy toward Chile is as calculated and deceptive in character as the covert destabilization policies of the past," Harrington said, referring to action by the Nixon Administration in 1970–73 to help overthrow the elected government of the late President Salvador Allende.

Harrington continued:

... And, I might add, these specific aid programs are utilized not necessarily because of Chile's overwhelming need for, say, 350 million tons of agricultural commodities, but rather because they provide a means for implementing a policy of support that has to be neither justified to nor debated by the Congress. In this way the administration can pursue its policy of unwavering support of the junta as if the legislative mandates on the issue were nonexistent.

Of the aid mechanisms presently employed by the administration that are currently beyond congressional control, Food for Peace is the most familiar. This past year, in an effort analogous to last year's blatantly political use of Food for Peace in which 50 percent of all U.S. food aid was diverted to just two countries, Cambodia and Vietnam, in a last minute subsidy of the war effort, the administration allocated to Chile—a non-MSA—83 percent—$57.8 million—of the total title I Food for Peace assistance for all of Latin America. For 1976, Chile has been allocated 85 percent—$55.1 million—of the total, of which $45.7 million has already been delivered. Honduras and Haiti, both MSA's, received 10 and 5 percent, respectively. Since Food for Peace commodities are sold in the host country—rather than donated—and thus rarely reach the poorest sectors in the recipient country, the aid is generally regarded as provided for political rather than humanitarian purposes. And, even more to the point, the sale of the commodities within the host country provides that government with local currency, thereby allowing them to conserve scarce foreign exchange for the purchase of other priority items on the international market, such as defense articles.

Not surprisingly, Chile in 1974 became the major customer in Latin America for U.S. weapons by ordering $75 million in defense articles, in excess of Brazil's orders by $6 million. In the same year, Chile's arms purchases from other countries exceeded $105 million. Included in this figure was $40 million for T-25 fighters from Brazil, $400,000 for anti-tank rockets from France, $66 million for two coastal submarines from West Germany, and $1 million in aerial bombs from Spain. Thus, in 1974 alone, Chile's international arms purchases exceeded $170 million and partially contributed to the 300 percent increase in the junta's military budget.

All of the 1974 U.S. orders, and more, is scheduled to flow into Chile either in the current fiscal year or beyond, for the State Department has been interpreting the ban on military aid enacted December 30, 1974, to mean that orders or agreements made prior to this date—or "already in the pipeline"—will be allowed to stand and deliveries of pipeline assistance will continue on schedule. In the first half of 1975, for example, despite the ban on military aid, Chile received about $14 million in defense articles under the foreign military sales program and $650,000 in military training under the military assistance program. In addition, the Chilean Government purchased almost $2 million in defense articles from private U.S. firms under the commercial sales program, purchases not prohibited by present legislation. Consequently, in the absence of any legislative action this year, all military aid already in the pipeline will be delivered in 1976 and beyond, commercial sales will continue, and cash sales under the FMS will resume.

According to the Department of Defense, the amount of military aid still in the pipeline as of September 30, 1975, totaled $102,754,000 in foreign military sales items and $14,000 under the military assistance program. More specifically, scheduled for delivery this spring are 18 Northrop F-5E Tiger II fighters—about $60 million in arms. With this on-schedule delivery alone, Chile will again rank, along with Brazil, as a major Latin American recipient of U.S. arms in 1976.

In addition, arms for cash in all probability will resume as soon as the mechanics of signing new contracts can be ironed out by the administration. The State Department's latest position on the issue holds that the ban on cash sales came to an end at the close of the fiscal year—June 30, 1975—and thus the sales could resume since no congressional authorization would be required for the transaction. Clearly, we are led to the rather obvious conclusion that, as they now stand, present legislative restrictions will have virtually no impact whatsoever on the flow of arms to Chile in the current fiscal year.

Arms purchase from Soviet reported. Chile bought anti-tank rocket-launchers from the Soviet Union through an agency in Czechoslovakia, according to a report in the Argentine newspaper La Opinion Feb. 25.

The U.S.S.R. had frequently denounced Chile's anticommunist military government for its allegedly widespread abuse of human rights. To "keep appearances" in the arms deal, La Opinion reported, Moscow had used not only the Czech agency Omnipol but other intermediaries in France and the Bahamas.

Cocaine traffic to U.S. cut. In an effort to maintain good relations with Washington, Chile turned over all its top drug-trafficking suspects to U.S. authorities and virtually eliminated the flow of Chilean cocaine to the U.S., the Washington Post reported March 1.

"Cooperation had been fantastic ever since the military regime came to power here," a U.S. drug agent in Santiago told the Post. The Chilean armed forces seized power in 1973.

However, some drug control officials in Chile were unhappy over what they considered to be light prison sentences imposed on drug merchants in the U.S., the Post reported. Chile also sought more U.S. drug-control equipment, according to the newspaper.

U.S. aid rejected. President Augusto Pinochet Ugarte announced Oct. 19 that his government had rejected a $27.5-million grant from the U.S. government because the U.S. Congress had made the grant conditional on an improvement in the Chilean human-rights situation.

"This act of not accepting a loan that came tied to political positions," Pinochet said, "has shown the dignity of [Chile] to the entire world, as a sovereign and independent nation."

The military government formally notified Washington Oct. 20 that it did not want any U.S. economic assistance. The U.S. Foreign Assistance Appropriations Act of 1977, signed by President Ford Oct. 1, had included the $27.5 million cited by Pinochet, plus some additional food grants to Chile.

The U.S. Congress had put a limit of $27.5 million on economic aid to Chile because of alleged torture and other repression by the military regime. Congress also had banned military sales or grants to Chile for the same reason. The Ford Administration had opposed both restrictions and asked for a total aid package of $100 million for Pinochet's government.

Arguing for the Administration, Secretary of State Henry Kissinger had said that the U.S. could maintain its influence in Chile only through a strong aid relationship. Washington could then use this influence to persuade Pinochet to curb political arrests and other human-rights violations, Kissinger said.

Foreign loans. Chile received loans from various foreign sources during 1976.

The World Bank Feb. 3 approved a $33 million loan to help Chile build a plant to process copper ore and by-products. The loan was supported by the U.S. but opposed by Great Britain, Sweden, Denmark, Norway and several international organizations including Amnesty International, which argued that aid should be denied to Chile until the government halted alleged abuses of human rights.

The executive directors of the World Bank Dec. 21 approved two loans to Chile totaling $60 million for a farm and agro-industry program and for improved electrical service.

The loans were approved by a large margin despite a negative vote by the director representing the Scandinavian countries and abstentions by five other directors with European constituencies. The U.S. voted in favor despite appeals from some congressmen for a negative vote on human-rights grounds. Hal Reynolds, the U.S. director, noted "concern" in Congress over Chile's human-rights situation but said the loans should be judged on economic merits alone and not on "political" grounds.

Chile received three loans from the Inter-American Development Bank: $38 million for agriculture and irrigation, reported Aug. 13; $21 million for an industrial credit program, reported Sept. 2, and another $38 million for irrigation and grazing, reported Oct. 22.

Chile borrowed another $25 million from a consortium of 14 financial institutions brought together by Libra Bank Ltd., an investment bank for Central and South America that was owned by Mitsubishi Bank Ltd. of Japan. The loan, earmarked for Chile's state agricultural-marketing company, was announced by Chilean officials Oct. 20. The announcement embarrassed Libra Bank, which had hoped to keep the loan secret to avoid publicity on the Chilean human-rights question, according to the Latin America Economic Report Nov. 5.

Andean Group membership dropped. Chile left the Andean Group Oct. 6 after trying unsuccessfully to change the group's limits on foreign investment and its common external tariff.

Chile had argued for the past year that because it needed to attract capital, it could not accept the group's restrictions on foreign investment, particularly the investment code known as Decision 24, which put a 14% limit on annual remittable profits. Group members had offered to raise the limit to 20%, but Chile had argued for no limit.

Chile also had opposed the common external tariff scheduled to be adopted by the group in 1978 as a move toward establishing an Andean common market.

Anaconda anti-Allende offer reported. Anaconda Co. and other U.S. firms active in Latin America secretly offered to funnel at least $500,000 through the U.S. State Department to help prevent the election of Salvador Allende as president of Chile in 1970, according to State Department documents examined by the New York Times Dec. 23.

The documents were provided to the Times by Edward M. Korry, former U.S. ambassador to Chile, and were independently verified by the newspaper. They showed that on April 10, 1970, Anaconda and other companies belonging to the Council for Latin America urged high State Department officials to intervene actively on behalf of Jorge Alessandri, Allende's conservative opponent.

The State Department rejected the offer of financial aid, the documents showed. There was no evidence that the offer was illegal, the Times said.

The documents provided the first published evidence that the council, now known as the Council of the Americas, had ever been secretly active on behalf of politicians in Latin America, the Times noted. Council members repeatedly had denied such activity.

C. Jay Parkinson, Anaconda's former board chairman and current president of the council, said he had "no recollection" of any offer of financial aid to Alessandri, the Times reported. Parkinson did recall attending the 1970 meeting, but he said the thrust of the presentation had been made by Jose L. DeCubas, then president of the council. DeCubas said that the council had "never offered any cash," but he added: "I don't know whether [council] members did it or not."

Colombia

Violence & Politics

Colombia remained under the emergency rule of a state of siege during much of 1976 because of political violence and labor and student unrest. The state of siege was lifted in June but reimposed in October.

Unrest resumes; state of siege retained. The government announced Feb. 5 that the state of siege would remain in effect indefinitely following a resurgence of civil unrest in Medellin and other cities.

The siege had been imposed in June 1975 amid a wave of kidnappings, guerrilla attacks and labor and student unrest. President Alfonso Lopez Michelsen had pledged Jan. 16 to lift it before the April municipal and departmental elections, but he reversed himself Jan. 29 under pressure from businessmen in Medellin who were alarmed by recent student riots.

Some 15,000 students at the University of Medellin had gone on strike Jan. 23 to demand administrative reforms, and students had stoned the city's business area, reportedly injuring 12 policemen. Police occupied the university Jan. 28 after further disturbances in which 20 students and 10 policemen were injured and some 100 students arrested. Eight students and 16 policemen were injured the next day as the clashes continued.

Medellin students called a new strike Jan. 30 as the disturbances spread to Cali, Popayan, Pasto and Buenaventura. Bombs exploded that night under a police car in Bogota, gravely wounding a policeman, and at the Spanish embassy in the capital, causing property damage but no casualties. Several students and policemen were injured Feb. 3 in further clashes in Medellin.

A student was killed and at least 30 civilians and policemen were wounded in Tulua (Valle del Cauca Department) Jan. 19 when rioting broke out during a demonstration by students and bank workers in favor of sugar mill workers who were striking for higher wages. A dry law was imposed in Tulua Jan. 20.

High school students in Buenaventura, in Valle del Cauca on the Pacific coast, clashed with policemen Jan. 21 during a demonstration against an increase in public transport fares. Several persons were reported injured. In Pasto, to the south near the Ecuadorean border, teachers clashed with police during a protest against the dismissal of 559 teachers who, according to the governor of Narino Department, were not needed and had been hired "to satisfy the bureaucratic appetites of local political chiefs."

Members of the leftist National Liberation Army reportedly attacked the municipality of Monte Libano (on the border between Antioquia and Cordoba Departments) Jan. 24, stealing food, supplies and money. One guerrilla was reported killed and four were reported captured during the assault.

Four sentenced in Rincon murder. Four men were convicted by a military court Jan. 20 and sentenced to long jail terms Jan. 30 for the September 1975 assassination of Gen. Ramon Rincon Quinones, inspector general of the armed forces.

Four others were acquitted in the controversial trial, in which defense attorneys claimed Rincon had been murdered not by the civilian defendants in the pay of the leftist National Liberation Army (ELN), as the prosecution claimed, but by soldiers under orders from top military leaders. The military leaders had sought to silence Rincon, who had found evidence of military involvement in the drug traffic, in the sale of arms to kidnappers and in the embezzlement of government funds, the defense lawyers charged.

An attorney for two of the convicted defendants, Juan Manuel Herrera, was arrested when the trial ended Jan. 20 but released the next day. He said secret police had dragged him from one court to another and finally freed him for lack of evidence.

The trial was denounced by nearly the entire Colombian legal profession, according to the London newsletter Latin America Jan. 30. The defense easily showed that nearly all the prosecution witnesses were unreliable, contradictory or in the pay of the army, and it noted that a colonel driving behind Gen. Rincon had neither attempted to stop the assassination nor reported it to the police, the newsletter reported. Fingerprints in the assassins' car belonged to none of the defendants, one of whom was in the hospital undergoing shock treatment for a psychological disorder on the day of the murder.

The four convicted defendants were sentenced to terms of 24–28 years at the Gorgona island prison.

Unrest grows. At least 14 persons were killed, scores were injured and hundreds arrested as labor and student unrest grew throughout the country in February, March and early April.

Bank and government employes, teachers and other workers struck for higher pay, students rioted against government repression and presumed leftist guerrillas carried out kidnappings, ambushes and assassinations. The government responded with new security measures, mass arrests, dismissals of striking workers, occupation of leading universities and charges that the unrest was directed by extreme leftists seeking to sabotage the municipal and departmental elections scheduled for April 18.

The trouble began to spread Feb. 12 when students and striking teachers rioted in Cali and Popayan. Four days later employes of the finance ministry began a nationwide strike for higher wages, which the government claimed it could not afford. The strike ended without a settlement March 2, after hundreds of strikers were fired or arrested and the government lost millions of pesos in uncollected taxes and customs revenues.

Workers struck Feb. 19 at three partly state-owned banks in Bogota and at the coffee and livestock banks in Barranquilla, Manizales, Cucuta and Cali. Hundreds of teachers struck at the National University in Bogota, and there was a general strike in Buenaventura, the major port on the Pacific coast, after police clashed with striking dockworkers.

Workers in the postal administration and the public works ministry joined the strike movement Feb. 26 while troops occupied finance ministry installations, three paralyzed banks and the major oil refinery at Barrancabermeja, where managers reportedly feared sabotage by striking workers. Students rioted that day in Medellin, Cali, Cartagena and Bucaramanga; hundreds of rioters were arrested in Medellin, and Cali was put under military control.

The Communist-led Colombian Syndical Workers' Confederation (CSTC) and the Liberal-affiliated Colombian Workers' Confederation (CTC) issued an unprecedented joint statement Feb. 28 vowing to work together "to eradicate injustice and immorality" and denouncing the government for recent food price increases "that accentuate the misery of the people."

(The statement resulted partly from outrage from labor leaders at the Feb. 15 kidnapping of CTC leader Jose Raquel Mercado by the M-19 guerrilla movement, which claimed to be the armed wing of the opposition National Popular

Alliance [Anapo]. The abduction was deplored by Anapo and the Communist Party, although the Communists denounced Mercado as "a callous anticommunist who rose to CTC leadership through corruption and terror.")

The CTC and CSTC joined several other unions March 16 in founding the National Solidarity Committee, a labor action group. Among the other founders was the Colombian Educators' Federation (Fecode), which led the teachers' strikes for higher wages.

The army occupied the National University March 2 after police clashed with thousands of student rioters. The assassination of three political leaders in different parts of the country—one each from the Liberal and Conservative Parties and Anapo—was reported the next day. A student was killed March 4 during riots in Medellin, occasioning protest strikes and marches March 9 at the major universities across the country.

Students and police clashed in Bogota and Cali March 16, and a policeman was shot to death in an ambush in Barranquilla. Clashes continued in Cali March 17, and in Pasto the army occupied Narino University to end student riots there.

President Alfonso Lopez Michelsen and his cabinet issued a set of strict new security measures March 18 under the existing state of siege. The measures provided, among other things, for the dismissal of student rebels, the suspension of striking government employes for as much as a year, and imprisonment of agitators for up to 180 days.

Guerrillas of the Colombian Revolutionary Armed Forces (FARC) kidnapped the wealthy industrialist Octavio Echavarria in Antioquia Department March 20. Four days later other abductors seized Francia Naranjo, daughter of the industrialist David Naranjo, killing a family bodyguard in the action. Echavarria was found dead of a bullet wound in Puerto Berrio March 25, and a suspected abductor of Francia Naranjo was found dead in Bogota, presumably having been killed by her fellow kidnappers.

(The leftist National Liberation Army [ELN] April 18 denounced the assassination of Echavarria by the rival FARC. This murder was a "villainous act" which "trampled on the Colombian revolutionary flag," the ELN charged. The ELN supported Cuban Premier Fidel Castro and the FARC backed the Soviet Union.)

Francia Naranjo was ransomed June 16; another kidnap victim, Camila Sarmiento, had been ransomed June 14. Their abductors were presumed to be ELN guerrillas. The London newsletter Latin America reported June 25 that the ransoms totaled more than $500,000.

Thousands of teachers struck March 25 to demand higher pay and denounce "military repression against students and teachers." Students rioted that day in Bogota, Medellin and Barranquilla, protesting the government's new security measures.

The government froze the funds of the teachers' union Fecode March 27 and dismissed more than 130 teachers in four departments for striking two days before. Fecode called a nationwide, 48-hour teachers' strike April 6-7 but few teachers observed it, according to press reports.

Students and police clashed in Medellin March 30 as students protested the updating of vacations to head off further unrest. A student was killed March 31 in clashes in Bogota; the army occupied the university that day and the government closed it down temporarily April 2.

Students in Bogota, Popayan and Villavicencio held protest marches April 1 against the Bogota student's death. There were new riots in Villavicencio April 2.

Labor leader murdered. Labor leader Jose Raquel Mercado was killed April 19 by guerrillas of the leftist M-19 movement who had kidnapped him two months before.

M-19 had issued a communique April 6 declaring that Mercado had been convicted in a "revolutionary trial" on charges of "treason" against Colombia and its working class. It said he would be executed April 19 unless the government revoked "repressive" labor legislation, reinstated workers fired for illegal strikes, and allowed newspapers to print an M-19 manifesto describing Mercado's "trial." The government refused to grant the demands or negotiate with the guerrillas.

The assassination was denounced April 19 by the government, the armed forces and the leftist opposition parties.

President Alfonso Lopez Michelsen held an emergency meeting with the National Security Council and declared afterward that the government would pursue Mercado's killers "indefatigably." Mercado's labor union, the Colombian Workers' Confederation, called its one million members out on strike April 21 to protest the murder.

At least 24 persons had been arrested in connection with Mercado's kidnapping before the assassination, it was reported April 9. Almost all were associated with the National Popular Alliance (Anapo), which denied any connection with M-19 although M-19 claimed to be Anapo's "armed wing." Among the detainees was Carlos Toledo Plata, an Anapo-bloc member in the House of Representatives.

Ruling parties win state, local vote. The ruling Liberal and Conservative Parties won more than 90% of the vote in elections for departmental (state) assemblies and municipal councils April 18.

The results were considered a repudiation of the leftist opposition parties, although voter absenteeism was 76%—one of the highest rates in Colombian history—and the offices at stake were relatively unimportant. (Real power was held by departmental governors and city mayors, all of whom were appointed.) The elections had been preceded by widespread strikes, riots, guerrilla attacks, kidnappings and assassinations. However, the country was calm on election day.

Preliminary returns reported by the Associated Press April 20 gave the Liberal Party 52% of the vote and the Conservatives 40%. The remaining 8% was shared almost equally by the National Opposition Union (UNO), dominated by the pro-Moscow Communist Party; the Revolutionary Independent Workers' Movement (MOIR), a Maoist group; and the National Popular Alliance, the populist movement of the late dictator Gustavo Rojas Pinilla.

The Liberal vote was split among three factions vying for control of the party before the 1978 presidential election. The faction of President Alfonso Lopez Michelsen won 19% of the Liberal vote, that of ex-Foreign Minister Julio Cesar Turbay Ayala won 29% and that of ex-President Carlos Lleras Restrepo, 31%. Turbay and Lleras sought the 1978 Liberal nomination; Lopez Michelsen was ineligible for reelection. (Liberal Sen. Estanislao Posada had proposed Jan. 4 that the constitution be amended to allow the reelection of Lopez, but Lopez rejected the idea Jan. 7 after it raised a furor among other Liberals and the press. The proposal was an apparent attempt to end serious Liberal Party divisions among followers of Lopez, Lleras and Turbay.)

The Liberals and Conservatives had campaigned as supporters of democratic rule in Colombia, while the leftist parties had called for a "protest vote" against the government. Roman Catholic priests across the country had urged their congregations April 16 to vote against the Marxist parties. Both UNO and MOIR complained of arrests of their campaigners despite government assurances of free leftist participation in the elections, the London Financial Times reported April 15.

The unrest which had plagued Colombia since the beginning of 1976 tapered off the week before the election. The last student riot occurred in Cartagena April 8, one day after a nationwide student strike to protest the military occupation of the National University in Bogota. (Soldiers who occupied the university claimed to have found "a veritable arsenal of Molotov cocktails, explosives and ammunition" on campus, according to the Financial Times April 15.)

State of siege lifted. The year-long state of siege was lifted by the Lopez Michelsen government June 22 despite the continuation of widespread civil unrest.

Violence increases. Student riots, guerrilla attacks and kidnappings, which had diminished just prior to the April 18 elections, resumed later.

Some unrest was attributed in press reports to inflation, which reached 16% in the first seven months of the year (against a government target of 15% for all of 1976).

Students rioted in Bucaramanga (Santander Department) July 7 to protest an increase in urban transport fares. Police and soldiers dispersed the rioters with tear gas after they broke the windows of shops and banks. The riots resumed July 27-28, leading to the death of a student and a policeman. Students rioted in Bucaramanga July 30 during the dead student's funeral, causing the government to impose a curfew in the city and to ban liquor sales. The measures were lifted Aug. 1.

Students in Cali (Valle del Cauca Dept.) also rioted July 13-14 to protest transport-fare raises. Other student disturbances occurred in Tunja (Boyaca Dept.) and Villaneuva (Cesar Dept.) July 27, in Medellin (Antioquia Dept.) July 29-31 and in Manizales (Caldas Dept.) Sept. 3. The army occupied Caldas University and imposed a curfew in Manizales Sept. 3 after students destroyed shops and automobiles to protest the dismissal of the university's rector.

Bombs exploded July 22 at a state transport office in Bogota and a bus terminal in Cali. Six more blasts occurred July 29-30 in Popayan (Cauca Dept.) and Medellin, and 10 other blasts were reported Aug. 4-6 in Bogota. The Bogota targets included banks, police stations and offices of U.S.-based companies.

Guerrillas of the pro-Soviet Colombian Revolutionary Armed Forces (FARC) occupied the hamlet of Sabanagrande (Santander Dept.) July 16, stealing food and money from its residents. The insurgents had killed a police inspector in the town of Belen, the London newsletter Latin America reported July 16. They also killed five peasants in the hamlet of Carare for allegedly being government informers, police asserted July 29.

(FARC in turn accused the army of torturing and killing hundreds of peasants in Antioquia Dept., according to a guerrilla communique printed by the leftist Colombian magazine Alternativa and cited by Agence France-Presse July 25.)

The government had prevented FARC from collecting a $150,000 ransom for Eric Leupin, the Dutch honorary consul in Cali whom the guerrillas had kidnapped in January 1975, the Associated Press reported June 17. Leupin, who was said to be in poor health, was held by FARC in inhospitable jungle areas, AP reported.

The government charged Aug. 6 that the student riots, guerrilla attacks and kidnappings were all part of a leftist plot financed from abroad. Finance Minister Rodrigo Botero Aug. 13 minimized the role of economic problems in the growing unrest, and asserted that the high rate of inflation was a temporary result of Colombia's rapid economic growth. The government lifted controls on imports of scarce goods Aug. 11 in an effort to force down prices.

Doctors strike. An estimated 7,000 doctors began an indefinite strike early in September to protest a Labor Ministry decree classifying employes of the Colombian Social Security Institute (ICSS) as public servants. The strike was finally settled Oct. 26 with the government yielding to many of the doctors' demands.

The strike had halted all but emergency services at major hospitals and clinics, denying health care to more than one million working-class families. The government declared the stoppage illegal, dismissed and arrested dozens of strikers, and banned liquor sales in major cities on weekends to reduce the number of violent incidents that caused injuries.

The strike was begun Sept. 6 by more than 4,000 doctors employed by the ICSS. Their union, the Medical Syndical Association (Asmedas), charged that classification as public employes was "denigrating" to doctors and would remove their right to strike and other labor benefits. Thousands of ICSS paramedical employes joined the stoppage Sept. 6. More than 2,000 doctors employed by the National Health Service and residents and interns employed by university hospitals went on strike Sept. 8-9.

The strike was supported by students in Bogota and Medellin who rioted sporadically Sept. 10-15, burning automobiles and fighting with policemen. More than 100 students were reported arrested by Sept. 15. The stoppage also was backed by the leftist National Opposition Union, which charged Sept. 9 that classification of the doctors as public servants would "annul 15 years of union struggle."

The strike was opposed by the Roman Catholic Church, which claimed the stoppage violated "medical ethics," it was reported Sept. 12. It also was opposed by many labor unions which noted that the doctors received high salaries and that the victims of their strike were poor persons.

President Alfonso Lopez Michelsen intervened in the crisis Sept. 13. In a nationwide television address, Lopez read a decree that moved the ICSS from the jurisdiction of the Labor Ministry to that of the Health Ministry, and said that he would ask Congress for extraordinary powers to reorganize the ICSS without altering the position of its doctors. He invited the doctors to resolve the strike "without victors or vanquished."

The strikers rejected Lopez' appeal Sept. 14, asserting the president had not abandoned the decree classifying them as public employes. Under the decree, the doctors charged, they would be denied job security and the rights to organize, to strike and to bargain collectively.

The strikers warned Sept. 19 that they would end even emergency medical services unless the government revoked the decree and released and reinstated jailed strike leaders.

State of siege reimposed. President Alfonso Lopez Michelsen reimposed a state of siege Oct. 7 to combat what he called a wave of subversive civil unrest.

Lopez had imposed the siege during riots in June 1975 and lifted it 12 months later despite a continuation of the violence. The new siege reportedly was forced on the president by the armed forces as a way to end the month-long strike by doctors at the Colombian Social Security Institute.

However, the strike did not end until Oct. 26, when the government granted several of the strikers' demands, including reinstatement of doctors dismissed during the stoppage.

The government imposed severe security measures under the new siege. Soldiers patrolled the major cities and military courts took charge of all cases of arson, sabotage, terrorism, kidnapping and extortion. Prison terms of up to 180 days could be imposed on persons convicted of inciting or participating in street disturbances.

Students vigorously protested the security measures, burning more than a dozen automobiles in Bogota and other cities. In response the government arrested scores of students and sent troops to occupy the National University in Bogota Oct. 16.

The government claimed the occupation was necessary because a cell of the National Liberation Army (ELN), the largest left-wing guerrilla group, was operating in the university. Officials noted that an ELN flag had been raised on campus Oct. 8 during a riot in which students burned four cars. Soldiers left the flag flying to justify continuing the occupation, according to press reports.

Most of the university's students boycotted classes Oct. 18, asserting they would stay on strike until the soldiers left the campus. The government responded by closing the university Oct. 20 and canceling the next semester Oct. 22.

Students rioted across Colombia Oct. 22 to protest the university's closing. The worst disturbances were in Medellin, where students burned a truck and clashed with police. Three students were wounded by police gunfire and two police officers were injured by students. More than 50 students were reported arrested.

A general assembly of National University students Oct. 25 vowed to "unite all the struggles [against] the government's reactionary policy" and to "combat categorically" the stage of siege. The government's Superior Council of Education Nov. 5 ordered the indefinite closing of the National University and the closing of residences for poor students from outside Bogota.

The government partially reversed itself Nov. 15, reopening the university but keeping the residences closed. Students in Bogota, Medellin and Palmira began a new boycott of classes Nov. 17, demanding that troops leave the National University and that the government reopen the residences for poor students.

Cabinet revised. The Lopez Michelsen Cabinet resigned Oct. 13 at the height of the unrest. The resignation of all Cabinet ministers followed the individual resignations of Labor Minister Maria Elena de Crovo, Interior Minister Cornelio Reyes and Justice Minister Samuel Hoyos Arango.

The reasons for the resignations of Reyes and Hoyos were unclear, but de Crovo's resignation was a direct result of the doctors' strike. De Crovo had infuriated the doctors by saying they were a-dime-a-dozen in Colombia and could be replaced easily, the London newsletter Latin America reported Oct. 1. The doctors retaliated by suspending the voluntary emergency service they had been offering during the strike. De Crovo resigned Oct. 10.

Lopez named a new Cabinet Oct. 19, replacing six of the 13 ministers. The Cabinet kept the traditional balance between the Liberal and Conservative parties, with six ministers from each party and one military man, Defense Minister Gen. Abraham Varon Valencia.

The new ministers were Rafael Pardo Buelvas (interior), Oscar Montoya Montoya (labor), Alvaro Araujo Noguera (agriculture), Sara Ordonez de Londono (communications), Raul Orejuela Bueno (health), and Victor Renan Barco (justice).

Barco resigned Nov. 17 after a Conservative congressman revealed that Barco had been sentenced to 30 days in jail in 1968 for an unspecified breach of ethics in his law practice. Barco was replaced as justice minister Nov. 19 by Cesar Gomez Estrada.

Other Developments

1975 legislation. As its 1975 session ended, Congress passed bills lowering the voting age to 18, legalizing divorce for persons married by civil ceremony, requiring foreign banks to be 51% owned by Colombians, and enacting urban and tax reforms, it was reported Jan. 2.

U.S. bribe scandal. Colombian personnel became implicated in the growing international scandals over bribery of foreign officials by U.S. corporations.

The Colombian government began an investigation Feb. 8 into reports that two air force generals had received illegal payments from Lockheed Aircraft Corp., which was alleged to have bribed officials in European and other countries as well. Venezuela's air force Feb. 10 began investigating reports that Lockheed had bribed some of its officers, and the Venezuelan government issued a report Feb. 14 naming seven persons who allegedly received illegal payments from Occidental Petroleum Corp.

The Colombian scandal broke Feb. 8 when newspapers in Bogota printed three letters released by the U.S. Senate's Subcommittee on Multinational Corporations, which was investigating illegal payments abroad by U.S. firms. The letters, addressed to Lockheed offices in Marietta, Ga. by two Lockheed officials in Colombia, Edwin Schwartz and Jose Gutierrez, discussed "sugar" (bribe payments) demanded by two Colombian air force generals and other officials in exchange for inducing the government to purchase Lockheed Hercules aircraft in 1968-69.

The generals—Jose Ramon Calderon and Armando Urrego, both former air force commanders in chief—allegedly exaggerated Colombia's defense needs to secure the purchases, for which they allegedly received some $200,000 from Lockheed. Both Calderon and Urrego denied the bribery charge and cooperated fully with the government investigation which began Feb. 8, according to press reports.

(Two other scandals involving Colombian officials and European companies were reported in the press. The Feb. 23 issue of Time magazine, reported that in the 1960s the West German firm Heckler and Koch had paid $200,000 to a committee of Colombian military officers to secure Colombia's purchase of army rifles which were later discovered to be inefficient and difficult to maintain. The Bogota newspaper El Bogotano reported Feb. 16 that the French firm Dassault had given its Colombian representative $200,000 to pay commissions related to Colombia's purchase of 18 Mirage jet fighters in 1972.)

The Colombian Supreme Court Sept. 1 took over the government's lagging investigation into bribes allegedly paid to Colombian military officers by Lockheed.

The court criticized the armed forces' prosecutor, who had been in charge of the case, for not making any progress in the seven-month probe. The prosecutor, Francisco de Paula Chavez, had said Aug. 23 that the investigation was stalled because of delays in translating Lockheed documents handed over to Colombia by the U.S. government June 22. There was only one translator working on the papers, and she worked only in the afternoons, de Paula said.

The documents indicated that Lockheed had bribed three Colombian air force generals to help secure Colombian purchase of Lockheed planes in 1968-69, the Mexican newspaper Excelsior reported Aug. 24. The generals were Jose Ramon Calderon and Armando Urrego, former air force commanders, and Federico Rincon Puentes, the current commander, Excelsior said.

Kissinger visits. U.S. Secretary of State Henry A. Kissinger paid a visit to Colombia Feb. 22-23 during a tour of Latin American countries.

Kissinger had flown Feb. 22 to Colombia, where students in Bogota and Medellin were rioting for the third day against his visit. He met Feb. 22 and 23 with President Alfonso Lopez Michelsen and Foreign Minister Indalecio Lievano Aguirre. Lopez said at a press conference with Kissinger Feb. 23 that Colombia supported Panama's efforts to gain control over the Panama Canal and Zone, and that it would recognize the MPLA in Angola. In response to a question, Lopez refused to condemn Cuban intervention in Angola and he made a veiled reference to U.S. intervention in Vietnam in the 1960s and early 1970s.

Action against narcotics. Colombia had joined Mexico, Panama and Costa Rica in agreeing to establish joint commissions with the U.S. to combat the illegal narcotics traffic, according to a statement Jan. 20 by two New York Congressmen, Lester L. Wolf (D) and Benjamin A. Gilman (R). Wolf said that he and Gilman had learned that the U.S. annually received $500 million worth of narcotics from Colombia.

In New York, meanwhile, 12 Colombians were convicted Jan. 26 of conspiracy to distribute Colombian cocaine and marijuana in the U.S. in what U.S. prosecutors described as "the biggest Colombian narcotics organization ever uncovered." Prosecutors said the organization distributed more than 20 pounds of cocaine per week in New York in 1972-74, with a weekly wholesale value of $250,000 and a street value of $2.5 million. U.S. authorities had seized $3\frac{1}{2}$ tons of the organization's marijuana with a wholesale value of $2 million, the prosecutors added.

Colombian government drugs agents in Cali seized 88 pounds of cocaine Jan. 27 after fighting a bloody gun battle with drug sellers which left one seller and one bystander dead and five other bystanders wounded. The cocaine was said to be worth as much as $25 million on the illegal market.

Police in Bogota had seized 22 pounds of cocaine Jan. 24, arresting seven alleged sellers including Jairo Montoya Escobar, an assemblyman in Risaralda Department. The seized drugs were said to be worth $8.2 million.

Police said the drug market had become so large that many farmers and wealthy landowners had given up traditional agriculture to grow marijuana, it was reported Jan. 28. Numerous secret airfields for the transportation of narcotics to the U.S. had recently been discovered in the northern regions of Guajira and Sierra Nevada.

Chile exiles charge harassment. A number of Chilean political refugees had been forced to leave Colombia under what exile sources called a policy of harassment by the Colombian government, the New York Times reported Feb. 1.

Those forced to leave included Pedro Ramirez, a former Chilean agriculture minister; Miguel Morales, former mayor of Santiago; Carmen Lasso, a former congresswoman, and Patricio Valdez, a sociology professor.

Valdez left Bogota Jan. 28 after security police denied him a good-conduct certificate he needed to have his visa renewed. He charged at the airport that security police and the visa department of the foreign ministry were trying to make life intolerable for Chilean refugees.

"We are told we must have a work contract to get a visa, but to get a contract we must already have a visa," Valdez asserted. "It is a vicious circle, on top of which they ask for other papers that are impossible to get, keep coming to our houses to search them and question us, interrogate our friends and employers and try to frighten us into leaving the country."

Security police denied Valdez' charges. A senior officer quoted by the Times asserted that Valdez had "abused Colombian hospitality" and that the police were "proceeding according to Colombian law and obeying the international conventions on asylum." The officer charged that "80% of [the Chileans] are not real refugees. They imagined persecution, wanted better economic opportunities, or were looking for adventure" when they sought asylum in Colombia.

Colombia had taken in hundreds of Chilean refugees after the 1973 military coup in Chile which ousted the leftist government of the late President Salvador Allende Gossens.

Cuban trade pacts signed. Cuba and Colombia had signed preliminary trade agreements covering steel, fish, paper and textiles following a visit to Cuba by a 70-man Colombian delegation headed by Alberto Galeano Ramirez, director of the Colombian Foreign Trade Institute, it was reported Feb. 20.

Colombian flood destroys dike. At least 47 persons were killed Oct. 6 in Pereira, Colombia when a dike, part of the city's aqueduct system, burst after a heavy rainstorm.

Colombian plane crash kills 37. A DC-3 passenger plane of the Venado Air Taxi line crashed Oct. 25 one minute after it of Bogota. All 37 persons aboard were killed. Aviation authorities attributed the accident to a fire in one engine. All the victims on the regional flight were Colombian.

Colombians in Venezuela illegally. Hundreds of Colombians were entering Venezuela daily and staying on illegally in hope of finding work in Venezuela's expanding economy, the New York Times reported Dec. 5.

Most of the illegal immigrants were peasants or other unskilled workers who lived in rural or urban poverty and took whatever jobs they could find—farm labor, shoe-shining, domestic service or any other work Venezuelans did not care to perform. Wages were considerably higher in Venezuela than in Colombia.

Ramon Ignacio Velasquez, head of the Venezuelan immigration bureau, estimated there were more than 300,000 Colombians living and working in Venezuela without papers. Other estimates put the total around 800,000, the Times said. Venezuela's population was 12.6 million; Colombia's was 24.7 million.

Cuba

Domestic & Economic Developments

Constitution approved. Cubans endorsed a new constitution in a national referendum Feb. 15.

The charter, approved by the First Congress of the Cuban Communist Party in December 1975, won 97.7% of the vote in the referendum, according to the government. The referendum was open to more than 5.5 million citizens over the age of 16. The last constitution, enacted in 1940, had not been followed officially since the revolution of 1959.

The charter declared that Cuba was a socialist state ruled by its people through a pyramid of elected assemblies culminating in the National Assembly of People's Power. It recognized the leading role of the Communist Party and institutionalized the social and economic changes brought about by the regime of Premier Fidel Castro since 1959.

The constitution recognized freedom of expression, the press, religion and association so long as they did not oppose the government or the principles of the revolution. It provided for state control of the information media, among other national sectors.

The charter was proclaimed Feb. 24 at a ceremony in Havana led by Raul Castro, the armed forces minister and first deputy premier. Castro announced that in the national referendum on the new charter Feb. 15, 5,602,973 citizens had voted, with 5,473,534 voting yes and 54,070 voting no.

Elections. Five million Cubans went to the polls Oct. 11 to elect 10,725 members of 169 municipal assemblies.

Candidates for the municipal assemblies had been selected in August by "assemblies of neighbors" in small villages, districts and groups of city blocks. Citizens over the age of 16 were eligible to vote.

Premier Fidel Castro said after voting Oct. 11 that the municipal assembly elections were "a significant step forward in the consolidation and institutionalization of the revolution."

The municipal assembly members Nov. 2 elected the nation's highest legislative body, the National Assembly of People's Power. Among the National Assembly's deputies were Castro, the 13 members of the Communist Party's Politburo, writers Alejo Carpentier and Nicolas Guillen, and Cuba's heavyweight boxing champion, Teofilo Stevenson.

The municipal delegates also elected members of the island's 14 provincial assemblies. Under the new constitution Cuba had 14 provinces of roughly equal size and population, and one special municipality, the Isle of Pines off the southwestern coast. Cuba previously had only six provinces.

The new administrative structure broke down as follows:

- Municipal assemblies would be responsible for schools, hospitals, stores, hotels, cinemas, public utilities and municipal transport. They also would select magistrates to preside over the municipal people's courts.
- Provincial assemblies would regulate intercity transport and provincial trade, and would elect judges to the provincial courts.
- The national assembly would control all basic industries, establish the national education curriculum and appoint supreme court judges. It would also act as the national legislature, considering all laws proposed by the Council of State.

Municipal and provincial delegates would serve $2\frac{1}{2}$-year terms and national delegates would serve five-year terms. All would continue in their existing jobs, receiving extra leave only when assembly meetings conflicted with normal work hours. The assembly jobs were unpaid but delegates would receive "a daily allowance equivalent to their salary and whatever additional expenses they may incur in the exercise of their duties." The Constitution stressed that assembly service carried no additional privileges or benefits, and that delegates could be recalled by their constituencies at any time.

The new structure was expected to reduce the state bureaucracy by 20%–25% and concentrate the remaining bureaucrats at the local level, according to the Oct. 29 London newsletter Latin America. Under the old system only 16% of Cuba's 250,000 state bureaucrats dealt with problems at a municipal level, while 38% operated at a regional level, Latin America said.

Assembly meets, names Castro president. The National Assembly of People's Power, Cuba's new legislature, convened in Havana Dec. 2, completing the reorganization of the Cuban government.

The assembly Dec. 3 elected Gen. Fidel Castro to be president of the new Council of State. The post effectively combined Castro's old office of premier, now abolished, and the presidency of the republic, heretofore held by Osvaldo Dorticos. Castro, who was also first secretary of the Cuban Communist Party, would be the "supreme power of the nation," according to a Cuban radio broadcast.

Dorticos fell in the hierarchy to be a member of the Council of State. Blas Roca, an old-line Communist, was elected president of the assembly Dec. 2.

In his opening speech to the assembly Dec. 2, Castro urged the 481 deputies to carry on a "tireless criticism of our work" and to avoid "all personality cults." Deputies should observe "the constant practice of self-limitation and modesty," in contrast to "the corrupt and haughty coterie [who had] betrayed Marxism-Leninism" in China, Castro said.

Castro sharply criticized members of the Organization of Petroleum Exporting Countries, charging that by raising oil prices they were "crushing underdeveloped countries." Castro denounced Saudi Arabia and Iran but praised what he called "progressive positions" taken by Venezuela, Algeria, Libya, Kuwait and Nigeria.

The assembly convened on the 20th anniversary of Castro's 1956 landing on the Cuban coast with an 82-member guerrilla force. Two years later the insurgents overthrew dictator Fulgencio Batista and established a largely ad hoc administration under Castro's leadership. The assembly meeting climaxed a process of systematizing the administration and sorting out the tasks of the Communist Party, the government and the labor organizations. Cuban administrative procedures now showed increased similarity to those of Eastern Europe, the Financial Times of London said Nov. 30.

Cuba gives up on oil production. Cuba had abandoned hope of producing oil in significant quantities and would build nuclear plants to satisfy its growing energy needs, according to the U.S. weekly Oil and Gas Journal March 2. Cuba produced only 3,000 barrels of crude oil per day, and was forced to import 150,000 barrels daily from the Soviet Union, the Journal reported.

Castro details economic situation. Fidel Castro Sept. 27 gave a detailed account of Cuba's economic problems, laying the principal blame on the sharp fall in world sugar prices.

In a speech before 500,000 persons in Havana, Castro noted that the price of sugar had dropped from 65.5¢ a pound in November 1974 to 7.5¢ a pound Sept. 23. In addition, Cuba was suffering a severe drought which had put sugar production 25% below target levels and affected Cuban agriculture across the board.

Because sugar brought Cuba more than 80% of its export earnings, the island faced a shortage of foreign exchange. Consequently, Castro said, Cuba would be forced to slow down its economic development, reduce trade with the West and increase its dependence on aid from Communist countries, especially the Soviet Union. Austerity measures would be imposed, including a cut in electricity output to conserve fuel; replacement of artificial-fiber imports with Soviet cotton, and reduction of the coffee ration from 43 grams a week to 30 grams (about one ounce).

Castro expressed gratitude for the Soviet Union's extensive aid to Cuba, saying: "Without the support of the Communist bloc and the Soviet Union, I don't know how a country like ours could solve its problems." He noted that Moscow was paying five times more than the world market price for Cuban sugar, was providing the island with all its oil and fuel and was selling Cuba wheat below world market prices.

The Soviet Union also was giving Cuba aid in the electrical, mechanical-engineering and steel sectors, Castro said.

(Cuba's problems were compounded by a fall in sugar production in Eastern Europe and the Soviet Union, which forced the Communist countries to take more Cuban sugar and left the island with less sugar to use in financing imports from the West. Moscow took 1.8 million tons of Cuban sugar in 1974 and 2.9 million tons in 1975, the Miami Herald reported Sept. 30. In addition, the Soviet Union had raised the price of petroleum it sold to Cuba by more than 40%, the Herald said.)

Castro charged that the U.S. had helped to drive down the price of sugar by tripling its import taxes to protect the U.S. sugar industry, thereby putting more sugar on the world market. This action was "brutal aggression," Castro charged.

Cuban Forces in Angola Assure Victory by MPLA

Cuban troops had started arriving in Angola in November 1975 to aid the Soviet-supported Popular Movement for the Liberation of Angola (MPLA) in a civil war against the U.S.-supported National Front for the Liberation of Angola (FNLA) and the National Union for the Total Independence of Angola (Unita). Ultimately, 15,000 or more Cuban troops were fighting for the MPLA in Africa, and they assured the MPLA of victory in the former Portuguese colony.

Cuba to continue supplying troops. Cuban Deputy Premier Carlos Rafael Rodriguez said Jan. 11 that Cuba would continue to provide troops to the MPLA regardless of any resolution which the Organization of African Unity might adopt regarding foreign intervention in Angola.

In an informal talk with U.S. correspondents in Havana, Rodriguez said Cuba would withdraw its support only if MPLA leader Agostinho Neto so requested. This was reiterated by Cuban Premier Fidel Castro in a Jan. 15 statement to foreign journalists.

The deputy premier, in his remarks, declined to comment on a U.S. government estimate that there were approximately 7,500 Cuban troops fighting alongside the MPLA.

He said Cuban aid had first become substantial in the spring of 1975 when the three Angolan movements' coalition government collapsed and the MPLA asked Havana to send advisors. Cuba had responded by sending 230 military advisors to train the MPLA forces and only stepped up its aid after "Oct. 23 [when] the South Africans suddenly came into Angola," Rodriguez stated.

Role of foreign forces seen mounting. The Johannesburg Star reported Jan. 20 that in fighting along the central Angolan battle front, Angolans were serving in an essentially supporting capacity to white foreign forces. In major battles at Cela—which, the Star said, pitted 3,000 Cuban-led MPLA soldiers against "thousands of white" troops supporting Unita fighters—

and Luso, as well as at other sites, this situation was regarded as prevalent, according to the Star.

Estimates of the number of South African and Cuban troops continued to change in statements from different quarters. The U.S. State Department said Jan. 16 that, though Cuba had committed 6,000–7,000 troops to the MPLA, Havana actually had a total of 9,500 troops in the area, a number of them stationed in the Congo, a major shipment point for Soviet arms deliveries.

The United Nations Security Council adopted a resolution March 31 condemning what it termed South Africa's aggression against Angola and calling on the South African government to pay compensation to the People's Republic of Angola for damages resulting from its intervention in the Angolan civil war.

The council vote was 9-0, with five abstentions by the U.S., Great Britain, France, Italy and Japan. China did not participate in the vote. The special Security Council session on Angola, which opened March 26, had been called earlier in the month by Kenya on behalf of the Organization of African Unity which had recently admitted the People's Republic of Angola, proclaimed by the MPLA, as a member.

The U.S. and other nations abstaining had objected to the resolution because it did not condemn as well the involvement of other states, particularly the Soviet Union and Cuba, in the Angolan war.

The Angolan representative, Pascal Luvalu, who said his government hoped to be admitted soon to the U.N., insisted March 26 that it was "ridiculous to speak of Soviet or Cuban interference" in Angola because the assistance they provided was neither part of any expansionist policy nor a violation of sovereignty.

The Cuban representative, Ricardo Alarcon Quesada, showed the Council photographs March 29 which he said depicted Chinese advisers in Angola, "close to the bandits of the CIA [U.S. Central Intelligence Agency]" and charged that China was acting as "the public relations agent of Africa's worst enemies." He said the victory of the "Angolan revolutionaries" had raised new hopes among the "millions of men and women who are oppressed in southern Africa," an allusion to the black majorities in white-minority ruled South Africa and Rhodesia.

William Scranton, the U.S. delegate, charged March 31 that Cuba and the Soviet Union were serving their own "global objectives" in intervening in Angolan affairs and said that more than 13,000 Cuban soldiers remained in Angola.

Scranton asked: "What are they doing there? Against what threat are they staying there? Who are the imperialists?" The Cuban representative contended, in response, that "imperialist" threats against Angola persisted.

Cuba defies Azores refueling ban. Despite objections from the Portuguese government, Cuba was using the Azores Islands to refuel aircraft carrying soldiers and arms to Angola, it was reported Jan. 18.

Portugal was officially neutral in the Angolan fighting, although some government sectors led by the foreign minister, Maj. Ernesto de Melo Antunes, supported the MPLA.

Cuban planes had refueled on Santa Maria Island in the Azores Dec. 20–30, 1975, but Portugal had subsequently barred Cuban stopovers there. The stopovers resumed Jan. 10 and continued Jan. 15 despite formal objections made by Portugal to the Cuban ambassador in Lisbon Jan. 13, according to reports.

The U.S. State Department said Jan. 19 that it had made strong protests against Cuban refueling in the Azores.

Cuban troop airlift reported halted. U.S. Intelligence sources cited by the Associated Press Feb. 5 said the Cuban airlift to Angola had been halted since Jan. 21 when the last planeload of Cuban soldiers arrived in Luanda aboard a Soviet IL-62 transport plane.

Portuguese government sources in Lisbon said Jan. 28 that Cuba had ceased to use the Azores as a stopover for the flights. The Portuguese government had expressed its "displeasure" to the U.S. ambassador in Lisbon Jan. 23 over a State Department announcement that the U.S. had been exerting pressure on Portugal to halt the Cuban refueling in the Atlantic islands.

A Canadian Foreign Ministry spokesman said Jan. 30 that Ottawa had barred Havana from using Gander International Airport in Newfoundland as a refueling point for its troop flights to Angola. The warning was sent to Cuba after Cuban aircraft twice had stopped at the airport en route to Angola, prompting a Jan. 23 protest from the U.S.

Kissinger: Cuba 'exports revolution.' U.S. Secretary of State Henry Kissinger had concluded that Cuba had resumed "exporting revolution" on its own initiative, now to Angola, the Sahara and possibly other places outside the Western Hemisphere, the New York Times reported Feb. 5.

However, Kissinger had decided not to express himself publicly on the issue, preferring instead to press the U.S.S.R. to end its intervention in Angola, the Times reported. Kissinger reasoned that he had no diplomatic leverage with Cuba, while he did have leverage with the U.S.S.R. because of the U.S.-Soviet detente, the newspaper said.

Kissinger reportedly had rejected the widely held theory that Havana had been forced by Moscow to send the 11,000 Cuban troops reported to be fighting for the MPLA. "I believe the Cubans went in there with flags flying," he was quoted as saying.

Kissinger was echoed by two unidentified Soviet officials quoted by the Times. "We did not twist their arms," said one official about the Cubans in Angola. "We didn't even have to twist their arms. The Cubans wanted to go in."

Both Soviet officials said Cuban military advisers had gone to Angola to train MPLA recruits in the spring of 1975, before Soviet advisers had appeared in the Angolan capital of Luanda, the Times reported.

Cuba had also sent military advisers to other countries in Africa and the Middle East, and there were unconfirmed press and intelligence reports that 300 Cubans were in Algeria to train and assist troops fighting against Morocco in the disputed Sahara, the Times noted.

Cuba's intervention in Angola was disturbing Venezuela and nations in the Caribbean, the Miami Herald reported Jan. 24. "Angola shows that [Cuban Premier Fidel] Castro has the capacity, the strength and the will to mount a large-scale military intervention," said a Venezuelan cabinet official quoted by the Herald. "If he can do it in Africa, so far from home, he also can do it anywhere in the Caribbean."

Some Venezuelan officials were convinced that Cuban airplanes taking troops to Angola were refueling in Guyana, Venezuela's neighbor on the eastern Caribbean coast of South America which recognized the MPLA government, the Herald reported. The presence of Cuban troops in Guyana would be a serious matter to Venezuela, which claimed more than half of Guyana in a territorial dispute, and to neighboring Brazil, the newspaper noted.

It was at Venezuela's initiative that the Organization of American States (OAS) had imposed its embargo on Cuba in 1964, after it was discovered that Cuba was aiding leftist revolutionaries against the Caracas government. The OAS had lifted the embargo in 1975, with many nations arguing that Cuba had stopped "exporting revolution" in the Western Hemisphere after the failure of Cuban guerrillas led by Ernesto "Che" Guevara who fought the Bolivian government in 1967.

Inside Cuba, the Angolan intervention had caused more complaining than any issue in recent years, according to diplomats quoted by United Press International Feb. 4. Complaints were voiced at Communist Party meetings, and some militia reserves had resisted recruitment for service in the African country, UPI noted.

The Cuban people had been told officially of the Angolan intervention only within the last two weeks, UPI reported, and no public mention had been made of Cuban casualties in the Angolan war.

Ford calls Castro an 'outlaw.' President Ford called Cuban Prime Minister Fidel Castro an "international outlaw" as he campaigned in Florida Feb. 28 for the support of Cuban-Americans in the March 9 U.S. Republican presidential primary.

Speaking at a naturalization ceremony in Miami for 1,121 persons, most of them Cuban refugees, Ford cited the Cuban military intervention in the Angolan civil war in declaring that the Castro regime was "acting as an international outlaw."

"My Administration will have nothing to do with the Cuba of Fidel Castro," he said. "It is a regime of aggression. And I solemnly warn Fidel Castro against any temptation to armed intervention in the Western Hemisphere. Let his regime, or any like-minded government, be assured the United States would take the appropriate measures."

The President pledged to "speed up" the process of naturalizing Cuban immigrants.

Kissinger stresses warning to Cuba. Secretary of State Henry A. Kissinger stressed anew March 22 his warning to Cuba that the U.S. "will not accept further Cuban military interventions abroad."

The warning was specifically related to the Cuban intervention in Angola and the possibility of any intervention in Rhodesia, where the white minority government was confronting demands by the black majority for rule.

In a speech in Dallas, Kissinger gave assurance that the U.S. would neither support the white minority government in Rhodesia nor condone foreign military intervention.

World peace was more likely to be threatened "by shifts in the local regional balances," Kissinger said, than by strategic nuclear attack. "We are not the world's policeman," he continued, "but we cannot permit the Soviet Union or its surrogates to become the world's policeman either."

Kissinger repeated his message at a news conference in Dallas March 23. "We stand strongly for majority rule and a rapid political change in southern Africa," he said, "not to be brought about by outside military forces." He refused under questioning by reporters to rule out any move by the U.S., including military invasion of Cuba, in the event Cuba ignored the warnings about new armed intervention in southern Africa. It would be "impossible for any senior official to put out ahead of time all the things the United States will or won't do and all the circumstances that may arise," he said. "We have pointed out the dangers to Cuba. We are serious about what I have said."

Cuba sets troop withdrawal. In a letter to the premier of Sweden, Cuban Premier Fidel Castro said Cuban troops would be withdrawn from Angola at a rate of 200 per week. By the year's end, Castro told Premier Olof Palme, Cuban forces in the southwest African nation would be reduced "drastically."

Castro authorized Palme, who received the letter May 21, to divulge its contents to U.S. Secretary of State Henry A. Kissinger. Kissinger, who was in Stockholm on an official visit, was notified of Castro's letter May 24.

The letter was the first indication that Cuba would conduct a pullout of the troops it had sent to Angola to aid the indigenous Popular Movement for the Liberation of Angola (MPLA) in its civil war against anti-Communist liberation movements and foreign forces.

Cuban President Osvaldo Dorticos May 26 indicated that the withdrawals would be carried out with the consent of Angolan President Agostinho Neto. Dorticos warned the U.S. not to demand evidence of the pullout.

Angolan Premier Lopo de Nascimento May 25 confirmed that some Cuban units were leaving the country. Information Director Luis de Almeida said that day that the MPLA had "appealed to Cuba for help... last fall and has now decided that the situation is sufficiently under control that the Cuban troops can begin to withdraw." Almeida said there were a total of 12,000 Cuban military forces in Angola, a figure regarded as low by Western analysts who estimated that as many as 15,000-18,000 Cuban troops were in Angola.

In Luxembourg May 25, Kissinger said the letter was "a positive development." He added, however, that the withdrawal rate of 200 soldiers a week "should be speeded up." U.S. officials said Kissinger had asked Palme to tell Cuba that the U.S. still insisted upon a total withdrawal of Cuban troops from Angola. The U.S. had said it would not consider recognizing the Luanda regime until such action were taken.

(According to U.S. estimates reported May 25 by the New York Times, if withdrawals of Cuban troops were to have begun at the end of May at a rate of 200 a week, at least 7,400 would remain in Angola at the year's end.)

In his letter, Castro also said Cuba had no intention of sending troops to other countries in southern Africa or in Latin America to aid "liberation movements." "I do not wish to become the crusader of the 20th century," Castro said.

In the letter, Castro said he was writing in response to an article by the Swedish premier in a Swedish newspaper, criticizing Havana for its military intervention in Angola.

Cubans & Soviets in Africa. A June 13 report in the New York Times described a Pentagon map that depicted the Soviet and Cuban military presence in Africa. Soviet personnel, arms and money were shown in Somalia, Uganda, Mozambique and the Sudan in eastern Africa; in Egypt, Libya and Algeria in northern Africa, and in Mali, Guinea, Nigeria and Angola in western Africa.

Fifty Cubans were placed in Somalia in military capacities and 310 in Guinea. The map showed 11,400 Cubans in Angola. However, an official of the North Atlantic Treaty Organization said the figure was higher, estimating it at about 15,000–16,000 Cubans. The official also noted that there had been no evidence of a Cuban withdrawal from Angola as had been signaled by Premier Fidel Castro.

Neto visits Cuba. Angolan president Agostinho Neto left Cuba July 29 after a seven-day official visit, the Miami Herald reported July 31.

At a July 26 rally marking Cuba's national day, Premier Fidel Castro pledged to increase the number of Cuban technicians and economic advisers in Angola. He said that a pull-out of Cuban forces from Angola was under way, but he assured Neto of continued Cuban military aid. (A U.S. State Department official quoted in the Sept. 22 Washington Post, reported that 3,000 Cuban soldiers had left Angola, leaving 10,000 still in the country.)

Angola war role detailed. An official version of Cuba's involvement in the Angolan civil war was written toward the end of 1976. (Excerpts were published by the Cuban news agency Prensa Latina Jan. 9, 1977 and reprinted by the Washington Post in three installments Jan. 10–11.)

The account was written by Gabriel Garcia Marquez, the celebrated Colombian novelist. Garcia Marquez, a communist, had visited Cuba several times in the past two years and had been in regular touch with President Fidel Castro.

Cuba's intervention in Angola, Garcia Marquez wrote, was "the end result of a continuous policy toward Africa." Since 1963 Cuba had given military aid to various black African liberation movements, notably the National Revolutionary Council of the Congo, which fought against forces of former Congolese Premier Moise Tshombe. Cuban revolutionary leader Ernesto (Che) Guevara fought alongside 200 Cuban troops in the Congo in April–December 1965, according to Garcia Marquez.

Cuban contacts with the Popular Movement for the Liberation of Angola (MPLA) reportedly began in 1965, when Angola was a Portuguese colony. MPLA leader Agostinho Neto, now president of Angola, visited Havana in 1966, Garcia Marquez wrote.

In May 1975, when the Portuguese were preparing to leave Angola and the MPLA was embroiled in a civil war with the National Front for the Liberation of Angola (FNLA) and the National Union for the Total Independence of Angola (UNITA), Neto reportedly asked for a shipment of Cuban arms. In July he asked Cuba to send instructors to open and run four military training camps, Garcia Marquez wrote. The Cuban government appealed to Otelo de Carvalho, then Portugal's chief of security, for permission to send the men to Angola, but Carvalho did not immediately reply, according to Garcia Marquez.

The decision to send troops to fight in Angola was made at a meeting of the Cuban Communist Party's top leaders Nov. 5, Garcia Marquez wrote. Cuba reportedly went ahead without Portuguese permission because it felt the MPLA was on the point of being defeated by the FNLA and South African mercenaries.

A Cuban battalion of 650 men was flown to Angola over 13 days beginning Nov. 7. The first flight carried 82 "well-trained warriors, with a high level of political and ideological formation," Garcia Marquez wrote. Cuban troopships followed, bearing thousands of soldiers plus armored vehicles, guns and explosives. They docked in Angola Nov. 27 and Oct. 4, 7 and 11.

Cuban instructors immediately set up the four training camps requested by Neto, and Cuban soldiers helped the MPLA drive FNLA troops from the outskirts of Luanda. Over the next few months more than 15,000 Cuban soldiers helped the MPLA drive its foes out of Angola and consolidate rule over the country. "Cuban aid reached such a level," Garcia Marquez wrote, "that at one point there were 15 Cuban ships on the high seas bound for Luanda."

The air and sea crossings were long and arduous because Cuba's planes and ships were old and overcrowded and because the U.S. intervened to hinder the Cuban aid effort, according to Garcia Marquez. U.S. threats reportedly forced Barbados and Guyana to deny refueling facilities to Cuban planes. And Cuban troopships "were the target of all sorts of provocations by North American destroyers, which followed them for days on end, and by war planes that buzzed them and photographed them," Garcia Marquez wrote.

President Castro followed the Angolan conflict closely. "At the start of the war, when the situation was especially pressing," Garcia Marquez wrote, "[Castro] stayed in the general staff command room as long as 14 hours at a stretch, without eating or sleeping, as if he were on the campaign. He followed the progress of battles, using colored indicators on wall-sized tactical maps, and was in constant contact with the battlefield high command [of the MPLA]."

Cuba's intervention in Angola was kept secret within the island until Castro acknowledged it at the December 1975 congress of the Cuban Communist Party. Families of soldiers fighting in Angola were ordered to reveal nothing, and some families did not even know that their relatives, who were officially on maneuvers, had been sent to Africa.

After the MPLA's success, Castro and Neto agreed in March 1976 on a Cuban troop-withdrawal program, Garcia Marquez wrote. "They decided that the withdrawal would be gradual but that as many Cubans as needed would remain in Angola as long as needed to build a modern and strong army, able to guarantee the future internal security and independence of the country without outside help," according to the Colombian author.

Garcia Marquez gave no figures on Cuban troop withdrawals.

Other Foreign Policy Developments

Comecon to build nuclear plant. Comecon, the Communist bloc's economic association, would build the first atomic power station in Cuba, the Soviet news agency Tass reported Jan. 6.

Under an agreement signed in Moscow in April 1976, the first stage of the plant would have "an output capacity of 440 megawatts." Cuban President Fidel Castro had said the plant eventually would have twice that capacity.

Soviet trade pact signed. Cuba and the Soviet Union signed a five-year trade agreement Feb. 6 which was expected to double the volume of trade between them, according to Cuban sources quoted by the Reuters news agency.

The pact, signed in Moscow, was Cuba's first long-term trade accord with a foreign country. More than half of the island's foreign trade was with the Soviet Union; trade exchanges between the two countries in 1976 would amount to about $3.4 billion, according to a protocol signed along with the five-year pact.

Torrijos in Cuba. Brig. Gen. Omar Torrijos, Panama's military strongman, visited Cuba Jan. 10–15 for talks with Premier Fidel Castro on bilateral issues and on Panama's negotiations with the U.S. over the future of the Panama Canal and Zone.

The two leaders signed an assortment of cultural and technical exchange pacts and agreed that Panama should be patient in the canal negotiations.

Torrijos thanked Castro Jan. 12 for advising him in recent years "not to fight on a hook" cast by the U.S., and he said Panama would continue to negotiate "calmly" for a new canal treaty. "We are—remember this—in a process of [national] liberation, and one of the means by which that can be reached is through negotiations," Torrijos declared Jan. 15.

Castro publicly advised caution on the canal issue Jan. 12, telling Torrijos: "Time is on our side in the struggle against the imperialists. The struggle of the Panamanian people is not very easy because Panama is small. But to the 1.2 million Panamanians we can now add nine million Cubans." As an example to Torrijos, Castro cited Cuba's tolerance of U.S. naval presence at Guantanamo Bay in eastern Cuba.

Torrijos was awarded Cuba's Jose Marti medal in a ceremony shortly after his arrival in Havana Jan. 10. He was accompanied on the trip by more than 200 Panamanians including workers, students, farmers, businessmen, military officers, folk dancers and Roman Catholic priests.

Trudeau visits Cuba during tour. Canadian Prime Minister Pierre Elliott Trudeau visited Cuba, Mexico and Venezuela Jan. 24–Feb. 2 in a bid to stimulate Canadian trade with the three Latin American nations and promote Canada's economic and political identity as a power in its own right, not just as part of a U.S.-dominated North American presence.

Trudeau came under sharp criticism from opposition politicians in Ottawa for his Cuban sojourn. To charges that he had, by his visit, condoned Cuban participation in the Angolan war, the prime minister responded in the House of Commons Feb. 3 that he had been "brutally frank" with Premier Fidel Castro on Canada's views on the Cuban role there, calling the intervention "a serious mistake." He maintained that cancellation of the scheduled visit would have constituted an "unproductive slight to Cuba."

During the Jan. 26–29 talks in Cuba, Castro had declared that relations between Ottawa and Havana were "better than ever." Canadian officials deemed the visit highly successful.

According to figures reported in the Toronto Globe and Mail Jan. 30, Canada ran a surplus of $75 million in trade with Cuba during 1975's first six months.

Colombia trade pacts signed. Cuba and Colombia had signed preliminary trade agreements covering steel, fish, paper and textiles following a visit to Cuba by a 70-man Colombian delegation headed by Alberto Galeano Ramirez, director of the Colombian Foreign Trade Institute, it was reported Feb. 20.

Kissinger on U.S.-Cuban relations. U.S. State Secretary Henry A. Kissinger toured Latin America Feb. 16–24 and then reported to the U.S. House Committee on International relations March 4. Among Kissinger's remarks regarding Cuba:

"...[W]e made clear last year on a number of occasions through many channels that we were prepared to normalize relations with Cuba, provided Cuba behaved as a responsible member of the international community. We even took some concrete steps such as easing the third-country boycott—that is, we removed from American companies domiciled in other countries in the Western Hemisphere, the prohibition against trading with Cuba.... However, after we made these iniatives, Cuba then took a very regressive attitude with respect to the sending of its troops to Angola. Therefore, we have stopped the process of normalization of relations with Cuba and under present circumstances no further progress is possible."

Kissinger was asked about the possibility that Cuba might intervene in Rhodesia. He said: "...[We] feel that Cuban military forces in this situation would present the gravest problems, and we cannot accept the principle that any state, much less a Western Hemisphere state, has the right to intervene in any crisis in any part of the world on its own, or has the right to intervene in these crises with military force. And therefore we would have to call on Cuba to act with great circumspection, because our actions cannot always be deduced from what we did in Angola."

Castro tours Eastern Europe, Africa. Premier Fidel Castro visited Yugoslavia, Bulgaria, Algeria and Guinea March 6–16, conferring with their presidents and with leaders of other African nations.

Castro made the stops on his return to Havana after attending the 25th Congress of the Soviet Communist Party in Moscow. He was accompanied on the trip by a large delegation including Deputy Premier Carlos Rafael Rodriguez and other members of the Politburo and the Central Committee of the Cuban Communist Party.

Castro arrived in Yugoslavia March 6, traveling immediately to the Adriatic resort island of Brioni for two days of talks with President Josip Broz Tito. Tito commended Cuba March 6 for its "broad contribution" to the victory of the Popular Movement for the Liberation of Angola in the Angolan civil war. However, press accounts noted that Tito, who reportedly disliked the Cuban and Soviet military buildup in Africa, referred to Cuba's aid to Angola as a nonaligned nation rather than to Cuban achievements on the battlefield.

Castro continued March 8 to Bulgaria, where he met with Communist Party First Secretary Todor Zhivkov. He moved on March 12 to Algeria, where he conferred for three days with President Houari Boumedienne and expressed Cuba's support for the republic recently declared in the Western Sahara by the Algerian-backed Polisario front. Castro met March 14 with Polisario leader Mohamed Lamine Ould Ahmed and with Oscar Montero, minister of state of Mozambique.

(In Algiers March 14 Castro rejected recent warnings by President Ford and Secretary of State Kissinger of the U.S. against further Cuban military adventures abroad. "In the first place," he said, "Ford is not my father ... We Cubans don't lose sleep over anything."

Castro arrived in Conakry, Guinea March 14 and met there March 15-16 with President Ahmed Sekou Toure and Presidents Agostinho Neto of Angola and Luis Cabral of Guinea-Bissau. A communique said the leaders "reviewed the struggle of the Angolan people against South Africa" and reaffirmed "the unity of progressive forces" against white minority regimes on the continent.

Pope favors progress effort. Pope Paul VI said March 25 that the Vatican "looks with sympathy on the efforts of the Cuban leaders to promote cultural, economic and social progress" among the Cuban people. The work of the Catholic Church in protecting human rights "finds fertile ground in Cuba due to its long tradition of Christian civilization," the pontiff added.

The pope spoke on receiving the credentials of Cuba's new ambassador to the Holy See, Jose Antonio Portuondo. The Vatican maintained full diplomatic relations with only one other Communist country, Yugoslavia.

Presence in Peru. Sen. Jesse Helms (R, N.C.) told the U.S. Senate April 27 that Cuba was engaged in a military build-up of "left-leaning" Peru. Helms said:

We know, for example, that the Soviets are heavily engaged in supplying arms and training to Peru. For several years now, the Soviet Union has made a strong investment in supporting the military system of the left-leaning government in Peru. The tremendous build-up of the Peruvian military machine has ominous implications for all of southern South America. Ironically, the United States itself has been also supplying arms to Peru without seeming regard for the leftist nature of the Peruvian government, and creating apprehension among our anti-Communist allies in South America. Indeed, the Secretary's recent visit to Peru, while excluding countries more inclined to anticommunism, seemed to confer a sort of benediction upon Peru's leftist policies.

For this reason, I have been deeply concerned about recurring reports indicating a sizable buildup of Cubans in Peru. If the Soviets, using the Cubans as their surrogates, choose to extend their adventures into the continents of the Western Hemisphere, then Peru would be the place to start. Peru itself could be converted into a Soviet satellite, Cuban style, and then used as a base to spread subversion throughout South America.

One year ago it was generally accepted that there were between 100 and 200 Cubans in Peru. But after the success of the Angolan operation, reports came from various sources indicating a growing Cuban presence in Peru. Rumors of this kind, of course, are frequent. But finally I received a report from a source I consider absolutely reliable that there are as many as 2,000 to 3,000 Cubans in

Peru. In my judgment, based upon my confidence in the source, the report was no rumor, but a report to be taken seriously.

On March 24, I met with the President of the United States and personally put a letter in his hands expressing the concern I had over such reports. On April 12, Gen. Brent Scowcroft, the Assistant to the President for National Security Affairs, responded to me on behalf of the President. He wrote as follows:

I have requested a thorough check of these reports and find that although there are rumors of larger numbers, we can confirm the presence of fewer than 100 Cubans in Peru. Most of these are associated with their Embassy in either a diplomatic, consular, or military capacity.

Mr. President, to be frank, I was astonished at this response. General Scowcroft actually seemed to imply that the Cuban presence had diminished in the past year. Yet a reliable source told me that there are more than 200 Cubans working on the large Olmos irrigation project in northern Peru alone, under the supervision of Soviet technicians.

Moreover, after checking further, sources in Peru have reported that there are not 2,000 to 3,000 Cubans, as I was told in March, but that there are actually 4,000 to 5,000 Cubans in Peru at this moment. Moreover, although they are disguised as technicians, I am told that they are prepared to switch to guerrilla warfare whenever they choose.

Nicaraguan infiltration. Cuba was also accused of involvement in Nicaragua.

The Nicaraguan government charged Nov. 16 that Cuba was training and infiltrating Nicaraguan leftists into Nicaragua for a guerrilla war against President Anastasio Somoza Debayle. The government also denied a recent charge by Cuban Premier Fidel Castro that Nicaragua was a base for Cuban exiles who staged attacks against Cuba and other countries that enjoyed good relations with the Castro government.

Cuba spurns OAS. Cuban Foreign Minister Raul Roa Sept. 14 reaffirmed Cuba's determination "never" to rejoin the Organization of American States.

Relations formed with Burma. Cuba established diplomatic relations with Burma Oct. 11.

U.S. businessmen visiting island. U.S. businessmen were visiting Cuba quietly, anticipating the day when relations between Havana and Washington were sufficiently improved to allow a resumption of normal commercial activities, the Wall Street Journal reported Sept. 27.

The visits were legal, but U.S. passports were not valid for trips to Cuba and U.S. money could not be used there without authorization. To circumvent these restrictions, Americans entered Cuba from such countries as Jamaica and Mexico using loose-leaf visas that could be discarded later. Cuban officials paid for the businessmen's expenses on the island.

The visitors generally avoided publicity, but it was known that executives of PepsiCo Inc. had recently been in Cuba, the Journal reported. Kirby Jones, a former aide to Sen. George McGovern (D, S.D.), told the Journal that he had escorted executives of five major U.S. corporations to Cuba in recent weeks and that he would chaperon officers of eight other U.S. companies in the next two months. The president of one commodities firm, I.S. Joseph Co. of Minneapolis, openly admitted having visited Cuba in 1975.

(The reported visit of PepsiCo officials to Cuba angered anti-Castro Cuban exiles in the U.S., the Journal reported. "A lot of Pepsi machines were ordered out of Cuban establishments" in Miami, a leader of Miami exiles told the Journal. A reporter for the Florida television station that reported the visit said one PepsiCo franchise had canceled about $300,000 worth of advertising with the station after the report.)

Cuba-Oswald link questioned. Associated Press (AP) reports on March 20 and 21 described recently released Central Intelligence Agency (CIA) documents concerned with the assassination of President Kennedy. One memo, from the CIA to the Warren Commission, charged with investigating the assassination of President Kennedy, said that a defector had told the CIA that Lee Harvey Oswald may have been in contact with Cuban intelligence officers seven weeks before killing Kennedy.

This information, together with the defector's assertion that the Cuban intelligence service tightened its security immediately after Kennedy's assassination, was given to the Warren Commission in May 1964. A CIA June 1964 memo remarked that the commission "saw no need to pursue this angle any further."

A CIA memo prepared in May 1975 for the Rockefeller Commission asserted, however, AP said, that it "was the opinion at the working level, particularly in the counter-intelligence component in the CIA, in 1964" that the Warren Commission report "should have left a wider 'window' for this contingency [the involvement of a foreign conspiracy in Kennedy's assassination]."

The 1975 memo specified two leads that it held the Warren Commission had not adequately followed up, AP said. One was testimony to the commission by a friend of Oswald, Nelson Delgado, that Oswald had told him in 1959 that he (Oswald) had contacts with Cuban diplomatic officials. The other lead was a statement allegedly made by Cuban leader Fidel Castro to a news correspondent on Sept. 7, 1963, that "U.S. leaders would be in danger if they helped in any attempt to do away with leaders of Cuba."

An AP report March 1 said that sources on the Senate Intelligence Committee had said that day that the committee had evidence that Earl Warren, head of the Warren Commission, had been informed of CIA attempts on Castro's life, but not until three years after the commission finished its investigation.

U.S. firm linked to Bay of Pigs raid. United Brands Co. of the U.S., then known as United Fruit Co., had actively participated in the 1961 Bay of Pigs invasion of Cuba at the request of the U.S. Central Intelligence Agency, according to a book published Oct. 21.

The book, titled "An American Company: The Tragedy of United Fruit," was written by Thomas P. McCann, a former vice president of the firm. McCann said United Fruit had dealt directly with the late Robert F. Kennedy, then U.S. attorney general, in planning the Bay of Pigs invasion. The CIA's main contact at the firm was the late J. Arthur Marquette, then vice president in charge of steamships and terminal operations, McCann said.

McCann quoted Marquette as saying that Kennedy "wanted us to supply two of our freighters to convey men, munitions and material during that invasion. The arrangements were made, and it was all very cloak and dagger: our own board of directors didn't know about it, and certainly only a handful of us with the company were party to the secret."

After the abortive invasion, McCann said, the logs of the two ships were sent to Washington, sealed with wax and then returned to the company. "As far as I know, they are still in company vaults—the official record of our participation in that fiasco permanently safe from public view," McCann said.

Burke Wright, United Brands' current public relations director, said he was unable to find anyone in the company who knew about its participation in the invasion, the Miami Herald reported Oct. 23.

Terrorism

Cubans blamed for U.S.-based terrorism. Militant pro-Castro and anti-Castro Cuban groups in the Miami area were engaged in terrorist activities in the U.S. and Latin America, according to testimony given before a U.S. Senate subcommittee in May and released Aug. 22.

The testimony was given before the Judiciary Committee's subcommittee on internal security by Lt. Thomas Lyons, a member of the Dade County Public Safety Dept., and Raul J. Diaz of the department's organized crime, terrorist and security unit. They said that as many as 50 Cuban groups of various political shadings had been operating in Miami at any one time, many of them involved in local actions in Cuba, Mexico and Central and South America.

Some Cuban exiles "use Dade County as a base for international terrorism against allied governments of Cuba, Cuban shipping, Communists, purported Communists and individuals who take a stand against their terroristic-type tactics," Lyons said. During the last two years there had been four homicides in

Dade County "with strong indicators on each that the motivations were political in nature and terroristic in design," he declared.

Diaz said that some pro-Castro groups had infiltrated exile organizations in Miami and made plans to assassinate Latin American diplomats and foreign ministers. He did not mention CIA efforts to use Cuban exiles in Florida to kill Premier Fidel Castro.

Antonio Gonzalez, an anti-Castro Cuban exile, had said Aug. 18 that there were as many as 500 pro-Castro agents operating in the Miami area. Gonzalez made the statement in Jacksonville in testimony at the trial of Rolando Otero, a fellow exile, on charges of exploding several bombs in Miami in 1975.

Gonzalez, testifying under a grant of immunity, said he and Otero had plotted to assassinate Castro during a planned visit to Venezuela, but Castro had called off the visit after the plot was discovered by agents of the Cuban government and the U.S.' Federal Bureau of Investigation. FBI agent Robert Ross, in testimony Aug. 17, had told the jury of the plot.

Cuban jetliner crashes after bombing. A Cuban passenger jet plunged into the Caribbean Sea Oct. 6 after one or more bombs exploded on board following takeoff from the island of Barbados. All 73 passengers and crew members were reported killed.

The bombing, attributed to Cuban exiles and Venezuelans who opposed Premier Fidel Castro, had wide repercussions. Castro blamed the sabotage on the U.S. Central Intelligence Agency and renounced an anti-hijacking treaty with the U.S.

At least 16 persons were arrested in Trinidad & Tobago and Venezuela in connection with the bombing. Trinidadian police Oct. 7 seized Hernan Ricardo and Freddy Lugo, two Venezuelan citizens who had boarded the Cuban jet in Trinidad Oct. 6 and left it in Barbados, returning to Trinidad the same day. The Cuban-born Ricardo admitted placing two bombs on the airliner, Trinidadian authorities said Oct. 18.

Ricardo and Lugo told Trinidadian police that they were employed by a private-detective agency in Caracas that was staffed by Cuban exiles. The Venezuelan government confirmed Oct. 14 that it had arrested 10 persons in connection with the bombing. Among them were Luis Posada, head of the detective agency, and Orlando Bosch, chief of the Command of United Revolutionary Organizations (CORU), an anti-Castro umbrella group. At least four more employes of the detective agency were reported to have been arrested in Caracas Oct. 15.

(CORU had been formed recently by Cuban Action, the Cuban National Liberation Front, the Bay of Pigs Veterans' Association, the April 17th Movement and the National Cuban Movement, according to U.S. intelligence sources quoted by the New York Times Oct. 11. The exile groups were based in Venezuela, Nicaragua, the Dominican Republic and Miami, it was reported Oct. 19.)

Bosch had been convicted of a bazooka attack on a Polish ship in Miami in 1968 and had been paroled by U.S. authorities after serving four years of a 10-year prison sentence. He had entered Venezuela in September by using a forged Costa Rican passport, Venezuelan authorities said Oct. 14.

Castro scores U.S., voids hijack pact— Castro declared Oct. 15 that he would cancel the 1973 anti-hijacking agreement between Cuba and the U.S. because the CIA had "participated directly" in the bombing of the Cuban airliner.

Speaking to several hundred thousand persons in Havana's Revolution Square, Castro said the bombing was carried out by "mercenaries" in the pay of the CIA. The U.S. agency was responsible for eight other 1976 attacks on Cuban officials or property abroad, Castro charged.

U.S. Secretary of State Henry Kissinger denied the charges Oct. 15. He said that "no official of the U.S. government, no one paid by the American government, no one in contact with the American government has anything to do" with the airplane sabotage. "We will hold the government of Cuba strictly accountable for any encouragement of hijacking and any encouragement of terrorism that may flow from its renunciation of the treaty," Kissinger said.

Castro said that Cuba would respect the treaty's terms until April 15, 1977, in compliance with a clause that required the parties to give six months' notice before cancellation. He added that he would be willing to discuss the agreement with the next U.S. administration "on the basis of a definite end of all acts of aggression and hostility against our homeland." Castro said that Cuba would never encourage air piracy and that it would continue to respect its anti-hijacking pacts with Canada, Mexico, Venezuela and Colombia.

Castro said the sabotage of the Cuban jet had been tied to the CIA by "absolutely reliable" Venezuelan journalists. He charged that Hernan Ricardo, who reportedly took credit for the bombing, was a CIA agent.

(Ricardo's connection to the CIA was not confirmed by other sources, but Cuban exiles and U.S. officials told the New York Times Oct. 20 that Posada and Bosch, under arrest in Venezuela in connection with the bombing, had been trained by the CIA and used in actions against the Castro government after 1960.)

Castro made it clear that he thought the CIA still sought to assassinate him. He said that the CIA had asked one of its agents in Havana to provide information about Castro's itinerary during a projected visit to Angola in November for that country's independence celebrations. The CIA operative was a double agent who had been passing information to the Cuban government for 10 years, Castro said.

Castro listed the eight other anti-Cuban terrorist attacks that he blamed on the CIA as:

■ An attack on two Cuban fishing boats April 6 by private launches from Florida. One Cuban fisherman was killed.

■ The bombing of the Cuban Embassy in Lisbon, Portugal April 22, in which two persons died.

■ The bombing of the Cuban mission to the United Nations in New York July 5.

■ The explosion of a bomb in a suitcase that was about to be loaded onto a Cuban airliner in Kingston, Jamaica July 9.

■ A bomb explosion July 10 in the offices of British West Indian Airways of Barbados, which represented the Cuban airline in Barbados.

■ The slaying of a technician of the Cuban National Fisheries Institute in Merida, Mexico July 23 during an abortive attempt to kidnap the Cuban consul there.

■ The abduction of two employes of the Cuban Embassy in Buenos Aires, Argentina Aug. 9.

■ A bomb explosion in the office of the Cuban airline in Panama Aug. 18.

Castro noted that all the attacks had followed Cuba's military intervention in the Angolan civil war, which had been sharply criticized by the U.S.

Venezuela discloses plots. Venezuelan police had discovered plans by right-wing Cuban exiles to carry out terrorist attacks in the U.S., Venezuela, Trinidad & Tobago, Barbados, Guyana, Panama and Colombia, the Caracas newspaper El Nacional reported Oct. 19.

Existence of the plans was confirmed by Venezuelan and U.S. officials who were quoted by the New York Times Oct. 20. Some of the attacks already had taken place, including the recent bombing of Guyana's consulate in Trinidad, El Nacional said. Guyana had an avowedly socialist government that enjoyed good relations with Cuba.

The plans were discovered in a police raid on the Caracas home of Luis Posada, the Cuban exile arrested in connection with the Oct. 6 Cuban airliner bombing. Police reportedly confiscated terrorist "equipment" in the raid.

Some of the terrorists had held high positions in the Venezuelan government, according to Venezuelan officials quoted by the Oct. 21 New York Times. Posada had held an important post in Venezuela's police intelligence agency until 1975. Venezuelan President Carlos Andres Perez, the officials added, had used the Cuban exiles to maintain contact with the Chilean military government, with which Venezuela had strained diplomatic relations.

Cuban exiles tied to Letelier slaying—Venezuelan police had linked Cuban exiles to the murder in Washington Sept. 21 of Orlando Letelier, the Chilean ex-

CUBA

Cabinet minister, El Nacional reported Oct. 19.

After arresting Orlando Bosch, leader of the anti-Castro group CORU, police learned that Bosch had told associates that the bomb that killed Letelier had been placed under his car by two Cuban exiles, Ignacio and Guillermo Novo.

The Novo brothers had been indicted in the U.S. in 1965 on charges of firing a bazooka at the United Nations, according to the Oct. 20 Washington Post. The indictments were later quashed on grounds that confessions had been taken from the Novos in violation of their constitutional rights. Guillermo Novo was convicted in 1974 in connection with a 1969 bombing incident and sentenced to six months' imprisonment and five years' probation, the Post reported.

A Venezuelan government source told the Post that the Chilean government had helped finance terrorism by Cuban exiles against the Castro government. "We've known it for years, but there's no way to do anything about it," the source said. That source and others told the Post that Orlando Bosch was one of several Cuban exiles who regularly made trips to Santiago, Chile.

U.S. intelligence sources also had received tips linking Bosch and CORU to Letelier's assassination, the New York Times reported Oct. 12. The sources said that the U.S. Federal Bureau of Investigation had learned that Cuban exile groups had carried a long-time grudge against Letelier for his role in improving relations between Cuba and Chile under the government of the late Chilean President Salvador Allende.

The U.S. State Department disclosed Oct. 15 that it had asked Venezuela to return Bosch to the U.S. for allegedly violating the terms of his parole. The U.S. did not make a formal request for Bosch's extradition, but asked Venezuela to put Bosch on a U.S.-bound airplane so he could be arrested on arrival.

Cuban airline office in Spain bombed. A bomb exploded Nov. 7 in the Madrid office of Cubana de Aviacion, the Cuban national airline, causing heavy damage but no casualties.

Responsibility for the blast was claimed by CORU.

A man claiming to represent CORU telephoned offices of the Associated Press in San Juan, Puerto Rico Nov. 9 and said the Madrid bombing was "a continuation of the war against [Cuban Premier] Fidel Castro." The caller said that Cuba "will be liberated only with the sweat and blood of its sons in exile."

In another development, Aldo Vera Serafin, a Cuban exile who had once served in Castro's government, was shot to death in a San Juan suburb Oct. 25. Vera had broken with Castro in the early 1960s and moved to Puerto Rico, where he had joined the Fourth Republic, an anti-Castro group said to have connections with Orlando Bosch.

Abuse of Political Prisoners

Kennedy scores regime on prisoners. U.S. Sen. Edward M. Kennedy (D, Mass.) criticized the Cuban government for refusing to allow representatives of international organizations to observe the condition of political prisoners on the island, the Miami Herald reported Aug. 28.

Kennedy said that several members of his staff had visited Cuba recently and asked the government to allow the International Red Cross, Amnesty International and the International Commission of Jurists to visit the island and make the inspection. The requests had been ignored, Kennedy said.

The staff members had been permitted to visit some prisons in which conditions appeared to be adequate, Kennedy said, but had been denied access to jails the government considered to be "maximum security" installations.

Kennedy, an advocate of normalized relations between the U.S. and Cuba, warned Havana that "the process of normalization . . . must inevitably include the conditions of human rights and of the political prisoners."

Abuse reported. The Inter-American Human Rights Commission, a unit of the Organization of American States, made public June 11 a report (its fifth) on the "cruel, inhuman and degrading" treatment given to political prisoners in Cuba.

Among treatment methods listed in the report:

(a) The political prisoner is put completely stripped into a freezing cold room;

(b) The political prisoner, again stripped, is put into a room with a very high temperature;

(c) The political prisoner is placed in a room just large enough to hold one person standing. He is kept there for a time calculated to cause terrible pain in his legs, which are supporting all his body weight. Often, the veins in the prisoner's legs rupture with all the dreadful consequences this brings on.

(d) The confinement of the political prisoner in hermetically-sealed rooms with the lights turned on for 24 hours—I repeat,—24 hours a day, so that the prisoner's mind is disturbed, he loses his sense of time and his sleep-cycle is upset, because he is hardly able to sleep on account of the brightness of the lights in the room.

(e) Continuous solitary confinement, which is also intended to break the political prisoner's spirit, so that he prefers to admit to any charge rather than continue to live under such conditions.

(f) The introduction of political police agents in prison cells for weeks and sometimes for months at a time, in order to spy on political prisoners, and, by pretending to be concerned about the accusations hanging over them, induce the prisoners to admit to the monstrous accusations of the State Political Police, and attempt to obtain confessions from the prisoners.

(g) The taking of political prisoners to places far from the detention centers, where death by firing squad is simulated with blank cartridges, or tracer bullets.

(h) The taking of political prisoners out to sea, in ships belonging to the Political Police, and placing around the prisoner's neck a thick rope with a slip knot, to the end of which is attached an anchor or concrete block, and threatening them with being thrown into the sea if they do not quickly confess that certain allegations made against them are true.

(i) Political prisoners are sometimes interrogated continuously, without rest, by successive teams of inquisitors, in order to break them down. When the political prisoner begs to be allowed to sleep, he is told that he may not sleep until he confesses.

(j) Political prisoners are sometimes subject to the application of the Russian symphony, which consists in strapping them to a chair, and then cracking a whip with great violence, producing a shattering, deafening noise which damages the ear-drum.

(k) As regards physical tortures, a frequent method is to take the political prisoner by the feet and submerge his head in a pool of water, so that he gradually suffers the symptoms of asphyxiation by drowning.

(l) Political prisoners are sometimes forced to remain standing, without being allowed to lean on anything, a procedure which disturbs the circulation of the blood.

(ll) Political prisoners are ordered to remain standing, with their legs apart, and are then beaten on the genitals with steel bands. This produces extreme pain, in view of the effects of these blows on such a delicate part of the human body.

(m) "Las tapiadas." This name has been given to female political prisoners in Cuba incarcerated in cells where they are isolated for violations of the iron discipline of the prison. In these cells there is no light and almost no water. The prisoners are kept naked in a very confined space. Their food is served to them at different times of day, so that they lose all notion of time. They may not receive visits or letters. They remain there, in a state of confusion, for weeks at a time.

Number of prisoners uncertain. No reliable statistics on the number of political prisoners held in Cuba were available outside the country. But Frank Greve and Miguel Perez reported in the Miami Herald May 23:

Seventeen years after the revolution, Cuba's jails still bulge with political prisoners. Premier Fidel Castro says 5,000 still are held from the revolution's first six years. Most neutral observers agree. But they add perhaps 15,000 prisoners, taken since 1965 for crimes with political overtones. Within Miami's exile community, where political emotion simmers on minor issues and boils on the subject of political prisoners, estimates sometimes rise above 100,000.

No matter the number, most adults in Miami's 400,000-plus Cuban exile community know somebody who is, or was, a Castro prisoner. That's not surprising. More than 100,000 persons were held at least briefly after the Bay of Pigs invasion in 1961. Most of those who could later fled to Miami.

Ecuador

Bloodless Military Coup

Rodriguez Lara overthrown. Gen. Guillermo Rodriguez Lara was deposed as president Jan. 11 in a bloodless coup led by the three armed forces commanders, who formed a governing junta.

The junta members were Vice Adm. Alfredo Poveda Burbano, the official leader, army Gen. Guillermo Duran Arcentales and air force Gen. Luis Leoro Franco. They imposed a state of siege and martial law, but vowed to turn over the government to civilians by 1977, as Rodriguez had pledged a month before.

The coup was denounced Jan. 12 by the Civic Junta, the conservative opposition coalition, which charged the new rulers had been hand-picked by Rodriguez Lara. It was also criticized by retired Col. Jorge Ceballos, a leader of the abortive September 1975 military coup, who declared from his hideout in northern Ecuador that he was "assuming command of the civilian-military uprising against the present government." However, the major cities were calm and no other opposition to the new regime was reported.

Rodriguez Lara had faced increasing opposition from the Civic Junta and sectors of the armed forces since the 1975 coup attempt. His position had been further undermined by student riots and a public transport strike Jan. 4–10 following the imposition of a 20% rise in urban transport fares.

Rodriguez effectively handed over power Jan. 9, but was not officially deposed for two days so he could attend the wedding of his daughter in Quito late Jan. 10, according to press reports. The government denied reports of the transfer of power Jan. 9 and arrested two cabinet officials—Public Works Minister Gen. Raul Puma Velasco and Education Minister Gen. Gustavo Vasconez—who publicly disclosed the overthrow but criticized the presence of Gen. Duran Arcentales on the junta.

Vasconez had said in a radio broadcast Jan. 9 that the coup had been carried out but that it was unacceptable for a "demagogue" and "leftist" like Duran to serve on the junta. He was expelled from the armed forces in addition to being arrested. Puma said from his jail cell Jan. 11 that Duran was "incapable of fully understanding the historical moment being lived by the people" and of "seeing that the government should protect the interest of the majorities." Other army officers also objected to Duran's membership in the junta, according to press reports Jan. 12.

The urban transport strike had begun Jan. 5, one day after the government increased transport fares and students in Quito damaged 40 buses—three of them with explosives—in protest. Striking bus owners in Quito and Guayaquil were joined Jan. 6 by the Ecuadorean Federation of Professional Drivers, who called an indefinite national strike until their safety against student rioters was guaranteed.

The cabinet resigned Jan. 7 as the strike entered its third day, partially paralyzing Quito, Guayaquil and Cuenca, and student demonstrations continued in the capital. The nation's three major labor federations refused to back the strike, demanding that the government rescind the fare increase to end the crisis. The increase was rescinded Jan. 10, after two persons were killed and six wounded in Cuenca in riots and clashes between policemen and civilian protesters the night before.

Rescinding of the increase ended the strike and student protests, but a bomb exploded Jan. 10 at the church where Rodriguez Lara's daughter was to be married, causing extensive damage but no casualties.

In an earlier development, the government had closed the television station Teleamazonas and arrested its manager and chief news editor Jan. 4, after the station, in a year-end news roundup, showed a photograph taken during the September 1975 coup attempt. The detainees were freed Jan. 8, after their arrest was denounced by the Guayaquil press.

Reporter ousted in narcotics issue. Pieter van Bennekom, a Dutch reporter working for United Press International, was ordered to leave Ecuador Jan. 13 for asking a question at a press conference Jan. 12 which linked Vice Adm. Alfredo Poveda Burbano, the titular head of the new military junta, to the illegal narcotics traffic.

Van Bennekom asked Poveda if he had any comment on an article in the New York Times April 21, 1975 which said Poveda had intervened to protect a narcotics dealer from prosecution. Poveda angrily denied having any ties to drug dealers and abruptly ended the news conference.

A police captain quoted in the Times article said Poveda, then Ecuador's government (interior) minister, had ordered him to make sure charges were dropped against Luiz Rivadeneira, who had been arrested with more than four pounds of cocaine paste in his possession. Soon afterwards Poveda was dismissed from the cabinet and transferred to the naval command.

New cabinet sworn. A cabinet of three civilians and 11 military officers was sworn in Jan. 14.

Civilians received the key portfolios of foreign affairs, finance, and industry and commerce, while military officers took over the natural resources (oil) and other ministries. Vice Adm. Alfredo Poveda Burbano, the junta leader, said the new government would follow a moderate political course, keeping Ecuador in the Organization of Petroleum Exporting Countries (OPEC), pursuing nationalist policies and fulfilling its pledge to yield power to elected civilian officials within two years.

The civilians in the cabinet were Armando Pesantes, foreign minister; Cesar Robalino, finance minister, and Galo Montano, industry and commerce minister. Pesantes was a career diplomat and former ambassador to Belgium. Montano was a business executive and Robalino, a former official of the natural resources ministry.

The new natural resources minister was Col. Rene Vargas, former manager of the state oil company CEPE. The other military officers in the cabinet—most of them colonels—included Col. Richelieu Levoyer, government (interior) minister, and retired Gen. Andres Arrata, defense minister.

Col. Vargas pledged a vigorous effort to increase Ecuador's oil exports, which had fallen by 11.6% and contributed to Ecuador's economic decline in 1975, the Miami Herald reported Jan. 17. The government would increase exploration and gradually exert more control over the petroleum industry, Vargas said.

Col. Levoyer pledged to make direct contact with the major political movements and to grant a partial amnesty to politicians who were imprisoned, exiled or in hiding, it was reported Jan. 16.

The military junta imposed press censorship late Jan. 12 but lifted it along with the state of siege Jan. 15 as the country continued calm and normal activity resumed. The censorship prevented the publication of further denunciations of the new government by newspapers, civilian politicians and dissident military officers.

The junta had been criticized Jan. 12 by the Conservative, Liberal and Christian Democratic Parties, all of which demanded a prompt return to civilian rule.

ECUADOR

The Christian Democrats spoke of the "bolivianization" of Ecuador, referring to the military regime in Bolivia which retained power despite periodic pledges to restore constitutional rule.

Several Ecuadorean newspapers had also criticized the coup Jan. 12, calling it a mere change of military commanders. El Universo said the government remained "a source of unease to Ecuadoreans who are anxious for the country to return to constitutional norms as soon as possible," while El Telegrafo said "Ecuador is experiencing one of the longest dictatorial lapses in its history." El Tiempo declared that "another chapter has ended in the chronicle of Ecuadorean frustration."

Meanwhile, students and workers demanded that the government raise wages by 50%, fix a minimum monthly wage of $120, freeze prices of essential articles and carry out the agrarian reform law, it was reported Jan. 14.

Government minister replaced. Government (Interior) Minister Col. Richelieu Levoyer was dismissed and replaced in office by Col. Bolivar Jarrin, it was reported June 12.

Levoyer was fired shortly after he had announced a government plan to end military rule by holding elections before February 1978. His dismissal apparently was not linked to the announcement, since Jarrin declared on assuming office that the plan would not be changed. Levoyer was replaced because he had antagonized traditional political groups with his "forthright style," the London newsletter Latin America said July 9.

Seven political parties expressed strong opposition to the elections plan, criticizing its vagueness and demanding that power be handed over to a civilian government immediately, it was reported Aug. 8. The parties, grouped in the "Democratic Institutionalist Front," included the Liberals, Conservatives and Velasquistas. The Velasquistas were followers of Jose Maria Velasco Ibarra, the exiled ex-president.

Parties to help write constitution. The military junta invited 14 political parties to help draft a new Ecuadorean constitution, and 12 of the groups accepted before the Oct. 11 deadline. The new charter was part of the junta's avowed plan to hand over power to a civilian government by 1978.

The two parties refusing to cooperate were the National Velasquista Movement of ex-President Jose Maria Velasco Ibarra and the Revolutionary Nationalist Party of former President Carlos Julio Arosemena. Their refusal appeared to break up a seven-party rightist coalition as the other five parties agreed to attend the constitutional talks. The coalition had been known variously as the Civic Junta, the Democratic Institutionalist Front and the Democratic Renovation Movement.

Right-wing parties would dominate the civilian representation at the talks. The major leftist group at the talks would be the Concentration of Popular Forces, led by Asaad Bucaram, the former presidential candidate and mayor of Guayaquil.

Oil Industry

Anglo yields oil installations. Anglo-Ecuadorean Oilfields Ltd. handed over its Santa Elena concession to the government Jan. 16 after its contract ended and the concession reverted to the state oil company CEPE.

The British firm had operated in Ecuador for 56 years, dominating the oil industry until the Texaco-Gulf consortium of the U.S. began exporting oil from the eastern Amazon region in 1972. Production from Anglo's 600 wells had declined steadily over the past 10 years, standing currently at 2,000 barrels per day.

Government to buy Gulf assets. The Ecuadorean government began negotiations Oct. 25 to purchase Ecuadorean Gulf Oil Co., the local subsidiary of Gulf Oil Corp. of the U.S.

The purchase would give the state oil firm CEPE a 62.5% share in Ecuador's petroleum production. Heretofore CEPE had held a 25% share in a joint venture with Gulf and Texaco Inc. of the U.S., each of which held a 37.5% share. Texaco reportedly would continue operating in Ecuador after Gulf sold out.

The negotiations followed a series of disputes before the government and Gulf. The disputes culminated in a government threat to expropriate Gulf's assets without compensation unless the company paid $53 million it allegedly owed the government. Gulf paid the money Sept. 30, hours before the government's deadline, but announced that it no longer wished to operate in Ecuador.

The money, according to the government, represented taxes and other obligations on Gulf exports since February. In withholding the funds, Gulf had charged that the government had taken crude oil "in excess of entitlements"; had withheld income taxes, profit-sharing and other taxes on Gulf in excess of legal requirements; had required Gulf to satisfy local demand for crude oil in excess of obligations and at a price resulting in substantial losses; had not made full payments on CEPE's purchase of equity participation in Gulf's producing and pipeline operations in Ecuador, and had not repaid other debts by CEPE.

Texaco had withheld about $11 million in payments to the government, claiming the government had underestimated production costs in Oriente jungle oilfields when it assessed Texaco's taxes. Texaco paid the money Aug. 20 after Col. Rene Vargas, the national resources minister, had warned that the government might cancel Texaco's oil concessions.

Texaco and Gulf had invested an estimated $264 million in their Oriente operations, including the Trans-Andean pipeline from the oilfields to the port of Balao on Ecuador's Pacific coast. The pipeline belonged to Texaco and Gulf, but the Ecuadorean government would buy it separately, excluding it from the negotiations over the purchase of Gulf's assets, according to the Sept. 17 Latin America Economic Report.

Labor & Other Unrest

Transport and agriculture strikes. Heavy transport workers went on strike throughout Ecuador June 21-26, demanding that the government abolish the U.S.-owned Cariben transport company, which loaded and unloaded ships in Ecuador's ports. The strike ended when the government threatened to arrest the strikers.

Coffee and plantain workers went on strike June 20 and were supported by government-employed agronomists and veterinarians who walked off their jobs. The government June 29 fired 600 agronomists for striking. The strikes paralyzed agriculture and livestock exports.

One-day police strike. Policemen struck in Quito July 15 to demand higher wages. The government arrested 13 high police officials the next day for allegedly organizing the one-day stoppage.

A government spokesman said July 16 that the strike had been "instigated" by "political groups" precisely when the regime was "trying to give [the policemen] what they wanted." Police wages were the lowest in Ecuador's armed forces.

School unrest. High-school students in Guayaquil began a 48-hour strike June 21 after a week of riots and clashes with police. The trouble had begun June 15 when police killed a 14-year-old student. The next day students stoned automobiles and shops in downtown Guayaquil. Policemen used tear gas to disperse them.

—Students rioted in the streets of Quito Oct. 28 to protest budget cuts at Ecuador's 16 universities. Police used tear gas to disperse the protesters, who erected barricades against traffic and threw gasoline bombs in the northern and central sectors of the city. The rector of Central University, the nation's largest, said that the universities were supposed to get 2% of Ecuador's annual oil revenues, but that the government had withheld the money for the preceding two years.

General strike in Riobamba. The Andean city of Riobamba was paralyzed Oct. 19-28 by a general strike called by professional, commercial and land-owning groups to protest government neglect of the city and surrounding Chimborazo Province.

Provincial authorities resigned soon after the strike began, apparently in support of the protest. The government arrested strike leaders and imposed martial law Oct. 21, after strikers rioted and clashed with police, leaving one person dead and several injured. However, the strike continued and protesters attacked the army troops that had been sent in when martial law was imposed. The government agreed Oct. 28 to free the arrested strike leaders and to institute a development program in Chimborazo.

The terms of the program were not announced, but they were apparently satisfactory to the strikers who ended the walkout that day. Strike leaders had demanded that the government develop education, transportation, electrification, health care, agriculture, forestry, industry and tourism in Chimborazo.

The province was among Ecuador's poorest and most neglected, according to press reports. Its illiteracy rate was 52.3%, the highest in the country. Its death rate was 15.9%, the infant mortality rate was 112.7 per 1,000 live births.

Quito had been barely affected by a general strike called Oct. 14 by the Ecuadorean Workers' Federation (CTE), the nation's largest trade union. The next-largest unions, the Ecuadorean Federation of Free Syndical Organizations and the Ecuadorean Union of Classist Organizations, refused to join the strike. The CTE had called the stoppage to protest "anti-labor legislation" and to support 1,200 workers at the La Internacional textile factory who had been on strike for 15 days to demand higher salaries and more social benefits.

Esmeraldas hit by strike, riots. Residents of the port city of Esmeraldas held a general strike Nov. 18–23 to demand better water and electricity service, completion of hospital and school buildings, more government aid to the local university and a greater local share of Ecuador's oil revenues.

The strike was accompanied by riots which led the government to impose martial law and a curfew. Four persons were wounded in disturbances in the city Nov. 18. Some stores were sacked Nov. 22 as food became scarce and prices rose.

The strike began after 12 houses in Esmeraldas were destroyed by a fire which firemen were unable to contain because of a lack of equipment. The incident symbolized the central government's neglect of the city and impoverished Esmeraldas Province, the strike leaders said.

Foreign bishops seized, expelled. Police invaded an international meeting of Roman Catholics in Riobamba Aug. 12 and arrested more than 50 priests and laymen on subversion charges. Among the detainees were 37 foreign clerics, including two archbishops and 15 bishops.

The foreigners, from the U.S. and 13 other countries, were freed Aug. 13 and expelled from Ecuador the next day. Their arrest and deportation were protested by the Latin American Episcopal Conference (CELAM) and by the bishops' councils of Ecuador and the U.S.

The Ecuadorean government charged Aug. 13 that the clergymen at the Riobamba meeting had been distributing subversive literature and had planned to interfere in the internal affairs of Ecuador and other countries. Several of the foreign priests had been expelled from their own countries, the government alleged.

The government's charges were denied Aug. 14 by two of the four American bishops who were arrested at Riobamba and expelled from Ecuador. Archbishop Robert F. Sanchez of Santa Fe, N.M. and Bishop Patrick Flores of San Antonio, Tex. said that the Riobamba meeting was the annual Latin American prelates' conference on the problems of poor people.

The action against the clerics was denounced by the Ecuadorean Episcopal Conference Aug. 14, by CELAM Aug. 16 and subsequently by the National Conference of Catholic Bishops, a U.S. organization. The bishops' conference protest was reported by the Washington Post Aug. 20.

Msgr. Alfonso Lopez Trujillo, CELAM secretary general, said that the action against the clergymen constituted "a violation of pastoral freedom." There was "a concerted campaign against the church" in most Latin American countries, where democracy had been "buried" in violations of human rights, Lopez said.

Archbishop Pablo Cardinal Munoz Vega, primate of the Ecuadorean church, said that the Ecuadorean government's charges against the clerics were a "total tergiversation." Munoz' accusation was in a letter delivered Aug. 16 to Archbishop Raul Cardinal Primatesta, president of the Argentine Episcopal Conference.

Archbishop Joseph L. Bernardin of Cincinnati, president of the National Conference of Catholic Bishops, called the Ecuadorean action "an unwarranted and unjustifiable intrusion by a state in the legitimate exercise of the pastoral ministry of the church," the Post reported.

Another protest was issued by Venezuelan Bishop Alberto Parra Leon, who suffered a heart attack in custody and was reported hospitalized in Ecuador Aug. 15. After returning to Venezuela, Parra said Aug. 23 that Ecuador's ruling military junta was composed of "three true beasts."

Javier Manrique, Ecuador's acting government (interior) minister, expanded on the government's charges against the clerics Aug. 25. In a nationwide television address, he read from three documents allegedly circulated at the Riobamba meeting which allegedly proved the meeting's subversive nature. One document accused Ecuador of having "carried out the ethnocide or murder of [its] Indians," while another analyzed ways of "altering the constitutional order and promoting civil disobedience," Manrique claimed.

Guatemala

Quake Devastates Nation

Earthquake hits Guatemala, Honduras. A major earthquake shook Guatemala and Honduras early Feb. 4, causing massive destruction and human casualties in the first country and severe damage but no casualties in the second.

The quake was also felt in El Salvador, where it caused damage in a town near the Guatemalan border, and in Mexico, where tremors were felt as far west as Mexico City but no damage was reported.

The greatest devastation occurred in Guatemala City, where the poorest neighborhoods were severely damaged, and in surrounding towns, several of which were reported completely destroyed.

By Feb. 18, the authorities had totaled 22,419 deaths and reported that at least 74,105 people had been injured in the earthquake. It was understood that the full toll would probably never be known. As many as 5,000 bodies might be buried under the rubble, officials said, and it was unlikely that they would all be found.

The earthquake registered 7.5 on the Richter scale, higher than the quake that destroyed much of Managua, Nicaragua in December 1972. The epicenter was said to be 30 miles southwest of Guatemala City between the towns of Siquinla and Escuintla.

The earthquake hit Guatemala City at 3:04 a.m. Feb. 4 and smaller tremors shook the capital throughout the day. In the southern or old part of the city, entire blocks of makeshift huts and adobe houses collapsed, filling the streets with rubble which later blocked rescue vehicles. The electricity and water supplies were cut off, as were communications with numerous other towns which were isolated by landslides and the collapse of bridges.

The government declared a state of "national catastrophe," mobilized the army and police, and began relief efforts under the National Emergency Committee headed by Defense Minister Gen. Fernando Romeo Lucas. President Kjell Laugerud Garcia flew over devastated areas outside the capital, reporting in a radio broadcast later Feb. 4 that he had found towns and villages totally destroyed.

Aid was immediately sent by the U.S., Venezuela, the U.N.'s Disaster Relief Office and the Organization of American States. Mexico and Colombia also pledged relief assistance, and the President of Nicaragua, Gen. Anastasio Somoza, reportedly flew to Guatemala to offer his country's aid. Doctors at Guatemala City's 200-year-old general hospital, which was badly damaged by the quake, sent out an urgent appeal for foreign medical supplies Feb. 5, noting that they had performed numerous operations under "highly questionable circumstances" in a tent set up alongside the hospital after its operating areas were largely destroyed.

The National Emergency Committee Feb. 4 urged residents of the capital to bury their dead immediately to avert an epidemic. Officials of the city morgue said the morgue was full and urged citizens to stop bringing in bodies.

The capital began returning to normal Feb. 5 as water and electricity were reconnected in the lightly damaged middle-class neighborhoods and some shops reopened to sell food and clothing at inflated prices. Thousands of residents of the city's poor sections were reported without food or water, but food, shelter units and other relief aid began arriving from abroad.

Outside the city, rescue teams reported severe damage and high casualties in the towns of El Progreso, Joyabaj, San Pedro Zacatepeque, San Juan Zacatepeque, Patzicia, Rabinal, Coban, Tactic and Salama, according to press accounts Feb. 5.

The major damage occurred in a 100-mile arc north and west of Guatemala City encompassing the departments of Guatemala, Chimaltenango and Zacatepeque, where virtually all the 340,000 residents were reportedly left homeless. The towns of Joyabaj, Tecpan, Patzicia, Chimaltenango, Comalapa, El Progreso, Zaragoza and San Miguel Jilotepeque were reported destroyed by the earthquake Feb. 4 and the towns of Mixco and San Lucas were reported levelled Feb. 6 by a tremor which registered 5.75–6 on the Richter scale.

More than 500 tremors of varying intensity shook the area Feb. 4–9, causing fresh landslides and the collapse of buildings damaged in the first earthquake, and keeping citizens in a state of near-panic, according to press reports.

Little looting or public disorder was reported in Guatemala City, although five alleged looters were executed by soldiers Feb. 8. President Kjell Laugerud Garcia had given soldiers orders to shoot looters on sight.

More than half of the recorded deaths (13,204) occurred in Chimaltenango Department northwest of Guatemala City. Relief workers there and in other devastated areas were sweeping away ruins and trying hurriedly to build new housing before the spring rains arrived. More than one million Guatemalans—more than one-sixth of the population—were left homeless by the earthquake.

Most of the injured had received basic medical care, leaving relief workers free to try to feed and shelter the homeless, it was reported Feb. 15. In addition to homes, the government must rebuild more than 1,000 schools, water systems in 75 remote villages, and numerous roads including the key highway from Guatamala City to the nation's Atlantic port, Puerto Barrios, observers said.

The government planned an initial housing reconstruction program financed with $17 million in foreign loans, $11.5 milion of which would be designated for rural areas, it was reported Feb. 22. Foreign aid continued to pour in to Guatemala; Venezuela pledged $20 million in reconstruction aid Feb. 11, and the U.S. Agency for International Development (AID), which had already contributed more than $3 million in relief funds, asked the U.S. Congress Feb. 18 to authorize $25 million in emergency aid to Guatemala. (The authorization was passed by voice votes of the U.S. House of Representatives April 12 and of the Senate April 13.)

(AID chief Daniel Parker flew to Guatemala at the request of President Ford Feb. 12 to assess the nation's relief needs. On his return to Washington Feb. 16 Parker said the earthquake's devastation was "just incredible. The real disaster is on the poor and the rural. Their shacks and shanties came tumbling down. Heavy tile roofs came tumbling down on them.")

More than 100 other countries contributed food, money, clothing and medical supplies, and some sent doctors and other relief workers. Guatemala continued to refuse aid from the British government, with which it disputed sovereignty over Belize (formerly British Honduras), but contributions from private British groups were accepted, it was reported Feb. 12.

Meanwhile, tremors continued to shake Guatemala City and outlying areas, keeping residents in a panic and leading many of the poor to sleep out in the open rather than return to damaged but not destroyed homes. However, the city continued its slow return to normality, with shops and stores reopening in increasing numbers and workers returning to their jobs in most industrial districts, where electricity

GUATEMALA

and water supplies were restored and factories resumed full operations.

(The earthquake had caused little damage to Guatemala's small but rapidly growing economy, the New York Times reported Feb. 24. Despite its huge death toll and its destruction in rural areas, the quake caused only superficial damage to light industries and it did not harm the Texaco refinery at Escuintla or the International Nickel Co.'s project at El Estor. Guatemala's chief agricultural exports—sugar, coffee and cotton, cultivated principally in the Pacific lowlands—were also unaffected by the disaster, according to the Times. In the highlands, where most of the Indian villages and towns were destroyed Feb. 4, family stocks were full from the corn and bean harvests completed in November. Much of the food was buried under debris, but some families were now digging it out, the Times noted.)

There was an upsurge of looting in Guatemala City and other areas, but hundreds of vigilante groups were formed to protect possessions in tents and abandoned homes, it was reported Feb. 16. Soldiers in Mixco outside the capital shot to death two alleged looters who tried to escape arrest Feb. 14. The two were reportedly ex-convicts freed along with many other prisoners after the earthquake destroyed jails in and outside the capital.

Quake laid to moving of North America—The Feb. 4 earthquake was caused by a westward movement of North America relative to the Caribbean region, according to a preliminary analysis by the National Earthquake Information Service of the U.S., cited by the New York Times Feb. 7.

The analysis was based on the widely accepted theory that the earth's surface was divided into gigantic plates whose movements relative to one another were largely responsible for earthquakes, volcanic activity and mountain formation, the Times noted. According to the Service, the Guatemala quake occurred as the North American plate moved westward along the Motagua fault, which ran inland from the Gulf of Honduras on Guatemala's Caribbean coast and was believed to be part of the boundary between the North American and Caribbean plates.

The North American plate consisted of the North American continent and all of the North Atlantic Ocean west of the Mid-Atlantic Ridge, while the Caribbean plate contained almost the entire floor of the Caribbean Sea plus the part of Central America to the west of it. Dividing the two plates, in addition to the Motagua fault, were the Cayman trench between Cuba and Guatemala and the Puerto Rican trench east of the Dominican Republic and north of Puerto Rico.

Other Developments

1976 budget. The government's budget for 1976 provided for record expenditures of $553.7 million, 39.4% higher than the figure originally proposed in 1975, it was reported Jan. 9. The government attributed the increase to inflation, particularly the high price of fuel.

Belize seeks U.N. guarantee vs. Guatemala. Prime Minister George Price of Belize was pressing Great Britain to seek a United Nations guarantee of Belizean independence and territorial integrity against the claims of Guatemala, it was reported Jan. 8. Price arrived in London Jan. 5 for conversations with British officials on the future of Belize, a British colony over which Guatemala claimed exclusive sovereignty.

IDB loans set. The executive director of the Inter-American Development Bank (IDB) announced Oct. 13 that the bank had allocated $135 million for development loans to Guatemala.

Rodolfo Martinez Ferrate said the credits would help finance construction of rural roads, hospitals and markets, expansion of the construction and fishing industries and promotion of rural electrification.

The IDB would lend Guatemala $105 million for the Pueblo Viejo hydroelectric project on the Chixoy River, it was reported Jan. 9. The sum was the largest ever authorized by the bank for a single financing.

Rightists control Congress. A right-wing alliance had wrested control of Congress from the less conservative coalition loyal to President Kjell Laugerud Garcia, the Washington Post reported July 18.

The alliance, formed in June, comprised the extreme rightist National Liberation Movement, led by Vice President Mario Sandoval Alarcon; the Central Aranista Organizada (CAO), which was loyal to ex-President Carlos Arana Osorio, and the centrist Revolutionary Party (PR). The group had an absolute majority in Congress and tight control of legislative committees, the Post reported. It was also supported by many military officers.

Luis Alfonso Lopez, a CAO member, had been elected president of Congress after Arana paid $5,000 to each of the 10 PR congressmen to vote for him, the London newsletter Latin America reported June 25.

Formation of the right-wing alliance left Laugerud's Democratic Institutional Party and the Christian Democratic Party as the effective opposition. Many members of the new majority, including Arana, had helped put Laugerud into office only two years before.

Guerrillas stage attacks. Members of the leftist Guerrilla Army of the Poor (EGP) attacked security forces and other targets in different parts of the country in July November.

Thirty armed insurgents attacked the eastern town of Olopa Nov. 13, killing two local landowners and then fleeing into the mountains with police in pursuit. Three days later guerrillas wounded two soldiers in a two-hour shootout in the mountains of the western department of El Quiche. Troops were combing those mountains in search of what they believed to be the guerrilla group's headquarters.

About 50 presumed guerrillas Nov. 20 destroyed 10 crop-dusting airplanes on a large farm on the southern coast. Before setting the planes on fire, the insurgents told a group of farmworkers that the action was a reprisal for "the poisoning of peasants" with the farm's pesticides.

Earlier, guerrillas in El Quiche had exchanged fire with military policemen Aug. 23 and killed two MP's Aug. 24. Insurgents July 9 had killed two soldiers in the hamlet of Tupoj and one in Ixcam.

The guerrilla attacks followed a resurgence of other political violence after a lull caused by the February earthquake. After March there was a sharp increase in murders and disappearances, mainly of minor leftist politicians, the Washington Post reported July 18. The victims were presumed to have been killed by police or government-backed paramilitary forces.

Two representatives of Amnesty International said that during their four-day visit to Guatemala in May, the local press reported more than 30 killings. An average of 11 bodies showing signs of torture were found daily throughout the country, the representatives said in their preliminary report, quoted by the July 23 London newsletter Latin America.

Amnesty International reported Dec. 13 that "extra-judicial detentions and executions" were a daily occurrence in Guatemala. The victims were believed to be petty criminals, peasants, members of opposition parties, trade unionists, journalists, students and teachers, Amnesty said. It estimated that more than 20,000 persons had been killed or had disappeared in Guatemala since 1966 as a result of action by government or semi-official forces.

Mexico

Lopez Portillo Succeeds Echeverria as President

Jose Lopez Portillo succeeded Luis Echeverria Alvarez as president of Mexico Dec. 1 after an election in which Lopez had campaigned actively for most of the year despite the fact that he had no real opposition for the post. As is traditional in Mexico, where the president serves a six-year term but may not run for reelection, the new president was hand-picked by the outgoing one. Mexico's only major party, the PRI (Partido Revolucionario Institucional, also known as the Institutional Revolutionary Party), had unquestioningly accepted Echeverria's designation of Lopez as its candidate and, therefore, the next president of the country.

Lopez Portillo elected president. Jose Lopez Portillo, candidate of the ruling Institutional Revolutionary Party (PRI), won a landslide victory in the Mexican presidential election July 4.

Lopez, a former finance minister, was the only candidate on the ballot. Two of the three small registered opposition parties had supported Lopez; the third had been unable to field a candidate because of internal disputes. The unregistered Communist Party ran a write-in candidate, Valentin Campa, who got comparatively few votes.

Lopez' victory was made official July 14. The Federal Electoral Commission said that he had received the highest vote total in Mexican history—17,695,043 ballots from an electorate of 25.9 million. Voter abstention was 28.6%, compared with 33% in the 1970 presidential election and 36% in the 1973 congressional vote, according to PRI officials.

Voters also elected 64 senators and 194 federal deputies.

Despite the absence of an opponent, Lopez campaigned vigorously for more than seven months. The PRI announced shortly before the election that during 221 days Lopez had traveled 50,000 miles, visited 924 cities, towns and villages, attended 453 political meetings, made 1,550 speeches and received 132,000 petitions.

Lopez made only general campaign statements, taking care not to upstage President Luis Echeverria Alvarez during his last year in office. Lopez described himself as a man of "neither the right nor the left." He called for more efficiency, honesty, organization and productivity in the Mexican government and economy.

In the closing speech of his campaign June 27, Lopez pledged to begin a thorough reorientation of the economy to increase production and achieve a higher standard of living for the Mexican masses. He said Mexico's most pressing economic problems were "the decreased growth rate, the public-sector deficit, the accelerated growth of the external debt, and the deficit in the balance of payments."

Mexico faced "years of saving, collective discipline and austerity" if it were to achieve "a balanced and just economic development," Lopez said. "Goods which are socially necessary and of strategic economic interest" should take precedence over consumer goods as production increased, he added.

"We have achieved in Mexico ... a backward and inefficient structure of production, confronted by a consumption structure that is one of the most advanced in the world—including a large publicity apparatus," Lopez said.

As means to raise productivity, Lopez said he envisioned:

■ Full use of installed capacity.
■ Regular and sustained expansion of effective demand and avoidance of the "stop-start" phenomenon in the economy.
■ A maximum of productive investment that could be financed with real internal and external non-inflationary resources.
■ Assurance that all savings generated by the productive process were invested in Mexico.
■ An equitable incomes policy, including tax reform and prevention of tax evasion and corruption.
■ A restructuring of the federal bureaucracy to increase government efficiency, eliminate duplicate jobs, facilitate economic and social planning and provide encouragement to the private sector.

Lopez inaugurated. Jose Lopez Portillo assumed the presidency of Mexico Dec. 1 with a call for national unity and strict austerity to overcome the country's acute economic crisis.

"Let us call an intelligent truce and recover our composure," Lopez said in an address to 5,300 Mexican and foreign guests at the National Auditorium in Mexico City. "Our first task is to get hold of ourselves and put an end to panic-stricken and frantic activity."

Lopez asked for austerity and pledged to combat inflation by strictly disciplining government spending. Inflation had reached about 30% in 1976. Lopez also called for a broadening of the distribution of wealth, opportunity and justice in Mexican society, and chided wealthy Mexicans who in their "insatiable greed for false riches" had taken their capital abroad, further eroding the weak Mexican peso.

"A few of the rich, who export capital, and a few of the poor, who export their labor, may leave Mexico," Lopez said. "But the rest of us are staying, and we can make our country a hell or a land where life is good. It is in our hands."

Lopez proposed more labor-intensive industry to combat unemployment and underemployment, which affected about half of Mexico's workers. He pledged fiscal reform to raise taxes on nonproductive capital holdings and lower them for low- and middle-income workers. The new president also said he would create a single ministry to oversee programming of the budget and public expenditures, consolidating the work of a number of different agencies.

Businessmen welcomed the moderation of Lopez' address. As an apparent result, the exchange rate for the Mexican peso rose Dec. 2 to 20 to the U.S. dollar. The peso had plunged to 28 to the dollar after it was floated at the end of August.

Lopez' speech was characterized as "well balanced" by U.S. Secretary of State Henry Kissinger, the New York Times said Dec. 3. Kissinger headed a 12-member delegation to the inaugural, one of 102 foreign delegations attending the ceremony.

(In addition to Kissinger's delegation, the U.S. was represented by Rosalynn Carter, wife of President-elect Jimmy Carter. She was the private guest of Lopez Portillo and his wife. Mrs. Carter, who brought a message of "special friendship" for Mexico from her husband, was treated with special deference by her hosts and other Mexican officials during her stay in the country Nov. 30–Dec. 2, press reports said.)

Lopez Portillo took office at a time of intense political and economic turmoil in Mexico. He inherited severe economic problems, including a foreign debt of more than $22 billion, a growing foreign trade deficit and a sharp fall in tourism, Mexico's chief source of foreign exchange. In addition, Lopez received indirectly some of the animosity aimed at former President Luis Echeverria Alvarez, who had picked Lopez as his successor.

In the closing months of his administration Echeverria had angered the middle

MEXICO

class and the business and landowning sectors by floating the peso, expropriating almost 240,000 acres of northern farmland and accusing the wealthy of undermining his economic reforms "in concert with foreign interests."

The northern farmland, expropriated toward the end of November, was handed over to peasants. Landowners and sympathetic businessmen called a strike to protest the move. In a further agrarian action Nov. 30, Echeverria signed titles making 32,000 peasant families the legal owners of nearly one million acres of land that many of them had worked for years.

Cabinet sworn in—President Lopez Portillo swore in his 19-man Cabinet Dec. 2. He gave the key political post of interior minister to Jesus Reyes Heroles, who was president of the ruling Institutional Revolutionary Party under Echeverria. The new finance minister, heading the government's economic team, was Julio Rodolfo Moctezuma Cid, who had served as secretary general of the Finance Ministry when Lopez Portillo was finance minister.

The new Cabinet ministers:

Interior—Jesus Reyes Heroles; finance—Julio Rodolfo Moctezuma Cid; presidency—Carlos Tello Macias; foreign affairs—Santiago Roel; defense—Felix Galvan Lopez; navy—Ricardo Chazaro Lara; national resources—Jose Andres de Oteiza; industry and commerce—Fernando Solana; agriculture—Francisco Merino; communications and transport—Emilio Mujica Montoya: public works—Pedro Ramirez Vazquez; water resources—Jesus Robles Linares; health—Emilio Martinez Manattou; education—Porfirio Munoz Ledo; labor—Pedro Ojeda Paullada; agrarian reform—Jorge Rojo Lugo; tourism—Guillermo Rosell de la Lama; regent of the Federal District—Carlos Hank Gonzalez; attorney general—Oscar Flores Sanchez.

PRI dominantes congressional vote. The ruling Institutional Revolutionary Party had won most of the seats in the July 8 congressional elections, according to official returns released July 16.

PRI candidates won 194 of the 230 seats in the Chamber of Deputies and 63 of the 64 seats in the Senate. Jorge Cruickshank, leader of the small Popular Socialist Party, became the first opposition candidate to win a Senate seat since 1929. He had run in coalition with a PRI candidate in Oaxaca State.

Echeverria rejected for U.N. post. Echeverria had hoped to become secretary general of the United Nations on leaving the Mexican presidency, but the U.N. General Assembly Dec. 8 reelected Kurt Waldheim to the post. Echeverria had offered himself as a Third World candidate.

The assembly's pro forma vote followed the Security Council's approval of Waldheim in secret balloting Dec. 7.

In the first round of balloting, Echeverria received four yes votes, four noes and seven abstentions. Waldheim was given 13 votes, with China casting a token veto to demonstrate its preference for a Third World candidate. Panama abstained because it too favored a Third World figure and also out of loyalty to a fellow-Latin American.

(Council members were permitted to vote for more than one candidate, and nine votes without a veto from the body's five permanent members, were required for a victory.)

On the second ballot, Waldheim received 14 votes as China switched and voted in favor. Panama again abstained.

Third-World diplomats, whom Echeverria had courted, had said he had displayed ignorance of important issues during a world tour in 1975, the Washington Post reported Oct. 5.

Press Control

Julio Scherer Garcia, the director of the Mexican newspaper Excelsior, was ousted from his post July 8, together with six close aides, in what was widely described as a government move to silence criticism.

Director of Excelsior forced out. Conservative employes of Excelsior, Mexico's leading newspaper, ousted its liberal director July 8 in what appeared to be the climax of a government campaign against the paper's independent political stance.

More than 200 reporters and other employes of Excelsior quit their jobs in protest when Julio Scherer Garcia, the director, and six of his top editorial and administrative aides were removed by a rebellious minority of the newspaper's 1,300-member cooperative.

Scherer was replaced by Regino Diaz Redondo, the editor of Excelsior's afternoon edition who, according to the July 11 Washington Post, had led a campaign against Scherer with the encouragement of and financial support from the Interior Ministry.

Excelsior's new management said in a front-page editorial July 9 that Scherer and his aides had been removed for committing "violations of the General Law of Cooperative Societies, its Code and the Constituent Bases of [Excelsior]." The vote to remove Scherer had been taken "democratically," without any "pressure" from the government, the editorial said.

Members of the ousted executive staff had told the Washington Post July 7 that the government was sponsoring a campaign to force Excelsior to drop its independent political stance. The latest incident in the campaign, they said, was the illegal invasion and occupation June 10 of land owned by Excelsior outside Mexico City.

The occupation was carried out by about 300 slum dwellers under the leadership of Humberto Serrano, a recently elected federal deputy and member of the ruling Institutional Revolutionary Party (PRI). Serrano said that the occupation would not end until Scherer was removed from the newspaper. The government refused to evict the squatters, who were fed from trucks belonging to the PRI and the Ministry of National Patrimony.

An editorial in Excelsior July 7 said the "passivity of the police authorities and the district attorneys" in the land occupation was "alarming." "We have to ask ourselves whether the government passivity is due to a lack of will or a lack of authority," the editorial declared.

Before the occupation, Excelsior had lost its advertising contract with the state-owned television station and its editors had been denounced in paid advertisements in the government newspaper and other Mexico City dailies. The advertisements were placed by phantom citizens' committees and presumably paid for by the government, according to Armando Vargas, an Excelsior correspondent quoted by the Washington Post July 14.

Vargas, in a letter to members of the U.S. Congress July 13, announced his resignation as chief correspondent of Excelsior and added:

On July 8, 1976, the freedom of the press as well as the dignity and integrity of hundreds of professional journalists suffered a devastating blow when the strongest, most prominent, and most influential newspaper of the country was stabbed in the back by the Government of Mexico.

The liberal editors, who for the last eight years have been trying to expand both the freedom of information and of opinion, were betrayed by a minority of conservative workers who succeeded in manipulating a number of the workers on the production staff. This minority, encouraged and supported by the Government of Mexico, the official political party of Mexico, and with the undeniable blessing of the President of Mexico, were only the perpetrators of a crime which implies enormous and terrible consequences for the Mexican social and political systems.

The eminent poet, Octavio Paz, who until that ill-fated day was the editor of Plural, the monthly literary magazine published by Excelsior, told me—"The transformation of Excelsior into a loudspeaker for the applause and eulogies to the powerful is a signal that the authoritarian shadow of darkness, already covering most of our Latin America, is advancing upon Mexico."

I was in Mexico from Wednesday, July 8, through Sunday, July 11. I lived through those tragic events. I remained with my colleagues and friends, witnessing the murder of a newspaper which up until then had been a proud example of what a free journalistic institution should be.

I refuse to be used as a legitimizer of this crime against freedom. I have a family. I am in a foreign country. I have no fortune. But dignity, integrity, and solidarity are concepts in which I believe as strongly as I despise their perversions.

Today I proudly join the ranks of the millions of unemployed, along with hundreds of my dear colleagues—editors, reporters, foreign correspondents, columnists, and photographers—who live and abide by the same principles and values which are cherished by any person who truly believes in freedom and democracy.

The Excelsior executives quoted by the Post July 8 attributed the government's campaign to Excelsior's editorial attacks on the regime for inefficiency, corruption, and slow progress in eliminating social injustices. The executives said that the campaign had begun at the end of 1975, after Excelsior effectively forced the resignation of then-Foreign Minister Emilio Rabasa by vigorously denouncing Mexico's support for United Nations resolutions against Zionism.

The Excelsior executives also linked the government campaign to the recent formation of a massive newspaper group that included the dailies El Sol and El

MEXICO

Universal, the Post reported July 11. Industry sources said that one of the group's principal shareholders was Mexico's outgoing president, Luis Echeverria Alvarez.

(Echeverria July 14 denied any personal or government involvement in the Excelsior management changes. "The present government has never, particularly now, bothered to take a position regarding an internal crisis of a newspaper cooperative," he said.)

Scherer and his aides were voted out of office at a meeting called July 8 by the minority conservative faction of the Excelsior cooperative. Scherer's supporters claimed to have the support of 812 of the cooperative's 1,302 members, but they walked out of the meeting to protest a procedural decision over vote-counting. The conservatives then voted against Scherer despite the lack of a quorum, and they threatened Scherer's backers until they left the Excelsior building. The Scherer group called a new meeting for July 21, but it was never held.

The changes at Excelsior were criticized in the foreign press, notably the New York Times and Washington Post. A Times editorial July 13 said "all that made [Excelsior] fresh, interesting and valuable in a democratic society has vanished to be replaced by conformist attitudes that would never have had a chance in the previous, genuine Excelsior." The editorial cited the government's involvement in the campaign against Scherer and compared members of the victorious conservative faction to "the bully boys of Lenin in 1917 or of Hitler in 1933."

An editorial in the Post July 14 charged that President Echeverria "has just managed to liquidate his country's one important independent center of political criticism, the newspaper Excelsior." The Post cited Echeverria's past role in encouraging a free press and asked: "As he prepares to step down, does he really want to be remembered as the man who killed Excelsior?" The editorial said:

This is not just another Third World situation in which a tinpot dictator seeks to close out alternative institutions and ideas. For Mexico is no ordinary Third World state. It is a country which, for all its economic disparities, has sustained a sophisticated "Western" intellectual and political life. The plain proof lies in the publication of a newspaper like Excelsior—the *old* Excelsior—and in the stability of a system which allows for the orderly rotation of political power. At the top, at least, Mexico has benefitted enormously, in terms of political dialogue and self-image alike, from cultivating this tradition. It has been a valuable substitute for a two-party system. Mexico has only one party and it has been a source of cultural vitality.

In an earlier article, in the July 11 issue of the Post, Marlise Simons had noted that Excelsior had frequently supported the government. Simons wrote:

For most of the past five years, Excelsior's Christian Democrat policies concurred with the government's own rhetoric on the abuses of over-concentrated wealth and the need for drastic social change.

On many issues considered taboo, however, Excelsior also attacked the government, noting for example that it had repressed independent union activity, that it was unwisely sustaining an over-valued currency and that it had failed explaining the violent deaths of 30 students in June 1971.

Last fall, the administration became angered by Excelsior's criticism of its handling of foreign policy, particularly on the issues of Spain's execution of several Basque terrorists, which the administration condemned, and of Mexico's support for a U.N. resolution equating Zionism with racism. The resignation of Foreign Minister Emilio Rabasa last December was directly related by observers to Excelsior's attack.

Since then, a broad propaganda offensive has been launched against Excelsior in the country's media, with growing evidence of government involvement in the campaign. One official was even quoted as complaining that "we gave you press freedom and now look what you do."

In apparent response to such criticism, Excelsior's new management charged in an advertisement July 26 that Scherer and his aides had inflated the expense accounts of former staff members, siphoned off cooperative money for personal use, mismanaged lands owned by the cooperative and shown favoritism to certain staffers. "It is now up to the attorney general's office to determine the degree of guilt of those responsible," the advertisement said.

The government prevented Scherer from traveling to the U.S. to inform congressmen and newspaper editors of the events surrounding his ouster from Excelsior, the Washington Post reported July 29.

Scherer planned to start a new newspaper, a news magazine and a news agency. He claimed to have sold more than $100,000 worth of shares in the ventures. However, press reports noted that since the government controlled communications and the distribution of newsprint in Mexico, it was unlikely that any of the ventures would succeed.

Leftist Activity & Terrorism

Leftists kill policemen. At least five policemen were killed and another five were wounded June 4 when gunmen in a passing automobile opened fire on about a dozen officers lined up for roll call on a sidewalk in the Mexico City suburb of Ciudad Azteca.

Police said the gunmen left leaflets signed by the Sept. 23rd Communist League, Mexico's largest urban guerrilla group. The league had been held responsible for another mass slaying of policemen May 6 and for the May 25 abduction of a foreign ambassador's daughter.

In the earlier slayings, nine policemen were shot to death in a Mexico City restaurant. Witnesses said that at least one of the attackers had identified himself as a league member. Six of the victims had been acting as bodyguards for the family of Olegario Vazquez Rana, a wealthy furniture executive.

The abduction involved Nadine Chaval, 16, daughter of Belgian Ambassador Andre Chaval, who was on her way to school in Mexico City when she was kidnapped. The league took responsibility for the abduction and claimed it had meant to kidnap the ambassador. Nadine was released May 29 after the league was paid a $408,000 ransom.

Soccer official kidnapped, freed for ransom. Juan de Dios de la Torre, an industrialist who headed the Mexican Football (Soccer) Federation, was kidnapped in Guadalajara March 8 by a group calling itself the Fidel Castro Guerrilla Command. He was released March 16 after payment of an undisclosed ransom. The guerrilla unit had not previously been noted publicly.

Guadalajara police capture 5 guerrillas. Police in Guadalajara said they had arrested five members of the People's Revolutionary Armed Forces, a small guerrilla group which was reported to have joined the Sept. 23rd Communist League in 1975, the Miami Herald reported May 6.

Student unrest. Police invaded the Autonomous University of Puebla May 4 and freed 10 hostages who had been held in a university building for two weeks by right-wing students.

The rightists, who demanded the resignation of the university's Communist rector, had killed one person and seized more than 50 hostages in taking over the building April 20. They subsequently released most of the hostages when riot police surrounded the university but did not attack for fear of provoking further violence.

A student was killed and about a dozen were wounded in fresh clashes between rightist and leftist students in Puebla April 28–29. The rightists charged April 29 that Rector Luis Rivera Terrazas had obtained arms, ammunition and explosives for leftist groups. Rivera denied the charge and urged the police to dislodge the rightists and free the hostages.

At the University of Sonora in Hermosillo, about 50 students were injured April 30 in clashes between rightists and leftists. Classes at the university had been virtually paralyzed for two months because of student unrest.

At the National Autonomous University in Mexico City, the nation's largest university, Rector Guillermo Soberon called April 28 for the elimination of right-wing paramilitary groups that had provoked bloody clashes with leftist and other students.

The groups, called "porros," were financed by powerful political interests and were used by deans at the university to maintain internal order, according to student sources cited by the French news agency Agence France-Presse. Porros had taken control of student organizations and sold arms and narcotics in the university, AFP reported.

In response to Soberon's appeal, the police had begun investigations and established "a system of vigilance in the schools," AFP noted.

Peasants, soldiers clash. Fifty-eight peasants and two soldiers were killed May

MEXICO

11-12 in gun battles in the municipality of Venustiano Carranza, Chiapas State.

The troops had been called in by the local mayor after peasants demanding land reportedly killed three prominent landowners. During the ensuing clashes the peasants cut telephone and telegraph wires, severing communications. Most of the peasants were armed with machine-guns, rifles and small arms, the Spanish news agency EFE said May 13.

The army had intervened in Sonora State April 8 to disarm and dislodge peasants who had occupied more than 1,000 acres of privately owned land. No one was reported injured in that action.

Luers downgrades leftist role. U.S. Deputy Assistant State Secretary (for Inter-American Affairs) William H. Luers told the International Political & Military Affairs Subcommittee of the U.S. House Committee on International Relations June 15 that leftist influence and terrorism in Mexico were weak and of little importance. He said:

With regard to Mexico, we believe that recent allegations that the Mexican Government is taking Mexico down the Chilean and Cuban road to socialism are unfounded. Those who make these allegations cite what they characterize as government supported land seizures, policies directed against foreign investment and the influence of Chilean exiles on government policies.

In discussing Mexico, it must be borne in mind that Mexico is a proudly independent country. The tenacity with which it holds to its independence is heightened by geography—it is our neighbor and highly sensitive to us and signs of any designs to undermine its independence. Decisions Mexico takes to respond to what it perceives as its internal problems are purely Mexican decisions. It does not seek or accept influence from foreign sources or proponents of alien ideologies. Its political system, which has evolved over the 66 years since the Mexican Revolution, is eclectic and unique.

The allegation that Chilean exiles are influential in the development of Mexican policy and actions can be looked at in context. Mexico has a long record of liberalism in granting political asylum. At the end of the Spanish Civil War, Mexico accepted many Republican exiles. It did the same after 1960 in accepting anti-Castro Cuban exiles, and following the overthrow of the Allende Government in Chile it accepted more than 100 prominent Chileans, plus a large number of their dependents, and assisted them in finding gainful employment.

Some of these exiles were given government positions. But there is no evidence that these or any other foreign advisors have significantly influenced the policies or programs of this large and resourceful nation. Mexico has a highly organized governing political party and a vast reservoir of educated technicians who are fully competent to run the nation.

With regard to internal far leftist organizations in Mexico, Communist and radical Marxist parties are legal but are small and weak. The government party—the PRI—has been successful in encompassing a wide spectrum of political thought and activity. Because Mexico's own revolutionary tradition is expressed by the PRI, it is difficult for the Marxist parties to build a following.

The Mexican Communist Party (PCM) has only an estimated 5,000 members, not enough under Mexican law to qualify for registration. Since 1968 when the Russians invaded Czechoslovakia, the PCM has followed a line relatively independent of Moscow. There is also evidence of strain within the party over the issue of the degree of support to be given to student activism.

The Popular Socialist Party (PSS) is a loosely organized party which claims 75,000 members. It has carefully refrained from advocating violence or opposing the goals of the Mexican Revolution. It has endorsed the PRI presidential candidate since 1958, while running some of its own congressional and gubernatorial candidates.

The PCM and the PPS have disavowed terrorism. The principal terrorist organizations in Mexico are the 23rd of September Communist League (which has been disavowed by the PCM), the Poor Peoples' Army, and the Peoples Armed Revolutionary Army. Strong Mexican government anti-terrorist measures resulted in an abatement of terrorism during 1975.

The 23rd of September Communist League is apparently the only group still active. They have claimed credit for several bombings, the murder of a police patrolman, and the recent kidnapping of the Belgian Ambassador's daughter. The 23rd of September League is an irritant to the GOM but not a threat to political stability. We know of no current Cuban connection to these terrorist groups.

Allegations that recent measures and actions by the Government of Mexico are "communist inspired," and against private domestic and foreign investment, do not hold up under scrutiny. There has, of course, been some controversy within Mexico over some of the government's recent proposals, a phenomenon that is inevitable in an open society in which various sectors do not always have identical interests.

With regard to alleged attacks on private property, the Government of Mexico has made it clear that it does not accept or tolerate violence as a means of furthering land reform any more than it will tolerate private land holdings in excess of the limits imposed by its Constitution. It has also acknowledged that the so-called "land invasions" are in part a result of the frustration of small farmers over their lack of adequate land. In a visit to Sonora on April 21, President Echeverria forcefully stated that the Government of Mexico would not tolerate land invasions and reaffirmed his government's commitment to the rule of law in regard to both squatters and property owners. The same theme has been sounded by Jose Lopez Portillo, the Presidential candidate of the ruling Institutional Revolutionary Party (PRI). Thus, while there have been land invasions, on occasion stimulated by leftist agitators, there is no official endorsement of such invasions.

Those who allege a drift towards Communism in Mexico also cite recent Mexican legislation—a Law on Human Settlements, which was opposed by some sectors in Mexico as an unconstitutional attack on private property. This law essentially gives authority to the government to regulate exploding urban growth through land use planning measures accepted in some industrialized countries. The Government of Mexico, in heeding the criticism expressed by some groups in Mexico, proposed some modifications of the original proposal by expressly stating that the law would not be used to expropriate private residences; by creating mechanisms to afford relief to property owners who might be affected; by excluding retroactivity; and by reaffirming its commitment to the concept of private property.

With regard to the general question of foreign investment, the Government of Mexico has made it clear that it wants and needs foreign investment that will be of benefit to Mexico's economy and development, but does not want investment that does not meet its needs. Foreign investors, including U.S. investors, continue to find investment attractive in Mexico, under the ground rules established by the Mexican Government. Mexico has a healthy and mixed economy with both private and public enterprise. The private sector within Mexico accounts for the largest part of total industrial production apart from petroleum, and the government continues to encourage its mixed economy. The long-range trend in Mexico, as in many countries of Western Europe, may well be toward greater state involvement in the dominant sectors of the economy. But we see little chance of dramatic shifts and anticipate that the private sector will continue to play a key role.

With regard to allegations that an "amnesty" of persons jailed as a result of student riots in 1968 is evidence of a trend towards Communism, it should be noted that most of the several hundred persons apprehended at that time have long since been released from jail on bail. The amnesty legislation was welcomed by both the left and right in Mexico as a measure which finally put the tragic events of 1968 to rest.

U.S. Congressmen warn of leftist trend. Thirty conservative members of the U.S. House of Representatives had warned U.S. President Ford May 5 of what they conceived to be a dangerous leftist trend in Mexico. In an Aug. 10 letter to Ford, 76 U.S. Congressmen renewed this warning to Ford. They said in the letter:

Since the fourteenth of April, at least thirty-five excerpts from the Mexican press have been inserted in the Congressional Record in a sincere effort to illustrate points of concern, and to provide the documentation which critics invariably demand—and invaribaly ignore.

It would be interesting to learn what favorable interpretation can be placed upon the following:

(1) The amnesty recenty provided for hundreds of Soviet agents who provided leadership for the bloody events of 1968, when hundreds of Mexicans were killed in summer-long disturbances.

(2) The placement of at least a thousand non-Mexican Communists and radicals in key government and journalistic positions in Mexico.

(3) The Mexican government's drive to increase political, economic, and "cultural" ties with every Communist nation on earth.

(4) The dismissal, by President Echeverria, of waves of terrorist atacks as mere "diversion" and "provocations" which are not the fault of self-proclaimed leftist revolutionaries.

(5) The recent changes in the Mexican Constitution to cut away the legal basis of private property.

(6) The recent introduction of Castroite textbooks, for compulsory use in all Mexican schools.

(7) The persistent employment of Communist, rhetoric, anti-American demagoguery, and calls for domestic class warfare from the highest Mexican officials.

(8) Government inaction in the face of thousands of land seizures taking place all across Mexico, often by armed gangs under non-Mexican leadership.

(9) Open declarations that collectivization of the counrtyside is the government's goal, combined with heavy government pressure on the rural population to join collectives.

Surely we are not expected to overlook the lesson of Cuba, when all our official "experts" and media pundits assured us that Fidel Castro had no intention of imposing Communism upon the Cuban people. As a result, the Cubans were enslaved, except for one Cuban in ten who escaped to the United States, and a Soviet base has been implanted ninety miles from Florida.

The present one-party government of Mexico is folowing a similar path. For moral and humanitarian reason alone, we should prefer not to see 65 million Mexicans forced to choose between slavery and exile. And for overwhelmingly important strategic reasons, we should prefer not to see what some Mexican writers can already visualize—a Cactus Curtain along the Rio Grande.

For all these reasons and more, we ask your assurance that the developing situation in Mexico is receiving the deep attention which it merits.

Jailed leftists escape. Six members of the September 23rd Communist League, the major Mexican terrorist group, escaped from the Jalisco State Penitentiary in Guadalajara in a violent operation that left two prison guards dead and another seriously wounded, police announced Jan. 23.

Alleged guerrilla leader killed. David Jimenez Sarmiento, alleged leader of the Sept. 23rd Communist League, was killed Aug. 11 when he and three other alleged guerrillas attacked the sister of President-elect Jose Lopez Portillo in Mexico City.

Police said that the attackers had opened fire on the automobile in which Margarita Lopez Portillo was being driven to work. Her bodyguards returned the fire. Sarmiento and one bodyguard were killed and three persons, including one attacker, were wounded in the shootout.

Police arrested more than 50 persons in raids in Mexico City after the attack, officials reported Aug. 12. The wounded attacker, Olivia Ledesma de Hernandez, was arrested not far from the site of the shootout, the London newsletter Latin America said Aug. 20.

Sarmiento's death led police to speculate that they would soon eliminate the Sept. 23rd Communist League and leftist terrorism in general, the New York Times reported Aug. 22. However, observers questioned whether the league in fact existed. They speculated that attacks attributed to the league might be acts of provocation by extreme rightists.

Unlike other leftist groups, the league never published political propaganda or manifestos explaining its actions, the Washington Post noted June 6. Its ransom demands for kidnap victims were always for money and never for the release of imprisoned colleagues. While other extreme leftist groups had earned some sympathy and admiration by kidnapping and denouncing high government officials, the league had provoked only public outcries by ambushing low-ranking policemen, the Post said.

Persons who recently had been arrested as league members had no history of political involvement, and leftist organizations and student groups said that they had never heard of them, the Post said. Mexico City newspapers had printed excerpts of a letter from seven imprisoned members of the original Sept. 23rd Communist League, founded in 1970. The letter said that the organization no longer existed, having "crumbled under the effect of repression and the exacerbation of its own internal contradictions," the Post reported.

Mexico City bombings. A number of bombs exploded in Mexico City late Nov. 29, causing police to increase security for the inauguration of President Jose Lopez Portillo Dec. 1.

The blasts, at buildings housing a travel agency, two banks, the Confederation of Chambers of Commerce and Johnson & Johnson, an American firm, injured two persons and caused an estimated $100,000 worth of damage. Police blamed the explosions on the Sept. 23rd Communist League, but offered no proof that the terrorist group had been responsible.

Economic Developments

Underemployment high. Underemployment was reported high at the beginning of 1976.

More than half of Mexico's workers were underemployed, either earning less than the national average minimum wage or unable to find full-time jobs, according to researchers at the College of Mexico cited by the Herald Jan. 21. In Mexico City 23% of men between the ages of 21 and 60 earned less than the minimum, while in rural areas the figure was close to 62%, the researchers reported.

Inflation down in '75. The inflation rate had fallen to 11.3% in 1975 from 20.6% the year before, according to statistics of the Bank of Mexico reported by the Miami Herald Jan. 18. In December 1975 the consumer price index had risen by less than 1% for the sixth consecutive month.

Oil. It was reported Jan. 2 that Pemex, the state oil company, planned to invest $640 million to build, in the state of Veracruz, one of the largest petrochemical complexes in Latin America. The complex was to include an ethylene plant with a 500,000-ton annual output.

Mexico's proved oil reserves totaled 6.03 billion barrels, enough for 15 years of internal consumption, according to a Pemex official quoted in the Latin America Economic Report Jan. 16. Only 12% of Mexico had been explored for oil, the Report noted.

In an Aug. 20 statement, Pemex said that new petroleum discoveries of "singular importance" had been discovered in the western state of Baja California Sur, with "very attractive possibilities for immediate development."

It was reported Aug. 31 that Pemex planned to increase crude-oil production at the Reforma fields in Chiapas State to 500,200 barrels per day by the end of 1976. The fields were producing 400,127 barrels per day at the end of 1975.

Foreign loans negotiated. A consortium of banks headed by the Deutsche Bank of West Germany would lend Mexico $300 million over five years, primarily to finance public sector investment, it was reported Jan. 2. The loan, announced in December 1975, was the largest single loan negotiated by Mexico in the year.

The Inter-American Development Bank approved three loans for Mexico totaling $81.8 million, it was reported June 18. The loans would help finance agricultural, water-service and tourism development projects.

Industrial developments. Among industrial developments announced in early 1976:

The steel company Altos Hornos de Mexico and the Brazilian state firm Cia. Vale do Rio Doce planned a joint venture to produce partially reduced iron for steel production, it was reported Jan. 9. Initial output would be 4 million tons per year beginning in 1980.

The government had bought the company Fertilizantes Fosfatados Mexicanos, which controlled about 80% of the world market in phosphoric acid, it was reported Jan. 23.

U.S.-Mexican session on joint problems. Representatives of the U.S. and Mexican governments and banks and industry in both countries agreed in San Antonio, Texas Jan. 26 to seek ways to resolve "some important differences in the political arena" in an effort to improve cooperation in investment, trade and industry. One problem cited by the U.S. delegation was Mexico's recent support for resolutions in the United Nations equating Zionism and racism.

The members of the U.S. delegation, headed by Sen. Jacob Javits (R, N.Y.), included Alden W. Clausen, president of Bank of America, and Robert Grimble, director of E. I. DuPont de Nemours International. The Mexican delegation, headed by Finance Minister Mario Beteta and Commerce and Industry Minister Jose Campillo Sainz, included Agustin Legarreta, president of the National Bank of Mexico.

Tire companies admit payoffs. Executives of Mexican tire companies said they had paid the former manager of the Mexican Chamber of Rubber Industries for his role in obtaining government approval of tire-price increases, according to a statement released by the Mexican attorney general's office and reported by the Miami Herald May 19.

The executives claimed that they had made the payment after prices were increased and that they had committed "no illegal act which could be interpreted as a bribe," the attorney general's office said. Prices were increased in 1974 and last February. Antonio Navarro, the former chamber manager, denied receiving any payment.

The U.S. Securities and Exchange Commission had charged in a suit May 10 that General Tire & Rubber Co. of the U.S., through its Mexican subsidiary, General Popo, had paid $240,000 in bribes to obtain price increases.

In an earlier development, Rollins Inc., a U.S.-based advertising firm, admitted March 3 that it had paid more than $100,000 in bribes to municipal authorities in Mexico City and that it "expected" to

MEXICO

continue making payments "because it is a custom" there.

200-mile offshore limit established. The government June 6 established a 200-mile offshore "economic zone," restricting fishing and mining off Mexico's Pacific and Gulf coasts and closing the Gulf of California to foreign fishermen.

A constitutional amendment gave the government control of all "exploitation" in the zone, including the harvest of marine life and minerals. The waters of the Gulf of California, which divided Baja California from mainland Mexico, became "interior waters" under Mexican jurisdiction.

Foreign fishing boats would be allowed in the "economic zone" only after purchasing government permits. Foreign fishing rights would be reduced and the long-range goal would be "total exclusion," Jorge Castaneda, Mexico's foreign affairs undersecretary, said.

U.S. Sen. Lawton Chiles (D, Fla.) told the U.S. Senate Aug. 3 that Mexico had been uncooperative in efforts to work out agreements on fishing grounds. He said:

Since the beginning of this country, and the early beginnings of our neighbor to the south, Mexico, fishermen of both countries have utilized the gulf. The gulf fishery moves in cycles and for that reason it is essential that our fishermen move from time to time in order to maintain a steady production and to keep our processing plants in full employment.

While we have recognized a 12-mile limit off the United States for fishing purposes, our fleets have historically fished up to 12 miles of the Mexican baseline, and Mexican vessels have done likewise off certain points of the United States.

Mexico recently declared a 200-mile limit to go into effect July 27, 1976. We have declared a 200-mile economic zone which will become effective March 1, 1977. Inasmuch as it is the stated position of the U.S. Government that U.S. shrimp fleet catches off Mexico have historically been from the surplus of shrimp over and above the Mexican fleet's actual catch records, it is a resource which should be readily available to continued fishing by U.S.-flag vessels.

This is especially significant in light of the fact that shrimp has a 1-year life span and after approximately 12 to 14 months will die a natural death if not harvested. Our distant water fleets have historically taken upward of 10 million pounds of shrimp off those fishing grounds, and these 10 million pounds have been an important factor in maintaining level and continuing employment in our processing plants.

Furthermore, Mexico, who has a desire to expand its fishing fleets, has had an opportunity to fish up to 12 miles of our baseline, and, under the statutory provisions of our 200-mile economic fishing zone would be permitted to continue doing so for such fish stocks where surpluses exist. In addition, our country represents a market for approximately $200 million worth of shrimp each year from Mexican production, and the bulk of all Mexican seafood production comes into our markets. However, in recent talks with Mexican officials, our Government and its industry representatives have been faced with an unsympathetic neighbor who has displayed no concern for our interest and needs, or the fact that a resource will waste. They have merely pointed to mathematical projections as justification for denying our fleets access to these fishery grounds where we have traditionally fished. They have ignored statesmanlike offers by U.S. industry representatives and have quoted our 200-mile economic zone provisions when beneficial to their cause, and ignored it when it tended to conflict with their interest.

Further, they have indicated a belief that the United States lacks the will and determination to enforce each and every aspect of that law—most notably those provisions which require embargoing seafood products from countries which refuse to negotiate in good conscience to provide access to fishery surpluses.

Peso floated. The Mexican government allowed the peso to float Aug. 31, ending its 22-year fixed parity with the U.S. dollar. After the peso fluctuated for nearly two weeks, the government Sept. 12 stabilized the exchange rate at 19.9 pesos to the dollar, an effective devaluation of 37% from the previous fixed rate of 12.5 pesos to the dollar.

(Devaluations of foreign currencies were calculated by the fall in their value relative to the U.S. dollar. Before the float, the Mexican peso was worth 8 U.S. cents; after the float, it was worth just over 5¢, for a devaluation of about 37%.)

The principal goal of the devaluation was to improve Mexico's balance-of-payments deficit, which had risen more than 400% since 1970 to about $4 billion, Finance Minister Mario Ramon Beteta said Aug. 31. Speculation against the peso had grown in recent months because of the deficit, Mexico's large foreign debt, its high inflation rate and a widespread belief that President-elect Jose Lopez Portillo would be forced to devalue the currency formally after he took office in December, according to the New York Times Sept. 1.

Mexico City bankers and businessmen welcomed the devaluation, the Times reported Sept. 2. They said the move might cause a short-term wave of inflation, but that it would eventually strengthen the economy.

To offset the devaluation's inflationary effect, President Luis Echeverria said Sept. 1 that the government would:

■ Adjust the salaries of civil servants and members of the armed forces.

■ Promote similar wage compensation for all other workers.

■ Enact "strict, and if necessary, extended control" of prices of consumer goods and raw materials.

■ Increase the interest rate paid to holders of small savings accounts.

■ Impose a surcharge on exports, canceling export tax credits.

■ Reduce import tariffs and eliminate "unnecessary controls" on imports.

■ Impose a special tax on "unusual or excessive profits arising from an exaggerated markup on prices of goods and services."

During the first week of the peso float the value of the currency fell sharply, prices soared and workers demanded substantial wage increases.

The Bank of Mexico was selling the dollar for 20.6 pesos Sept. 2 and for 20.45 pesos Sept. 3. Over the Sept. 4–5 weekend, with banks closed, black-market dealers in tourist areas sold dollars for 27 pesos and bought them for 19. Some shopkeepers set their own rates. A large music store, which sold musical scores that were imported from the U.S. and marked with U.S. prices, set its rate at 22 pesos to the dollar.

Prices rose sharply despite pleas from the government and the closing of 490 shops for hoarding or hiking prices without authorization, the Journal of Commerce said Sept. 7. Prices on items from food to furniture were up 20%–60%, the newspaper reported. Some stores doubled the price of fresh vegetables, according to the Sept. 9 Miami Herald.

As a result, workers demanded large wage increases.

Implementing its anti-inflation measures, the government ended an 11%–16% export-tax subsidy Sept. 1 and imposed stiff new export taxes Sept. 8. New taxes to discourage imports also were imposed Sept. 8, ranging from a 2% levy on airplane parts to 75% on rugs, jewelry and other luxury items. The new duties were criticized as unnecessary by Jorge Sanchez Mejorada, president of the Confederation of Industrial Chambers, and Joaquin Pria Olavarrieta, president of the National Chamber of Processing Industries, the Journal of Commerce reported Sept. 13.

Echeverria, in an appearance at a Mexican trade fair in San Antonio, Tex. Sept. 7, defended the peso float and the government's subsequent financial measures. He said Mexico was striving to strengthen its domestic monetary situation by helping its manufacturers capture a larger share of the U.S. market.

The fair, called MexFair '76, was the largest held by Mexico in the U.S., with several thousand products exhibited by more than 750 companies. The items ranged from sophisticated electric goods to delicate hand-made artisan ware. Mexico had held a trade fair annually in San Antonio since 1972.

(Mexico's trade deficit with the U.S. had decreased 13.1% in the first half of 1976, compared with the first six months of 1975, the Journal of Commerce reported Sept. 8. Mexico's overall trade deficit had fallen 12.4% in the January–June period, the Journal reported Aug. 23. About 60% of Mexico's exports went to the U.S.)

Foreign Affairs & Other Developments

Conditions set for Spain ties. Jose Lopez Portillo, presidential candidate of the ruling Institutional Revolutionary Party, said Mexico would not resume diplomatic relations with Spain until there was "a clear and broad democratic opening" in Madrid and Spanish exiles could "return home with dignity," it was reported Jan. 10.

In an apparent overture to Spain after the death of Generalissimo Francisco Franco, Mexican National Patrimony Minister Francisco Javier Alejo had conferred for two hours with Spanish Foreign Minister Jose Maria de Areilza in Paris Dec. 17, 1975. However, Areilza reportedly had told him the time was not ripe for a renewal of relations because some senior military and government officials in Spain were still bitter about Mexico's denunciations of the Franco government after it executed several convicted terrorists in September 1975, accordng to the New York Times.

It was Alejo's meeting with Areilza—and not the controversy over Mexico's support of a United Nations resolution equating Zionism and racism—which had caused the resignation in December 1975 of Mexican Foreign Minister Emilio Rabasa, who was angered by the selection of Alejo for such an important diplomatic mission, according to the Financial Times of London Jan. 8.

Prison torture detailed. Witnesses testified at a U.S. congressional hearing Jan. 15 that hundreds of American citizens held in Mexican jails were tortured, sometimes with U.S. agents looking on approvingly.

Many American prisoners were arrested in Mexico without charges or evidence, and were beaten, shocked with electrical wires and forced to pay thousands of dollars to unscrupulous lawyers and corrupt officials, the witnesses charged.

One witness, Mrs. Charles Harrison of Santa Ana, Calif., read a statement by her daughter, Karen, who had been arrested at the Mexico City airport with her husband. A U.S. agent identified as Arthur Sedillo had watched the husband tortured with electric shock and had recommended that he and Karen "cooperate fully with the Mexican government, as they were serious as could be about taking people for rides or throwing me in the river," Karen's statement said.

The hearing was held in Los Angeles by Rep. Barry M. Goldwater Jr. (R, Calif.), who said that despite mounting concern over the treatment of U.S. prisoners in Mexico, "sometimes you have to hit the State Department over the head to get their attention. This is another whack with the two-by-four."

Americans flee Mexican jail. Fourteen American prisoners escaped from the jail in Piedras Negras (Coahuila State) and crossed the U.S. border safely March 12 after they had been freed by three raiders who surprised prison guards at gunpoint.

The raid was led by Donald Fielden, an unemployed Dallas truck driver, and financed by Dr. Sterling Blake Davis, a Dallas psychologist and father of one of the escaped prisoners, the Dallas Times Herald reported May 9. Fielden told the newspaper his fee had been $5,000.

Fielden surrendered to federal authorities in Dallas May 13 and was charged with exporting a firearm to Mexico without a license. He was freed on $5,000 bail. Mexico asked the U.S. to extradite the escaped prisoners, all of whom had been held on narcotics charges, it was reported May 15. The U.S. gave no indication that it would comply.

Following the escape the deputy chief of the Piedras Negras jail was fired and at least eight other jail employes were placed under investigation by the Mexican attorney general's office, it was reported March 18.

Four nations vow antidrug effort. Mexico, Colombia, Panama and Costa Rica had agreed to establish joint commissions with the U.S. to combat the illegal narcotics traffic, according to a statement Jan. 20 by two New York congressmen, Lester L. Wolff (D) and Benjamin A. Gilman (R).

Wolff said he and Gilman had learned that the U.S. annually received $1 billion worth of Mexican heroin and cocaine and $500 million worth of Colombian narcotics. He noted that by March "17,000 opium fields in Mexico" would be in bloom.

Wolff commended Mexico for using herbicides in a new campaign against illegal opium poppy cultivation, but added that he was "very disappointed that to this point only 10%–15% of the Mexican poppy fields have been destroyed."

Mexico, which supplied an estimated 70%–90% of the heroin consumed in the U.S., had launched a broad campaign against the narcotics traffic in December 1975 in close collaboration with agents of the U.S. Drug Enforcement Administration, the New York Times reported Jan. 2. The results of the program's first month showed a sharp increase in the amount of pure heroin seized and poppy fields destroyed, according to the Times.

To carry out the program, 200 Mexican agents had been trained over the previous year by French, British, U.S. and Mexican specialists. Most of their equipment was donated by the U.S.—including 27 helicopters, nine fixed-wing aircraft and two aerial photographic systems—but the campaign was run exclusively by Mexico, with about 20 U.S. agents exchanging information with their Mexican counterparts, the Times reported.

U.S. Attorney General Edward Levi had visited Mexico secretly Dec. 29, 1975, conferring with Mexican Attorney General Pedro Ojeda Paullada on the narcotics traffic and delivering a message from President Ford to Mexican President Luis Encheverria Alvarez, the Mexican newspaper Excelsior reported Jan. 19. Ford had said a few days earlier that he had spoken personally with Echeverria about the drug problem, though he did not specify when.

■ Mexican officials said March 5 that they had broken up a major drug ring with U.S. connections, arresting 23 persons and seizing more than $14 million worth of cocaine and heroin. Three of those arrested were Colombians who allegedly brought narcotics into Mexico.

■ Sources of the oversight and investigations subcommittee of the U.S. House of Representatives' Interstate and Foreign Commerce Committee said April 14 that Mexican drug merchants were trading narcotics for arms stolen from U.S. military bases. Hundreds of U.S. weapons including M-16 rifles had been confiscated from arrested drug dealers, the sources said.

Opium poppy fields destroyed. Mexico and the U.S. announced June 8 that most of the opium poppy fields in Mexico—the major source of heroin entering the U.S.—had been destroyed in an intensified joint eradication campaign.

The campaign's effect might not be "fully felt" in the U.S. heroin market in 1976, according to U.S. Attorney General Edward Levi. He and Mexican Attorney General Pedro Ojeda Paullada announced the campaign's success at a press conference in Washington.

The announcement followed reports that the campaign was endangered by growing friction between narcotics agencies of the two countries, the Washington Post noted June 9. A Post correspondent in Mexico reported that Mexican officials were angry at what one characterized as "insolent and inept behavior" by U.S. Drug Enforcement Administration (DEA) officials in Mexico.

Mexican sources charged that "American agents and agents provocateur are acting against our wills and behind our backs" to engage in entrapment of narcotics dealers and other activities that were illegal in Mexico, the Post reported.

The charges were denied in Washington by Ojeda Paullada and by DEA Administrator Peter Bensinger. However, some DEA officials said privately that Mexico had certain complaints about U.S. activities. The officials said that the U.S. had acted on these complaints and resolved them.

Alejandro Gertz, head of the Mexican anti-drug campaign, had charged March 16 that the DEA was inefficient and uncooperative and that the U.S. was making Mexico the scapegoat for its "own inability" to break up American drug rings. Gertz spoke in reply to U.S. Rep. Lester L. Wolff (D, N.Y.), who had said March 15 that high Mexican officials were protecting drug merchants. Wolff added March 17 that the drug traffic had political protection not only in Mexico but in the U.S. and other countries.

Defending the Mexican campaign, Gertz declared: "The narcotics problem won't be resolved until the American market is wiped out. Why do so many U.S. authorities want to discuss the market problem here in Mexico instead of over there?"

Following Gertz' protest the U.S. State Department praised Mexico March 18 for its "intense effort" to curb the flow of heroin into the U.S.

U.S.-Mexican Interparliamentary Conference. U.S. and Mexican legislators participated in the 15th Mexico-U.S. Interparliamentary Conference, which was held Feb. 25–29 in Atlanta, Ga. Developments of the conference, according to a summary provided by Sen. Mike Mansfield (D, Mont.):

The work of the Conference was organized into two Committees: Political Affairs and Economic and Social Affairs.

Committee I—Political affairs

During the committee's discussions on bilateral relations it was agreed that generally, Mexico-United States relations were good if not excellent. At the broader level, however, the Mexican delegates pointed out considerable differences of opinion which reflect the global political, military, and economic interests of the United States.

After considering Cuban intervention in Angola, the Mexican delegation reaffirmed the country's traditional opposition to intervention in the internal affairs of one country by another.

The Organization of American States and the proposed amendment to the Rio Treaty were reviewed in detail by the Mexican delegation during the committee meeting. This review demonstrated the considerable lack of consensus among the OAS countries on such matters as ideological pluralism, sovereignty over natural resources, and collective economic security. Specifically, the Mexican delegates affirmed their country's conviction that collective economic security is vital to the peace and well being of the hemisphere. Regarding the proposed amendments to the Rio Treaty, the U.S. delegates expressed some reservations, whereas the Mexican delegation explained that Mexico regarded the treaty as an alliance for cooperation rather than a military pact.

In reference to narcotics control, discussants expressed the view that major efforts were being undertaken by both countries. Both delegations praised President Echeverria's proposal to establish parallel national commissions to oversee the drug traffic curtailment efforts.

The committee's consideration of the Law of the Sea focused on efforts within the United Nations to obtain a comprehensive law of the sea agreement, and on national legislation creating 200-mile fishery or economic zones. Both delegations expressed hope that the United Nations would complete its work on these issues this year.

The subject of human rights elicited concern from U.S. delegates regarding the treatment of Americans in jail in Mexico, and from the Mexican delegation over the detention of Mexican aliens in the United States. Both delegations agreed that all nations could do better in implementing the U.N. Declaration on Human Rights.

Committee II—Economic and social affairs

The first topic discussed was inflation and development. Commenting on worldwide inflation and the adverse effects on Mexico's balance of payments when the costs of manufactured goods rise, the Mexican Chairman emphasized the importance of a more equitable international economic system to reduce the impact of recessions in the developed countries on the less developed ones. This world economic situation heightened the U.S. appreciation for the interdependence of nations, an appreciation demonstrated by the recent, major U.S. contribution to the International Monetary Fund (IMF). Attention was also called to Secretary Kissinger's address to the Seventh Special Session of the U.N. General Assembly in September 1975, which proposed various measures to improve the economies of developing countries.

On bilateral exchange of goods and services, a U.S. delegate suggested the possibility of negotiating long-term agreements whereby Mexico would provide crude oil exports to the United States of certain key Mexican products. The Mexican delegation stated that although their recent oil discoveries did not put them on the scale with the Middle East, they expected exports of crude oil to increase significantly in the future.

Considerable discussion was also devoted to Mexico's "twin plants" Border Industry Program which was established in 1965 to alleviate high unemployment along the border. The Mexican delegation pointed out that the activities of these 550 plants had slowed by January 1975 but a U.S. delegate noted that this was a result of the recession, in the United States and higher costs in Mexico.

In his opening statement, the Mexican Chairman observed that the Charter of Economic Rights and Duties of States, originally proposed by President Echeverria, had been adopted by the United Nations on December 12, 1974. Essentially, the charter removed the concept of economic cooperation from good will and gave it a standing in international law. The U.S. delegation responded, noting that the United States and other industrialized countries, had objected only to certain provisions regarding foreign investment, expropriation, primary commodities, producer cartels, indexation of prices and similar provisions. Because certain amendments had not been accepted, universal adherence to the Charter had not been established. At the request of the Mexican delegation, members of the U.S. delegation in Committee II agreed to discuss the Charter with officials in the U.S. executive branch.

Tourism was mentioned by the Mexican delegation as an industry which continues to be important to the Mexican economy. The recent decline of American tourists and tourists receipts was regretted, although it was understood that this was a consequence of worsening economic conditions in the United States.

The Mexican delegation noted the efforts to stimulate American interest in travel to Mexico and the establishment of centers to prepare Mexicans for employment in the tourist industry. An American delegate noted that some of the decline in U.S. tourists to Mexico could be attributed to Mexico's support of the so-called "Zionism" resolution in the United Nations. Moreover, he cited the lack of competitive air fares as another deterrent to tourists. On the other hand, the Mexican decision to rescind the 15 percent restaurant tax for foreign visitors was a welcome development. Finally, the Mexicans again suggested that the $100 customs exemption for returning U.S. residents be increased, especially in view of recent inflationary factors.

The Mexican delegates expressed dissatisfaction with the U.S. Trade Act of 1974. Particularly, the delegates noted that restricting the application of the General System of Tariff Preferences would work to the detriment of Mexican exports since textiles, footwear, electronic parts, steel, and glass were exempted from coverage. The Mexican delegates also dealt with certain nontariff restrictions, such as import quotas, which severely curtail Mexican exports of cotton and tomatoes.

The U.S. delegates, observed that trade restrictions were two-sided, citing lemon oil as well as other deciduous fruits as items which have long been excluded from the Mexican market, even though they do not compete with Mexican production. In 1974, moreover, American-produced beef, dairy products, and quarterhorses were subjected to high tariff rates, until somewhat modified in 1975. The U.S. delegation also cited the Mexican system of licensing as another obstacle to free trade as well as the de facto tariffs implied by the Mexican pricing structure. In conclusion, the U.S. delegation stated that an easing of trade regulations was unlikely unless reciprocated by the Mexicans. Responding to Mexican criticisms, the U.S. delegation noted that Mexico in particular, and Latin America in general, could expect substantial benefits from the new GSP provision of the trade act.

Efforts to promote a common Latin American economic system (SELA) were outlined in a paper by a Mexican delegate, noting that Mexico had led a one year initiative before the adoption of the Charter in October 1975, by twenty-three Latin American countries, including Cuba. Members of the U.S. delegation welcomed the assurance that SELA was intended to enhance cooperation, not divisiveness, among all nations of the hemisphere.

In discussions on migratory workers, the Mexican delegate recalled that the Organization of American States (OAS), at its tenth regular meeting, had adopted the term "non-documented migratory worker" as preferable to the terms commonly used. The U.S. delegates agreed that the new term was to be commended since it tended to reaffirm the principle of work as a fundamental right. The U.S. delegation pointed out, contrary to popular belief, that two-thirds of the migratory work force was engaged in non-agricultural pursuits.

Both delegations cited the October 1974 meeting between President Echeverria and President Ford as a positive step on this issue. At the meeting, President Echeverria noted that a long term solution to the problem depended upon the improvement of economic conditions in Mexico, noting that Mexicans emigrated because of domestic population pressures, the relative unproductiveness of Mexican agriculture, and higher salaries in the United States. Moreover, he noted that this emigration often occurred at Mexico's expense through the loss of better qualified and more productive Mexican workers to U.S. industrial centers.

The U.S. delegation, though in agreement with the above observations over the long run, felt that the establishment of a new "Bracero" program would be a reasonable temporary solution. While Senators from agricultural states favored this approach, it was strongly opposed by U.S. organized labor. It was suggested that the bracero issue be discussed by labor representatives of Mexico and the United States to encourage understanding of the issues involved.

Finally, the U.S. delegation noted that the Rodino bill, which would impose criminal penalties for the hiring of illegal aliens, had passed the House of Representatives on two different occasions and that the United States Supreme Court had upheld a similar California state law. It was agreed that the adoption of such laws would discourage the hiring of Mexicans and or Mexican-Americans especially in doubtful or borderline cases.

In reference to education, the Mexican delegation stressed the importance of learning the history of neighboring countries to improve social and political relations. In particular, it was suggested that bilingual education be encouraged and that similar ideals and historical parallels of Mexico and the United States be pointed out to students. The establishment of the Third World University, which was to open soon pursuant to a UNESCO declaration, was discussed, with U.S. delegates expressing considerable interest. The United States Chairman observed that one problem in the United States was the lack of equal educational opportunities for Mexican-Americans. For instance, despite a shortage of doctors in the United States, degrees from Mexican institutions, especially in medicine and dentistry, were still not being recognized in the United States. Both delegations agreed that student and technical exchange programs should be encouraged.

The U.S. delegates also cited recent developments in solar energy which might prove applicable to the desalinization of water, a problem which affects both Mexico and the United States. Responding to the U.S. comments on the northward flow of sewage from Mexicali in Baja California to San Diego, California, the Mexican delegates stated that the Mexican Government had assumed full responsibility for the problem and had taken some initial corrective steps which had been successful.

At the close, the respective Chairmen of the two delegations expressed full agreement on the usefulness of the Interparliamentary mechanism for increasing mutual understanding of complex problems and respect for the positions of both countries in international affairs.

Hurricane cracks dam; death toll at 630. A 30-foot-high earthen dam in La Paz, Mexico burst Oct. 1 when the resort port city of 60,000 was struck by Hurricane Liza. At least 630 persons were known to have died and more than 350 others were missing, officials said Oct. 6. The Cajoncito River dam collapsed under the force of 130-mile-an-hour winds and five and a half inches of rain and released a five-foot wall of water on the city's shantytown where 10,000 persons lived.

President Luis Echeverria ordered an investigation of the dam's collapse and promised that a new concrete one would replace it. Local officials had charged that the four-year-old dam was poorly constructed, at a cost of $260,000, and was "a permanent menace." The disaster left 30,000 to 70,000 homeless.

La Paz, 700 miles south of San Diego, Calif., was the capital of the state of Baja California Sur.

Trains collide in Mexico. An excursion train collided with a freight train Oct. 10 in the Sierra Madre of northern Mexico. The district attorney's office said Oct. 12 that 15 persons died in the crash, state police put the toll at 19 and the Red Cross put the figure at 24. Two Americans and two Britons were among the dead. The accident was caused by the failure of the passenger train engineer to heed a stop signal, officials said Oct. 12.

Panama

Domestic Affairs & Foreign Involvement

Torrijos in Cuba. Brig. Gen. Omar Torrijos, Panama's military strongman, visited Cuba Jan. 10–15 for talks with Premier Fidel Castro on bilateral issues and on Panama's negotiations with the U.S. over the future of the Panama Canal and Zone.

The two leaders signed an assortment of cultural and technical exchange pacts and agreed that Panama should be patient in the canal negotiations. Agreement on the canal issue undermined leftist Panamanian students who sought an immediate takeover of the canal, according to press reports.

Torrijos thanked Castro Jan. 12 for advising him in recent years "not to fight on a hook" cast by the U.S., and he said Panama would continue to negotiate "calmly" for a new canal treaty. "We are—remember this—in a process of [national] liberation, and one of the means by which that can be reached is through negotiations," Torrijos declared Jan. 15.

Castro publicly advised caution on the canal issue Jan. 12, telling Torrijos: "Time is on our side in the struggle against the imperialists. The struggle of the Panamanian people is not very easy because Panama is small. But to the 1.2 million Panamanians we can now add nine million Cubans." As an example to Torrijos, Castro cited Cuba's tolerance of U.S. naval presence at Guantanamo Bay in eastern Cuba.

(Torrijos had been cautioned against making any comments hostile to the U.S. by Sen. Jacob Javits [R, N.Y.], who visited Panama on the eve of the general's departure for Cuba, it was reported Jan. 11. Javits told Torrijos that Cuba's intervention in the civil war in Angola had "absolutely aborted" prospects for a normalization of relations between Washington and Havana.)

U.S. and Panamanian negotiators insisted talks for a new canal treaty were proceeding on schedule, but both sides had privately agreed not to press the talks toward a conclusion during 1976, a U.S. election year, the Washington Post reported Jan. 17. There was hostility in the U.S. Congress to abandonment of U.S. sovereignty over the canal, and President Ford's Republican challenger, former California Gov. Ronald Reagan, had turned the canal into a campaign issue, charging the Ford Administration was selling out U.S. power in the Western Hemisphere, the Post noted.

Torrijos was awarded Cuba's Jose Marti medal in a ceremony shortly after his arrival in Havana Jan. 10. He was accompanied on the trip by more than 200 Panamanians including workers, students, farmers, businessmen, military officers, folk dancers and Roman Catholic priests.

Regime exiles critics; businessmen strike. The government exiled 11 critics of its policies Jan. 20, provoking business executives in Panama City and Chiriqui Province to begin an indefinite protest strike Jan. 21.

The dissidents, sent to Ecuador, were described by the regime as right-wing subversives, but they included Alberto Quiros Guardia, the socialist owner of the radio station Radio Impacto. The other exiles were conservative business leaders and independent lawyers who had criticized the government's social and economic policies and its handling of negotiations with the U.S. for a new treaty to govern the Panama Canal and Zone.

The exiles were among 15 persons reportedly arrested Jan. 15 after business leaders and lawyers held a conference in David (Chiriqui Province) at which the government's agrarian policies and its suppression of civil and political liberties were criticized. The government charged Jan. 20 that its detractors at David had planned "to undermine the security of the state, above all in economic and farming matters."

The regime charged Jan. 21 that the exiles had also tried to undermine the canal treaty negotiations in cooperation with Arnulfo Arias, the exiled former president, and Ronald Reagan, the U.S. Republican presidential candidate. A government communique cited a recent meeting in Florida between Reagan and Arias at which Reagan allegedly said the canal negotiations would be easier if Panama were led by Arias and not Brig. Gen. Omar Torrijos, the current military strongman.

(A spokesman for Reagan asserted his meeting with Arias "was a social meeting, brief, and at no time did Reagan promise Arias support or anything else," the Miami Herald reported Jan. 23. "To try to connect [the meeting] with what is going on now [in Panama] is ridiculous," the spokesman said.)

The Panamanian Association of Business Executives (Apede) and the National Council of Private Enterprise (Conep) denounced the exile of the critics Jan. 21 and its members began in indefinite protest strike. The groups cited the prohibition against the expatriation of Panamanians in the 1972 constitution, which had been approved by Torrijos. Apede added that some 115 persons had been arrested recently for political reasons.

The government declared the strike illegal Jan. 22, but Apede claimed to have closed down 65% of the banks, factories and business offices in Panama City and to have "completely paralyzed" Chiriqui Province. The government issued a list that day of the 11 exiles, who included Ruben Dario Carles, vice president of Chase Manhattan Bank in Panama and former finance minister; Antonio Dominguez, recently elected president of the chamber of commerce; and Ivan and Winston Robles, leaders of the Independent Lawyers' Movement.

Business leaders denounced Torrijos in an open letter published by the newspaper El Tiempo Jan. 22, accusing him of taking "pseudopatriotic" positions to "silence critical voices which demand that Panama's position regarding the canal be maintained and that individual guarantees be respected." They apparently referred to Panama's acceptance of the U.S.' desire not to sign a new treaty in 1976, while President Ford was running for election.

The strike waned in Panama City Jan. 23 as all banks opened and only businesses linked to the exiles remained closed, but the stoppage remained 60% effective in Chiriqui, according to the news agency LATIN. That night some 500 supporters of the government attacked Apede headquarters in Panama City, breaking windows and wrecking automobiles parked outside.

The strike was reportedly 100% effective in Chiriqui Jan. 25, leading the government to impose a curfew and begin extended negotiations with the strikers. Apede headquarters in Panama City were attacked again that night by some 100 persons whom Apede's president, Carlos Gonzalez de la Lastra, described as "policemen in civilian dress."

Following the failure of the negotiations Jan. 26 the government charged the strikers were trying to force the return of ex-President Arias and it threatened to revoke the naturalization cards of Apede members born abroad. This effectively ended the strike in Panama City, according to press reports, but the stoppage continued in Chiriqui. Gonzalez de la Lastra charged in a newspaper interview that Gen. Torrijos ran a "tyrannical"

PANAMA

government without any effective political or civil liberties.

The National Guard occupied Apede headquarters Jan. 29, wrecking the offices and expelling but not arresting the business leaders who had met there continuously since the strike began Jan. 22. Gonzalez de la Lastra called the occupation a "flagrant violation of the constitution and the laws of the Republic of Panama."

Ex-President Arias attempted to return to Panama Jan. 29, but he was turned back in Miami by officials of Pan American Airways who showed a letter from Torrijos asserting Arias would be refused admission in Panama and returned to the U.S. at Pan American's expense.

United Brands signs land sale pact. United Brands Co. of the U.S. signed an agreement under which it would sell the government all the land it owned in Panama and lease back enough land to maintain current banana production of 22 million boxes per year, it was reported Jan. 8.

The U.S. firm would sell its 100,000 acres for $151,500 and lease back 37,500 acres, paying the government $2 million each year in rents and fees. Panama agreed to keep the banana export tax at 35¢ per box and to continue to levy the normal income tax of 50% on profits earned in Panama. Panama also had the option to buy the buildings, equipment, trucks and other facilities still owned by United Brands on the banana plantations.

Tack replaced. Juan Antonio Tack resigned April 1 as foreign minister and Panama's chief negotiator in talks with the U.S. over the future of the Panama Canal and Zone. He was replaced by Aquilino Boyd, Panama's ambassador to the United Nations.

The government said Tack quit "for strictly personal reasons." However, the London newsletter Latin America had reported Jan. 16 that Tack was "intensely" disliked by the U.S. State Department, and the Miami Herald noted April 4 that he had taken a more nationalist stance in the canal talks than Brig. Gen. Omar Torrijos, Panama's military strongman.

Students riot. Students rioted in Panama City Sept. 10, 15 and 20, prompting charges by the government that U.S. Central Intelligence Agency had organized a "destabilization" campaign against the regime of Brig. Gen. Omar Torrijos.

The U.S. denied the charges, and observers linked the riots to discontent over Panama's economic problems, repression of student protesters and the suspension of talks with the U.S. for a new Panama Canal treaty.

Press reports said that the disturbances posed a serious threat to Torrijos because student radicals had provided most of his non-military support. Without them, the general was backed mainly by the National Guard, although there were some reports of support among peasant groups, the New York Times said Sept. 23.

Pro- and anti-Torrijos high-school students fought with rocks and fists in the streets of the capital Sept. 10, in the worst mob violence in Panama in more than a year. The pro-government students protested the third anniversary of the military coup in Chile, and their adversaries denounced a recent rise in the prices of milk and rice. Store windows were smashed during the battles.

More windows were broken Sept. 15 when students from the National Institute, an anti-Torrijos stronghold, rioted in defiance of a government ban on all demonstrations. Riot police broke up the disturbance and the government ordered all high schools closed until Sept. 20.

U.S. involvement denounced—The Panamanian government charged Sept. 17 that the riots were part of a CIA "destabilization" plan against Torrijos. Foreign Minister Aquilino Boyd handed U.S. Ambassador William Jorden a formal protest note accusing the U.S. armed forces stationed in the Canal Zone of interfering in Panama's internal affairs. Boyd said that an American serviceman and two civilian employes of the U.S. Defense Department had been arrested for "active participation" in the student disturbances.

The U.S. Embassy subsequently issued a statement denying U.S. involvement in the riots and expressing "regret that unfounded allegations have been made which can only impact unfavorably on the friendly relations between the U.S. and Panama and affect adversely the ongoing negotiations between our two countries."

The U.S. armed forces' Southern Command in the Canal Zone also denied involvement in the disturbances, adding, "Unfortunately, these allegations and arrests have created a potentially dangerous situation and forced us to place a personnel-movement limitation on Southern Command members and their dependents." Since Sept. 10, the 40,000 Americans living in the Canal Zone had been urged by local armed forces radio and television stations to stay away from downtown Panama City.

Boyd's protest note said the three American "agents" under arrest were Pfc. Bernard Lowell Jameson, Hector Downs and Rogelio Garcia. U.S. officials told the New York Times Sept. 18 that Garcia and Downs were Panamanians. Garcia worked as a warehouseman at Howard Air Force Base in the Canal Zone, and Downs was unemployed, the officials said.

The Panamanian government said that about 15 persons had been arrested in the disturbances, but student and diplomatic sources said Sept. 17 that close to 100 persons had been jailed. Twenty persons were arrested Sept. 16 in a night raid on the offices of an independent labor group. Eusebio Marchovsky, a prominent Social Democratic lawyer, had been arrested Sept. 15.

The government appeared to soften its charges against the U.S. Sept. 19 as Vice President Gerardo Gonzalez said: "We're not accusing any government of participating in the troubles, but we are saying that elements of this government were involved and we must try them according to the law." However, the government radio network charged again that there was a CIA "destabilization" plan and accused the U.S. of "arrogance, aggression and blackmail." The U.S. formally rejected the charges in a note delivered by Jorden Sept. 21.

The disturbances resumed Sept. 20 when 500–1,000 students from the National University were attacked by police and soldiers as the students marched toward the center of Panama City shouting, "Down with bourgeois repression" and "Reduce the cost of living." At least 50 persons were arrested, and classes at the university were suspended indefinitely.

(More than 70 persons arrested for looting during the September student riots were sent to a penal colony, the New York Times reported Sept. 23.)

Panama heightened its charges against the U.S. Sept. 22 as Foreign Minister Boyd charged that Canal Zone residents who favored continued U.S. sovereignty over the zone had "the mentality of the whites of southern Africa." The U.S., Boyd said, should "end discrimination and racism [in the zone] in work, housing, in schools and the hospitals, all segregated by race..." U.S. Secretary of State Henry Kissinger should offer to relocate the families of 3,500 American employes in the zone in a fashion similar to his reported plan to relocate Rhodesian whites, Boyd added.

(The Panama Canal Co. denied Boyd's charge of discrimination, saying that housing in the zone was being integrated and that U.S. and Panamanian schools there would be combined gradually beginning in 1976, the Washington Post said Sept. 23.)

Boyd said it was important that the talks for a new Panama Canal treaty be resumed immediately. If President Ford should lose the November election, "then he would be a lame duck, and [Democratic candidate Jimmy] Carter wouldn't be able to talk either until next spring," Boyd said. "We cannot delay that long."

Boyd denied that Torrijos' rule was threatened by growing economic pressures and unconfirmed reports of spreading government corruption. Some observers believed that leftist students had rioted in mid-September because they had lost faith in Torrijos' promises of popular reforms, the Washington Post reported Sept. 23.

Economic problems. Among Panama's economic woes, according to the Sept. 27 Miami Herald:

- Unemployment in the urban areas of Panama City and Colon had risen to an officially estimated 9%, compared with 5% in 1975.

- Panama's growth rate had fallen below 2% in 1975 from 8% in the late

1960s and early 1970s. The value of permits issued for new private construction in the first six months of 1976 was the lowest for any six-month figure since Torrijos seized power in 1968.

■ One of the worst Panamanian droughts of the 20th century had reduced agricultural production. A fall in rice production had contributed to the controversial rise in rice prices.

Canal Controversy

Negotiations at standstill. The U.S.-Panamanian talks on the future of the Panama Canal were reported to have stalled early in 1976 despite new negotiations in Panama Feb. 7–22. The reason for the impasse, according to most press reports, was the presidential campaign in the U.S., in which Republican challenger Ronald Reagan was accusing President Ford of "selling out" U.S. security and interests in Panama and the Western Hemisphere.

Ford answered Reagan by asserting in Peoria, Ill. March 6 that the U.S. would "never renounce national defense interests nor its interests in the operation of the canal." He repeated the assertion in Texas April 10. However, Ford's statements appeared to contradict the U.S.' avowed intention eventually to hand over to Panama sovereignty over the canal. Reagan said April 13: "Apparently the only people who aren't aware of the giveaway that's being planned are the real owners of the canal—the people of the United States."

(Brig. Gen. Omar Torrijos, Panama's strongman, accused the presidential candidates April 21 of "irresponsibility" in dealing with the Panama Canal issue. Panama's Foreign Minister Aquilino Boyd, interviewed on the CBS-TV "Morning News" program April 16, said that Ronald Reagan was "wilfully deceiving the people" of the U.S. and "inflaming patience in my country." The U.S. had purchased rights only "for a specific purpose in Panama, for the construction, maintenance and protection of the Panama Canal," Boyd said. "Panama has never given up sovereignty.")

The Panama Canal subcommittee of the U.S. House of Representatives held hearings April 6–8 on the negotiations and other issues relating to the canal. It heard secret testimony April 8 from Ambassador at Large Ellsworth Bunker, who headed the U.S. negotiating team in the canal talks.

Rep. Leonor K. Sullivan (D, Mo.), who chaired the hearings, said April 8 that the canal negotiations would not be completed soon because, according to Bunker, "there's quite a bit to be done." She asserted she supported the 1903 treaty which gave the U.S. control of the canal "in perpetuity," and she accused the Ford Administration of trying to transfer sovereignty over the canal in a "veiled and piecemeal fashion," without Congressional authorization.

Sullivan said she was concerned over some concessions already made to Panama, such as the flying of the Panamian flag in the Canal Zone and the "executive" leasing of zone property to Panama.

Rep. Gene Snyder (R, Ky.) April 13 released portions of Bunker's subcommittee testimony, which indicated that the Ford Administration intended "to give up the Canal Zone after a period of time" and to give up control of the canal itself after a longer period. Bunker said in a telephone interview with The Herald that it had always been "perfectly clear" that Panama eventually would gain control of the zone, the Herald reported April 15.

White House Press Secretary Ron Nessen said April 15 that the Ford Administration sought a treaty that would "protect American interests" in the Canal Zone "for the useful life of the canal, probably for about 30 to 50 years." He said the U.S. had decided to negotiate a new canal treaty following the Panamian riots in 1964 which left 24 persons dead and hundreds injured.

Gen. Torrijos said in an interview March 7 that if the canal talks failed, Panama "would have to resort to violent incidents" to gain sovereignty over the zone. "We have set 1977 as the goal" for a new treaty, he said. "Patience has its limits."

In a related development, Venezuelan President Carlos Andres Perez declared June 22 that the U.S. Bicentennial would "only be marred by a fact which is dissonant with the best traditions of the U.S. I am referring to the colonial enclave of the Panama Canal Zone." Perez said that "the best homage to [George] Washington and to the thousands of anonymous heroes of the U.S. independence would be to proclaim to an admiring world that the U.S. is restoring to Latin America, that they are returning to their legitimate owners, that portion of [Panama]."

Kissinger on situation. U.S. Secretary of State Henry A. Kissinger discussed the U.S.-Panama talks March 4 in testimony before the U.S. House Committee on International Relations. Kissinger said:

"Three [U.S.] administrations have been discussing this issue for 10 years because it is not, contrary to some allegations, a problem between us and an individual leader in Panama. It is an issue that has affected the whole Western Hemisphere and which could poison our relationship with the entire Western Hemisphere and put us into an extremely complicated position. We are negotiating with the government of Panama to see whether it is possible to come to an arrangement that protects our vital interests with respect to the operation and security of the canal.... [T]he negotiations are now going on, and they are proceeding because we do not want a guerrilla war in the Western Hemisphere without having made every effort to find a solution that protects our vital interests. I cannot yet tell you whether such an agreement is possible because we are in the process of negotiating it.

"... [T]he danger we see is that the countries of the Western Hemisphere will unite with Panama in a policy of political and military harassment of the United States in Panama. Now, there is no question that the Panama Canal is vital to the United States.... The question is whether we can come to an agreement that would find the right support in the Western Hemisphere, that protects our security concerns and at the same time removes the dangers that I have described. It is not an issue between them and us; it is an issue for the whole Western Hemisphere."

Canal Co. 'sickout.' Some 700 U.S. employes of the Panama Canal Co. called in sick March 15–20 in what amounted to a wildcat strike against austerity measures proposed recently by the U.S. Army, which owned the company.

The "sickout" by teachers, canal pilots and tugboat captains caused the closing of schools in the Canal Zone and a backup of as many as 175 ships outside the canal. The proposed austerity measures, devised by the Army in anticipation of a $14 million Panama Canal Co. deficit in 1976, included a wage freeze and elimination of the "tropical differential" which gave the company's 3,600 U.S. employes greater wages and benefits than its 11,000 Panamanian workers.

The strikers returned to work late March 20 after the Canal Zone's governor, Maj. Gen. Harold R. Parfitt, agreed to oppose the austerity measures and to institute some form of collective bargaining for Panama Canal Co. employes. The company later said it would seek a toll increase to cover mounting losses, which it attributed to the world economic slump and to unexpectedly strong competition from the reopened Suez Canal.

A further cause of the "sickout" was fear among company employes that they would lose their jobs and privileges when the U.S. and Panama signed a new canal treaty, according to press reports. Brig. Gen. Omar Torrijos, Panama's military strongman, said March 22 that the new treaty would respect the rights of U.S. workers.

The Panamanian government had noted March 18 that no Panamanian workers were striking in the Canal Zone. The Washington Post charged in an editorial March 25 that the job action showed the "irresponsibility" of U.S. residents of the Canal Zone "who profit personally from maintenance of the status quo."

Meanwhile, President Ford March 23 ordered into effect a new ship-measuring system for vessels using the canal that would increase toll revenues by as much as $6.5 million per year. Ford excluded the proposed counting of deck-stowed cargoes—especially containers and lumber—which had brought protests from the shipping industry, according to the Journal of Commerce March 26.

Canal toll increase sought—The Panama Canal Co., the U.S. agency that administered the canal, had asked President Ford to approve a 20% increase in canal toll rates to offset an anticipated $12 million operating loss in fiscal 1977, it was reported Oct. 5. The increase, which could not take effect under company rules until Nov. 15, would follow a 20% rate hike approved by former President Richard M. Nixon in 1974. The new hike had been opposed by a committee of the Organization of American States, it was reported Aug. 26. It was supported by Panama, which had long charged that the Panama Canal Co. kept toll rates artificially low to subsidize international—and particularly U.S.—shipping.

In fiscal 1976, commercial traffic through the canal had declined 10.5% to 12,160 ships, and toll revenues had fallen 5.4% to $134.22 million, according to preliminary figures released by the canal company and reported by the Miami Herald July 9.

New canal talks set. The U.S. and Panama agreed Oct. 7 to resume negotiations within two weeks for a new treaty to govern the Panama Canal and the Canal Zone.

The agreement was announced after U.S. Secretary of State Henry Kissinger met with Panamanian Foreign Minister Aquililino Boyd in New York.

Gen. Torrijos had denounced both President Ford and Democratic candidate Jimmy Carter for their statements on the canal issue in their televised debate on foreign policy Oct. 6. Torrijos charged Oct. 7 that the two candidates had showed "great irresponsibility toward the people of the U.S. by the superficial way in which they discussed the most explosive subject in relations between the U.S. and Latin America."

Attacking Carter's pledge that he would "never give up complete control or practical control" of the Canal Zone, Torrijos said: "I want to remind Carter that the word 'never' is one that has been wiped out of the political dictionary since the liberation struggles."

"Ford," Torrijos continued, "claims credit for not having any young American fighting in any part of the world. But in Panama, 20,000 soldiers of the [U.S. Army's] Southern Command sleep in tension, with their rifles and canteens ready, waiting for Latin America to reclaim the sovereign rights it is being denied in the negotiations."

Torrijos declared Oct. 11 that Panamanians were neither "bootlickers nor midgets," and that if the canal negotiations failed, "we will have enough courage to eradicate the [U.S.] intruders by force." Speaking to a crowd about 50 yards from the Canal Zone, Torrijos said: "Imperialism is over there with its 14 military bases, but even if they were 64, they would never destroy our people's yearning for freedom."

The canal talks were deadlocked on the duration of a new treaty, the defense role the U.S. would have in insuring the safety of the canal, language to insure that the canal would not be closed, the right of the U.S. to widen the canal, and the size and position of land and water areas needed to operate the canal, the New York Times reported Oct. 8.

Status of negotiations. A guide to the issues involved in the canal dispute was published by the Council of Americas, an association of 230 major U.S. corporations with investments in Latin America. The guide gave this description of "the status of the negotiations":

The most recent round of negotiations began in June, 1974. By September, 1976, agreement in principle had been reached on four major issues:

The new treaty with Panama will have a fixed termination date.

Under a new treaty, jurisdiction over the Canal Zone will pass to Panama gradually. The United States will retain the right to use areas necessary for the operation, maintenance nad defense of the canal.

During the life of the treaty, the United States will have the primary responsibility for operating the canal. Panamanians will gradually assume larger roles in day-to-day operations until Panama takes full responsibility for operations when the treaty expires.

The United States will have primary responsibility for the defense of the canal during the life of the treaty. Panama will grant the United States use rights for defending the waterway and will participate in its defense as fully as possible.

Several other issues remain to be resolved. These concern the economic benefits Panama will derive from the canal, the right of the United States to expand the canal, the area the United States needs for canal operation and defense, an acceptable formula to insure the canal's neutrality after the treaty expires, the rights of United States citizens in the zone, and finally, the duration of the new treaty.

The guide also gave this summary of "the economic picture":

The Panama Canal has always been of considerable value to United States commerce. In 1975, about twelve percent of all United States export and import waterborne tonnage used the Panama route. Forty-five percent of the cargo moving through the canal came from the United States, and 23 percent was bound for United States ports.

Despite such statistics, however, the canal is not considered the critical United States trade route that it once was. A Library of Congress study indicates that there are many alternative routes for most important products and commodities. And the use of larger vessels and other means of transportation may serve to limit canal traffic in the future. Nevertheless, for shippers of certain commodities—coal and coke, for instance, and petroleum products—and for certain regions of the United States, the Panama Canal remains an important commercial link.

The canal is more important to the commerce of Panama and some other Latin American nations than it is to that of the United States. More than 29 percent of Panama's foreign trade passes through the canal. Some 25 percent of its foreign exchange earnings and nearly 13 percent of its gross national product are directly or indirectly attributable to the waterway.

More than 50 percent of the foreign trade of Nicaragua, El Salvador, and Ecuador moves through the canal, as does more than 25 percent of the exports and imports of many other Latin American nations.

Of course, the canal's importance extends far beyond the hemisphere, for 5 percent of the world's seaborne trade uses it. Trade between the East Coast of the United States and Asia accounts for nearly 40 percent of the total canal traffic and is therefore, the major canal trade route.

Of total canal traffic moving from the Atlantic to the Pacific, some 12.5 percent is bound for the West Coast of the United States, 10.5 percent for South America and nearly two-thirds for Asia, principally Japan. About two-thirds of the traffic from the Atlantic to the Pacific originates in the United States.

Of the goods which passed from the Pacific to the Atlantic in 1975, only 12.5 percent originated in the United States. Most of the goods originated in South America—24 percent—or in Asia—37 percent. The remaining tonnage started out in Canada, Central America or Oceania. About 39 percent of all this West to East trade through the canal was destined for United States east and Gulf Coast ports. Another 40 percent was bound for Europe.

Most of the cargo moving through the canal is industrial raw materials and grains, which lend themselves to shipment by sea. Among such cargoes, fossil fuels—coal, coke, and petroleum—predominate, accounting for about 36 percent of the annual traffic. By contrast, finished products—iron and steel manufactures, for instance, or machinery and equipment—represent less than 10 percent of the canal's tonnage.

Currently, there are fewer than 15,000 transits through the canal each year, and its capacity is estimated at 26,000 transits a year. Projections suggest that this capacity will not be reached until early in the next century.

In case a greater capacity is required, two options have been considered. A third lane of locks could be added to the existing canal at an estimated cost of $1.7 billion, or a new sea-level canal could be built at an estimated cost of more than $5 billion. Thus far, there has been no conclusive evaluation of the economic or military need for or the technical feasibility of either expansion project.

Paraguay

Abuses of Human Rights

The 22-year presidency of Gen. Alfredo Stroessner, the most lasting dictatorship in Latin America so far, has been marked with repeated allegations of repression. According to observers, a fresh wave of repression—replete with mass arrests, and charges of killing and torture of political prisoners—got under way late in 1975 and increased in intensity in 1976.

Communist leader seized. The French Communist newspaper L'Humanite reported Jan. 31 that Miguel Angel Soler, a leader of Paraguay's outlawed Communist Party, had been arrested in Paraguay several months before and was feared dead. The French Committee of Solidarity with Paraguay said rumors had circulated in the Paraguayan army and interior ministry that Soler had "died resisting interrogation" by authorities, according to the Cuban newspaper Granma Feb. 17.

Drinan on abuses. U.S. Rep. Robert F. Drinan (D, Mass.), in a statement in the U.S. Congressional Record March 3, denounced the Stroessner regime for its abuses of human rights. Drinan said:

The actions of the regime receive a measure of internal legitimacy through the implementation of article 79 of the 1967 Constitution. This provision and a similar one in the previous Constitution enable Stroessner to rule under a state of siege. When a state or siege is in force—as it has been since Stroessner came to power in 1954—the President has extraordinary powers. Among these are the banning of public demonstrations and meetings, abrogation of certain civil rights, authorizing arbitrary arrest and banishment, search and seizure of private homes, and detention without warrants. The regime has claimed that the state of siege is necessitated because of a persistent Communist threat.

With the assistance of this constitutional provision, the Stroessner regime has established a policy of detaining people without charge. Amnesty International has determined the number of long-term political prisoners to be 150. Of these only two are known to have been tried: Prof. Antonio Maidana and Alfredo Acorta. They were both convicted and sentenced to terms of 2½ and 1 year respectively, for their role in the general strike of 1958. Upon the expiration of their sentences the Stroessner regime invoked Public Law 294—the precursor of article 79—to keep them in prison. Both Maidana and Acorta are still being held today. Amnesty International brought the case of Professor Maidana before the Inter-American Commission on Human Rights in 1972. The following year the Commission appealed to the Stroessner regime to release Maidana. This appeal has not been answered.

Other individuals known to have been detained by the Paraguayan Government include two American citizens: Msgr. Roland Bordelon and Kevin Cahalan. These two men, both representatives of the Catholic Relief Service, were visiting a Catholic community, San Isidro de Jejui, when it was raided by the military. Monsignor Bordelon, in a letter to the Paraguayan Foreign Minister, complained of the fact that he and his associate were detained for 56 hours without being charged. During this period of time they were not allowed to contact the American Embassy. It was only after the Embassy learned of their detention that they were released. Paraguayans arrested in that same raid were detained for up to 6 months and were released only after vigorous protests by the Paraguayan Catholic Church.

The recent arrest of the eminent anthropologist, Dr. Miguel Chase Sardi, and three of his colleagues, Victorio Suarez, Mauricio Schwartzman, and an unidentified secretary, is yet another example of the regime's detention policy. These four people were involved in a project to educate the Ache Indians—the Marandu project. They have now been detained for over 3 months without charges being filed against them. The International League for the Rights of Man has documented both their detention and the fact that Chase Sardi has been tortured.

The Stroessner regime also follows a policy of widespread random arrests. These arrests are usually short term in nature and are used mainly to intimidate the general population. This policy is also used to intimidate opponents. The regime has attempted to intimidate Prof. Luis Resck in this manner. Their failure in this case is obvious from the fact that they have arrested Resck over 90 times.

The regime also engages in severe forms of torture. Amnesty International has reported that—

> The prolonged beating for periods of up to two hours non-stop with whips and sticks, burning of sensitive parts of the body with cigarettes, and the removal of fingernails are all common forms of torture used.

The two most severe forms of torture are the picana electrica and la pileta. Picana electrica consists of applying electric shock treatments to sensitive parts of the body. La pileta—known as "the bath"—consists of repeated submerging of the prisoner's head in a tub containing water filled with filth and excrement. Amnesty International has documented the death of Juan Jose Farias by this torture.

The conditions of the prisons is yet another example of the regime's disregard for fundamental human rights. Political prisoners are held in groups between 3 and 15 in cells 12-foot square. These prisoners are not allowed to receive letters or medical treatment. The only visitors they may receive are members of their immediate families and then only for 5 minutes per week.

The treatment of the Indians in Paraguay has sparked a great deal of international attention in the past few years. In 1973, the University of Bern Switzerland released a copy of a letter it had sent to the Stroessner regime. This letter charged the regime with an intentional governmental policy to exterminate the Ache Indians. They claimed that the government condoned manhunts, pillaging, mass murders, and slave trading of the Indians. The University of Bern used the studies by Mark Munzel and Miguel Chase Sardi to document its claim. The Marandu project was a response to these atrocities and an attempt to educate the Indians to the ways of modern Paraguay. The effort was started with the cooperation of the regime, but now it and the fate of the Indians are tied to the fate of Chase Sardi.

Another indication of the low regard in which Paraguayans hold the Stroessner regime is the number of Paraguayans in voluntary or forced exile. Amnesty International determined that 800,000 or one-third of the present population are now in exile. Among these people are many who were involved in protecting human rights in Paraguay.

The freedom of the press in Paraguay remains quite restricted. Any paper that is able to exert any effective opposition to the regime is rapidly closed down. This is reported to have been the reason for the closings of Comunidad and El Radical.

While the Stroessner regime has been dealing with its internal opponents in this manner, it has been continually receiving military assistance from the United States. From 1970 to 1975 the Stroessner regime received $13,532,000 in military assistance from the United States. The administration request for 1976 shows a marked increase to $8,800,000. The Department of Defense in its "Congressional Presentation Document for Fiscal Year 1976" claimed that one of the major objectives of this assistance

PARAGUAY

is to increase the internal security capabilities of the Stroessner regime.

Along with donating money and equipment the United States has trained many of the Paraguayan forces. Since 1950, we have trained almost 1,500 members of the Paraguayan military. The number of trainees has also shown a marked increase in recent years to the point where we have averaged almost 100 soldiers a year the last 3 years.

The United States has provided this assistance despite the fact that Paraguay faces no real external or internal threat. The last time Paraguay was involved in a war was in 1935 when it defeated Bolivia in the Chaco war. Its relations with its neighbors remain relatively cordial. In recent years it has embarked on joint ventures with each of its powerful neighbors Brazil and Argentina. It has begun a major hydroelectric project with Brazil, and Amnesty International reports that its police and military have begun to cooperate with Argentina to arrest political opponents.

There, also, does not seem to be any internal threat that would necessitate this military assistance. Paraguay has been free of guerilla movements and its Communist Party has not been at all effective since the general strike of 1958.

The fact that Paraguay has neither an external nor an internal threat refutes the necessity of the American military assistance program. Why does the Stroessner regime need this equipment and training other than to further suppress its own people?

Mass arrests reported. More than 1,000 persons were arrested in Paraguay after an April 3 shootout in Asuncion between police and leftist guerrillas, according to sources cited May 8 by the Associated Press.

The guerrillas, two of whom died in the shootout, belonged to the Politico-Military Organization (OPM). The government claimed that the group had links to the Roman Catholic Church and to the People's Revolutionary Army, Argentina's Marxist guerrilla movement.

(There were more shootouts between Paraguayan police and both Paraguayan and Argentine revolutionaries April 4-6, the London newsletter Latin America reported May 7. About 30 guerrillas died in the action, including three top leaders of the OPM, the newsletter said. Five policemen were reported to have died in the action.)

Those arrested after the shootouts came mostly from poor neighborhoods of Asuncion, the AP said. Paraguayan and foreign Catholic priests and Paraguayan staffers of a service program run by the Christian Church of the U.S. were among those arrested.

One of the priests was identified as the Rev. Jose Miguel Munariz, a Jesuit who was arrested April 11 and expelled from Paraguay April 19. Five members of the Christian Church's Friendship Mission were arrested April 10 and a sixth was seized April 23.

The government had closed Cristo Rey, a Jesuit school in Asuncion, at the end of March, arresting 28 teachers on charges of teaching Marxism and promoting guerrilla activities, AP reported May 8. The detainees included one French and six Spanish Jesuits, four of whom were deported. The Rev. Pedro Arrupe, superior general of the Jesuit order, denounced the Paraguayan government May 10 for allegedly violating the human rights of Jesuits.

In a related development, the International League for the Rights of Man charged in New York April 5 that the Paraguayan government had throttled a service project for Paraguayan Indians by arresting its director and four senior staff members at the end of 1975. There was evidence that the project workers had been tortured after their arrests, Morris B. Abram, a league representative and former U.S. delegate to the United Nations' Human Rights Commission, said.

The service program, called the Marandu project, was sponsored by the Catholic University of Asuncion and was funded by the Inter-American Foundation of the U.S. Its director was Miguel Chase Sardi, a distinguished Paraguayan anthropologist.

The Paraguayan government claimed that Sardi and his colleagues had been arrested for aiding Communist subversives. It denied that they had been mistreated, the New York Times said April 6.

Abram and other league representatives called for a cutoff of U.S. aid to Paraguay under a federal law prohibiting help to governments that committed gross violations of human rights. The group denounced the U.S. State Department for continuing to support the Paraguayan regime and for allegedly covering up evidence of mass arrests, torture and threatened annihilation of the Paraguayan Indian population.

(Professor Richard Arens of Temple University, a league representative, accused the Paraguayan government of killing or enslaving Ache Indians until their population was reduced from 10,000 to a few hundred.)

The State Department denied covering up evidence of human rights abuse in Paraguay and said it had expressed U.S. concern to Paraguay over Sardi's arrest.

Amnesty International said in a message to the OAS General Assembly June 4:

Another wave of repression was launched by the Paraguayan authorities in early April, 1976, after the alleged discovery of a new guerrilla network, called the Organizacion Politico-Militar (OPM). Similar waves of violent repression in Paraguay have been carried out in the past. A conservative estimate says that about 350 people were arrested during April 1976. The Police Investigation Department—a place noted for the continuing use of barbaric torture was still crowded with many of the 200 people reportedly arrested or disappeared in late November and throughout December 1975. On March 17, 1976, Amnesty International sent a letter to the OAS Inter-American Commission on Human Rights urging an investigation of reports of gross violations of human rights in Paraguay, citing 55 cases of persons arrested and maltreated late last year.

The Inter-American Commission on Human Rights of the Organization of American States estimated that there were some 1,000 political prisoners in Paraguay, most of whom had not been charged and were not permitted lawyers, the New York Times reported June 9. In the previous six weeks, the Times said, at least two prisoners—Mario Scherer, a student, and Mario Arzamendia, a newspaper vendor—had been tortured to death.

The prisoners included peasants, professors, students, shopkeepers, opposition politicians and others, according to the Times. They were generally arrested in raids against alleged "Communist conspiracies," although Paraguay's Communist Party was tiny and virtually inactive and the country had no leftist guerrilla movement.

Church scores government. The bishops' council of the Roman Catholic Church of Paraguay issued a document July 12 accusing the government of a wide range of abuses of priests and other Paraguayans.

The document, apparently provoked by the mass arrests in April and May, denounced indiscriminate repression of students and peasants; the torture and disappearance of political prisoners; government intervention in church colleges and police raids on other church educational institutions; the imprisonment of priests, seminarians and lay members; the expulsion from Paraguay of eight priests, and the existence of a broad government campaign to defame the church.

This "violence of the system," the document concluded, was responsible for social protest in Paraguay, especially among the country's youth. A "critical" attitude by the church was more necessary than ever, the bishops asserted. They demanded that the government restore their freedom to carry out ecclesiastical duties.

Other Developments

Navy commander replaced. Adm. Hugo Gonzalez was replaced as navy commander after a clash between a brigade of Paraguayan marines and a group of Argentine border guards, apparently over arms smuggling, the London newsletter Latin America reported March 5.

Paraguay's navy commander traditionally controlled the arms traffic with Argentina, according to the newsletter. The Argentine armed forces reportedly were concerned over growing evidence that Paraguayan smugglers were selling arms to Argentina's major terrorist groups—the left-wing People's Revolutionary Army and two right-wing assassination squads, the Argentine Anticommunist Alliance and the Liberators of America.

(The armed forces were also concerned over the smuggling of Argentine automobiles into Paraguay, Latin America reported. According to the Buenos Aires newspaper La Opinion, quoted by the newsletter, 70% of all the cars in Asuncion came from Argentina, and 50% of these were stolen.)

Foreign minister resigns. Foreign Minister Raul Sapena Pastor resigned March 8 because of health problems, after

PARAGUAY

more than 20 years in office. He was then replaced by Alberto Nogues, his undersecretary for the past eight years, who had served as acting foreign minister for the last three months while Sapena recovered from two operations.

Stroessner reelection planned. The National Assembly voted July 16 to amend the Paraguayan constitution to allow the reelection of President Alfredo Stroessner.

An assembly resolution, passed 80-17, called for a constituent assembly to meet in February 1977 to change the article in the charter which forbade the reelection of a president who had served two consecutive terms. Stroessner, who seized power in a military coup in 1954, was serving his fifth five-year term as chief executive. The next presidential election was scheduled for 1978. The two-term restriction had been put into effect in 1967, after Stroessner had served three terms.

Stroessner's was the most durable dictatorship in Latin America. His Colorado Party held two-thirds of the seats in the National Assembly. The remaining seats were held by three opposition parties—the Liberals, the Radical Liberals and the Febreristas—which were hamstrung by the periodic arrest of their members on suspicion of subversive activities.

World Bank loan. The World Bank had approved a loan of $157 million over the next five years for various projects in Paraguay's agricultural, cattle-raising, industrial, educational and transport sectors, it was reported Feb. 27. The bank would provide 70% of the financing for these projects and the Paraguayan government, the other 30%.

Foreign investments set. Companies from Great Britain and Japan would invest $70 million in Paraguay's paper and cellulose industry, the Latin America Economic Report said April 30.

Bowater, a British firm, would put $50 million into a cellulose-and-paper plant using bagasse, a plant residue, and New Orient Industries of Japan would invest $20 million in a plant using bamboo.

Paraguay's first steel mill, with an initial output of 100,000 tons per year, would be built by a consortium formed by the state-owned company Sidepar, with 60% of the shares, and the Brazilian firms Tenenge and Coferraz, it was reported Jan. 16. The new company, to be known as Acepar, would have a total investment of $50 million. Its output was expected to cover Paraguay's internal needs, supply the Itaipu complex and leave a surplus for export to Brazil.

Other economic developments. Among other economic developments:

A recent confidential document by the Central Bank criticized the size of Paraguay's foreign debt in relation to its gross national product, it was reported Feb. 13. The debt stood at $616.6 million on June 30, 1975, representing 68% of the GNP. Exports in 1975—worth $175 million—were 30% of the total debt, according to the Latin America Economic Report.

Paraguay's inflation rate for 1975 was 6.7%, one of the lowest in Latin America, according to Central Bank figures reported March 5. However, the figures did not take into account price rises in the Alto Parana region, near the Brazilian border, where commercial activity surrounding the building of the Itaipu hydroelectric complex had pushed prices to 100% above those in Asuncion, according to the Latin America Economic Report.

Peru

Domestic Developments

Austerity measures set. Economy Minister Luis Barua Castaneda announced a series of economic austerity measures Jan. 12 to combat the nation's trade and fiscal deficits, maintain the current level of investment and reduce the gap between the rich and the poor.

The measures included tax increases, a rent freeze, abandonment of government fuel and food subsidies, cuts in non-essential imports and government purchases, and ceilings on wage increases and top salary levels. The wage regulations—a special $18.50 raise in the monthly wage with a $37 ceiling on further increases—were protested by some labor unions.

The pro-government Peruvian Revolutionary Workers' Confederation criticized the wage ceiling Jan. 23, asserting it would prevent salary increases from compensating for price rises, and bank and insurance workers struck against the austerity measures the next day. The opposition Peruvian Workers' Confederation called a general strike Feb. 2-3, but press reports said few of the union's workers responded. The government charged Feb. 2 that labor protests were part of a "counterrevolutionary" subversive plan against which it would act "energetically and decisively."

Barua Castaneda noted Jan. 12 that Peru's imports in 1975 had increased from $1.9 billion to $2.5 billion while exports had decreased from $1.5 billion to $1.4 billion. "The foreign debt becomes a millstone to Peru," he said. The country's foreign reserves had fallen to $150 million by the end of the year, Barua added.

The stagnation in exports was caused by the fall of copper and other mineral prices on the international market, the hiatus in iron ore exports due to the nationalization of Marcona Mining Co. of the U.S., and the decline of Peru's fishing industry following a reduction of the expected anchovy catch, according to press reports.

To benefit the depleted national treasury, Barua announced an end to fuel and food subsidies—which would increase the price of gasoline from 33¢ to 50¢ per gallon and the price of food by a similar proportion—and an increase in the top level of income tax from 44% to 65%. Corporation taxes were increased and taxes were imposed on cooperatives, social property and foreign travel. A revaluation of real estate was ordered to increase the tax base.

Government ministries were ordered to cut expenditure on non-salary items by 5%, and imports of alcoholic drinks and newsprint were ordered cut by 30% and 15% respectively. Imports of foreign films and "frivolous magazines" were also ordered cut, and government policing of importers was planned to insure that they used their foreign currency in accordance with declared intentions.

Labor & economic events. Among other labor and economic developments of early 1976:

The Federation of Mining and Metallurgical Workers held a national strike Jan. 19-20 to demand that the government release two miners and four other labor leaders it arrested in December 1975. The union claimed Jan. 20 that all its 70,000 members had participated in the stoppage.

The Peruvian Graphic Workers' Federation ended a nine-day strike Jan. 24 which had kept 15,000 workers away from their jobs and prevented the publication of several newspapers. The strikers won all 13 of their demands including the reinstatement of 10 workers dismissed earlier.

The government Feb. 4 revoked a decree forbidding a union to strike unless two-thirds of its members voted in favor, and requiring unions to record the names, addresses and votes of all members in any strike vote. The decree, first issued in 1913, had been reactivated by the government in October 1975, causing a number of unions to hold protest strikes.

The Inter-American Development Bank approved a $37.6 million loan to help Peru build a highway across the Andes mountains, it was reported Jan. 23. The bank later approved a $32.3 million loan to help finance the Cuzco regional electric power system and expand the Machu-Picchu hydroelectric plant, it was reported Jan. 30.

Peru would sell Venezuela one million tons of iron ore in 1976-77, it was announced Feb. 10.

Belaunde interrupts exile. The former Peruvian President Fernando Belaunde Terry began a 15-day visit to Peru Jan. 4, ending an exile which began in 1968 when he was overthrown by the armed forces. At a press conference Jan. 5, he praised President Gen. Francisco Morales Bermudez but called on Morales to set a date for the restoration of democratic rule. Although sanctioned by the military regime, Belaunde's visit was denounced by the government-controlled press.

Cabinet shuffled. President Francisco Morales Bermudez revised his cabinet Jan. 31 as a number of officials reached their scheduled retirement from the armed forces.

Gen. Jorge Fernandez Maldonado became premier, war minister and army commander, replacing Gen. Oscar Vargas Prieto, who remained in the government as controller general despite retiring from active military duty. Fernandez, a former mines minister, was considered among the most radical members of the military group that seized power in 1968 under Gen. Juan Velasco Alvarado, the former president. As premier, Fernandez was first in line to succeed Morales as chief executive.

Gen. Luis Cisneros became interior minister, succeeding Gen. Cesar Campos, and Gen. Arturo La Torre was named mines minister, replacing Gen. Luis Vera.

In a further cabinet shift Feb. 3, Morales swore in three ministers without portfolio: Gen. Cesar Rosas, head of the national public administration institute; Gen. German Velarde, chief of the social mobilization agency Sinamos; and Gen. Jose Soriano, chief executive of the Bayovar chemical complex.

Convicts executed. Three men were executed by firing squad—one Jan. 23 and the other two Feb. 4—after they were convicted of killing policemen during attempted robberies. The executions were the first since the death penalty was restored in 1974 for persons convicted of sexually assaulting minors or of killing policemen or civilians in the course of a robbery.

Foreign magazines banned. The government prohibited the importation of 23 foreign publications—a majority of them women's magazines and children's comic books—on grounds that they threatened the "intellectual, moral and civic growth of the population," it was reported Feb. 3.

Two of the magazines, Cosmopolitan and Vanidades, both published in the U.S., had been banned in January. The other forbidden publications included Batman and Mighty Mouse comics.

Regime to keep control of newspapers. The government announced July 21 that it would retain control indefinitely over the nation's major newspapers because "adequate conditions have not been achieved to permit their transfe.... to significant sectors of the organized population."

Five of the seven "socialized" (nationalized) newspapers in Lima were to have been handed over to "organized sectors"—such as labor and peasant groups—July 27.

Military rebellion fails. Troops loyal to President Francisco Morales Bermudez July 9 crushed a barracks rebellion led by Gen. Carlos Bobbio Centurion, commander of the Peruvian Military Instruction Center.

Bobbio and an undisclosed number of troops under his command occupied the center after Bobbio refused orders from Gen. Jorge Fernandez Maldonado, then army commander, to retire from the service. Paratroopers attacked the center and forced Bobbio to surrender after a brief exchange of gunfire. No one was hurt in the action, according to press reports.

Fernandez had asked Bobbio to retire after Bobbio publicly criticized Fernandez and the government's economic policies. Bobbio favored drastic economic measures to solve Peru's current crisis, and an increased role for the private sector in Peru's economy, the newsletter Latin America reported July 16.

Leftist Cabinet members removed. President Francisco Morales Bermudez revised his Cabinet July 16, dismissing the last prominent left-wing reformists from the government.

The move was an apparent response to pressure from conservative army and navy officers and from foreign bankers with whom Peru was negotiating large loans, according to reports in the London newsletter Latin America July 30 and the New York Times Aug. 4. The government had moved steadily to the right since August 1975, when Morales succeeded Juan Velasco Alvarado as president.

Morales also replaced Gen. Luis La Vera Velarde as army chief of staff with Gen. Pedro Richter Prada, a conservative.

The new Cabinet, sworn in July 17, comprised five new ministers and 13 holdovers from the previous Cabinet. Morales created a new post, minister of integration, and named Rear Adm. Jorge DuBois Gervasi as its first occupant. DuBois had been head of the National Integration Office.

Replaced in the Cabinet shuffle were Gen. Jorge Fernandez Maldonado, the premier, war minister and army commander; Gen. Miguel Angel de la Flor, foreign minister; Gen. Enrique Gallegos, agriculture minister, and Adm. Isaias Paredes, housing minister. They were succeeded by men who were considered politically more conservative.

Fernandez Maldonado had been considered the most radical Cabinet member. As mines minister under Velasco Alvarado, he had supervised the nationalization of foreign mining and other companies. He was replaced as premier, war minister and army commander by Gen. Guillermo Arbulu Galliani, who was described July 23 by the newsletter Latin America as "vehemently anti-Communist."

De la Flor had shaped Peru's foreign policy of support for the nonaligned nations' movement and for the interests of developing countries. He was replaced by Jose de la Puente Radbill, a conservative civilian economist and career diplomat. De la Puente said he would not attend the forthcoming meeting of nonaligned nations in Sri Lanka, the New York Times reported Aug. 4. He said he would work to improve relations with the right-wing military governments in neighboring countries.

Gallegos, a close associate of Fernandez Maldonado, was replaced as agriculture minister by Gen. Luis Arbulu Ibanez. Paredes was succeeded as housing minister by Adm. Geronimo Cafferata Marazzi.

Unrest preceded Cabinet revision—The Cabinet reorganization followed unrest in Lima at the beginning of July over the government's new economic austerity measures.

The Lima unrest had steadily declined under a state of emergency declared by the government. Striking micro-bus drivers had returned to work July 7, schools had reopened July 12, and workers at the Manufacturas Nylon factory had ended their strike July 15. However, rioters in the northern city of Cajamarca smashed windows and burned automobiles July 12 to protest recent price increases.

The government used the state of emergency July 13 to outlaw "all types of strikes or stoppages" and all unauthorized "political, social or labor union meetings." The arrests of more than 35 journalists and political and labor leaders were reported July 19–30.

United Press International reported July 19 that more than 30 journalists and labor union leaders had been arrested in recent days for unspecified political offenses. Among them was Hugo Blanco, the Trotskyite political leader and former peasant organizer, who was arrested and expelled from Peru July 10. Blanco arrived in Sweden July 11.

The arrest of Augusto Zimmerman, former press secretary to ex-President Velasco Alvarado, was reported July 23 by Latin America. Several leaders of a fishermen's union were arrested July 24 as they prepared to hold a press conference to protest the denationalization of the anchovy-fishing fleet. The arrest of Gustavo Espinoza, former secretary general of the General Confederation of Peruvian Workers, was reported by Latin America July 30.

Army officers, journalists seized. At least five army officers had been arrested for attempting to organize a coup to reinstate the ousted premier, Gen. Jorge Fernandez Maldonado, the London newsletter Latin America reported Aug. 13.

The arrested officers, like Fernandez, were left-wing reformists. Right-wing soldiers who had revolted against the government at the beginning of July had not been arrested, the French newspaper Le Monde noted Aug. 27.

Another 10 officers had been arrested in Iquitos on orders of Gen. Gonzalo Briceno, who would shortly become commander of the first military region in Piura, Latin America reported Aug. 13. No reason for the arrests was reported.

Carlos Urrutia, a prominent journalist, also was arrested. Urrutia, director of the banned magazine Marka, was seized Aug. 17, after the Lima newspaper Expreso published a letter in which he protested government actions against newspapers, magazines and reporters.

The government Aug. 25 ordered the arrest of Rafael Roncagliolo, president of the Peruvian Newspapermen's Federation, on charges of "subversion." Roncagliolo was a critic of President Francisco Morales Bermudez. The Lima newspaper El Comercio had published a letter from Roncagliolo's wife charging that Roncagliolo had been under "incessant persecution" from persons claiming to be army officers, the news agency Latin reported Aug. 25.

In other arrests, 127 persons were seized Aug. 23 when police cleared the National Engineering University in Lima, which had been occupied by rebellious students. The university's rector had suspended classes for a week, charging that professional agitators had imposed a reign of terror in classrooms. Interior Ministry officials said that weapons, explosives and subversive pamphlets were found in the university after the police cleared it. Most of the arrested students were released after the police checked their identifications.

The newspaper La Prensa reported Aug. 28 that another 200 students and workers had been arrested Aug. 27 when they staged a protest demonstration at San Marcos University in Lima. The object of their protest was not reported.

The National Federation of Mining and Metallurgical Workers charged Aug. 16 that police had arrested 40 labor leaders and other workers as they prepared to strike at the copper and zinc mines of the state company Centromin. The government averted the strike by declaring it illegal and awarding miners a pay increase of about 28%. The miners had demanded 100%.

All arrests were made under the state of emergency, which the government Aug. 1 extended for one month. A curfew remained in effect in Lima, and strikes remained banned.

Foreign Military Aid

U.S. military training reported. Despite formally cool relations between Lima and Washington, the Peruvian armed forces had made good use in recent years of the military training facilities offered by the U.S. Defense Department, according to a report by the North American Congress on Latin America (Nacla), cited in the London newsletter Latin America Jan. 16.

The only U.S. Army Special Forces (green berets) mobile training team specializing in counterinsurgency to be sent to Latin America in the past three years was in Peru during the first half of 1975, Nacla reported. In addition, the U.S. Army's "School of the Americas" in the Panama Canal Zone had trained 278 Peruvians in "basic combat and counterinsurgency" and 631 Peruvians in "internal security operations" in 1970-75, according to the report. In each course the Peruvians totaled more than 50% of the students, Nacla said.

Kissinger on Soviet arms aid. U.S. State Secretary Henry A. Kissinger, testifying March 4 before the U.S. House Committee on International Relations, said that the Soviets "supply arms to Peru largely because we [the U.S.] refuse to supply arms to it, and it is one of the problems that is raised if too stringent restrictions are placed on the sale of arms. I do not have the impression that the Soviet Union is in any way dominant vis-a-vis the government of Peru. The government of Peru is very nationalistic, very proud of pursuing an independent course, and while it is closer to the Soviet Union than some of the other Latin American countries, it also made great efforts while I was there to show its friendship to the United States. So, I would not say that the Soviet Union has a dominant role in Peru."

Helms on Cuban & Soviet involvement in Peru. Sen. Jesse Helms (R, N.C.) told the U.S. Senate that the U.S.S.R. might be using Cuba as its "surrogate" in Peru. Helms said:

We know, for example, that the Soviets are heavily engaged in supplying arms and training to Peru. For several years now, the Soviet Union has made a strong investment in supporting the military system of the left-leaning government in Peru. The tremendous build-up of the Peruvian military machine has ominous implications for all of southern South America. Ironically, the United States itself has been also supplying arms to Peru without seeming regard for the leftist nature of the Peruvian government and creating apprehension among our anti-Communist allies in South America. . . .

For this reason, I have been deeply concerned about recurring reports indicating a sizable buildup of Cubans in Peru. If the Soviets, using the Cubans as their surrogates, choose to extend their adventures into the continents of the Western Hemisphere, then Peru would be the place to start. Peru itself could be converted into a Soviet satellite, Cuban style, and then used as a base to spread subversion throughout South America.

One year ago it was generally accepted that there were between 100 and 200 Cubans in Peru. But after the success of the Angolan operation, reports came from various sources indicating a growing Cuban presence in Peru. Rumors of this kind, of course, are frequent. But finally I received a report from a source I consider absolutely reliable that there are as many as 2,000 to 3,000 Cubans in Peru. In my judgment, based upon my confidence in the source, the report was no rumor, but a report to be taken seriously.

On March 24, I met with the President of the United States and personally put a letter in his hands expressing the concern I had over such reports. On April 12, Gen. Brent Scowcroft, the Assistant to the President for National Security Affairs, responded to me on behalf of the President. He wrote as follows:

I have requested a thorough check of these reports and find that although there are rumors of larger numbers, we can confirm the presence of fewer than 100 Cubans in Peru. Most of these are associated with their Embassy in either a diplomatic, consular, or military capacity.

Mr. President, to be frank, I was astonished at this response. General Scowcroft actually seemed to imply that the Cuban presence had diminished in the past year. Yet a reliable source told me that there are more than 200 Cubans working on the large Olmos irrigation project in northern Peru alone, under the supervision of Soviet technicians.

Moreover, after checking further, sources in Peru have reported that there are not 2,000 to 3,000 Cubans, as I was told in March, but that there are actually 4,000 to 5,000 Cubans in Peru at this moment. Moreover, although they are disguised as technicians, I am told that they are prepared to switch to guerrilla warfare whenever they choose.

Purchase of Soviet planes planned. Peru planned to buy 36 late-model fighter-bombers from the Soviet Union, according to U.S. officials quoted by the New York Times Aug. 19.

The purchase had been under negotiation for several months and had been discussed when a high-level delegation from the Soviet air force secretly visited Lima for nine days in early July, the U.S. officials said. Peruvian Foreign Minister Jose de la Puente told reporters Aug. 23 that an agreement had not been concluded.

Moscow had offered Lima good terms for the $250-million purchase of the 36 Sukhoi SU-22 fighter-bombers, U.S. sources said. Peru reportedly would be allowed to pay off the sum over 10 years at an annual interest rate of 2%, with a year of grace. Lima had received generous terms when it bought 200 Soviet T-55 tanks in 1973.

The plane purchase would represent the largest single acquisition of foreign aircraft by a Latin American country since World War II. Peru's air force was currently equipped with French Mirage fighters, British Canberra combers and U.S. A-36 attack planes.

U.S. officials told the New York Times they were reluctant to discuss the plane purchase in detail because this might upset negotiations for a $200-million short-term loan to Peru by a group of U.S. banks. The loan was considered crucial to Peru's troubled economy.

Other Communist-bloc arms—U.S. Rep. Larry McDonald (D, Ga.) commented on Peru's Soviet plane deal in a statement in the Oct. 1 Congressional Record. McDonald also discussed other Communist-country arms acquired by Peru. He said:

Earlier this year, I called attention to Peru's recent, heavy acquisitions of weaponry from the Soviet Union, in connection with our policy on military sales which is so biased against Chile. At that time, I pointed out that Peru has a 6-to-1 advantage in numbers of tanks—about 400 tanks, versus 76 for Chile. The contrast in quality makes the odds even greater. Chile is still equipped with M-4 Shermans, whereas Peru has added, to its 60 Shermans, at least 250 Soviet T-54/55's plus 100 French AMX-13 tanks.

Peru also has three batteries of Yugoslav 105 mm howitzers, and eight truck-mounted SAM's which would be quite dangerous to Chile's essentially subsonic Air Force.

Puerto Rico

Controversy Over Status

Controversy continued through 1976 over the ultimate status for Puerto Rico. Proposals ranged from complete independence, through various suggestions for revision of Puerto Rico's status as a commonwealth of the U.S., to acceptance of the island as a state of the U.S.

Dellums proposes independence. Rep. Ronald V. Dellums (D, Calif.) introduced in the U.S. House of Representatives July 1 a joint resolution pledging Congress to "recognize and accept without reservation the inalienable right of the people of Puerto Rico to self-determination and independence." He charged in a statement in the Congressional Record that "Puerto Rico is still a classical colony of the United States." Dellums said in his statement:

The United States acquired Puerto Rico by military invasion and conquest. When the United States entered the Spanish-American War in 1898, Puerto Rico had just won almost complete independence from Spain through the Autonomic Charter. In that year, the United States invaded Puerto Rico. In December, the Treaty of Paris was signed, and Spain ceded Puerto Rico, Cuba, and the Philippine Islands to the United States as booty of war. The United States set up a military government on the island. Despite all the new laws passed by the U.S. Congress since that date, Puerto Rico today lacks even the basic powers granted to it by Spain in 1897, including the right to establish its own currency, to set tariffs on imports—even from Spain—to enter into commercial treaties, and to establish its own postal system.

In 1917, the Jones Act, or the Law of Federal Relations between Puerto Rico and the United States, was passed. It unilaterally abolished Puerto Rican citizenship and imposed U.S. citizenship on the Puerto Rican people, even though their only popularly elected governing body, the House of Delegates, had passed a resolution firmly opposing U.S. citizenship for Puerto Rico.

The classical colony is one where the people of the land have neither the power to make laws that govern them, nor the power to revoke them. The Jones Act made the Puerto Rican people subject to the laws of the United States, stipulating that unless otherwise stated, the statutory laws of the United States * * * shall have the same force and effect in Puerto Rico as in the United States.

Today, the Puerto Rican Legislature may pass laws only in the areas expressly transferred to it by Public Law 600, a 1951 amendment to the Jones Act. The U.S. Supreme Court can revoke decisions of the Puerto Rican Supreme Court if it is determined that they countervene the Constitution or a law of the United States.

Despite the subsequent changes in the form of local government for Puerto Rico, the United States still controls these fundamental areas of Puerto Rican life: Citizenship, foreign relations, foreign commerce, immigration and emigration, currency, defense, the postal service, labor relations, transportation and communication. A 1965 report by the School of Public Administration of the University of Puerto Rico showed that there are 12 Federal agencies with 53 subdivisions and 12 regulative Federal agencies operating on the island, all to administer U.S. Federal laws.

Puerto Rico is still a classical colony of the United States.

This colonial control has direct and pervasive effects in the most important areas of national life: Monetary currency, defense policy, and economic production. Because the government has no control over its own currency, the material basis of independence does not exist. Puerto Rico is condemned to suffer the effects of economic policies taken without consultation and without considering the effect on the Puerto Rican people.

In defense Puerto Rico is assumed to have no direct interests of its own. It serves only our interests, and in return has to tolerate the presence of a huge, repressive, and dangerous Military Establishment.

In considering the framework of commercial relations between the two countries, all the basic decisions are made by agencies of the U.S. Government. We are so used to this situation that we do not see that this implies the most flagrant neglect of the interests of one of the parties, namely Puerto Rico.

None of these areas of U.S. prerogative—citizenship, currency, defense, and market—constitute "common agreements." The concept "common" implies an agreement between equals, and such agreement takes place when it is in the mutual interest of both parties. Puerto Rico is in no way an equal, sovereign nation, freely entering into a relationship with the United States. Far from being in the interest of both parties, these "common agreements" are clearly in the political, economic and military interest of the U.S.A., and are a severe abridgement of the welfare and freedom of the Puerto Rican people.

Some have argued that the present Commonwealth government, which "delegated" these vital areas of defense, currency, citizenship, market, and foreign relations to the United States, was agreed to by the Puerto Rican people by referendum, and that the majority of the Puerto Rican people do not support independence.

We do not want to debate what particular "status" the Puerto Rican people support for their country. That is their choice. It is not the issue for us. For this Government, and in particular, this Congress, what is at issue is the fact that no people can carry out their right to exercise self-determination regarding their political future unless and until they are a free and sovereign nation first. That is, Puerto Rico must be independent first, in order then to be able freely to choose what its relations with other countries, peoples, and governments should be. . . .

The referendum held in 1952 offered the people of Puerto Rico only two alternatives; To keep the old arrangement, or to approve the new Constitution of the Free Associated States. The election was run by the administration in power. It was held while the island was occupied by U.S. troops, in a period when the pro-independence forces had been violently repressed. Finally, the U.S. Congress never committed itself to being bound by the results of the referendum. For all of these reasons, this referendum is not valid under international law.

With the exception of the fact that "independence" was included as an alternative, these same criteria apply to the plebiscite held on the island in 1967. In addition to these conditions invalidating the plebiscite, it was not supervised by the United Nations, and it was conducted by the defenders of the status quo, who had a great deal of influence over the mass media and complete control over the repressive apparatus. More than 60,000 native U.S. citizens and naturalized foreigners were allowed to vote, and the election was held under the eye of the CIA and the FBI present on the island.

The commonwealth form of government did not make Puerto Rico self-governing. As we have shown, the fundamental areas of Puerto Rican life are still controlled and regulated by the U.S. legislative, judiciary, and executive structures.

The fact is that U.S. colonial involvement on the island represents a clear and present threat, restraint and coercive force preventing the Puerto Rican people from exercising their right to self-determination.

The Puerto Rican people are denied the right to vote for the President of the United States or for voting representatives in either House of Congress, yet are subject to all the laws passed by the Congress, unless Congress otherwise rules, and their local laws can be unilaterally abrogated or changed by Congress.

'Permanent union' compact offered. Sen. Henry M. Jackson (D, Wash.) introduced in the U.S. Senate Sept. 22 a joint resolution to establish "a Compact of Permanent Union between Puerto Rico and the United States." The resolution incorporated "in large part," Jackson said, the recommendations made in 1975 by a Puerto Rican-U.S. advisory group that had studied the problem for two years. A memorandum included with the resolution explained major details of the proposal. According to the memo:

The proposed Compact contains 19 sections, most of which simply confirm present law and policy. The United States' unfettered responsibility and authority with respect to foreign affairs and defense affecting Puerto Rico is explicitly stated; Puerto Rico may, however, enter into certain defined international agreements, and participate in specialized agencies of international organizations, unless the President determines that to do so would be inimical to the foreign relations of the United States. Common citizenship, a common currency, and a common market are affirmed.

The principal changes in existing law which would be effected by the Compact are:

(a) As to the applicability of Federal laws—

The current law (Section 9 of the Puerto Rico Federal Relations Act of 1950, which carries forward the language of 1900 and 1917 statutes) provides:

"That the statutory laws of the United States not locally inapplicable, except as hereinbefore or hereinafter otherwise provided, shall have the same force and effect in Puerto Rico as in the United States".

In other words, there is presently a presumption that U.S. statutes apply to Puerto Rico, unless they are "locally inapplicable". Specific language in given U.S. statutes reverses this presumption.

The problem with the presumption is that it runs contrary to the spirit of the Commonwealth idea—which emphasizes local autonomy and internal self-government for the people of Puerto Rico.

The Compact would change the presumption in the following ways:

(i) Current laws of the United States which are applicable to Puerto Rico, and future amendments of such laws, shall continue to be applicable, except insofar as they are changed by the Compact or incompatible with it.

(ii) Laws (other than those covered under (i) above) enacted after the effective date of the Compact shall not be applicable to Puerto Rico unless they explicitly refer to Puerto Rico and are compatible with the Compact.

(iii) Prior to the enactment of any legislation applicable to Puerto Rico, including an amendment to a currently applicable law (i.e., under (i) above) the Governor of Puerto Rico may submit to the President objections to its applicability to Puerto Rico. If the President finds that applying the legislation to Puerto Rico would be inconsistent with the Compact or is not essential to the interests of the United States, he may suspend the application of the law to Puerto Rico. If he does so, he must inform Congress of his action. Congress may then reverse this Presidential action by passing a concurrent resolution within 60 days.

(iv) A similar process is provided in the case of Federal rules and regulations. If Puerto Rico notifies the relevant Federal department or agency that it objects to the application of the rule or regulation to Puerto Rico, its objection will prevail unless the department or agency finds that application is necessary to the interests of the United States and is compatible with the Compact.

(v) On the initiative of the President, and with the concurrence of the Governor, the Compact makes possible the transfer to Puerto Rico of the total or partial performance of functions vested by law in the United States. In such cases, Puerto Rico will bear the administrative expenses associated with the performance of the transferred functions. Further, Congress is empowered to provide for the administration of legislation by Puerto Rico, to the end that appropriated funds may be adapted to the special needs and conditions on the island.

(b) As to tariffs—

As under current law, Puerto Rico is prohibited from imposing tariffs or duties on articles imported from the United States, and the United States will not impose such tariffs or duties on articles imported from Puerto Rico.

After coordinating with the Federal authorities concerned, Puerto Rico may levy, increase, reduce, or eliminate tariffs and quotas on articles imported directly into Puerto Rico from foreign countries or transshipped through the United States. so long as mutually agreeable procedures are established to avoid conflict with the United States' international obligations, and so long as other statutory conditions are met.

Puerto Rico may also, under the Compact, import materials duty free for subsequent shipment and sale to other parts of the United States, provided that the F.A.S. (free at side) shipping price contains at least 35% value added in Puerto Rico.

The purpose of this is to provide a new incentive for industries to locate in Puerto Rico, similar to those available to Guam and the Virgin Islands. It will also equalize Puerto Rico's relative advantage with other developing areas—which, under the 1974 Trade Act, have been afforded duty-free entry of products to which they add a substantial part of the value. It is those areas who are now Puerto Rico's chief competitors in labor-intensive industries.

Despite the progress made through "Operation Bootstrap", and despite the heavy trade between the mainland and the island (in 1974 Puerto Rican shipments to the U.S. totalled $2.8 billion, while imports from the United States amounted to $2.7 billion), Puerto Rico remains one of the poorest areas of the United States, with a per capita income only 40% of the United States average. It has been deeply affected by the U.S. recession (making its products harder to sell on the mainland), by inflation (making its imports from the U.S., particularly food, more costly at a time when its unemployment rate has exceed 20%), and by the quadrupling of petroleum prices (it is totally dependent on imported crude oil). If it is to renew the upward movement of its economy, it must be given a degree of flexibility with regard to trade and tariffs. An economically stronger Puerto Rico will be better able to provide for its people, thus reducing the burden on U.S. taxpayers and enhancing its position in the Caribbean.

Puerto Rico's long-standing exemption from Federal income taxes is retained.

(c) As to submerged lands—

The Compact substantially adopts the language of Public Law 600 of 1950, with regard to Puerto Rico's entitlement to property ceded to the United States by Spain in 1898. As in P.L. 600, the United States is expressly granted the right to continue to use for Public purposes such lands as are now so used.

The Compact then provides that bodies of water in and around Puerto Rico and its adjacent islands: "together with the submerged land underlying the same seaward to the limits of the continental shelf as may now or hereafter be recognized by the laws of the United States or international law as belonging to or appurtenant to the States or Puerto Rico, are and shall be the property of Puerto Rico".

(d) As to the entry of aliens into Puerto Rico—

While the United States immigration laws will continue to apply to Puerto Rico, the Compact provides a means by which the President and the Governor of Puerto Rico may agree on measures to limit the number of aliens in specified categories who may be admitted to Puerto Rico as permanent residents, or to permit aliens in other categories to be admitted to Puerto Rico as permanent residents. The Congress is empowered to deny effect to these measures by concurrent resolution.

Puerto Rico has one of the highest population densities in the world. It is also experiencing severe unemployment. Yet because it also has the highest living standard of any Latin American community, it has attracted large numbers of immigrants, particularly from the Caribbean area. It is important that Puerto Rico have some means of controlling this immigration, subject to approval by the President and Congress.

(e) As to the language of court proceedings—

The Compact provides that proceedings, pleadings, and records in the United States District Court for Puerto Rico shall be in Spanish, unless the Court, in the interest of justice and the effective administration of its work, shall otherwise determine in particular cases.

(f) As to responsibility for environmental quality—

As is the case with the states under Federal environmental laws, the primary responsibility for protecting and improving the quality of Puerto Rico's environment is to be Puerto Rico's. The Compact establishes the presumptive validity of Puerto Rico's environmental regulations, which are not to be disapproved or superceded by Federal regulations, unless they are determined to be clearly injurious to public health and safety. Since Puerto Rico is more than 1,000 miles from the mainland, and since economic conditions on the island are demonstrably different from those in the States, the Compact gives Puerto Rico both the authority and responsibility to protect its environment in a manner consistent with those geographical and economic conditions, while retaining Federal oversight and authority to correct abuses.

Ford backs statehood. President Ford Dec. 31 advocated statehood for Puerto Rico.

In a statement issued in Vail, Colo., Ford recalled that the Ad Hoc Advisory Group on Puerto Rico, appointed by the U.S. President and the governor of Puerto Rico, had recommended in 1975 a new compact of permanent union.

Ford said that he had concluded "that the proposed compact, significant and important though it is, does not advance as rapidly as it might freedom and opportunity for the American citizens of Puerto Rico."

He proposed that the people of Puerto Rico and the U.S. Congress "begin now to take those steps which will result in statehood for Puerto Rico." Ford said he would submit to Congress legislation to that effect.

Mixed reaction in Puerto Rico—In San Juan Dec. 31, incoming Gov. Carlos Romero Barcelo lauded Ford for "defending our right to equal citizenship."

"The news that the President will recommend to Congress that Puerto Rico be admitted as the 51st state," Romero Barcelo said, "should put the lie to claims heard here so frequently that the U.S. would never grant statehood to Puerto Rico even though the Puerto Ricans

PUERTO RICO

should request it after a democratically held referendum."

Romero Barcelo had campaigned as an advocate of statehood but had pledged not to take any action to achieve it during his four-year term. Instead, he said, that period would be used as an educational time for a plebiscite on statehood issues that would be held after he left office. In a 1967 plebiscite, 60.4% of the voters approved a commonwealth status, 38.9% statehood and .6% independence.

Gov. Rafael Hernandez Colon, who lost the election to Romero Barcelo, deplored Ford's move as contrary to U.S. commitments to the Puerto Rican people's right to self-determination.

"The people of Puerto Rico," Hernandez Colon said, "have never ceded that right to President Ford and they do not do so now." Hernandez Colon was an advocate of continued commonwealth status.

Former Gov. Luis Munoz Marin, chief architect of Puerto Rico's commonwealth status, issued a statement expressing "profound disagreement" with Ford's position.

Other Developments

Economic summit talks held, Ford warns Cuba not to meddle in Puerto Rico. The leaders of seven industrialized nations met in Dorado Beach, Puerto Rico June 27–28 for summit talks on economic problems. President Ford used the occasion to speak out against Cuban efforts to alter Puerto Rico's status.

Security was extraordinarily tight at the resort hotel where the conference was held, 20 miles west of San Juan. Prior to the opening session June 27, about 10,000 persons demonstrated peacefully outside the gates of the hotel compound. The demonstrations were organized by the Puerto Rican Socialist Party, which demanded independence for the island.

Arriving in San Juan June 26, Ford warned Cuba not to meddle in U.S.-Puerto Rican relations. Without naming Cuba, Ford said: "There are those who seek to distort the facts, to mislead others about our relations with Puerto Rico. The relation is clear and open. We are proud of the relationship that we have developed and we invite the world to examine it."

Noting that Puerto Rican voters had approved commonwealth status for their island in a 1967 national referendum, Ford said that critics of the U.S.-Puerto Rican relationship should grant their citizens the same freedom of choice.

"Those who might be inclined to interfere in our freely determined relations should know that such an act will be considered an intervention in the domestic affairs of Puerto Rico and the U.S.," Ford said. "It will be an unfriendly act which will be resisted by appropriate means."

U.S. officials confirmed later that the warning was intended for Cuba and said the phrase "appropriate means" encompassed diplomatic pressures and economic sanctions.

Romero Barcelo elected governor. In elections held Nov. 2, San Juan Mayor Carlos Romero Barcelo of the pro-statehood New Progressive Party (NPP) was chosen governor of Puerto Rico. He won an upset victory over Gov. Rafael Hernandez Colon and his Popular Democratic Party, which supported continuation of Puerto Rico's Commonwealth status.

With 111 of 113 precincts counted, the vote was 657,900–623,759; the Independence Party polled 72,715 votes. The NPP also won 40 of Puerto Rico's 78 mayoralties, compared with only three in 1972, and for the first time captured control of both state legislative bodies.

During the campaign, Romero Barcelo focused on Puerto Rico's severe economic problems, particularly the 20% unemployment rate.

Wiretapping charges probed. Federal and Commonwealth authorities were investigating charges that the government-owned Puerto Rico Telephone Co. had violated the rights of hundreds of citizens and engaged in political espionage through extensive, illegal wiretapping of private telephone conversations, the New York Times reported Nov. 27.

The charges were first made by the Puerto Rican Socialist Party, whose newspaper, Claridad, had reported July 30 that the telephone company's "Observations Department" periodically recorded calls in "various parts of the country, for no clear reason."

Socialist leader Juan Mari Bras charged at a press conference Aug. 2 that the telephone company had made "thousands of feet" of unauthorized recordings, including one of a conversation between two Socialist leaders. Mari Bras played that tape and five others for reporters. Then he called for the dismissal of Salvador Rodriguez Aponte, the phone company's president.

The Commonwealth government claimed the tapes were part of a "quality control" program but it discontinued the program Aug. 6. The government appointed a special prosecutor to look into the case, it was reported Aug. 4. He obtained Mari Bras' tapes Nov. 10 after a drawn-out court dispute.

Puerto Rico's Civil Rights Commission also investigated the case. In a report issued Sept. 13, the commission termed the tape-based monitoring system unconstitutional, saying the legal ban on wiretapping was "absolute." But, the commission said, it had found no evidence that the taping was done for purposes other than quality control.

The tape scandal apparently played some role in the November elections, in which Gov. Rafael Hernandez Colon was defeated by Carlos Romero Barcelo of the New Progressive Party. Romero had promised to try to sell the telephone company back to private enterprise, the Times reported Nov. 27.

Uruguay

Military Depose Bordaberry, Mendez Appointed President

President Juan Maria Bordaberry of Uruguay, criticized abroad as presiding over "the charnel house of Latin America" and as allowing the military to have virtually free rein in the violation of human rights, was deposed by the armed forces in mid-1976 in dispute over policy.

Bordaberry ousted. The armed forces removed President Juan Maria Bordaberry June 12, citing "irreconcilable" differences over Uruguay's political future.

The presidency was assumed temporarily that day by Vice President Alberto Demicheli, who was also chairman of the Council of State.

All Cabinet ministers remained in their posts except Housing Minister Federico Soneira, a personal friend of Bordaberry. The military reaffirmed its support for the austerity program of Economy Minister Alejandro Vegh Villegas.

Bordaberry, with military support, had ruled by decree since June 1973 when he dissolved Congress and the labor unions. He had been elected to a five-year presidential term in November 1971 in an election marred by charges of vote fraud in Bordaberry's favor.

In a communique announcing Bordaberry's removal, the military leadership charged that Bordaberry did not respect "the deep democratic convictions of our citizenry." The statement noted that Bordaberry had suggested that Uruguay's political parties be abolished, an act for which "the armed forces do not wish to share . . . historical responsibility."

Bordaberry had proposed in December 1975 that a corporate "new state" be established in Uruguay with a major role for the armed forces written into the constitution. While the military should direct policy, a team of civilians could execute it, Bordaberry suggested. He proposed that his own presidential term be extended for three years beyond its March 1977 expiration date.

Top military leaders rejected the proposal and named a committee of representatives to negotiate with Bordaberry over Uruguay's political future. The negotiations were abandoned after two months when the president demanded that the military chiefs instead of their representatives meet with him, the Associated Press reported May 7.

(Bordaberry's proposed "new state" was also rejected by Economy Minister Vegh Villegas, AP reported. Vegh said the abolition of political parties would facilitate political organizing by the outlawed Communist and other left-wing parties. He suggested instead a gradual return to rule by the major traditional parties, the Blancos and Colorados. Both groups were officially in "recess.")

U.S. Rep. Edward I. Koch (D, N.Y.) had said that Bordaberry had told the military junta in a memo that Uruguay "is not a democracy anymore." Koch inserted in the U.S. Congressional Record May 5 the following excerpts (as recorded in Excelsior, Mexico City, April 11) from Bordaberry's memo:

Today the dialogue between the President of the Republic and the Armed Forces is the only direct dialogue possible. The Armed Forces must make it clear whether they are ready to accept in principle the role that the President reserves for them. . . .

The power of the political parties and the power of the Armed Forces exclude each other. . . . a new order of power (must be established) in which the Armed Forces shall support the new government in replacement of the political parties . . .

It (the government) will have to extend the power, instead of limiting it as did previous Constitutions, because the enemy of personal liberty is not the government but by a danger coming from outside the country . . .

Government actions alone will determine whether the Constitution is good or bad, not whether these actions are unconstitutional, discussions which used to paralyze government actions in the past.

There is a need for a higher and permanent entity, a Supreme National Council in addition to the National Security Council for any important political decision-making, whose existence would allow the Armed Forces to take an immediate action in case of danger. The government would have the authority in this entity, supported by the consensus which comes about when the governing functions are carried out without interference from particular interests, either from the labor unions or the economy.

The political parties would represent the authorized opinion but would not be allowed to grab power in the traditional manner: through agitations or the press.

The legitimacy of voting has been gradually degenerating into the illegitimate creed that after obtaining electoral victory, there would exist a complete freedom of action even against the national will and interest. This is not a democracy anymore.

Bordaberry met with the military chiefs May 21 and June 1, but they were unable to compromise. The chiefs told the Council of State June 10 that Bordaberry would resign by June 27, the third anniversary of the closing of Congress. To speed the resignation, the army told the news media June 11 not to disseminate any statements from the president's office. Bordaberry refused to quit, and he was overthrown the next day.

Demicheli, two days after becoming president, announced June 14 that Uruguay would be returned to democratic rule, but not before 1979. The Blancos and Colorados would eventually be allowed to resume activities, but the Communist Party would remain banned. There would be a bicameral legislature, with the lower house composed of elected business and labor leaders.

Bordaberry June 13 resumed management of his large cattle ranch outside Montevideo.

New president named. The ruling National Council July 14 chose Aparicio Mendez, a conservative lawyer and former health minister, to be Uruguay's new president.

Mendez had been chairman of the National Council since it was officially formed June 27. He had previously been vice chairman of the Council of State, whose 25 members, along with 20 top-ranking military officers, composed the National Council.

At his first press conference July 15, Mendez said he planned a "civic purge" to root out any Marxists remaining in political institutions, public administration and the universities. But the purge would not entail "cutting off heads and dividing the country," he added.

Uruguay's traditional political parties, the Blancos and Colorados, would eventually play a role in the "new order" he intended to establish, Mendez said. Military sources had said earlier that the two parties would be allowed to select Mendez' successor after they were purged of "professional politicians."

Mendez' administration would apparently be under tight military control. United Press International had reported June 19 that the Uruguayan president's press office would henceforth be supervised by the head of the president's military household.

Uruguay would also get a new constitution, according to a military document reported by UPI. The charter would disavow "the concept of class struggle," it would allow "non-political labor unions" for "factories and companies only" and it would outlaw "strikes and lockouts."

(A spokesman for Montevideo's business community had told the Mexican newspaper Excelsior June 21 that leaders of the armed forces and of Uruguay's 20 largest companies had agreed that the government should continue its ban on all union activities.)

Mendez inaugurated, politicians banned. Mendez began his five-year term Sept. 1. He immediately decreed the suspension for 15 years the political rights of the leaders of all existing parties.

The ban on political leaders was occasioned by "the subversion and inertia of the political parties that led to shedding of innocent blood, limitation of liberties, collapse of security and administrative chaos," according to Mendez' decree. The ban was necessary to "prepare for the incorporation of new generations to political life through the traditional parties," the decree said.

The sanctioned leaders included Wilson Ferreira Aldunate, former presidential candidate of the Blancos; Jorge Batlle, former candidate of the major faction of the Colorado Party; Jorge Pacheco Areco, former president of Uruguay and Colorado leader; and all candidates of the leftist Broad Front coalition who ran on the ticket headed by retired Gen. Liber Seregni in the 1971 general elections.

Ferreira Aldunate, an outspoken critic of the military-civilian government, was living in exile. His arrest was ordered Aug. 5 by the Uruguayan armed forces on unspecified charges of subversion. An unidentified aide of Ferreira later took political asylum in the Mexican embassy in Montevideo, the Mexican newspaper Excelsior said Aug. 21.

A new Uruguayan Cabinet had been appointed Aug. 27, the French newspaper Le Monde said Aug. 29. Most members of the previous Cabinet were reappointed, but Economy Minister Alejandro Vegh Villegas was replaced by his top aide, Valentin Arismendi.

Vegh had told associates that he wished to leave office because he disagreed with government policies and wished to place himself "in reserve" for the future, Excelsior reported Aug. 11. Vegh was named Aug. 27 to the legislative Council of State, whose 25 members also served on the National Council.

Excelsior said that Vegh felt that Mendez' term of office was too long and that the armed forces' timetable for return to civilian rule was too slow. He also felt that it was a mistake for the government to persecute Ferreira Aldunate, whom Vegh considered not an "enemy" but a "political adversary" who could be "an ally under certain circumstances," the newspaper said.

Vegh had leaked news of his planned departure as a "trial balloon" to test the political reaction, Excelsior reported Aug. 11. Within hours, the newspaper said, the value of the Uruguayan peso fell sharply in trading on foreign exchange markets and businessmen pressured the economy minister to stay on. Vegh took the reaction as a sign of future political strength and reaffirmed his plans to quit and protect his reputation, Excelsior said.

In another political development, Uruguay's outgoing president, Alberto Demicheli, in a farewell speech Aug. 31, praised the armed forces. He said that if the military had not closed Congress and suspended the activities of political parties in 1973, the parties would have led Uruguay "into communism."

(A special committee headed by Uruguayan Interior Minister Gen. Hugo Linares restored the political rights of ex-President Juan Maria Bordaberry and five other politicians, it was reported Oct. 7. The six had been among thousands of political leaders whose rights were suspended by Mendez in his Sept. 1 decree.)

Abuses of Human Rights

Political arrests & torture charged. Amnesty International charged Jan. 13 that the government had arrested 600 to 700 persons in Uruguay for political reasons in October and November 1975, and many had been tortured in custody. Argento Estable, an alleged Communist sympathizer, had died in December after being tortured by soldiers, and Alberto Altesor, a former Communist Party leader, had disappeared after being arrested in October in a hospital where he was recovering from heart surgery, Amnesty reported.

Officials of the Soviet embassy in Montevideo had informally complained to the government about its strong anti-communist campaign and its public charges that Moscow had provided direct aid to the Uruguayan Communist Party, it was reported Jan. 10.

Youth groups banned. The government Jan. 20 banned two Christian youth groups—the Universal Federation of Christian Student Movements, based in Geneva, Switzerland, and the Frontier Internship, based in New York. They were charged with carrying out pilot programs for foreign leftist refugees in Uruguay and giving economic aid to Uruguayans emigrating for political reasons. The government charged the Universal Federation supported Cuba's educational reforms under Premier Fidel Castro.

Arrests mount, fugitives seek asylum. Meanwhile, political arrests reportedly continued in Montevideo and dozens of citizens took political asylum in foreign embassies to avoid detention. Some 20 doctors were seized along with two retired leftist army colonels, Carlos Zufriategui and Pedro Montanez, the Cuban press agency Prensa Latina reported Feb. 9. Several young military officers were arrested for alleged ties to the Communist Party, it was reported Feb. 28, and the singer Tabare Etcheverry was also detained, according to a report March 4.

(Most Communist Party leaders had been arrested following the discovery in December 1975 of party hideouts containing arms, ammunition, explosives and lists of party members, it was reported Feb. 24. Eight Communists had been tried by a military court for alleged subversive activities, according to the Montevideo radio station Radio El Espectador Jan. 17.)

Twenty-four persons were reported March 3 to have taken political asylum in foreign embassies in Montevideo, 20 in Mexico's embassy and the other four in Colombia's. Six of the refugees flew to Mexico March 5, and another eight followed March 12. By then the Mexican embassy had accepted another 70 refugees and the Colombian embassy another four, according to press reports.

Bombs exploded Jan. 11 at a hotel, nightclub and marina in Punta del Este, causing property damage but no casualties. A leftist group calling itself "Operation Aurora" took credit for the blasts. Retired Gen. Liber Seregni, leader of the outlawed leftist Broad Front coalition, was reported rearrested at his home near Punta del Este the same day.

Human rights abuse charged. Amnesty International began a worldwide campaign to publicize alleged abuses of human rights in Uruguay, notably the arrest, torture and killing of political prisoners.

Amnesty's office in London published a report Feb. 19 charging that 22 political prisoners had been tortured to death in Uruguay between May 1972 and November 1975, and two more prisoners had been killed since then. The president of Amnesty's chapter in Mexico City issued a list of the first 22 victims March 5, and the organization's London office issued two photographs March 11 which allegedly showed Uruguayan prisoners being tortured.

Uruguay's military-led regime refused to reply to the charges except to assert Feb. 18 and again March 11 that it did not recognize Amnesty's "legal or moral authority."

Amnesty's Feb. 19 report asserted that Uruguay had the world's highest proportion of political prisoners to total population, with 6,000 prisoners out of 2.5 million inhabitants. One of every 50 Uruguayans belonged to either the armed forces or the police force, the report added. The political prisoners were said to include workers, students, doctors, former members of Congress, union leaders, lawyers and teachers, most of them Communists but some of them Christian Democrats and members of the traditional center-right parties.

"The most sinister aspect of the Uruguayan repressive apparatus is the generalized and systematic use of torture, which constitutes a routine practice in the case of political prisoners," the report said. It listed various forms of torture used by the Uruguayan army and police including the "sawhorse," in which a prisoner was stripped and placed astride a sharp-edged, moving metal bar; and the "submarine," in which a prisoner was submerged in a tub of water and excrement.

The photographs released by Amnesty March 11 were said to have been sent from Uruguay by an unidentified army officer who said he had taken part in the torture but now felt revulsion for it.

The president of Amnesty's Mexican section, Alicia Escalante de Zama, issued a list March 5 of the 22 Uruguayans allegedly tortured to death in 1972-75. The victims included Edison Marin, a peasant and member of the outlawed National Liberation Movement (Tupamaros) allegedly torn to pieces by police dogs; Aldo Perrini Guala, drowned by the "submarine" method; and Dr. Carlos Alvariza, killed when his body was repeatedly thrown against a cement wall. Mrs. Zama said Amnesty would send an appeal to Uruguayan President Juan Maria Bordaberry to restore human rights, signed by 5,000 Mexicans.

Amnesty International reported in London May 10 that it had forwarded to Bordaberry a letter protesting human rights abuse in Uruguay. The letter was signed by 40 prominent human rights activists in the Soviet Union, including Andrei Sakharov, Andrei Amalrik and Alexander Ginsberg.

Wilson Ferreira Aldunate, the former presidential candidate of the Uruguay's Blanco party, said he had "no doubt" that the Uruguayan government had ordered the recent slaying in Argentina of Zelmar Michelini and Hector Gutierrez Ruiz, two former Uruguayan legislators, Excelsior, a Mexico newspaper, reported May 28. Ferreira arrived in France May 31 after taking political asylum earlier in the Austrian Embassy in Buenos Aires.

Venezuela suspends ties. Venezuela suspended diplomatic relations with Uruguay July 6, a week after alleged Uruguayan security officers invaded the grounds of the Venezuelan embassy in Montevideo and abducted a Uruguayan woman who was seeking asylum there.

Venezuela charged before the Organization of American States July 8 that Uruguay had committed a "clear violation of the right of asylum and of the sovereignty of states." The Uruguayan government newspaper La Manana denied the charge July 9 and asserted that Venezuela had joined an "international campaign against Uruguay."

According to Julio Ramos, Venezuela's ambassador in Montevideo, a Uruguayan woman had rushed into the embassy's garden June 28 shouting that she wanted asylum. Franklin Becerra, an embassy official, went to her aid. Then three plainclothed Uruguayan security officers entered the yard, struck Becerra and dragged the woman out by her hair. They put her in an automobile and drove her away.

Ramos immediately protested the incident to the Uruguayan government and demanded that the woman be returned to the embassy. The government replied June 29 that it regretted the incident but that the woman's abductors "do not belong to any official dependency, either police or military."

Uruguay promised to investigate the incident thoroughly; however, authorities arrested the police guard assigned to the Venezuelan embassy, making it impossible for him to make public statements on the identities of the abductors, the Miami Herald reported July 1.

In a further Venezuelan protest, Ramos stayed away from official joint ceremonies July 5 paying homage to the Uruguayan national hero Artigas and celebrating Venezuela's independence day. Uruguay reacted by declaring Ramos and Becerra personae non gratae. Venezuela then told Uruguay it was suspending diplomatic relations and officially announced the action July 6.

The Venezuelan government said July 6 that a private investigation by Ramos and Becerra had determined that the abducted woman was Elena Quintero de Diaz, 31, a schoolteacher. (The Uruguayan government had no comment other than to say that day that Diaz had left Uruguay in 1975 and had not "returned legally.")

The Venezuelan statement identified only one of Diaz' abductors, and then only by the nickname "Cacho." Uruguayan exile sources in Paris told the Mexican newspaper Excelsior July 7 that two of Diaz' abductors were "Cacho" Deniz and Jose Marquez, both police intelligence officers.

Ramos and Becerra returned to Venezuela July 7. They left the embassy in the hands of Colombian diplomats. The embassy continued to shelter five Uruguayans seeking political asylum in Venezuela, according to press reports.

Meanwhile, 106 Uruguayan political refugees flew from Montevideo to Mexico City June 24-July 2. The refugees, includ-.

ing five airforce officers, had taken asylum in the Mexican embassy in Montevideo in the preceding months. The air-force officers July 2 denounced Uruguay's "military dictatorship."

Torture reported common. The International Commission of Jurists said July 16 that torture of men, women and children by Uruguayan authorities was an everyday practice. The percentage of the national population under arrest was probably higher in Uruguay than in any other country, the commission added.

(Three nude bodies were found Sept. 6 floating in the River Plate near the Uruguayan city of Colonia, which was across the river from Buenos Aires, Argentina. The victims bore signs of torture and had their hands tied behind their backs with wire. They were presumed to have been killed by either Uruguayan or Argentine right-wing terrorists. Seventeen such corpses had been found on the Uruguayan side of the river since April 22.)

Mendez disavowed his comments Oct. 10 and the government confiscated that day's edition of La Manana. The reporter who had conducted the interview said that he had recorded the president's comments but had been forced to turn over the tape to Gen. Eduardo Zubia, chief of the second military region, which was based in San Jose, where the interview took place. The reporter said that in the interview Mendez had "gone further" on an off-the-record basis.

Lt. Gen. Julio Vadora, the Uruguayan army commander, denied Oct. 12 that the government violated human rights. "No one will teach us to respect the rights of the vanquished," he said, apparently referring to jailed leftists who were said to be the principal victims of torture.

El Pais and La Manana carried editorials Oct. 15 denouncing U.S. Rep. Edward Koch (D, N.Y.), the leading advocate of the ban on military aid to Uruguay. The newspapers printed transcripts of the congressional hearings on the aid-ban amendment, followed by editorial rebuttals.

At a hearing held Aug. 4 by a U.S. House subcommittee on international organizations, Hewson A. Ryan, deputy assistant secretary of state for inter-American affairs, testified that the U.S. had "a treaty-like obligation" to provide military aid to Uruguay. However, after persistent questioning from Rep. Donald M. Fraser (D, Minn.), the subcommittee's chairman, Ryan admitted that no such obligation existed.

Shortly after his testimony Ryan was transferred from the State Department's second-ranking post in Latin American affairs to become the department's senior inspector of the U.S.-Mexican border. He denied that the transfer was related to his testimony, the Washington Post reported Sept. 20.

Koch had told the subcommittee that "since the [Uruguayan] military is responsible for [the country's] systematic repression, our provision of military assistance . . . for 'internal security' purposes makes us accomplices in the repression," the Post reported. Koch said he hoped the aid ban would end the Uruguayan human-rights violations reported by Amnesty International, the International Commission of Jurists and other groups.

"But even if that does not result," Koch said, "I do not believe that the American people want to continue to support military despotism where the U.S. has no national security interests at stake."

Koch said in a statement inserted in the Congressional Record Aug. 10:

Perhaps the most tragic consequence of our policy is the case of Uruguay. Known as the "Switzerland of Latin America" because of its democratic and progressive traditions, it was subject to severe economic and political strain to the 1960's. An economic decline was coupled with the growth of the Tupamaros, a leftwing urban guerrilla group, who nearly destroyed all political order. The United States reacted by providing assistance to the police and military of Uruguay. By 1973 the military had won the battle against the terrorists. But a momentum had been established. Legitimate civilian control was lost as the military continued its drive for power. Using "subversion" as a pretext, the military has created a horribly repressive police state, jailing 5,000 Uruguayans, many of whom are peaceful and democratic opponents of the dictatorship. One in every 500 Uruguayans is a political prisoner. Since 1973 the United States has continued its military aid and increased economic support to the Uruguayan regime, despite repeated reports of widespread use of torture, reports which have been documented by Amnesty Interna-

URUGUAY

tional and the International Commission of Jurists. **The State Department appears to uncritically accept the Uruguayan Government's assertion that the repression is temporary but necessitated by internal threats.**

Supporting the aid ban Sept. 28, Sen. Frank Church (D, Idaho) charged that Uruguay had become "a torture chamber," surpassing "even Chile in the ferocity of its repression." Church said that 50,000 Uruguayans, or one out of each 500 citizens, recently had been jailed or temporarily detained.

Economic Developments

Inflation at 51.9%. Inflation in Uruguay for the 12 months that ended March 31 was 51.9%, according to statistics released by the national university's economics department and cited May 14 by the Latin America Economic Report.

The rise in the cost of living in March was 2.6%, the department said. The government had put the increase at 1.8%.

Wages, prices raised. The government July 3 announced a 20% wage increase and a series of price increases in basic consumer goods ranging from 4.6% for flour to 22.5% for rice. The wage raise was retroactive to July 1.

Wages had been frozen for the preceding six months under the austerity measures of Economy Minister Alejandro Vegh Villegas. The cost of living in Uruguay had risen by 44% in the 12 months that ended May 31, with a 1.4% increase in May, according to figures of the national university's economics department, cited July 2 by the Latin America Economic Report.

—The Uruguayan Trade Association reported Oct. 8 that the cost of living had risen 24.1% in January–August, with the major increases occurring in food prices.

—The government decreed a 6% wage increase Oct. 8 and a 14% rise in gasoline prices Oct. 11.

Soviet pact. Despite its anti-Communist stance, Uruguay signed a trade agreement with the Soviet Union, which included a $20-million Soviet loan for the purchase of machinery, according to the Latin America Economic Report April 20. In 1975 Uruguay's exports to the Soviet Union were worth $65 million while its imports were worth $9 million.

Trade deficit. The value of Uruguay's imports in 1975 again exceeded the value of Uruguay's exports.

Uruguay's foreign trade balance showed a $172.6-million deficit in 1975, according to government figures cited July 9 by the Latin America Economic Report. Exports were worth $383.8 million and imports, $556.4 million. Kuwait was the biggest source of imports, with a total value of $99.9 million. Brazil was the second leading supplier of imports, with $71.8 million, and provided the biggest market for Uruguayan exports, buying goods worth $65.4 million.

Peso devalued. The government devalued the peso by 1.94% Oct. 8. It was the 16th "mini-devaluation" of 1976, for a total peso depreciation of 30.42% since the beginning of the year.

Venezuela

Foreign Affairs

Kissinger visits. U.S. State Secretary Kissinger visited Venezuela in February during a six-country tour of Latin America.

The tour began Feb. 16 in Caracas, Venezuela. More than 20,000 police and national guardsmen were on hand for Kissinger's arrival, having dispersed hundreds of anti-Kissinger student demonstrators in the city only hours before. Kissinger met Feb. 16 and 17 with President Carlos Andres Perez and his foreign minister, Ramon Escovar Salom, and he made a major address Feb. 17 offering a six-point plan for U.S. cooperation in solving economic and other problems in the Western Hemisphere.

The plan, which offered no major new U.S. initiatives, committed the Ford Administration to: recognize that the more industrial nations in Latin America needed support and capital in their efforts to participate in the world economy; continue foreign aid to the neediest countries still "oppressed by poverty and natural disaster"; support regional and subregional organizations such as the Andean Group, the Central American Common Market and the Caribbean Common Market; negotiate all disputes on the basis of equality; support hemispheric collective security arrangements; and modernize the Organization of American States.

"It is time for all of us in the hemisphere to put aside slogans and turn from rhetoric to resolve," Kissinger told a group of businessmen, legislators and others in announcing the plan. The U.S. felt that it continued to have a "special relationship" with Latin America, he said, though in the past Washington had not "taken sufficiently into account that Latin America had experienced years of frustration in which lofty promises by the United States had been undone by the gradualism of the American political system, which responds less to abstract commitments than to concrete problems."

President Perez said Feb. 17 that he and Kissinger had discussed trade, oil and Cuban intervention in Angola, among other issues. The talks were reportedly cordial but cool. Perez said Kissinger had agreed to press for changes in the U.S. Trade Reform Act and to support the Latin American Economic System (SELA), and Kissinger said Venezuela and the U.S. generally agreed on the issue of Angola and Cuba. The U.S. and Venezuela issued a joint communique Feb. 17 envisioning closer cooperation in energy research, educational development and narcotics control.

A student was killed in Caracas Feb. 17 as demonstrations continued against Kissinger's visit and protesters clashed with national guardsmen. Students and police clashed again the next day, leading authorities to close the major university campus and most high schools.

Perez on tour. President Carlos Andres Perez went on an international tour Nov. 16–30, visiting the United Nations in New York and then traveling to Italy, Great Britain, the Soviet Union, Switzerland, Spain and Portugal.

Perez conferred with leaders of his host countries and signed trade and other economic agreements with four of the nations. During the tour he repeatedly promoted the economic independence of Third World countries and defended the right of the Organization of Petroleum Exporting Countries (OPEC) to raise oil prices.

Perez addressed the U.N. General Assembly Nov. 16. He said that OPEC's price increases were not "for the exclusive benefit of OPEC members," but represented "an irrevocable decision to dignify the terms of exchange and to revalue the raw materials and basic products of the Third World." He pledged to promote within OPEC an "automatic mechanism" to help poor nations buy oil at its current high prices.

Perez condemned colonialism, terrorism, racial discrimination and other abuses of human rights. He vigorously denounced apartheid in South Africa and announced that Venezuela was severing commercial relations with the Pretoria government. He also urged the U.S. to return to Panama complete sovereignty over the Canal Zone.

Perez visited Italy Nov. 17–21. He conferred with President Giovanni Leone Nov. 17, with Premier Giulio Andreotti and other leaders Nov. 18, and he had an audience with Pope Paul VI Nov. 20. At the end of his visit Perez signed a pact that would expand economic ties between Venezuela and Italy. He said Venezuela would deposit an unspecified sum of dollars in the Italian banking system to help alleviate Italy's acute economic crisis.

The Venezuelan leader flew to London Nov. 21 and began consultations with British political leaders and business executives the next day. Venezuela and Great Britain Nov. 23 signed a cooperation agreement that covered energy, transportation, the smelting of iron ore and manufacture of steel, petrochemicals, agriculture and fisheries, health and social services, environment and ship-building. Perez expressed faith in the strength of the British economy and said Venezuela would continue to deposit part of its reserves in British banks.

Perez continued to Moscow Nov. 24. He held three days of talks with Soviet President Nikolai Podgorny which he characterized as "very positive" but "frank and sometimes tough." Venezuela and the Soviet Union signed an agreement Nov. 26 that provided for general economic and technical exchange and included an oil interchange under which one party could ship its oil to the other party's customer to reduce shipping time and expenses. Under the arrangement Venezuela would be able to send oil directly to Cuba.

Perez criticized both the Soviet Union and the U.S. during his Soviet visit. At a state dinner in the Kremlin Nov. 25, he chided Moscow for not participating in the Conference on International Economic Cooperation (North-South Conference) in Paris. At a press conference at the Venezuelan Embassy in Moscow Nov. 26, Perez charged that the U.S. and the Soviet Union were not doing enough to end the armaments race.

He warned that "the time in which the Soviet Union and the U.S. made the decisions for everyone is over. The solid unity of the Third World gives us a new power of decision."

Perez flew to Switzerland Nov. 27, where he addressed a meeting of the Socialist International at the Geneva headquarters of the International Labor Organization. He traveled to Spain the next day, paying an unofficial 18-hour visit to King Juan Carlos I and Queen Sofia.

Perez completed his tour Nov. 29–30 in Portugal. He conferred with Premier Mario Soares and other leaders and addressed the National Assembly Nov. 29. In the address Perez pledged Venezuelan support for Portugal's fledgling democracy and vowed that Venezuela would continue to accept Portuguese immigrants. Venezuela and Portugal signed an agreement Nov. 30 under which Caracas would supply oil to Lisbon on easy credit terms. "Several Venezuelan groups will arrive in Portugal [soon] to study investments," Perez added before departing for Venezuela.

Colombians immigrate illegally. Hundreds of Colombians were entering

Venezuela daily and staying on illegally in hope of finding work in Venezuela's expanding economy, the New York Times reported Dec. 5.

Most of the illegal immigrants were peasants or other unskilled workers who lived in rural or urban poverty and took whatever jobs they could find—farm labor, shoe-shining, domestic service or any other work Venezuelans did not care to perform. Wages were considerably higher in Venezuela than in Colombia.

Ramon Ignacio Velasquez, head of the Venezuelan immigration bureau, estimated there were more than 300,000 Colombians living and working in Venezuela without papers. Other estimates put the total around 800,000, the Times said. Venezuela's population was 12.6 million; Colombia's was 24.7 million.

Economic Developments

Oil industry nationalized. The oil industry was formally nationalized Jan. 1 in a ceremony at Lake Maracaibo attended by top government officials and representatives of foreign nations including members of the Organization of Petroleum Exporting Countries (OPEC).

President Carlos Andres Perez raised the Venezuelan flag over the nation's first productive well, Zumaque No. 1, drilled in 1914 by Shell Caribbean Oil Co. He noted that the nationalization process, though "difficult," had been carried out "in a climate of friendship and peace."

"We are not nationalizing because we will earn more money," Perez declared. "We are nationalizing because oil is the nation's basic industry . . . and it is neither convenient nor acceptable that [it] be in foreign hands." He said OPEC members should use oil not as a weapon but as an instrument to correct injustices and further the dialogue between rich and poor countries which "got off to a good start in the recent North-South conference in Paris."

Perez added at a news conference Jan. 2 that the nationalization would facilitate creation of a Venezuelan "social democracy" which would "halt the concentration of wealth in the hands of a few" and provide "a genuine distribution of goods, above all to the least powerful classes."

The oil industry earned Venezuela $7.6 billion in 1975, or more than 80% of the nation's income.

Under the nationalization, all oil companies were absorbed by the state monopoly Petroleos Venezolanos (Petroven), which thus became the largest single supplier of crude oil to the U.S. Venezuela sold the U.S. more than 1 million barrels of oil daily, or more than one-third of the U.S.' oil imports.

Some foreign companies would remain in Venezuela to provide technical assistance and advice to subsidiaries of Petroven, and most of the 500 foreigners employed by the foreign firms would continue to work for the new Venezuelan companies. Exxon Corp. of the U.S. announced Jan. 6 that it had signed a contract to purchase an annual average of 965,000 barrels of oil per day from Petroven and to provide a wide range of services to Lagoven, the Petroven subsidiary operating the assets formerly owned by Creole Petroleum Corp., Exxon's Venezuelan affiliate.

Meanwhile, oil production was reported dropping sharply, having fallen to 1.75 million barrels per day in mid-December 1975 from the average of 2.4 million barrels a day in the first 11 months of the year. Production in 1976 might average 1.5 million barrels per day or less, the Wall Street Journal reported Jan. 7.

The production drop was generally attributed to declining demand and full storage tanks, though the government ascribed the fall to its desire to take over the industry with low stocks of oil, the London newsletter Latin America reported Jan. 2. The foreign oil companies had told the government they could not sell more than 1.4 million barrels per day at current Venezuelan prices because of the reduced world demand, but they had offered to buy as much as 2.36 million barrels a day from Venezuela at lower prices, Latin America noted.

In another oil development, Occidental Petroleum Corp. of the U.S. reported Jan. 1 that it was writing off its entire $73.4 million investment in Venezuela. The government had not offered to compensate Occidental for its nationalized assets because of reports that Occidental had bribed government officials.

Oil developments—Venezuela raised its oil export prices by an undisclosed amount Oct. 1. It was the fourth increase since the oil industry was nationalized Jan. 1, when the average price for Venezuelan crude was $10.97 per barrel. Prices had been increased July 1 by 10¢-15¢ per barrel for medium-gravity crudes and by 25¢-27¢ per barrel for high-sulfur residual fuel oils. Officials of the Mines and Hydrocarbons Ministry said the average price of Venezuelan crude could reach $11.40 per barrel by the end of 1976, the Wall Street Journal reported Sept. 3.

■ The government had completed planning for its long-awaited petrochemical development project, according to the June 11 Latin America Economic Report. The project, to cost $2.32 billion, comprised four main petrochemical complexes, two in western and two in eastern Venezuela. All were expected to be in operation by 1981.

■ The Venezuelan Scientific Research Institute announced Sept. 9 that it had developed a new way to transform sulfur-laden "heavy" crude oil into more marketable, sulfur-free "light" petroleum. The discovery would make it easier for the state oil company to develop the huge Orinoco tar belt which stretched across eastern Venezuela.

Bribe scandals. Military and civilian officials in Venezuela were implicated in February in a growing scandal over bribery of foreign officials by U.S. firms.

The air force began an inquiry into alleged Lockheed Aircraft Corp. bribes Feb. 10, after the Mexican newspaper Excelsior Feb. 7 printed an internal Lockheed letter noting that the company had paid for a visit to Disney World, Florida in 1974 by a Venezuelan lieutenant colonel, J. M. Laurentin, and his family.

Venezuelan President Carlos Andres Perez Feb. 14 gave his attorney general an official report on alleged bribes by Occidental Petroleum Corp., whose assets were nationalized by the Venezuelan government Jan. 1 along with those of all other foreign oil companies. The report said that in order to secure oil exploration contracts from the previous Venezuelan government, Occidental had paid $1.6 million in bribes to seven persons including Alberto Flores Ortega, then a Mines Ministry official and currently Venezuela's minister to the Organization of Petroleum Exporting Countries (OPEC).

(Venezuelan newspapers reported Feb. 17 that to secure oil contracts in 1971, Occidental had made payments to relatives of a number of officials, including $106,400 to Alberto Flores' father.)

A Caracas judge Nov. 16 dismissed charges against six persons accused of conspiring to use illegal means to obtain oil contracts for Occidental Petroleum.

Judge Carmen Romero de Encinoso ordered the immediate release of five of the accused who had been arrested in July. The sixth defendant, Chandra Takur, an Indian economist, was believed to have fled the country after learning of his indictment.

Encinoso also closed a police investigation of eight persons in connection with the case. Two of the suspects had died during the probe.

The five released from prison Nov. 16 were Alberto Flores Ortega and Alberto Flores Troconis, the father of Flores Ortega; Jose Toro Hardy, a Venezuelan oil executive; Luisa Rondon de Rivero Vasquez, widow of a Venezuelan businessman, and John Askew, an American.

The case involved the award to Occidental of three 123,500-acre oil concessions in Southern Lake Maracaibo in 1970.

A Venezuelan congressional panel had issued a report June 8 saying that Askew, a former consultant to Occidental who lived in Venezuela, had made payments to the other defendants from $3 million in fees he received from the U.S. company. The money was to have been used to win favors for Occidental, but the defendants had not been in a position to influence government decisions on oil-service contracts, the report concluded.

The congressional panel said that because of Occidental's "irregular" activities, the company should not be compensated by the government for its nationalized Venezuelan assets.

Armand Hammer, Occidental's chairman, denounced the panel's report June 10. He said that its charges had no "supportive evidence," and that its recommendation against compensation for Occidental was "contrary to the constitution of Venezuela."

Hammer acknowledged that Occidental had paid Askew $3 million, but he said the money had been paid for "valuable

VENEZUELA

services" rendered by Askew and not for "an irregular purpose."

Occidental again July 14, after the seven arrest warrants were issued, denied any wrongdoing. The company said it "didn't direct, authorize or have any knowledge of alleged attempts to bribe Venezuelan officials."

Foreign banks arrange $1-billion loan. The Royal Bank of Canada and eight other international banks in the U.S. and Europe were arranging a $1-billion loan to the Venezuelan government, a spokesman for the Canadian bank announced Sept. 15.

The loan, described as the largest private credit ever granted to a Latin American government, would be used to refinance the maturing short-term foreign debt of several autonomous institutions in Venezuela. These included the National Housing Agency, the Venezuelan Petrochemical Institute, and Nitraven, the state petrochemical company.

The loan would carry about 7.5% interest over seven years. The fluctuating interest rate would be computed by adding 1.125% to the London interbank offer rate, which was usually adjusted every six months. On Sept. 15 the rate was quoted as 6.125%.

Besides the Royal Bank of Canada, the managers of the loan were four U.S. and four European banks. The U.S. lenders were Citicorp International Ltd., Morgan Guaranty Trust Co. of New York, Chemical Bank and Continental Illinois National Bank and Trust Co.

In a related development, two Venezuelan banks joined forces with British and Kuwaiti banks Sept. 17 to form Araven Finance Ltd. The new company would channel long-term development funds into Venezuela, provide a range of financial services to the Venezuelan economy and promote joint ventures between Venezuelan and Arab interests, the Journal of Commerce reported Sept. 20. The founding partners were Morgan Grenfell and Co. Ltd. of Great Britain, Kuwaiti International Investment Co. of Kuwait, and Banco Latino and Banco del Centro Consolidado of Venezuela.

World Bank lauds economic actions. A confidential World Bank study of the Venezuelan economy said that the government had been "highly successful" in handling the "serious and immediate problems arising from the sudden expansion of the country's financial resources," the New York Times reported Oct. 16.

The study, an interim report, said that Venezuela's "successful global economic management of the last three years needs now to be complemented with well-designed policies and measures in the fields of petroleum policy, fiscal reform, manpower and industrial and agricultural development."

Due to an increase in petroleum prices, Venezuelan treasury revenues had risen from $3.82 billion in 1973 to $9.53 billion in 1975, and official expenditures had kept pace with income. The expansion of government spending had produced pressure on prices through burgeoning demand and an upward adjustment of wages, the study noted. Inflation was estimated at 16% in 1974 and 13.32% in 1975. (The inflation rate for the first six months of 1976 was estimated at 7.1%, according to the Aug. 6 Latin America Economic Report.)

If government expenditures continued to rise, the study said, there would be an annual fiscal gap of about $3.5 billion over the 1976-80 period. Nevertheless, Venezuela's balance of payments "would not constitute a serious problem during the period," the study added.

Pilot strike. Venezuelan airline pilots struck Sept. 14-30 to protest bad working conditions and the "unsafe" state of the country's airports. The government declared the strike illegal and arrested strike leaders, but it eventually agreed to improve conditions for the pilots. However, 23 pilots were fired by their employers for being "troublemakers." The companies affected were two domestic airlines—Linea Aeropostal Venezolana and Aerovias Venezolanas S.A.—and Venezuela's international airline, Viasa.

Electricity firm nationalized. The government nationalized the Canadian International Co., the main supplier of electricity to western Venezuela, which had four subsidiaries in the country's major oil-producing regions, it was reported Nov. 12. The firm received $100 million in compensation.

Unrest & Violence

Students riot. Students rioted in San Felipe (Yaracuy State) and other cities Feb. 14-25 after two San Felipe students were killed, apparently by policemen, during a demonstration to demand improved facilities at a local school.

The protests were intensified by student hostility to U.S. Secretary of State Henry Kissinger, who visited Caracas Feb. 16-18.

San Felipe was virtually paralyzed Feb. 16 as transport workers and shopowners went on strike to protest the students' deaths. The fathers of both victims were transport workers. There were fresh riots that day in San Felipe as the dead students were buried.

All political parties denounced the killing of the students, and Interior Minister Octavio Lepage told the victims' parents that the culprits would be punished. The opposition Popular Electoral Movement demanded the dismissal of the governor of Yaracuy and his police chief, whom it held responsible for the deaths. The governor was later removed by the federal administration in Caracas.

Riots continued in San Felipe Feb. 17 as the national guard, which had occupied the city for several days, struggled to maintain order. Twenty-eight persons had been injured since Feb. 14 and 150 had been arrested, including 10 municipal policemen presumed to be linked to the killing of the students. Police charged that outside agitators and "saboteurs" were encouraging the rioters, and the Caracas newspaper El Nacional reported that persons in civilian dress were seen firing on student demonstrators in San Felipe and that others claiming to be guerrillas of the National Liberation Armed Forces (FALN) were attacking national guardsmen. Nevertheless, shops and businesses in the city reopened Feb. 17 and transport workers returned to their jobs.

The unrest spread Feb. 17 to Merida and Maracaibo, where students stoned businesses, and to Coro, Tucupita, Valencia, Barcelona and Barquisimeto. Students in Caracas damaged 23 buses and sacked a local office of the ruling Democratic Action Party Feb. 18. The next day there were student protests in Guarenas, where seven buses were burned, in San Fernando de Apure, where five persons were injured, and in at least 13 other cities including 11 state capitals.

Torture death, deputies' arrest scored. A furor was touched off in Caracas in late July and early August when a political prisoner was tortured to death and two federal deputies were arrested in connection with the February abduction of William Niehous, a U.S. business executive.

The controversy began July 27 when the government disclosed that a leftist prisoner had died July 25 after being interrogated by agents of Disip, Venezuela's police intelligence squad. Newspapers and opposition politicians reported that there were signs of torture on the body of the victim, Jorge Antonio Rodriguez, leader of the small Venezuelan Socialist League. The government ordered a "rigorous" investigation of the incident and Aristides Lander, Disip chief, resigned.

Opposition parties, notably the Movement to Socialism, charged July 27 that other political prisoners also had been tortured. The Justice Ministry ordered medical checks for three prisoners July 28, and it admitted July 30 that two of them had been tortured.

Interior Minister Octavio Lepage said July 27 that Rodriguez had been "a contact" with the guerrilla group that had kidnapped Niehous. Lepage said that Rodriguez and two other alleged contacts were arrested July 20 when police intercepted several million dollars in ransom money being passed on to them by presumed agents of Niehous' employer, Owens-Illinois Inc.

Lepage said that two left-wing federal deputies, Salom Mesa Espinoza of the People's Electoral Movement and Fortunato Herrera, formerly of the Democratic Republican Union, also were involved in Niehous' kidnapping. The two were arrested Aug. 3, touching off further protests from opposition parties because deputies were immune from arrest.

President Carlos Andres Perez defended the arrests Aug. 5. He said that they were made by military officers under provisions of the military code that authorized the arrest of civilians who formed

VENEZUELA

part of an armed group. They were the first arrests of legislators since 1963, when two deputies were seized for alleged connections with guerrilla groups. Those arrests too were ordered by Perez, who was then interior minister.

Payment of the ransom would have satisfied the third demand by Niehous' kidnappers. The other two demands were payment of a $116 bonus to each of Owens-Illinois' 1,600 employes in Venezuela, and financing of the publication of a manifesto by the guerrillas in foreign newspapers. Owens-Illinois had met both demands, it was reported April 6.

The Venezuelan government seized Owens-Illinois' assets April 6 in reprisal for its financing of the manifesto's publication. Government officials said that the company would be paid "just" compensation for its nationalized property.

The government had closed a television station for 72 hours and seized one issue of a Caracas newspaper after each disseminated unauthorized reports on the kidnapping, it was reported April 6. The television station had broadcast an interview with a woman who claimed to be in contact with the kidnappers.

In a related development, Tito Gonzalez Heredia, second-in-command of the Red Flag guerrilla group, was fatally wounded in a gun battle with Disip agents in Caracas, the London newsletter Latin America reported July 2.

Niehous kidnap probe stalled. The Venezuelan government admitted Oct. 9 that there were no new leads in its investigation of the William Niehous kidnapping.

Four persons were awaiting military trial in the case, including two opposition congressmen, Salom Mesa Espinoza and Fortunato Herrera.

Following a heated congressional debate on the arrests, the Supreme Court had asked Aug. 12 to see all documents related to the case. The court ruled Aug. 25 that the arrests were unconstitutional but that there was enough evidence to warrant continued investigation of the congressmen on suspicion of the crime of "military rebellion." The court recommended that the congressmen be held under house arrest until the Delegated Commission of Congress voted on whether to lift their parliamentary immunity.

The commission voted to lift the immunity Aug. 26. The vote against Mesa Espinoza was 12–11, with all government delegates voting to lift his immunity and all opposition delegates voting not to. The vote against Herrera was 20–3.

The Supreme Court's intervention had been requested by Attorney General Jose Ramon Medina, who had disputed President Carlos Andres Perez' contention that the kidnapping constituted an act of "military rebellion" and therefore justified the congressmen's arrest. Newspapers on the right and left unanimously had condemned the arrests, according to the Aug. 20 London newsletter Latin America.

Nearly 400 persons had been detained in the Niehous case, most of them under the military code of justice, which allowed indefinite arrest without trial or recourse to civil appeal courts, Latin America reported.

Meanwhile, Niehous' professed kidnappers, the Argimiro Gabaldon Commandos of the Group of Revolutionary Commandos, said in a communique that the U.S. executive was still alive, Latin America said Aug. 20. Niehous' wife, showing little confidence in the Venezuelan police investigation, offered a $500,000 reward for information leading to the discovery of her husband's whereabouts.

Owens-Illinois Inc., Niehous' employer, was at odds with the Venezuelan government over the terms of the nationalization of its Venezuelan subsidiary, the Journal of Commerce reported Nov. 1.

Business sources in Caracas told the Journal that the government and the U.S. company were deadlocked over the designation of a three-man board to arbitrate the nationalization. Owens-Illinois wanted the board to decide whether the nationalization actually would be permitted, while the government insisted that the board only decide the amount of indemnization to be paid to the U.S. company. The board reportedly would comprise a company representative, a government delegate and an impartial representative, perhaps from the International Chamber of Commerce.

Owens-Illinois initially had demanded almost $165 million for its installations, which represented about 70% of Venezuela's annual glass-manufacturing capacity, the Journal reported. Venezuela had countered with a $25 million offer—representing the net book value of Owens-Illinois' assets in the country. The company then lowered its demand to $100 million, the Journal said.

Diplomatic sources in Caracas called the nationalization a "prime irritant" in U.S.-Venezuelan relations, the Journal said. The U.S. State Department reportedly had expressed displeasure over Venezuela's handling of the affair.

Political prisoners on hunger strike. An undisclosed number of political prisoners had been on a hunger strike for three weeks, demanding that they no longer be treated as military offenders, the London newsletter Latin America reported Oct. 1.

Attorney General Jose Ramon Medina had urged military authorities to take the demand seriously, but his recommendation had not been acknowledged by the Defense Ministry, the newsletter said. Eighteen prisoners reportedly were seriously ill as a result of the strike.

The government denied that there were any political prisoners in Venezuela, but 54 prisoners were being held under the military code of justice, instituted in the early 1960s to combat leftist guerrillas. All were charged with varying degrees of "military rebellion," but only seven had been tried and sentenced, according to an Amnesty International report cited by Latin America. Forty had been held for more than a year without formal charges, Amnesty International said.

Venezuela indicts 4 in Cuban jet crash. A district judge in Caracas, Venezuela Nov. 2 charged four Cuban exiles with the murder of 73 persons who died Oct. 6 when a Cuban passenger jet crashed in the Caribbean Sea after two bombs exploded on board.

Judge Delia Estaba Moreno issued indictments for "qualified homicide and manufacture and use of war weapons" against Orlando Bosch, Luis Posada, Hernan Ricardo and Freddy Lugo. All pleaded not guilty. All but Bosch were naturalized Venezuelan citizens.

Bosch and Posada had been arrested in Caracas a few days after the Cuban jet crashed. Ricardo and Lugo had been arrested in Trinidad & Tobago Oct. 7 and deported to Venezuela Oct. 26. Their deportation suggested that the five nations affected by the plane crash—Trinidad, Venezuela, Cuba, Barbados and Guyana—had decided that Venezuela should try the alleged saboteurs.

Representatives of the five nations had met in Trinidad Oct. 21–22 but had issued no statement on their talks. Sources close to the talks told newsmen that a majority had wanted Barbados to try the suspects but that Barbados had refused in apparent fear that the trial would hurt tourism.

In the face of sharp criticism from the other countries, Barbados asserted that there was insufficient evidence for an indictment—despite confessions reportedly written by Ricardo and Lugo in Trinidad—and that the crash had occurred outside Barbados' three-mile offshore territorial limits. (The wreckage was found Oct. 25 about five miles from the island.)

Trinidad also declined to hold the trial, claiming that it lacked enough policemen to conduct a thorough investigation. Cuba was ruled out for undisclosed reasons, and Guyana's only connection to the tragedy was the 11 Guyanese nationals killed in the crash. Venezuela apparently agreed to hold the trial despite its reported fear that the proceedings would anger the large Cuban-exile community in Caracas.

The Venezuelan indictment did not say whether the defendants would be tried in civil or military court. An impartial civil trial was considered unlikely because the civil courts were openly political and some of the defendants had ties to the Venezuelan police and government, the Washington Post reported Oct. 31. Venezuelan judges were appointed by the ruling Democratic Action Party, were allowed to make their investigations in secret and were not required to explain their decisions. Defendant Luis Posada was a former operations chief of Disip, the Venezuelan political security police, which was in charge of the local investigation of the Cuban jet crash.

(The Venezuelan police and government also had ties to other Cuban exiles who supported actions against the Cuban government, making a fair civil trial of the alleged saboteurs even less likely, the Miami Herald noted Oct. 24. Hildo Folgar, a Cuban-born gynecologist, was a personal friend and family physician of Venezuelan President Carlos Andres Perez. Orlando Garcia, another Cuban exile, was deputy director of Disip and security adviser to Perez. Bernardo Viera Trejo, a public relations man who reportedly had been seen with Orlando Bosch, had worked for Perez' presidential campaign in 1973.)

Lawyers for the four defendants said that it would be very difficult to prove the prosecutor's case. They noted that there was no evidence that the explosion that caused the Cuban jet to crash was caused by a bomb. They also said that if a bomb were the cause, there was no proof that the bomb was manufactured by the defendants. Sebastian Alvarez, attorney for one of six other Cuban exiles who were arrested in the case and later released without charge, said Nov. 2 that the only evidence in the case was the "divination" of the judge.

Nevertheless, an investigator in the case told the Caracas newspaper El Nacional Oct. 30 that the government had "more than 50 proofs" of conspiracy by the defendants. The Cuban Embassy in Caracas said Nov. 4 that it had given Venezuela additional evidence including bomb fragments recovered from the plane's wreckage by Cuban divers.

Among the evidence against the defendants, according to press reports:

■ A taxi driver taking Hernan Ricardo and Freddy Lugo to their hotel in Trinidad Oct. 6 heard them discussing the plane's bombing and laughing over it, the Washington Post reported Nov. 3.

■ Trinidadian police said they had proof that Ricardo had contacted Luis Posada from the hotel. Police also said that both Posada's girlfriend and his secretary in Caracas had confirmed that they had passed on this message from Ricardo to Posada: "The truck has left with a full load," the Post reported. (The truck and load presumably referred to the Cuban plane and the bombs.)

■ Ricardo had cabled Cuban exiles in Caracas during his brief stay in Barbados Oct. 6, asking for a "considerable" sum of money, El Nacional reported Oct. 30. Some of the money was sent to him, the newspaper said.

■ Trinidadian police confiscated baggage belonging to Ricardo. The baggage contained floor plans of the Cuban embassies in Venezuela, Mexico and Jamaica and plans of various airports in the Caribbean with their schedules of foreign flights, El Nacional reported Oct. 31.

Ricardo and Lugo, both of whom were professional photographers, told the Caracas newspaper El Mundo Oct. 26 that they had gone to Barbados only to check camera prices. Trinidadian police said Oct. 22 that Ricardo the previous day had tried to commit suicide in jail by slashing a wrist. He was taken to a hospital that day and released soon afterward.

Joseph Leo, an FBI agent attached to the U.S. Embassy in Caracas, had been in contact with Bosch's alleged fellow saboteurs, Luis Posada and Hernan Ricardo, the Washington Post reported Oct. 25.

The report, confirmed by the U.S. Embassy, appeared to contradict U.S. Secretary of State Henry Kissinger's recent assertion that "no one in contact with the American government has had anything to do" with the crash of the Cuban jetliner Oct. 6.

Leo had maintained "a casual acquaintance with Luis Posada when Posada was a Disip official," an embassy spokesman told the Post. Leo had helped Ricardo obtain a one-year U.S. business visa earlier in 1976 for a trip to Puerto Rico on a photographic assignment for Vision magazine, the spokesman said. Vision denied any association with Ricardo, the Post noted.

Leo's name and telephone number also appeared in the appointment book of a third alleged saboteur, Freddy Lugo, the Post said. The U.S. Embassy spokesman denied that Leo had had any personal contact with Lugo.

Leo's contacts with the alleged saboteurs first had been raised by Guyanese Premier Forbes Burnham, who charged Oct. 17 that the U.S. was ultimately "responsible" for the Cuban plane crash. Burnham accused the U.S. of attempting to "destabilize" his socialist government.

Burnham's charges caused a sharp deterioration of ties between the U.S. and Guyana, U.S. State Department officials said Oct. 21. Frederick Z. Brown, a State Department spokesman, charged Oct. 20 that "the Burnham speech contained bald-faced lies." A Guyanese spokesman replied Oct. 21 that the U.S. had "overreacted" with "crudity and rudeness."

Venezuela expels U.S. journalists—Three U.S. journalists who flew to Venezuela to report on the plane-sabotage case were detained by police after their arrival Oct. 21 and deported to the U.S. the next day.

Venezuela gave no explanation for the action against Taylor Branch, a columnist for Esquire magazine; John Rothchild, a free-lance writer accompanying Branch, and Hilda Inclan, Latin American affairs reporter for the Miami News. The Washington Post reported Nov. 1 that the journalists had been expelled because they recognized Ricardo Morales Navarrete, the Disip officer in charge of security at Maiquetia International Airport, as a Cuban exile who had been a paid informant of the U.S. Federal Bureau of Investigation in Miami in the late 1960s.

Morales had been a key witness against Orlando Bosch in 1968 when Bosch was convicted of firing a bazooka at a Polish ship in Miami. A few years later a bomb had exploded in Morales' car in Miami, and Morales had blamed Bosch for the attack. Morales had moved to Venezuela in 1975. Since then, there were conflicting reports that Morales had patched up his differences with Bosch and that he had lured Bosch to Venezuela for arrest, according to the Oct. 24 Miami Herald. Morales refused to confirm or deny either report, the Herald said.

Cuban exiles deny link to Letelier slaying. Venezuelan police denied recent reports that Orlando Bosch had told them that two Cuban exiles, Guillermo and Ignacio Novo, had planted the bomb that killed former Chilean Foreign Minister Orlando Letelier in Washington Sept. 21, the Washington Post reported Oct. 21.

Guillermo Novo, who lived in Union City, N.J., denied Oct. 20 that he or his brother had been involved in Letelier's assassination.

A spokesman for the Institute for Policy Studies, which had employed Letelier at the time of his death, said Oct. 18 that the FBI was sending one or two agents to Venezuela to investigate possible links between Cuban exiles there and Letelier's murder. The FBI refused to confirm or deny the report, the Washington Post said Oct. 20.

Other Areas

BAHAMAS

Opposition. Chester Wallace Whitfield was elected leader of the opposition Free National Movement Jan. 12, following the resignation of former leader Kendal Isaacs. Whitfield had stayed out of active politics since his party was defeated in the 1972 general elections.

Foreign firms. Many firms incorporated in the Bahamas had announced plans for shutting down operations before Feb. 1, when they were due to be taxed under new legislation because they were not owned 60% or more by Bahamians, it was reported Jan. 22. The government's gradual removal of tax breaks for foreign banks, financial conglomerates and other businesses had caused many corporations to move to the nearby Cayman Islands, still a British colony.

Bahamas. Michaiah Shobek, a U.S. citizen, was hanged Oct. 19 for murdering three American tourists in the Bahamas in 1974. Shobek, a 22-year-old handyman from Milwaukee, said that he had killed the tourists on orders from God. He was buried in a pauper's grave outside Nassau.

BARBADOS

BLP wins elections; Adams takes office. The opposition Barbados Labor Party (BLP) won 17 of the 24 seats in the House of Assembly (parliament) in elections Sept. 2. J. M. G. (Tom) Adams, party leader, was sworn in as prime minister Sept. 3.

Adams succeeded Errol Barrow, who had served as prime minister since 1961 and had led Barbados to independence from Great Britain in 1966. Barrow's Democratic Labor Party (DLP) won the remaining seven parliament seats Sept. 2, losing its previous 17–7 majority.

The BLP had campaigned for a free national health service, elimination of both a 5% sales tax and corporate and trade taxes, a charter for women and a program to fight unemployment. Adams had charged that unemployment had reached 28%, while Barrow had put it at 13.7%.

The BLP also had accused the DLP of becoming arrogant, lethargic and corrupt after so many years in office. Barrow, the BLP charged, had insulted and threatened leaders of religious and other groups that had opposed constitutional changes pushed through parliament by the DLP in 1974. One of the changes "gave the political element considerable voice in the appointment of [Barbados'] chief justice and other judges," the Miami Herald said Aug. 28.

The BLP also charged that DLP members had accepted payoffs to approve the establishment in Barbados of a bank owned by Sidney Burnett Alleyne, a London-based Barbadian and self-styled financier, the Herald reported.

The DLP campaigned on what it called its record of stability and social and economic progress. Barrow noted that he had diversified the Barbadian economy, once totally dependent on the sugar crop, by developing tourism and light manufacturing industries. Barbados, the DLP noted, had remained politically and socially stable under Barrow while some Caribbean states, such as Jamaica and Grenada, had experienced civil unrest and others, such as Guyana, had moved politically to the left.

Adams called for national unity after being sworn in as prime minister Sept. 3. He said: "We will continue our policy of independence and [we] have no plans to change Barbados' present attitude toward Western countries, the nonaligned countries or on issues on which Barbados will be called to take a stand in the United Nations." He indicated that Taiwan would be asked to close its embassy in Bridgetown unless it dropped its "unrealistic" insistence that its Republic of China government represented the people of China.

Adams, 44, was the son of Sir Grantley Adams, who was prime minister of the West Indies Federation during its brief existence from 1958–62.

Americans deported in 'plot.' Prime Minister J.M.G. Adams announced Oct. 25 that two U.S. citizens had been deported from Barbados for allegedly participating in an anti-government plot.

Adams said that the Americans, Robert Virgo and Gerry Cappadoro, had conspired with two members of the opposition Democratic Labor Party (DLP) and with a "notorious" Barbadian who had been arrested in Martinique aboard a yacht laden with guns and ammunition. Police in Martinique identified the Barbadian as Sidney Burnett Alleyne, head of the defunct Alleyne Mercantile Bank in Bridgetown, the Miami Herald reported Oct. 28. Allegations that Alleyne had bribed members of the DLP had contributed to the party's defeat in the September parliamentary elections.

Adams said Oct. 25 that Virgo and Cappadoro had been arrested at the home of Earl Glasgow, a former aide to Earl Barrow when Barrow was prime minister and DLP leader. Barrow denied that the DLP had anything to do with the alleged conspiracy, it was reported Nov. 12.

(Barrow had resigned as DLP leader and been replaced by Frederick Smith, the former education minister, the London newsletter Latin America said Sept. 24.)

BELIZE

Prime Minister George Price of Belize was pressing Great Britain to seek a United Nations guarantee of Belizean independence and territorial integrity against the claims of Guatemala, it was reported Jan. 8. Price arrived in London Jan. 5 for conversations with British officials on the future of Belize, a British colony over which Guatemala claimed exclusive sovereignty.

Representatives of Britain and Guatemala met in Panama City Sept. 21–22, with Price sitting in the British delegation, to discuss Belize's future. No details of the talks were disclosed, but British officials said relations between Great Britain and Guatemala had improved dramatically in recent months, the London newsletter Latin America reported Oct. 15. Representatives of Guatemala and Belize held their first bilateral talks Oct. 26–28 in San Pedro Sula, Honduras. The meeting covered economic questions but no details were disclosed.

Great Britain wanted to grant independence to Belize, but Belize would not accept it without a guarantee of military protection against invasion by Guatemala. London seemed unwilling to make the guarantee, and Belize had said it would accept protection from the U.S. or another country, the Oct. 4 Miami Herald said.

Diplomatic sources quoted by the Herald believed that Guatemala's demand for full control of Belize had been hardened by recent reports of oil deposits off the Belizean coast.

COSTA RICA

Discontent. About 100 persons were arrested in San Jose Jan. 9 for rioting in front of the presidential house to protest a 25% increase in urban transport fares. Fifty-four of the detainees were reported freed Jan. 10. Before the riot, unknown arsonists had set fire to three buses in the capital.

President Daniel Oduber charged Jan. 16 that labor, popular and student organizations in Costa Rica were increasingly infiltrated by communists who were responsible for recent political unrest.

Leading associations of businessmen had expressed strong opposition to recent increases in taxes and in the foreign exchange rates for luxury imports, it was reported Jan. 20.

Kissinger on tour. U.S. Secretary of State Henry Kissinger visited Venezuela, Peru, Brazil, Colombia, Costa Rica and Guatemala Feb. 16–24, conferring with their presidents on trade and other bilateral and international issues.

Kissinger arrived Feb. 23 in Costa Rica, where Foreign Minister Gonzalo Facio hailed him as "one of the greatest architects of world peace" and some 30,000 student demonstrators denounced him as "the principal architect" of the military coup in Chile in 1973. Facio praised the U.S. policy of detente with the Soviet Union and said Costa Rica proudly counted itself as a U.S. ally.

Kissinger also met in Costa Rica Feb. 24 with the foreign ministers of Honduras, El Salvador, Panama, Nicaragua and Guatemala. He had planned to hold a summit conference there with all Central American presidents, but the meeting had been canceled Feb. 17 after the leaders of Guatemala, El Salvador and Honduras declined to attend because of what they described as pressing domestic matters.

Figueres accused. A court-appointed receiver in New York accused ex-President Jose Figueres of a role in a plan to loot $24 million from Capital Growth Co., a mutual-fund group based in Costa Rica that once had 16,000 public investors, the Wall Street Journal reported Sept. 22.

Michael Armstrong, the receiver for Capital Growth, filed suit in U.S. District Court seeking a $24-million judgment against Figueres and four other defendants. The suit charged, among other things, that in 1968, when Figueres was running for president of Costa Rica, Capital Growth bought 40% equity for $2 million in a failing Costa Rican company controlled by the Figueres family. The Costa Rican firm's stock was "virtually worthless," the suit charged.

After the transaction, Clovis McAlpin, Capital Growth's president, obtained a Costa Rican passport and was appointed to a Costa Rican diplomatic post. McAlpin, who was facing tax problems with the U.S. Internal Revenue Service, moved Capital Growth's main office to Costa Rica.

'Vesco Law' repealed. The Costa Rican Legislative Assembly Nov. 2 repealed a 1974 law that gave the Costa Rican president final say on whether an extradition application could be received by the courts.

The measure was known popularly as the "Vesco Law" because it was assumed to have been tailored to protect Robert L. Vesco, the fugitive American financier who lived in Costa Rica and was a friend of President Daniel Oduber and ex-President Jose Figueres.

Vesco exercised considerable power in the ruling National Liberation Party (PLN), which had elected Oduber and Figueres to the presidency, the London newsletter Latin America said Oct. 29. Vesco's lawyer was Gonzalo Facio, the former foreign minister who was seeking the PLN presidential nomination in 1978.

DOMINICAN REPUBLIC

Spanish royalty visit. King Juan Carlos I and Queen Sofia of Spain visited the Dominican Republic May 31–June 1 en route to the U.S. The king met in the Dominican Republic with President Joaquin Balaguer.

Haitians expelled. Dominican military brigades recently rounded up and expelled about 4,000 Haitians who had been living illegally in the Dominican Republic, according to Dominican press reports cited Oct. 24 by the news agency LATIN.

Officials of the National Frontiers Council had expressed fears that the Dominican Republic was experiencing "a peaceful invasion" from Haiti, which shared the island of Hispaniola with the Dominican Republic. About 400,000 Haitians were living illegally in the Dominican Republic, according to a university professor quoted by LATIN.

Some observers felt mass repatriation of Haitians might harm the Dominican sugar harvest, which relied partly on cheap Haitian labor, LATIN said.

Opposition groups coalesce. Five opposition parties had agreed to form a united front against the reelection of President Joaquin Balaguer in 1978, the London newsletter Latin America said Nov. 12.

The groups were the Democratic Quisqueyan Party, the National Civic Union, the Social Christian Revolutionary Party, the National Conciliation Movement and the Democratic Integration Movement, according to the newsletter.

Government to buy more of gold-mining firm. The government signed an agreement Dec. 15 to buy an additional 26% equity in Rosario Dominicana S.A., a gold-mining concern. The purchase would bring the government's share of Rosario's outstanding stock to 46%.

The other 54% would be divided equally between two U.S. firms, Rosario Resources Corp. and Simplot Industries Inc. Under the Dec. 15 agreement each firm would sell 13% of its equity in Rosario to the government and each would be paid $3.7 million—the book value of the shares sold.

The agreement also stipulated that Rosario would be subject to a new income tax on gold and silver mining amounting to 5% of net income, Rosario Dominicana announced. The pact confirmed the terms under which Rosario's Pueblo Viejo gold mine currently was operated. The mine, one of the largest in the Western Hemisphere, was brought into production in 1975. In the first quarter of 1976 it was producing gold at the rate of 350,000 ounces a year.

The government and Rosario had argued for more than a year over whether Rosario would develop the large Los Cacaos deposit adjacent to Pueblo Viejo. The Dec. 15 agreement left the question open.

Philip Morris payoffs detailed. The Dominican affiliate of Philip Morris Inc. of the U.S. apparently paid $1,000 a month to President Joaquin Balaguer in 1973, according to internal company documents cited by the Wall Street Journal Dec. 28. Balaguer denied receiving the money.

The affiliate, E. Leon Jimenes (ELJ), also paid $16,000 to a Dominican tax officer in 1975 for a favorable ruling and $120,000 to various Dominican legislators to secure passage of a certain bill, the documents showed.

Eduardo A. Leon, ELJ president, said payoffs were necessary to insure corporate survival and profitability in the Dominican Republic. ELJ's payments were "chicken feed" compared to payments made in other countries by Lockheed Aircraft Corp. of the U.S., Leon asserted.

Leon said that ELJ contributed money to all major Dominican political parties, but mainly to Balaguer's Reformist Party, the Journal reported. He refused to estimate the total contributed, saying only: "I have a free hand to do anything I want. Philip Morris doesn't have to know everything we do."

Corporate payments to political campaigns were legal in the Dominican Republic.

EL SALVADOR

Earthquake. El Salvador suffered some damage from the earthquake that hit Guatemala Feb. 4.

In El Salvador, the earthquake cut roads and highways and caused damage in the town of Apulo, just across the Guatemalan border.

Government sweeps elections. The ruling National Conciliation Party (PCN) swept the congressional and municipal elections March 14, winning all 54 deputies' seats and 261 mayoralties at stake in the voting.

The major opposition group, the National Opposition Union (UNO), did not campaign, having withdrawn its candidates to protest the October 1975 electoral law and allegedly arbitrary actions by the government's Central Electoral Council. However, the council refused to sanction the withdrawal, keeping UNO candidates on the ballots and enabling the PCN to claim victory over the opposition.

(UNO was a coalition of the Christian Democratic Party, the National Democratic Union and the Revolutionary National Movement. The outlawed Communist Party was allied with the Christian Democrats although it was not officially part of UNO.)

The 1975 electoral law required candidates to register personally, rather than by proxy, and it allowed the invalidation of a party's entire list of candidates if any one candidate did not register properly. The requirement of personal registration "gave the authorities far more than the normal opportunities for intimidation... which were put to good use," according to opposition members cited by the London newsletter Latin America April 2.

As a result, UNO was able to get only 89 of its 261 lists approved, Latin America noted. In addition, the electoral council invalidated the UNO list for San Salvador on the grounds that one candidate owed money to the government, which he paid upon notification, and another was under contract to the regime, to build a soccer field, the newsletter reported.

The campaign was marked by government denunciations of the opposition and by bombings by left-wing guerrillas. The PCN charged repeatedly that UNO was taking orders and money from abroad, and President Arturo Molina charged March 8 that the opposition was infiltrated by "international Communists" and "false Christians."

Bombs exploded throughout El Salvador Feb. 26-March 13, causing no casualties but some property damage, notably to PCN offices. Credit for most of the blasts was claimed by the Maoist People's Revolutionary Army (ERP), which denounced the electoral process as a fraud.

(The ERP had suffered another division in its ranks and one of its members had been put to death as a result, according to a clandestine communique reported by the Spanish news agency EFE April 4. The split was the fifth or sixth since the small organization was founded in 1970, according to EFE. Splits in the ERP had already produced the Workers' Revolutionary Organization, the National Resistance Armed Forces and other breakaway groups that had not yet chosen names.)

Defense minister nominated to be president. Col. Carlos Humberto Romero had been selected presidential candidate of the ruling National Conciliation Party for the March 1977 elections, it was reported July 5. Romero resigned as defense minister to accept the nomination.

Rodriguez found guilty of gun-sale conspiracy in U.S. Col. Manuel Alfonso Rodriguez, former staff chief of El Salvador's armed forces, was convicted in New York Oct. 8 of conspiring to sell 10,000 submachine guns to U.S. Treasury agents posing as underworld figures. He was sentenced in U.S. District Court in Manhattan Nov. 23 to serve 10 years in prison.

Rodriguez had been arrested May 15 while still serving as chief of staff.

The Salvadoran government declined to defend Rodriguez. It said May 17 that he had not been on an official mission when he was arrested. Rodriguez was replaced as military chief May 22 by Col. Armando Leonidas.

Rodriguez was arraigned in U.S. District Court in Manhattan May 16 and held in $3 million bail. Six co-defendants—one Salvadoran and five U.S. citizens—were held in total bail of $2.8 million.

According to a complaint filed by Joseph F. Kelly, special agent of the U.S. Treasury Department's Bureau of Alcohol, Tobacco and Firearms, the defendants had conspired to purchase the firearms in the U.S., then sell them to Kelly and other U.S. agents "who posed to the defendants as underworld crime figures."

Rodriguez, the complaint said, had signed a purchase order and State Department export application claiming that the arms were to be used for "the national defense of El Salvador." (The State Department did not approve the application, and no weapons were delivered.)

Rodriguez and five co-defendants were arrested in a Mount Kisco, N.Y. motel by Kelly after he had paid $75,000 to Rodriguez and $25,000 to two of the other defendants. The funds were to have paid for the arranging of the false papers, Kelly's complaint said. The seventh defendant was arrested May 17 at Kennedy International Airport in New York City when he returned from a vacation.

The defendants were all charged with conspiracy to defraud the State Department, to violate the National Firearms Act, and to defraud the U.S. Treasury of $2 million in taxes that would have been owed on a legal domestic arms sale. The seven had planned to sell the guns for $2.8 million, the complaint said. There would have been a subsequent "larger multimillion dollar order if the initial venture proved successful," the complaint added.

The defendants denied the charges but the complaint said that Kelly had tape recordings of six meetings of the accused conspirators, including the last at which the payoff and arrests were made.

In addition to Rodriguez, the defendants were: Miguel D. Celis, a resident of El Salvador described as a Panamanian businessman; Raymond J. Geraldo of Fort Lee, N.J., described as a "former trade nominee for El Salvador"; Frank G. Alvarez of Dix Hills, N.Y., marketing director for Latin America for Mott Haven Truck Parts of the Bronx, N.Y.; Dominick Cagianese, of West Hempstead, N.Y., a Mott Haven employe; Robert Michaelson of Plainview, N.Y., president of Wittington Imports Ltd. of Great Neck, N.Y.; and Irwin Tobocman of New York City, a food broker. Cagianese was the defendant seized at Kennedy Airport.

Honduras, El Salvador OK arbitration. Honduras and El Salvador agreed to submit to an arbitrator the border dispute that had simmered since their brief but bloody war in July 1969.

The 14-point agreement, signed Oct. 6, was described as a first step toward a peace pact between the two countries. It was hailed as "historic" by Alejandro Orfila, secretary general of the Organization of American States (OAS).

Sporadic border clashes had occurred July 14-22, on the seventh anniversary of the so-called "Soccer War" between the two countries. Following a formal ceasefire July 22, Honduras and El Salvador agreed Aug. 12 to demilitarize the four areas where the clashes had taken place and to leave the maintenance of public order there to OAS military observers.

GRENADA

Gairy narrowly reelected. Prime Minister Eric Gairy and his ruling Grenada United Labor Party (GULP) won a narrow victory over the opposition People's Alliance in national elections Dec. 7.

GULP lost five of its 14 House of Assembly seats to the Popular Alliance. The House's 15th seat was retained by the sole independent incumbent who recently had joined the alliance.

The Popular Alliance—a coalition of the leftist New Jewel Movement and two conservative groups, the Grenada National Party and the United People's Party—had made Gairy the major issue in the campaign. The alliance had charged that the prime minister was erratic, authoritarian and responsible for Grenada's current economic stagnation.

Granadan nutmeg and cocoa exports were bringing high prices, but the once-thriving tourist industry had been crippled by widespread unrest in 1973. A special commission of inquiry had found Gairy responsible for the unrest. More recently, the tourist industry had been hurt by Grenada's support of a United Nations resolution against Zionism, which caused a boycott of Grenada by North American Jewish tourists.

Producers of bananas, Grenada's largest export crop, were experiencing difficulties because of the declining value of the island's currency, the East Caribbean dollar. The government was thought to be running a deficit of up to EC$20 million, according to the Dec. 7 Financial Times of London.

Among other issues raised by the Popular Alliance during the campaign:

■ Gairy was protecting three Americans wanted by the U.S. Federal Bureau of Investigation on charges of passing bad checks at U.S. racetracks. The three apparently had entered Grenada under false names and had befriended Gairy. When Grenadan Attorney General Desmond Christian began proceedings against the Americans earlier in 1976 on charges of illegally entering Grenada, Gairy ordered him to drop the case. The Guyanese-born Christian refused, so Gairy declared Christian a prohibited immigrant and had him deported.

■ Innocent Belmar, the former Grenadan police superintendent, had been fired from his post after a commission of inquiry blamed him for widespread police brutality. However, Gairy praised Belmar warmly and selected him as a GULP candidate for a House seat in the Dec. 7 elections.

GUYANA

Opposition backs government. Ex-Premier Cheddi Jagan, leader of the opposition People's Progressive Party (PPP), said Feb. 21 that the party was giving "critical support" to Premier Forbes Burnham and his People's National Congress (PNC).

The PPP thus abandoned its longstanding antagonism toward Burnham, who had taken power in 1964 after Jagan was overthrown by strikes and riots covertly supported by the U.S. and Great Britain. The PPP had boycotted Parliament since the fraud-ridden 1973 elections, but it was expected to return to the legislature in time for celebration of the 10th anniversary of Guyana's independence in May.

Jagan said the PPP would join the PNC in fighting unspecified foreign interference in Guyana, but it would not support Burnham "unconditionally."

The PPP and PNC, the only significant political groups in Guyana, were both avowed Marxist-Leninist parties. Both had sent representatives to the First Congress of the Cuban Communist Party in Havana in December 1975.

Cuba, China military presence denied. The government vigorously denied foreign reports that Guyanese paramilitary forces were being trained by Cuban and Chinese advisers.

The reports originated in Brazil, Venezuela and the U.S. The most detailed of them, a "confidential report" quoted by the Venezuelan magazine Resumen Feb. 23, alleged that Guyana had three paramilitary installations, and a fourth under construction, where Cuban and Chinese advisers assisted in the "political indoctrination, military training and agricultural instruction" of thousands of Guyanese youths. Other Guyanese traveled to Cuba for training and indoctrination, Resumen reported.

Resumen's article was immediately denounced by government officials in Georgetown and Guyanese representatives in Venezuela and Brazil. Foreign Minister Frederick Wills called the article "wicked and malicious," it was reported March 3, and other officials charged it was part of a U.S.-inspired "destabilization" campaign against Guyana's socialist government, it was reported March 10.

The Washington Post reported March 10 that there was no evidence of Cuban or Chinese military presence in Guyana, although there were camps where Guyanese teenagers underwent voluntary paramilitary training and instruction in Guyanese history and culture, the government's cooperative socialist doctrine, and agricultural methods.

Resumen's "confidential report," the Post added, had been leaked by the Venezuelan embassy in Georgetown, which received it from Patrick Tenassee, a Guyanese employe of the American Institute for Free Labor Development (AIFLD) and long-time opponent of Premier Forbes Burnham. The AIFLD had received more than $11 million in contracts from the U.S. State Department's Agency for International Development since 1968 to strengthen labor organizations throughout Latin America, the Post reported. It had also provided cover in Uruguay for operatives of the U.S. Central Intelligence Agency, according to the Post.

(Resumen later continued what amounted to a campaign against Burnham's government, it was reported March 12. It alleged the establishment of a police network in Guyana "on the model" of the Soviet NKVD, and it called the Burnham regime "totalitarian and racist." Resumen's Feb. 23 article on the paramilitary camps had said the great majority of youths receiving training there were blacks. Although blacks controlled the Guyanese government, they were outnumbered in the population by East Indians.)

Burnham admitted March 3 that there were Cuban, Chinese and East German advisers in Guyana, but he said they worked only on agricultural and industrial projects. The youth camps, he added, were run by the Guyana National Service, which trained jobless youths for work.

The reports on the youth camps followed concern in Venezuela, Brazil and the U.S. over rumors that Georgetown had allowed Cuban aircraft to refuel in Guyana en route to Angola to deliver Cuban soldiers to fight in the African nation's civil war. Burnham denied the rumors March 6, but he said he would consider allowing Cuban planes to refuel in Guyana if they were carrying soldiers to aid Mozambique in its current conflict with Rhodesia. Burnham called for a united international front against Rhodesia's white minority government.

Booker nationalization set. Premier Forbes Burnham announced Feb. 23 that the British-owned Booker Group, the last major foreign conglomerate operating in Guyana, would be nationalized May 26, on the 10th anniversary of Guyanese independence.

"We shall be bringing to an end an empire, an epoch which dates back to 1815," Burnham said. He noted that while Booker accounted for 40% of Guyana's exports and more than 25% of its gross national product, the company had not brought any capital into the country in the last 10 years.

The Booker Group, a subsidiary of Booker-McConnell Ltd. of Great Britain, was mainly involved in growing and processing sugar cane, but it also participated in many other sectors of Guyana's economy including fishing, printing, engineering, electronics, insurance, livestock and dairy products and commercial banking. Its nationalization had long been demanded by the opposition People's Progressive Party, with which the government had recently been reconciled.

Representatives of Booker and the government recently agreed to begin talks on the amount of compensation Guyana would pay for the company's assets, it was reported Feb. 15.

An agreement had also been reached for Guyana to purchase the major assets of Sprostons (Guyana) Ltd., an engineering and shipbuilding subsidiary of Alcan Aluminium Ltd. of Canada, it was reported Jan. 30.

Government school takeover OK'd. Parliament approved a bill enabling the government to take over all schools in Guyana, the Miami Herald reported Oct. 1.

The measure, passed by an overwhelming majority of the legislature, had been bitterly opposed by the Roman Catholic and Anglican churches. The churches had owned and run more than half of the 608 nursery, elementary and secondary schools that now passed into the government's hands.

Premier Forbes Burnham hailed the bill as an "historic measure" that would allow the government to "carry out its proper task of reorienting society," introducing "truly socialist content" in the educational system.

The bill embodied amendments to the Education Act and to Guyana's Constitution, which stated that "every religious community shall be entitled, at its own expense, to establish and maintain places of education." Foreign Minister Frederick Wills said that the Constitution must be adapted to suit "particular circumstances and conditions," the Herald reported.

The Catholic Standard, a weekly church publication, called the takeover of the schools an "ominous development." "What is most alarming is the speed with which our Constitution can be changed," the Standard said. "With little discussion, with no opportunity for the people to be informed of arguments and to express an opinion, their sacred rights can be abrogated overnight."

The government said that it would pay compensation only to schools whose owners had made personal sacrifices in acquiring them. This did not include church schools, Burnham declared, because their purchase and upkeep had been paid for by the public. Burnham's argument was disputed by Alan Knight, the Anglican archbishop of the West Indies. He said that Christians had contributed to the schools "as part of the church and not as the public."

The takeover of the schools was supported by the People's Progressive Party (PPP), which was nominally in the opposition but generally backed the government. However, the bill did not incorporate the PPP's suggestion that Guyana's schools be modeled on Cuban and Soviet schools and include the teachings of Marx and Lenin in the curriculum, the Herald reported.

HAITI

Cabinet shuffled. President Jean-Claude Duvalier April 1 replaced six of his 11 Cabinet ministers including Interior and Defense Minister Paul Blanchet, who had been considered the most powerful Haitian after the chief executive.

Blanchet was succeeded by Pierre Biamby, private secretary to the president and to his late father, President Francois ("Papa Doc") Duvalier. The other new Cabinet members were Social Affairs Minister Achille Salvant, Public Works and Transportation Minister Fernand Laurin, Agriculture Minister Remillot Leveille, Education Minister Raoul Pierre-Louis and Public Health and Population Minister Willy Verrier.

The Cabinet changes resulted from a campaign against liberal officials by influential associates of "Papa Doc," according to the Manchester Guardian April 6 and the London newsletter Latin America April 9. This group included Simone Duvalier, widow of the late president; Luc Desyr, chief of the secret police, and Henri Siclait, head of the Regie du Tabac (state food agency).

Blanchet had enacted a number of reforms including a mining code, controls on foreign land ownership, and new taxes on the bauxite operations of Reynolds Metals Co. of the U.S. However, the land controls had been flouted and $7 million of the extra revenue from Reynolds had disappeared into the Duvaliers' foreign bank accounts, according to the newsletter Latin America.

Blanchet's replacement, Biamby, had been a leader of the Tonton Macoutes, Francois Duvalier's feared personal security force.

(The Cabinet changes were also linked in press reports to an apparent assassination attempt on Jean-Claude Duvalier in January. Duvalier reportedly was taken to the U.S. naval base in Guantanamo Bay, Cuba, for brief treatment after the incident.)

Duvalier bribe request alleged. The owner of Translinear Inc. of the U.S. charged that President Jean-Claude Duvalier demanded a $1 million payment after the company won a contract to develop tourism on the Ile de la Tortue off the Haitian coast, according to the Spanish news agency EFE March 2.

William Crook, owner of Translinear and a former U.S. ambassador to Australia, said Translinear had refused to make the payment and Haiti had subsequently canceled its contract, according to the report.

Crook's allegations were publicized at hearings of a U.S. Joint Economic subcommittee March 2 and 5.

The charges were denied by Haitian Ambassador to the U.S. Georges Salomon, who asserted in letters to the press March 3 that "the allegation of bribes in the mentioned case is an outright fantasy apparently directed to mislead the honest opinion in Congress and the press and to put some kind of pressure on the government of Haiti to enter into a deal or contract it resisted as sensitive and encroaching upon the sovereignty and priviliges of the nation." Salomon said:

A careful examination of the published statements made at the hearings indicate that apparently Translinear in its anxious attempts to win by all means the contract, came across an unnamed businessman (I quote) "who purported to be a member of the Government", but was only eager to exploit the excessive anxiety of the Firm.

But in no case as indicated in the statements made at the hearings, an official of the Haitian Government has been directly or indirectly involved in bribes or has attempted to solicit improper payments from Translinear Inc. which did not signed in the past or has not signed by now any contract with the Government of Haiti for any Free port facilities in La Tortue Island.

Kennecott pact signed. Kennecott Copper Corp. of the U.S. said March 24 that it had signed an agreement with the Haitian government for continued exploration, development and mining on Haiti's northern coast. The company reportedly had found indications of a sizable copper orebody in Haiti, according to the Wall Street Journal March 25.

Refugees reach Miami. More than 100 Haitian refugees crowded in a 16-meter sailboat reached Miami Aug. 30 and asked for political asylum in the U.S. The group's leader said they had sailed from Port-au-Prince 16 days before, leaving at night to evade police patrols. A U.S. immigration official said the Haitians wanted to live in the U.S. for "economic reasons."

Siclait dismissed, expelled. A spokesman for President Jean-Claude Duvalier announced Sept. 7 that Henri Siclait had been removed as director of the Regie du Tabac, the state domestic trading monopoly.

Duvalier later denounced the "scandalous opulence" of Siclait's life-style and had Siclait and 40 of his aides expelled from Haiti, it was reported Sept. 24. The president ordered an accounting of the Regie's revenues and announced that the funds henceforth would be used "progressively to reduce Haiti's dependence on foreign aid."

The Regie's estimated annual revenue of $30 million traditionally had been used to support the Tontons Macoutes (the president's personal police force), to pay off government supporters and to enlarge the Duvalier family's Swiss bank accounts, the London newsletter Latin America said Sept. 24. The U.S. had long sought a reform of the Regie to make the Duvalier government more acceptable internationally, the Washington Post reported Sept. 18.

Other personnel changes—Among other changes in Haitian government personnel:
—Trade and Industry Minister Antonio Andre was replaced by Wilner Pierre-Louis, it was announced Sept. 7.
—Rosalie Adolphe was named supervisor general of the Volontaires de la Securite Nationale (Tontons Macoutes), a new post, it was reported Aug. 17. She was a former aide to the late Francois Duvalier, the president's father, and a former commander of the Fort Dimanche political prison. (A dozen Tontons Macoutes had been killed in April by three men who then fled to the Dominican Republic and later to Jamaica, it was reported Aug. 27. The killings resulted in more than 200 arrests in Port-au-Prince.)

Amnesty declared. President Duvalier Sept. 30 declared an amnesty for 251 prisoners convicted of political and other crimes. He made the announcement after visiting several penitentiaries in Port-au-Prince.

Amnesty International had charged earlier that prison conditions in Haiti were "among the most inhuman in the world." An Amnesty report, cited in the Washington Post June 23, said human rights were "constantly abused" by the Duvalier government.

HONDURAS

Constitutional rule. The Liberal and National Parties expressed "moderate optimism" Jan. 6 about a government plan, announced at the end of 1975 by President Gen. Juan Alberto Melgar Castro, to restore constitutional rule by the end of 1979.

The parties asserted, however, that civilian government could be reestablished sooner. They said Melgar's "good faith" would be reflected in the composition of the projected council which would prepare election bylaws.

Both parties were experiencing internal struggles between their governing factions and more liberal dissidents, the Spanish news agency EFE reported Jan. 11.

Earthquake hits Guatemala, Honduras. A major earthquake shook Guatemala and Honduras early Feb. 4, causing massive destruction and human casualties in the first country and severe damage but no casualties in the second.

In Honduras, the earthquake destroyed much of the towns of Santa Barbara,

Santa Rosa Copan and Pofradia near the Guatemalan border. Electric power was cut in at least a dozen cities and towns, and major industries were damaged in San Pedro Sula and Puerto Cortes. Police said 29 houses collapsed in Puerto Cortes and one entire neighborhood was flooded by broken water and sewer mains. Honduras was still recovering from the devastation of Hurricane Fifi, which killed as many as 10,000 persons and destroyed agricultural land in the north in 1974.

Pulp-&-paper development. The government of Honduras, the Venezuelan Investment Fund and the Inter-American Development Bank agreed in Cancun, Mexico, May 15 to finance a $415 million forestry development program in the pine forests of Olancho, Honduras. The goal was to establish a pulp and paper plant in Honduras that would produce 203,000 tons of linerboard and 28,000 tons of corrugated paper annually for banana cartons.

United Brands' bribes. The U.S.' United Brands Co. disclosed Dec. 10 that an internal investigation into a $1.25-million bribe paid to a Honduran official in 1974 also had uncovered $1.2 million in previously undisclosed payments to foreign officials and a $300,000 slush fund that may have been used to pay off union officials.

The report was filed under a U.S. court order in an agreement with the U.S. Securities and Exchange Commission. The SEC had brought suit against United Brands after the Wall Street Journal reported payment of the Honduran bribe. The SEC had been investigating United Brands since the suicide of its chairman, Eli M. Black.

In its detailed report on the Honduran bribe, United Brands said that in May 1974, Black had offered then-President Gen. Oswaldo Lopez Arellano several hundred thousand dollars to reduce his country's banana tax. Lopez turned down the offer, the report said.

Abraham Bennaton Ramos, Honduran economics minister, then approached company officials to talk about the tax, saying it could be reduced if he were paid $5 million. United Brands rejected the payment as too high but Black subsequently agreed to a $2.5-million payment, of which half actually was paid. The report concluded that payment of the bribe was "a unique aberration rather than part of a pattern."

JAMAICA

State of emergency declared. The government declared a nationwide state of emergency June 19, after six months of political and other violence had claimed more than 100 lives.

The emergency gave the police and army broad powers of search and seizure, under which they arrested more than 300 persons including members of the opposition Jamaica Labor Party (JLP). Most of the detainees were released after questioning; only 51 were reported still in custody July 6.

The government claimed June 19 that it had discovered an arms cache in Trench Town, a slum in Kingston where much of the recent violence had taken place. The previous day Herb Rose, a top official of the JLP, had resigned from the party and charged that it was planning "a whole strategy of violence" to win the projected 1977 parliamentary elections.

"I have seen young men being trained and brainwashed to commit murders, to destroy property and personal effects of innocent and impoverished people who are singled out only because they are of a different political persuasion," Rose asserted at a press conference in Kingston. The JLP denied his charges as false and malicious.

Prime Minister Michael Manley charged June 29 that evidence of a terrorist plot against his government had been found in the homes of Peter Wittingham, a prospective JLP candidate for Parliament, and Sen. Pearnel Charles, one of the party's three vice presidents. Both men were being interrogated at army headquarters in Kingston, it was reported June 30.

JLP leader Edward Seaga said that the state of emergency might be a step taken by the government to turn Jamaica into a Cuban-style socialist state that would be part of a "Red axis" in the Caribbean, the

London Times reported June 23. Seaga implied that the government had fomented violence so that it could impose the state of emergency and cancel the 1977 elections.

The government had been claiming for two months that the violence was part of a "destabilization" campaign against Manley's socialist regime by conservative Jamaicans, the U.S. government and U.S. businessmen. This charge was echoed by Earl Barrow, the prime minister of Barbados, the Financial Times of London reported May 25.

Jamaican Foreign Minister Dudley Thompson told the Mexican newspaper Excelsior June 20 that the "destabilization" campaign was being directed by the U.S. State Department and abetted by the U.S. press. The press had widely reported Jamaican violence, causing a decline in visits to the island by U.S. tourists. Thompson attributed the U.S. hostility to Manley's leftist policies and Jamaica's current friendship with Cuba.

(The U.S. was upset over conflicts between the Jamaican government and U.S.-based bauxite companies and over Cuba's role in training Jamaican security officers, the London newsletter Latin America reported May 14. JLP leader Edward Seaga had gained important allies in Washington by denouncing Cuba in Jamaica, the newsletter said.)

Despite the government's claims, much of the violence in Kingston appeared to be caused by armed gangs from the youth wing of the People's National Party (PNP), Prime Minister Manley's political movement. PNP youths clashed often with gangs belonging to the JLP.

Members of the PNP's "Tel Aviv" gang fought with members of the JLP's "Skull" gang in April, causing one death and many injuries, Latin America reported May 14. The president of the PNP's youth movement asserted that 20 of its members had been killed in recent weeks by right-wing terrorists, the newsletter said.

Some of the violence was perpetrated by common criminals, according to numerous press reports. Burglars were blamed for the slaying June 15 of Fernando Rodriguez, the Peruvian ambassador in Kingston.

The government had imposed a dusk-to-dawn curfew in Kingston May 10 after six tenement houses were burned to the ground and residents attacked firemen in a section of West Kingston. The violence had begun when tenants of the buildings attacked demolition crews that had come to tear down the tenements to make way for government housing.

PNP wins elections. Prime Minister Michael Manley and his ruling People's National Party (PNP) won a decisive victory Dec. 15 in elections for Jamaica's House of Representatives—the lower chamber of Parliament.

The PNP won 48 House seats, 11 more than it had won in 1972 when the last elections were held. The opposition Jamaica Labor Party (JLP) won the other 12 seats, losing three from its 1972 total.

The vote was considered a strong endorsement of Manley's socialist policies and a repudiation of the JLP, which had criticized the government's growing control of the economy and Manley's close ties with Cuban Premier Fidel Castro.

Manley appealed for unity Dec. 16 and said Jamaica must make great sacrifices to emerge from its economic recession. The days of "frills and soft options" were over, he said.

Manley denied that his large margin of victory was a mandate to move more rapidly toward socialism. However, the PNP's left wing was growing, and its three leading figures—Arnold Bertram, D. K. Duncan and Anthony Spaulding—had been elected to the House by solid majorities, Reuters noted Dec. 16.

The PNP had pledged during the campaign a top-priority effort to bring the "pillars of the economy" under state control and to implement a national development plan. It emphasized the government's achievements since 1972 in education, housing, health care, literacy, land reform, cooperative development and youth facilities. The party also promised to improve relations with the U.S. and work for a normalization of ties between the U.S. and Cuba.

Shortly before the elections, the government granted salary increases to nurses and teachers, announced a reduction in taxes for middle-class taxpayers in 1977, placed a subsidy on flour and other basic foods and added $11 million to the "impact program" that provided short-term jobs for the unemployed.

OTHER AREAS

The JLP had charged during the campaign that "private rights [were] at the mercy of the state" and that Manley, in league with Castro, was attempting to communize Jamaica. The opposition party also said that Castro had placed Communist agents among the scores of Cuban technicians, engineers, teachers, doctors and farmers who had come to Jamaica in recent months under a technical cooperation pact between the two islands.

The JLP had noted that unemployment was rising and that Jamaica's earnings from tourism and bauxite and sugar exports were falling. The government's high-taxation policies and left-wing image had brought the business community to the verge of bankruptcy, the JLP charged.

(Unemployment in Jamaica had reached an average of 25% and was as high as 50% in some poor areas of Kingston, according to press reports. Tourism had declined 11.7% in January-September, according to government figures reported Nov. 15. Bauxite ore production was down 29%, bauxite exports had fallen 10% and alumina exports were down 47%, according to the Oct. 1 Latin America Economic Report. The decline in alumina exports was due to a sharp drop in world demand and to lengthy shutdowns in Jamaica's major alumina plants because of labor disputes.)

In response to the JLP criticism, the government charged that businessmen who backed the opposition had committed economic sabotage. Mining Minister Horace Clarke asserted that more than $200 million had been taken out of Jamaica illegally in the previous two years, the London newsletter Latin America reported Nov. 12. Several business leaders ran for the House of Representatives on the JLP ticket.

The campaign was marked by sporadic shootouts which took the lives of about 15 persons, according to press reports. The violence was mostly between the armed youth groups of the PNP and JLP. PNP candidate Ferdie Neita was shot and wounded and JLP candidate Colin Williamson was roughed up by a mob Dec. 13. Williamson's car was firebombed and one of his aides was slashed with a machete.

(Bob Marley, the reggae [Jamaican popular music] singer, and three members of his troupe were shot and wounded Dec. 3 by gunmen who invaded Marley's home in Kingston. Marley gave a free concert at a government rally Dec. 5.)

Nevertheless, the government claimed that violence had declined sharply since the state of emergency was imposed in June. Authorities were holding 470 persons under the emergency, the Dec. 17 London Times said. JLP leader Edward Seaga had charged that most of the detained were members of his party, it was reported Dec. 15.

Jamaican newspapers were exercising self-censorship to avoid being shut down under the emergency measures, the London Times reported Oct. 12. Cowed by Section 35 of the measures—which allowed the arrest without warrant of anyone "concerned in acts prejudicial to public safety or public order or in the preparation or instigation of such acts"—newspapers were printing little opposition criticism of the government and were printing unedited the security forces' bulletins. The Daily Gleaner, Kingston's leading newspaper, had dropped its bylines to protect individual journalists.

The government imposed direct censorship shortly before the elections, ostensibly to reduce violence. The army and police announced Dec. 12 that political literature must be submitted to security forces six hours before publication or broadcast.

The joint army-police command banned all political meetings and rallies Dec. 14. The next day, after sporadic violence at polling places, the ban was extended for 30 days.

Cuba hails Manley victory—The official Cuban newspaper Granma welcomed the PNP's election victory Dec. 16, describing Manley as "a sincere friend of the Cuban revolution." The election result was "of special importance, as it was gained despite bold attempts by imperialism and internal reaction to destabilize [Manley's] government," Granma said.

NICARAGUA

Guerrilla leaders killed. Two top leaders of the leftist Sandinista National Liberation Front were killed in shootouts with National Guard (army) troops Nov. 7 and 9, according to Nicaraguan authorities.

Carlos Fonseca Amador, a founder of the guerrilla group, was reported killed Nov. 9. Two days before, troops reportedly had slain Eduardo Contreras Escobar, another Sandinista leader, and four fellow guerrillas. Contreras had flown to Cuba in December 1974 after leading an assault on the home of a wealthy Managua businessman and forcing the government to send to Cuba at least 12 imprisoned Sandinistas.

The Nicaraguan government charged Nov. 16 that Cuba was training and infiltrating Nicaraguan leftists into Nicaragua for a guerrilla war against President Anastasio Somoza Debayle. The government also denied a recent charge by Cuban Premier Fidel Castro that Nicaragua was a base for Cuban exiles who staged attacks against Cuba and other countries that enjoyed good relations with the Castro government.

In earlier guerrilla developments:

—The Nicaraguan government had approved safe-conducts to Mexico for four Sandinistas who had taken asylum in the Mexican Embassy in Managua, the London newsletter Latin America reported Sept. 10.

—Military authorities said June 28 that Cesar Augusto Salinas, Sandinista chief in northern Nicaragua, had been killed in a clash with National Guard troops June 25.

TRINIDAD & TOBAGO

Industrial plan. The government would invest up to nearly $200 million on an eight-year industrialization program, it was reported Jan. 2. Priorities for 1976 included construction of an iron and steel complex, a natural gas pipeline, a polyester fiber factory and two fertilizer plants, and expansion of an existing cement factory. The program was made possible by large surpluses in public revenue from the rise in Trinidad's oil prices and production.

PNM wins elections. The ruling People's National Movement (PNM) won the general elections Sept. 13, giving Prime Minister Eric Williams a fifth consecutive five-year term of office.

The PNM won 24 of the 36 seats in the House of Representatives. The leftist United Labor Front (ULF) won 10 seats, becoming the major opposition party, and the moderate Democratic Action Congress (DAC) won the two seats from Tobago. There were 271 candidates from nine parties vying for the seats.

An estimated 56% of the 595,991 eligible voters cast ballots, compared with a 28% turnout in the 1971 elections, which had been boycotted by the main opposition parties. The eligible voters included about 69,000 persons aged 18–21 who were enfranchised for the first time.

The elections were the third since Trinidad & Tobago became politically independent in 1962 and the first under the new Constitution which was implemented Aug. 1. The new charter, replacing the 1962 Constitution, made Trinidad & Tobago a republic in the British Commonwealth. Queen Elizabeth II would be replaced as chief of state by a president to be elected by the two houses of the Trinidad & Tobago Parliament, but the Privy Council in London would remain the republic's highest court of appeal.

The ULF's strong showing in the elections presaged an ideological battle in the House of Representatives, according to press reports. The ULF, formed in 1975 with support from the working classes, had avowedly Communist aims. The PNM was considered moderate, and Williams was committed to partnership with multinational corporations to develop Trinidad & Tobago's natural resources.

The PNM had campaigned on what it called its record of economic prosperity, rapid industrial development, improvements in education, growth of respect for Trinidad & Tobago in foreign countries, and preservation of Trinidadian democracy. The government had diversified the Trinidad & Tobago economy by investing revenues from oil and sugar exports in the development of automobile and household-appliance industries and the expansion of the republic's prosperous tourist industry.

The opposition parties had accused the government of mismanaging public funds and failing to reduce the high unemployment rate, estimated officially at 17% and unofficially at 30%-35%. The opposition had also stressed the poor condition of roads throughout the two-island nation, an irregular water supply, poor telephone service and other problems.

The elections posed the strongest challenge to Williams in his 20 years in office, and the PNM's victory was attributed partly to the fragmentation of the opposition. The ULF would be the first serious opposition force in the House of Representatives since the 1966-71 term, when the Democratic Labor Party held the 12 opposition seats. The PNM held all the House seats after the boycotted 1971 elections, losing two of the seats later when two PNM representatives bolted the party.

Index

A

AAA—See ARGENTINE Anticommunist Alliance
ABEL Amaya, Mario—45
ABOUREZK, Sen. James (D, S.D.)—77
ABRAM, Morris B.—151
ACEPAR (Paraguayan/Brazilian steel firm)—153
ACHE Indians (Peru)—150-2
ACORTA, Alfredo—149
ADAMS, M. G.—185-6
AFRICA—103. See also countries
AFRICAN Development Fund (ADF)—20
AGENCY for International Development (AID) (U.S.)—120
AGOSTI, Brig. Orlando—23
AGRICULTURE—19, 62-3, 85, 94-5, 132, 153, 190
    Agrarian reform—125
    Coffee—8, 17, 62, 116, 121
    Drought—99, 145
    Earthquake damage—121
    Food exports—17
    Grain—26
    Harvest—26
    Migratory workers—138
    Strikes—116
    Sugar—17, 20, 99, 121, 192
ALBUQUERQUE Queiroz, Ayrton de—56
ALCAN Aluminium, Ltd. (Canada)—63, 192
ALEJO, Francisco Javier—135
ALESSANDRI, Jorge—81, 86
ALGERIA—103

ALLANA, Ghulam Ali—70
ALLENDE, Hortensia Bussi de—79
ALLENDE, Jose Antonio—28
ALSOGARAY, Alvaro—27
ALTOS Hornos de Mexico (Mexican steel firm)—132
ALVAREZ, Frank G.—190
ALVAREZ, Sebastian—183
ALVAREZ Penaranda, Gen. Raul—50
ALVARIZA, Dr. Carlos—171
ALVEAR, Bishop Enrique—10, 73
AMNESTY International (AI)—10-2, 38-41, 57, 74, 149-52, 170-3, 182, 192
ANACONDA Co. (U.S.)—86
ANCHORENA, Manuel de—47
ANDEAN Development Corp.—19-21, 85-6
ANGELELLI, Enrique—45
ANGLICAN Church—192-3
ANGLO-Ecuadorean Oilfields, Ltd.—115
ANGOLA, People's Republic of—99-104
ANTUNES, Maj. Ernesto de Melo—100
ARAUJO Noguera, Alvaro—93
ARAUZ Castex, Manuel—24, 47
ARAVEN Finance, Ltd.—179
ARAYA, Bernardo—77
ARBULU Galliani, Guillermo—157
AREILZA, Jose Maria de—135
ARELLANO Stark, Gen. Sergio—81
ARENS, Richard—152
ARGENTINA:
    Agriculture—26. Anticommunist Alliance (AAA)—11, 28, 38-40, 42-3, 152. Anti-Semitism—40-1, 46. Automobiles—26, 37
    Crime—33-4

Economy—17, 25, 32, 37; foreign investment & controls—32, 36-7; inflation—24-6, 31-3, 37, 47; monetary developments—17, 26, 31, 36
 Falkland Islands—25, 46-7.
Food—47
 Government & politics—1, 24-5, 32-6; cabinet changes—24-5, 32; military coup (including pre-coup developments)—23-31. Gas pipeline—36
 Human rights abuses & torture—3-4, 37-45
 Labor, unions & strikes—23, 25-6, 28, 31, 35-6
 Nazis—40-1
 Oil—26, 33. Other political violence—11, 24, 28-31, 151-2; see also 'Human rights abuses & torture' and 'Military coup' above
 Press & censorship—23, 27, 34, 42, 46
 Taxes—36. Tourism—26. Trade—26, 36-7
 Unemployment—32, 37
ARGENTINE Anticommunist Alliance (AAA)—11, 28, 38-40, 42-3, 152
ARGENTINE National Socialist Front (FNSA) (neo-Nazi group)—41
ARIAS, Arnulfo—142
ARMS Purchases & Sales—17, 84, 93, 159
ARMSTRONG, Michael—187
AROSEMENA, Carlos Julio—115
ARROSTITO, Norma—46
ARRUPE, Rev. Pedro—151
ARZAMENDIA, Mario—152
ASHE, Derick—46-7
ASKEW, John—178-9
ASSASSINATIONS—See under POLITICAL Violence, Terrorism & Guerrilla Activity
ATOMIC ENERGY—104
AUSTRIA—16, 46, 69
AUTOMOBILE Industry—26, 37, 63, 82
AVIATION—93-5, 109-10, 159-60, 178-9, 182-3
AZORES Islands—100

B

BACA, Alberto Martinez—35
BACHMAN, Maria Elena—69
BAEZA, Jose—27
BAHAMAS—185
BALAGUER, Joaquin—188
BALBIN, Ricardo—16
BALDOVINOS, Carlos M.—45

BANADOS, Rev. Christian—67
BANK of Montreal—53
BANKS & Banking—85, 93, 132, 179
BANQUE Canadienne Nationale (Canada)—53
BANZER Suarez, Gen. Hugo—50-2
BARBADOS—185-6
BARBIE, Klaus—49
BARCO, Victor Renan—93
BARNET, Richard—78
BARRIENTOS Ortuno, Rene—18, 50, 52
BARROW, Earl—185-6, 196
BASSO, Lelio—4
BAUXITE—20, 63, 193, 196-7
BAY of Pigs Veterans' Association—109
BEAUSIRE, Marie Anne—69
BECERRA, Franklin—171
BELIZE—121, 186
BELMAR, Innocent—191
BENSINGER, Peter—136
BERDICHEVSKY, Gen. Jose—81
BERMUDEZ, Morales—15
BERNARDIN, Archbishop Joseph L.—117-8
BERNARDINO, Bishop Angelico—56
BERTRAM, Arnold—196
BESSONE, Diaz—37
BETETA, Mario Ramon—134
BIAMBYN, Pierre—193
BICUDO, Helio—59
BIDEGAIN, Oscar—35
BIRNS, Laurence R.—41
BIRTH Rate—117
BLANCHET, Paul—193
BLANCO, Hugo—158
B'NAI B'rith—63
BOBBIO Centurion, Carlos—157
BOLIVIA: Disasters—53. Corruption—18. Economy—17, 19, 52-3. Foreign relations—8, 18-9, 52. Government & political violence—49-52. Human rights & torture—3-4. Labor unions & strikes—50-1. Natural gas—53
BOOKER-McConnell, Ltd. (British firm)—192
BORDABERRY, Juan Maria—167-8
BORDELON, Msgr. Roland—150
BOSCH, Juan—4
BOSCH, Orlando—79, 109, 111, 182-4
BOTERO, Rodrigo—91
BOWATER (British firm)—153
BOYD, Aquilino—143-4
BRANCH, Taylor—184
BRANDAO, Evil—59
BRANDT, Willy—16
BRAZIL:
 Agriculture—8, 26, 63; coffee—8,

INDEX

62. Arms sales—84. Automobiles—63
Censorship—56. Corruption—18
Disasters—63
Economy—61-3, 153; monetary developments—17
Foreign relations & trade—26, 62-4; U.S.—4, 7-8, 18
Government & politics—1, 51-2, 55-61
Health—64. Human rights & torture—3-4, 11-2, 38, 41, 55-60
Oil—62
Unemployment—63
BRAZILIAN Anti-Communist Alliance (AAB)—57-60
BRAZILIAN Communist Party (PCB)—56, 59
BRAZILIAN Democratic Movement (MDB)—55-6, 61-2
BRONER, Julio—31
BROWN, Frederick Z.—183
BRUERA, Ricardo—32
BUCARAM, Asaad—115
BUKOVSKY, Vladimir—79-80
BUNKER, Ellsworth—145
BURBANO, Alfredo Poveda—113-4
BURMA—107
BURNHAM, Forbes—183, 191-3
BUSSI, Gen. Antonio—42
BUSTAMANTE, Jose Luis—52

C

CABRERA, Manuel—76
CADEMARTORI, Jose—80
CAFIERO, Antonio—25
CAGIANESE, Dominick—190
CAHALAN, Msgr. Kevin—150
CALABRO, Victorio—24, 30
CALDERON, Jose Ramon—18, 93-4
CALLAGHAN, James—47
CAMPA, Valentin—123
CAMPORA, Hector—35
CAMUS, Bishop Carlos—76
CANADA—100-1, 105
CANADIAN International Co.—179-80
CAPELLINI, Jesus Orlando—32
CAPITAL Growth Co. (U.S.)—187
CAPPADORO, Gerry—186
CARPENTIER, Alejo—97
CARRIO, Genaro—71
CARTER, Jimmy—80, 147
CASALDALIGA, Bishop Pedro—58
CASSIDY, Sheila—65-7
CASTELLO Branco, Carlos—57
CASTELO Soto, Eduardo—43
CASTEX, Arauz—25
CASTILLO Velasco, Jaime—10, 73, 76

CASTRO Fidel—97-8, 102-6, 109-10, 141, 196-8
CASTRO, Raul—97
CATHOLIC Church, Roman—28-9, 40-3, 45, 58-67, 73-7, 80-1, 91, 106, 117-8, 151-2, 192-3
CEJAS, Jesus—45
CELIS, Miguel D.—190
CENSORSHIP—See PRESS & Censorship
CENTRAL America—8. See also country
CENTRAL Intelligence Agency (CIA)—79, 107-10, 143-4
CENTROMIN (Peruvian state mining firm)—158
CEPE (Ecuador state oil firm)—115-6
CEPERNIC, Jorge—35
CHAVAL, Nadine—128
CHEMICAL Bank (U.S.)—179
CHILE—49-50
Agriculture—85. Arms purchase—84
Censorship—72. Cuban exiles & terrorism—110-1, 184
Drugs—84-5
Economy—17, 82-3, 85-6. Education—82
Foreign relations & trade—20-1, 34, 52, 82-6
Government & politics—81-2. Human rights & torture—3-4, 8-15, 38-41, 65-81
CHILES, Sen. Lawton (D, Fla.)—133
CHINA, Communist (People's Republic of)—191-2
CHRISTIAN, Desmond—191
CHRISTIAN Church (U.S.)—151
CISNEROS, Luis—156
CITICORP International, Ltd. (U.S.)—179
CLARKE, Horace—197
CODELCO (Chilean state copper firm)—82-3
COFERRAZ (Brazilian steel firm)—153
COFFEE—8, 17, 20, 62, 116, 121
COLOMBIA:
Arms purchase—93
Coffee—8. Cuban trade—95
Disasters—95. Drugs—21, 135
Economy—17, 90-1, 93, 95. Emigration problem—175-6
Foreign investments & trade—93, 95
Government & politics—90, 92-4
Human rights abuses—3-4
Kidnappings—87-91
Population—95
Refugees—94-5

Unrest—87-92. U.S. relations—7-8, 18, 94
COLOMBIAN Revolutionary Armed Forces (FARC) (guerrilla group)—89
COLOMBIAN Social Security Institute (ICSS)—91-2
COLOMBIAN Syndical Workers' Confederation (CSTC)—88-90
COMECON (Communist bloc economic association)—104
COMIBOL (Bolivian state mining company)—53
COMMUNICATIONS—19
COMMUNISTS & Communism—33, 56-9, 77, 88-9, 97-8, 123, 129-30, 149, 151-2, 160, 169-70, 187, 189
COMPORA, Hector—33
CONTINENTAL Illinois National Bank & Trust Co. (U.S.)—179
COPPER—20, 82-3, 155-6, 158, 194
CORDOVA-Claure, Ted—50
CORTAZAR, Julio—4
CORU (Cuban anti-Castro group)—79
CORVALAN, Luis—79-80
CORVALAN Nanclares, Ernesto—24
COSTA Rica—21, 69, 94, 135, 187
CREOLE Petroleum Corp.—177
CRIME—185, 189-91
CROOK, William—193
CRUICKSHANK, Jorge—125
CUBA:
  Agriculture—99. Atomic Energy—104
  Canada—105. Canal zone dispute—141
  Economy—17, 99. Exiles & terrorism—79, 108-11, 182-4
  Foreign relations & trade—95, 99, 104-5, 141, 196-7; Angola—99-104; military intervention—106-7, 159, 191-2, 196-8; Soviet Union—99, 104; U.S.—100-2, 105, 107-10
  Government & politics—97-8
  Human rights & torture—3, 10, 14, 111-2
  Political prisoner exchange—80
CUBAN Action—109
CUBAN National Liberation Front—109

D

DALLA Tea, Gen. Carlos—32
DASSAULT (French firm)—93
D'AVILA, Gen. Ednardo—56-7
DAVIS, Dr. Sterling Blake—135
De ALMEIDA, Luis—102
'DEATH Squads': Argentine Anticommunist Alliance (AAA)—11, 28, 38-40, 42-3, 152. Brazilian Anti-Communist Alliance—57-60
De CARVALHO, Otelo—103
De CROVO, Maria Elena—92-3
DeCUBAS, Jose L.—86
De DIAZ, Elena Quintero—171
De DIOS de la Torre, Juna—128
De la FLOR, Miguel Angel—157
De la PUENTE Radbill, Jose—157, 160
DELLUMS, Rep. Ronald V. (D, Calif.)—161-2
DEMICHELI, Alberto—167, 169
De NASCIMENTO, Lopo—10
De PAULA Chavez, Francisco—93
DESALINIZATION—138
De ZAMA, Alicia Escalante—170
DIAZ, Raul J.—108
DINA (Chilian secret police)—75-9, 81
DISASTERS—1, 6, 53, 62-3, 95, 99, 119-22, 139, 188-9, 194-5
DIVORCE—93
DISIP (Venezuelan security police)—180-4
DOMINGUEZ, Antonio—142
DOMINICAN Republic—3-4, 17, 187-8
DORTICOS, Osvaldo—98, 102
DRINAN, Rep. Robert (D, Mass.)—41, 149-50
DROUGHTS—26, 63, 99, 145
DRUGS & Narcotics—21, 84-5, 94, 114, 135-7
DuBOIS Gervasi, Jorge—157
DURAN Arcentales, Gen. Guillermo—113
DURRANT, Patricia—8, 72
DUVALIER, Jean-Claude—193-4

E

EARTHQUAKES—119-122, 188-9, 194-5
ECHAVARRIA, Octavio—89
ECHEVERRIA Alvarez, Luis—21, 123-5, 138-9
ECONOMY—17, 24-5, 36, 47, 61, 63, 90-1, 93, 98-9, 121, 123-4, 131-3, 138, 144-5, 153, 155-7, 165, 173, 175-9, 185, 187-8, 190, 192-8
  Aid (economic)—83-6
  Foreign trade—See under 'F'; see also LATIN American Economic System (SELA)
  Monetary developments—17-20, 26, 31, 36, 63, 83, 124, 133-4, 173, 190
ECUADOR: Labor & other unrest—114, 116-8. Military coup—113-5. Monetary developments—17. Oil—115-6

INDEX

ECUADOREAN Episcopal Conference—117
ECUADOREAN Federation of Free Syndical Organizations—117
ECUADOREAN Union of Classist Organizations—117
ECUADOREAN Workers' Federation (CTE)—117
EDUCATION—20, 82, 116, 192-3
EDUCATIONAL, Scientific & Cultural Organization, United Nations (UNESCO)—15-6
ELECTIONS—97-8, 185-6, 189-92, 198-9
ELECTRICITY—19, 99, 117, 121, 156, 179-80
EL SALVADOR—188-90
ENERGY & POWER—99, 155-6, 173, 175-6. See also specific sources (e.g., ATOMIC ENERGY; GAS, Natural)
ENRIQUEZ Espinosa, Edgardo—38-9
ERB, Patricia—45
ERP-August 22 (Argentine guerrilla group)—42
ESCOVAR Salom, Ramon—5
ESPINOZA, Gustavo—158
ESTABA Moreno, Judge Delia—182
ESTADO de Sao Paulo, (Brazilian newspaper)—60-1
ESTRADA, Diaz—82
ETCHEVERRY, Tabare—170
EURO-Latinamerican Bank, Ltd.—53
EUROPEAN Brazilian Bank, Ltd.—53
EUROPEAN Community (EC)—36-7
EXCELSIOR (Mexican newspaper)—125-8
EXXON Corp. (U.S.)—177
EYZAGUIRRE, Jaime—10, 73
EYZAGUIRRE, Jose Maria—69

F

FABIANO Sobrinho, Nelson—55
FACIO, Gonzalo—6
FALKLAND Islands—25, 46-7
FARIAS, Juan Jose—150
FEDERAL Bureau of Investigation (FBI), U.S.—78-9, 183
FERNANDEZ Maldonado, Jorge—156-8
FERTILIZANTES Fosfatados Mexicanos—132
FIAT Automotive Co.—45
FIDEL Castro Guerrilla Command (Mexican group)—128
FIELDEN, Donald—135
FIEL Filho, Manoel—56
FIGUERES, Jose—187

FISHING Industry—133, 137, 155, 158, 192
FLOODS—95
FLORES, Bishop Patrick—117
FLORES Labra, Fernando—77
FLORES Ortega, Alberto—18, 178
FLORES Troconis, Alberto—178
FNLA—See NATIONAL Front for the Liberation of Angola
FOLGAR, Hildo—182-3
FONSECA Amador, Carlos—198
FOOD—47, 63, 83-5, 121
FORD, Gerald—101-2, 130, 145-6, 164-5
FOREIGN Trade—3-9, 17, 20-1, 26, 36-7, 62-4, 82, 85-6, 91, 95, 134, 138, 148, 153, 173, 176, 190, 197
FORESTRY—195
FRANCE—77, 84, 93
FRASER, Rep. Donald M. (D, Minn.)—41, 172
FREI, Eduardo—81-2
FRENZ, Bishop Helmut—74
FRERS, Arturo Keolliker—46

G

GAIRY, Eric—190-1
GALEANO Ramirez, Alberto—95
GALLARDO, Jorge—50
GALLARDO, Samuel—50
GARABAGLIA, Juan Carlos—30
GARCIA, Orlando—183
GARCIA Marquez, Gabriel—103-4
GAS, Natural—36, 53, 198
GATTO, Alberto Marcelo—55, 57
GEISEL, Ernesto—4-5, 55, 58-9, 61
GELBARD, Jose—35
GENERAL Popo (Mexico)—132
GENERAL Tire & Rubber Co. (U.S.)—132
GERALDO, Raymond J.—190
GERMANY, West—132
GERTZ, Alejandro—136
GILMAN, Rep. Benjamin A. (R, N.Y.)—21, 94, 135
GOLD—188
GOLDWATER Jr., Rep. Barry M. (R, Calif.)—135
GOMES Monteiro, Gen. Dilermando—56-8
GOMEZ, Julio—32
GOMEZ Estrada, Cesar—93
GONZALEZ, Ana Maria—43
GONZALEZ, Antonio—109
GONZALEZ, Carlos Hank—125
GONZALEZ, Gerardo—144
GONZALEZ, Julio—23

GONZALEZ de la Lastra, Carlos—142–3
GONZALEZ Heredia, Tito—181
GONZALEZ Videla, Gabriel—81
GRAIN—26
GREAT Britain—25, 41, 46–7, 63, 65–7, 85, 115, 120–1, 153, 176, 186, 192
GRENADA—190–1
GREVE, Frank—112
GRINDLAYS Bank, Ltd.—53
GROUP of Revolutionary Commandos (Venezuelan guerrilla group)—181
GUARDO, Ricardo—24
GUATEMALA: Belize claims—121, 186. Earthquake—1, 6, 119–22, 194–5. Economy—121. Government & politics—121–2. Human Rights & torture—3–4. Terrorism—122
GUERRILLA Army of the Poor (EGP) (Guatemala)—122
GUEVARA, Ernesto "Che"—49
GUEVARA, Nacha—27–8
GUILLEN, Nicolas—97
GUINEA—103
GULF Oil Co. (Ecuador)—115–6
GULF Oil Corp. (U.S.)—18, 52, 115
GUTIERREZ, Jose—18, 93
GUTIERREZ, Nelson—66, 69
GUTIERREZ Ruiz, Hector—38, 171
GUYANA—183, 191–3
GUZETTI, Rear Adm. Cesar Augusto—11, 32, 41

H

HADDAD, Rev. Antonio—56
HAITI—84, 188, 193–4. Human rights—3–4
HAMMER, Armand—178–9
HARGUINDEGUY, Gen. Albano—32
HARKIN, Rep. Thomas (D, Iowa)—71
HARRINGTON, Rep. Michael (D, Mass.)—83–4
HARRISON, Mrs. Charles—135
HEALTH & Medicine—64, 91–2, 117, 119–20
HECKLER & Koch (West German firm)—93
HELMS, Sen. Jesse (R, N.C.)—29, 106–7, 159
HENRIQUE Simonsen, Mario—63
HERNANDEZ Colon, Gov. Rafael—166
HERRERA, Fortunato—180–1
HERRERA, Juan Manuel—88
HERRERA Latoja, Gen. Francisco—82
HERRERAS, Casildo—24–5
HERZOG, Vladimir—11, 56–7
HIJAKINGS—See POLITICAL VIOLENCE, Terrorism & Guerrilla Activity
HIPOLITO, Bishop Adriano—58
HONDURAS: Border dispute—190. Bribe scandal—195. Earthquake—119, 194–5. U.S. aid—84
HOUSING—18, 20, 47, 120
HOYOS Arango, Samuel—92
HOZ, Jose Martinez de—32–3, 36–7
HUMAN Rights Abuses—See under POLITICAL Violence, Terrorism & Guerrilla Activity
HUMBOLDT, Ciro—50
HUMPHREY, Sen. Hubert (D, Minn.)—77
HURRICANES—139

I

IGLESIAS, Enrique—16–7
IGNACIO Domingues, Gen. Oswaldo—59
IMMIGRATION & Emigration—95, 138, 175–6
INCLAN, Hilda—184
INDIANS—60, 118, 121, 150–2
INTER-American Commission on Human Rights (OAS)—8–15, 72–4
INTER-American Development Bank (IDB)—18–20, 36, 52–3, 85, 121, 132, 156
INTER-American Foundation (U.S.)—151
INTER-American Press Association (IAPA)—16
INTER-Continental Hotel (Brazil)—63
INTERNAL Revenue Service (IRA) (U.S.)—187
INTERNATIONAL Coffee Agreement—8
INTERNATIONAL Development Bank—See WORLD Bank
INTERNATIONAL League for the Rights of Man—150–1
INTERNATIONAL Monetary Fund (IMF)—17, 31, 36, 137
INTERNATIONAL Tin Agreement—8
IRON—20, 26, 132, 198
IRRIGATION—85
ITAIPU (Paraguayan hydroelectric complex)—153
ITALY—176

J

JACKSON, Sen. Henry M. (D Wash.)—163
JACOVELLA, Tulio—27

INDEX

JAGAN, Cheddi—191
JAMAICA—72-3, 195-7.
　Economy—196-7. Civil unrest & violence—195-6. Government & politics—196-7. Unemployment—196-7
JAPAN—153
JARRIN, Bolivar—115
JAVITS, Sen. Jacob (R. N.Y.)—132
JESUITS—151
JEWS & Judaism—40-1, 46, 63, 190
JIMENEZ de Arechaga, Justino—71
JOHNSON & Johnson (U.S.)—131
JORDEN, William—143
JORGENSEN, Anker—16, 46
JUAN Carlos I, King (Spain)—187
JUSTINIANO, Horacio—81

K

KELLEY, Joseph F.—189
KENNECOTT Copper Corp. (U.S.)—194
KENNEDY, Sen. Edward M. (D, Mass.)—4, 39, 64, 75-6, 94, 111
KERENSKY, Alexander—82
KISSINGER, Henry—4, 6-8, 63-4, 74, 85, 102-2, 105, 109, 146, 159, 175, 183, 187
KLEIN Jr., Guillermo Walter—33
KLIX, Brig. Jose Maria—32
KNIGHT, Alan—193
KOCH, Rep. Edward I. (D, N.Y.)—40-1, 168, 172
KONDER, Rodolfo—56
KORRY, Edward M.—86
KRAISELBURD, David—46
KRAISELBURD, Raul—46
KREISKY, Bruno—16, 46
KUBITSCHEK, Juscelino—61

L

LABOR Developments, Union & Strikes—23, 25-6, 28, 31, 33, 36-7, 50-1, 63, 87-92, 114, 116-7, 124, 142-3, 146, 155-8, 168-9, 173, 179. Unemployment—63, 83, 95, 177, 196-7
LANDER, Aristides—180
LANUSSE, Alejandro—35-6
LANUSSE, Maria Caride de—29
LASTIRI, Raul—35
LATIN American Economic System (SELA)—3
LATIN American Episcopal Conference (CELAM)—117
La TORRE, Arturo—156
LAUGERUND Garcia, Kjell—6, 122

LAURENTIN, J. M.—18, 178
LEIGH Guzman, Gen. Gustavo—81
LEON, Eduardo A.—188
LEON, Luis—27
LEPAGE, Octavio—180
LETELIER, Orlando—77-8, 110-1, 184
LEUPIN, Eric—91
LEVI, Edward—21, 136
LEVOYER, Richelieu—115
LIBEROFF, Dr. Manuel—11, 38
LIBYA—103
LIENDO, Gen. Albano—32
LIENDO, Gen. Horacio—32
LIEVANO Aguirre, Indalecio—5-6
LINARES, Hugo—169
LINEA Aeropostal Venezolana (airlines)—179
LLERAS Restrepo, Carlos—90
LOCKHEED Aircraft Corp. (U.S.)—18, 93-4
LONG, Pablo Fernandez—29
LOPES de Souza, Ney—60-1
LOPEZ, Luis Alfonso—122
LOPEZ Michelsen, Alfonso—87, 89-94
LOPEZ Rega, Jose—31, 35
LOZANO, Domingo—45
LUDER, Italo—24
LUERS, William H.—129-30
LUGO, Freddy—109-182-3
LUTHERAN Church—74
LUVALU, Pascal—100
LYONS, Lt. Thomas—108

M

MABONI, Rev. Florentino—60
MACONDES, Regina—38
MAGALHAES da Silveira, Alexandre—56
MAIDANA, Prof. Antonio—149
MALEK, Gustavo—35-6
MALI—103
MALNUTRITION—17, 38
MANDATE of History & the Demands of the Future, The (book)
MANLEY, Michael—195-7
MANRIQUE, Javier—118
MARCONA Mining Co. (U.S.)—155
MARI Bras, Juan—166
MARIN, Edison—171
MARINHO, Roberto—58
MARLEY, Bob—197
MARQUEZ, Gabriel Garcia—4
MARQUEZ, Jose—171
MARTINEZ Ferrate, Rodolfo—121
MASSERA, Emilio—23
MASSUE, Sadi Conrado—35
MATOS, Huber—79
MATTEI, Gen. Fernando—82

M'BOW, Amadou Mahtar—16
McALPIN, Clovis—187
McCANN, Thomas P.—108
McDONALD, Rep. Larry (D, Ga.)—160
McNAMARA, Robert—71
MEAT (beef)—26, 36-7
MEDICAL Syndical Association Union (Asmedas)—91-2
MEDINA, Jose Ramon—182
MELASCO Ibarra, Jose Maria—115
MELGAR Castro, Juan Alberto—194
MENDEZ, Aparicio—168-9, 172
MENDOZA, Gen. Cesar—81
MENENDEZ, Gen. Benjamin—37
MERCADO, Jose Raquel—88-9
MERCURIO El (Chilian newspaper)—73
MERINO Castro, Jose Toribio—80
MESA Espinoza, Salom—180-1
METALS & Mining—8, 20, 26, 50-3, 63, 82-3, 132, 153, 155-6, 188, 193-4, 196-8
MEXICAN Chamber of Rubber Industries—128
MEXICAN Communist Party (PCM)—129
MEXICO:
    Agriculture—125, 138
    Disasters—139. Drugs & narcotics—21, 135-6
    Economy—3, 17, 131-4, 137-8; monetary developments—133-4
    Foreign relations—132, 134-5; U.S. & trade —18, 129-30, 132-3, 135-9; bribery scandal—18
    Government & politics—123-5
    Human rights & torture—135, 137
    Leftists & terrorism—128-31
    Oil—132, 137
    Political corruption—132-3. Press censorship—125-8
    Territorial waters—133, 137
    Unemployment—131
    Zionist resolution—126-7, 132, 138
MIAMI, Fla.—108-9
MICHAELSON, Robert—190
MICHELINI, Zelmer—11, 38, 171
MIGUEL, Lorenzo—23-4, 31
MILLAS, Jorge—82
MILLER, Rep. George (D, Calif.)—71
MIRA, Benjamin—82
MITTERRAND, Francois—46
M-19 (Columbian guerrilla group)—88-90
MOCTEZUMA Cid, Julio Rodolfo—125
MOFFETT, Rep. Toby (D, Conn.)—71
MOFFITT, Michael—77
MOFFITT, Ronni Karpen—77
MOLINA, Arturo—189
MONDELLI, Emilio—25, 31
MONTANEZ, Pedro—170
MONTEALEGRE, Hernan—10, 74, 76-7
MONTECINO, Lillian—78
MONTENEGRO, Oscar Luis—38
MONTES, Jorge—79-80
MONTONEROS (Argentine terrorist group)—28-31, 42-6
MONTOYA Escobar, Jairo—94
MONTOYA Montoya, Oscar—93
MORAES Neto, Prudente de—58
MORAIS Penido, Geraldo Maria de—59
MORALES, Miguel—94
MORALES Bermudez, Francisco—156-7
MORALES Navarrete, Ricardo—184
MORGAN GUARANTY Trust Co. of N.Y.—179
MORRIS, Ivan—10
MOVIMIENTO Democratico Brazileiro (MDB)—11
MOZAMBIQUE—103
MPLA—See POPULAR Movement for the Liberation of Angola
MULLER, Amaury—55
MUNARIZ, Rev. Jose Miguel—151
MUNOZ Ledo, Porfirio—125
MUNOZ Vega, Pablo Cardinal—117
MUNZEL, Mark—150
MURTINHO, Helber—59

N

NARANJO, David—89
NARANJO, Francia—89
NATIONAL Council of Private Enterprise (Conep)—142
NATIONAL Cuban Movement—109
NATIONAL Earthquake Information Service (U.S.)—121
NATIONAL Front for the Liberation of Angola (FNLA)—99-100, 103-4
NATIONAL Intelligence Directory (DINA) (Chilean security forces)—9-10, 73, 75-6
NATIONALIZATION—155, 177-80, 192
NATIONAL Liberation Army (ELN) (Bolivian guerrilla group)—49
NATIONAL Liberation Army (ELN) (Colombian guerrilla group)—87, 89, 92
NATIONAL Liberation Front (Nicaraguan guerrilla group)—197-8
NATIONAL Liberation Movement (Tupamaros) (Uruguayan guerrilla group)—171
NATIONAL Union for the Total Independence of Angola (Unita)—99-100, 103
NAVARRO, Antonio—132
NAZIS—40-1

INDEX

NEITA, Ferdie—197
NESSEN, Ron—145
NETO, Agostinho—103-4
NEW Orient Industries (Japan)—153
NEW Progressive Party (NPP) (Puerto Rico)—165-6
NICARAGUA—197. Cuban Intervention—107. Human rights & torture—3-4
NIEHOUS, William—180-1
NIGERIA—103
NORTHROP Corp. (U.S.)—18
NORWAY—63
NOVO, Guillermo—184
NOVO, Ignacio—79, 111, 183

O

OCCIDENTAL Petroleum Corp. (U.S.)—18, 93, 177-9
ODUBER, Daniel—187
OIL—18, 26, 33, 52, 62, 82, 93, 98-9, 115-6, 132, 137, 155, 176-9, 198
OJEDA Paullada, Pedro—21
OLABARRIETA, Alberto—30
OLSEN, Rear Adm. Kaare—65
OLSON, Carl—46
OLSON de Oliva, Chris Ana—45-6
ORDONEZ de Londono, Sara—93
OREJUELA Bueno, Raul—93
ORFILA, Alejandro—9-10, 14-5, 71, 73
ORGANIZATION of American States (OAS)—8-15, 70-6, 101, 107, 111-2, 137-8, 190
ORGANIZATION of Petroleum Exporting Countries (OPEC)—176-8
ORTIZ Mena, Antonio—18-9
OSWALD, Lee Harvey—107-8
OVANDO Candia, Gen. Alfredo—50
OWENS-Illinois, Inc.—180-2

P

PAINO, Savador Horacio—31
PALME, Olof—46
PANAMA: Canal dispute—1, 6, 9, 104-5, 141-8. Civil unrest & strikes—142-4. Cuban relations—141. Drought—145. Drugs—21, 135. Economy—144-5. Unemployment—144. U.S. relations—141-4
PANAMA Canal Co.—144, 146-7
PANAMANIAN Association of Business Executives (Apede)—142
PAPAGNO, Rogelio—35
PARAGUAY: Agriculture—153. Catholic Church—151-2. Defense—151. Economy—17, 153. Foreign trade—153. Government & politics—12, 153. Human rights & torture—3-4, 149-52. Press & censorship—105-2. U.S. aid—150-1
PARDI, Rear Adm. Julio—32
PARDO Buelvas, Rafael—93
PARKER, Daniel—120
PARKINSON, C. Jay—86
PARRA Leon, Bishop Alberto—118
PASCAL Allende, Andres—69
PAUL, Pope—42, 106
PAULLADA, Pedro Ojeda—136
PAVON, Guillerom—43
PAZ, Juan Carlos—25
PAZ, Octavio—126
PEMEX (Mexican state oil firm)—132
PEMJEAN, Enrique—81
PENIDO Burnier, Rev. Joao Bosco—58
PEOPLE'S Alliance—190-1
PEOPLE'S Revolutionary Armed Forces (Mexican guerrilla group)—128-9
PEOPLE'S Revolutionary Army (ERP) (Argentine guerrilla group)—33-4, 42-4, 151-2
PEOPLE'S Revolutionary Army (ERP) (Salvadoran guerrilla group)—189
PEPSICO Corp. (U.S.)—107
PEREDA Asbun, Juan—49-50
PEREIRA Araujo, Jose Cortez—60
PEREIRA de Araujo Neto, Benvenuto—60
PEREZ, Carlos Andres-3, 5, 16, 18, 145-6, 175-8, 180-1
PEREZ, Miguel—112
PERON, Juan Domingo—26
PERON, Maria Estela Martinez de—1, 23-8, 30-1, 35
PERRINI Guala, Aldo—171
PERU: Cuban intervention—106-7, 159. Economy—17, 155-7. Fishing industry—155, 158. Foreign relations—16, 52. Government & politics—156-8. Labor & civil unrest—155-8. Military rebellions—157-8. Press & censorship—156-8. Soviet arms aid—159-60. U.S. military aid—158-9
PETROBRAS (Brazilian state oil firm)—61
PETROVEN (Petroleos Venezolanos) (Venezuelan state oil firm)—177
PHILIP Morris, Inc. (U.S.)—188
PINOCHET Ugarte, Augusto—9, 33, 67, 70, 73, 76-7, 81-2
PINTO, Edras—81
POLITICAL Corruption—18, 33, 35-6, 132-3, 165-6, 177-9, 186-8, 193-5
POLITICAL Violence, Terrorism & Guerrilla Activity: Assassinations—11, 27-30, 43,

45-6, 49-50, 77-81, 87-90, 109-11, 184
  Border disputes—190
  Civil unrest & violence—58, 87-9, 91-2, 180-4, 187, 190, 195-6. Cuban exiles & terrorism—108-9, 182-4
  Hijack pact—109-10
  Human rights abuses, imprisonment & torture—3-4, 8-15, 33-5, 37-44, 46, 56-60, 65-81, 111-2, 122, 135, 137, 149-52, 169-73, 180-1, 194
    Kidnappings (including kidnap-murders)—28, 30, 38-46, 49-50, 57-8, 87-91, 122, 128, 131, 180-2, 184
  Military rebellions—23-4, 30-1, 157-8
  Other guerrilla activity—1, 27, 30-1, 42-6, 49-50, 87-91, 109, 122, 128, 131, 151, 170, 180, 182-3, 189, 197-8; see also specific group, e.g. MONTONEROS, NATIONAL Liberation Armed Forces (FALN), PEOPLE'S Revolutionary Army (ERP), REVOLUTIONARY Left Movement (MIR). Other terrorism—24, 27-31, 42-4
  Police action—27-31, 38-9, 41-6, 49-51, 75-81; AAA—11, 28-31, 38-9, 43; Brazilian Anti-Communist Alliance (AAB)—57-8; 'Death Squads'—42-3, 45-6, 57-60; Disip—180-4
POLITICO-Military Organization (OPM) (Paraguayan guerrilla group)—151
POPULATION—95
POSADA, Estanislao—90
POPULAR Movement for the Liberation of Angola (MPLA)—99-104
PORTUGAL—100
POSADA, Luis—109, 182
POVERTY—16-7, 117, 119-20
PRATS Gonzalez, Carlos—78
PRECHT, Rev. Cristian—67
PRESS & Censorship—23, 27, 34, 38, 42, 46, 56, 72, 125-8, 150-2, 156-8
PRICE, George—121, 186
PRIETO, Arnaldo—61
PRIMATESTA, Raul Francisco Cardinal—28-9
PUERTO Rican Socialist Party—165-6
PUERTO Rico—161-6
PUERTO Rico Telephone Co.—165-6
PULP-&-PAPER—195

Q

QUADROS, Jose de—57
QUESADA, Ricardo Alarcon—100
QUIETO, Roberto—42
QUIJANO, Raul—24, 47

R

RABASA, Emilio—126-7
RAMIREZ, Pedro—94-5
RAMOS, Abraham Bennaton—195
RAMOS, Julio—171
RAQUEL Mercado, Jose—89-90
RASKIN, Marcus—78
RAUSCH, Bishop James—78
REAGAN, Gov. Ronald (Calif.)—141-2, 145
RED Brigades of Workers' Power (Argentine guerrilla group)—29-30
RED Flag (Venezuelan guerrilla group)—181
RED September (Chilean guerrilla group)—77
REFUGEES—38-40, 43-4, 69-70, 94-5, 194
REQUE Teran, Gen. Luis—50
RESUMEN (Venezuelan magazine)—191-2
REUSS, Rep. Henry (D, Wis.)—71
REVES Heroles, Jesus—125
REVOLUTIONARY Independent Workers' Movement (MOIR)—90
REVOLUTIONARY Left Movement (MIR) (Chilian guerrilla group)—69, 77
REVOLUTIONARY People's Vanguard (Brazilian guerrilla group)—58
REYES, Cornelio—92
REYES, Col. Rafael—29
REYNOLDS, Hal—85
REYNOLDS Metals Co. (U.S.)—63, 193
RHODESIA—102
RICARDO, Herman—109-10, 182-3
RICE, Patrick—42
RINCON Puentes, Ferderico—94
RINCON Quinones, Gen. Ramon—88
RIVERA Terrazas, Rector Luis—128
ROA, Raul—107
ROBLEDO, Angel—24, 27
ROBLES, Ivan—142
ROBLES, Winston—142
RODRIGUEZ, Carlos Rafael—99
RODRIGUEZ, Jorge Antonio—180
RODRIGUEZ, Manuel Alfonso—189-90
RODRIGUEZ Lara, Gen. Guillermo—113
ROMERO Barcelo, Gov. Carlos (Puerto Rico)—164-6, 189
ROMO, Oswaldo—70, 74
RONCAGLIOLO, Rafael—158
RONDON de Rivero, Luisa—178
ROSARIO Dominicana S. A.—188
ROSARIO Resources Corp. (U.S.)—188
ROSAS, Cesar—156
ROSSETTI, Nadyr—55
ROYAL Bank of Canada—179

INDEX

RUCKAUF, Carlos—35
RUIZ, Gutierrez—11
RUSSELL Tribunal, Bertrand—3-4
RYAN, Hewson A.—172

S

SAKHAROV, Andrei—79, 171
SALINAS, Cesar Augusto—198
SALOMON, Georges—193
SANCHEZ, Archbishop Robert F.—117
SANCHEZ, Ruben—49
SANTANA Machado, Luiz—56
SANTIAGO da Silva, Manoel—59
SANTUCHO, Mario Roberto—44
SAPENA Pastor, Raul—152-3
SARDI, Dr. Miguel Chase—150-1
SARMIENTO, Camila—89
SARMIENTO, David Jimenez—131
SAVLOFF, Guillermo—28
SCHERER, Mario—152
SCHERER Garcia, Julio—125
SCHWARTZ, Edwin—18, 93
SCHWEITZER, Miguel—69
SCRANTON, William—100
SEAGA, Edward—195-7
SEBURGO Silva, Jorge—81
SECONDE, Reginald—65
SECURITIES & Exchange Commission (SEC) (U.S.)—195
SEDILLO, Arthur—135
SELA—See LATIN American Economic System
SEPT. 23rd Communist League (Mexican guerrilla group)—128-9, 131
SEREGNI, Liber—170
SHIPS & Shipbuilding—192
SHOBEK, Michaiah—185
SICLAIT, Henri—194
SIDEPAR (Paraguayan state steel firm)—153
SILVA Henriquez, Raul Cardinal—67, 76-7
SIMON, William—9, 73
SIMONS, Marlise—127
SIMONSEN, Mario Henrique—62
SIMPLOT Industries, Inc. (U.S.)—188
SNYDER, Rep. Gene (R, Ky.)—145
SOARES, Rev. Francisco—29
SOARES, Mario—46
SOBERON, Rector Guillermo—128
SOBRINO Aranda, Luis—27
SOCIALISTS & Socialism—46, 180
SOFIA, Queen (Spain)—187
SOLANA, Fernando—125
SOLARI Yrigoyen, Hipolito—45
SOLER, Miguel Angel—149
SOMALIA—103
SONEIRA, Federico—167

SORIA, Carmelo—80-1
SORIANO, Jose—156
SOUSA, Daniel—59
SOUSA, John Philip—70-1
SOUTH Africa—100
SPAIN—63, 111, 134-5
SPAULDING, Anthony—196
SPROSTONS (Guyana) Ltd.—192
STEEL—63, 132, 153, 198
STEVENSON, Teofilo—97
STOCKS & Bonds—37
STROESSNER, Alfredo—149-53
SUDAN—103
SUGAR—17, 20
SULE, Anselmo—16
SULLIVAN, Rep. Leonor K. (D, Mo.)—145
SWEDEN—46, 85

T

TACK, Juan Antonio—143
TAIANA, Jorge—35
TAKUR, Chandra—178
TALAMANTE, Olga—43
TAPIA, Col. Julio—82
TARQUINI, Jose Miguel—29
TAXES—36, 93
TELLO Macias, Carlos—125
TENASSEE, Patrick—191
TENENGE (Brazilian steel firm)—153
TERAN Ortuno, Sgr. Mario—50
TERRITORIAL Waters—133, 137
TEXACO, Inc. (U.S.)—115-6
THIRD World Movement—29
TIME (magazine)—76
TIN—8, 53
TITO, Josip Broz—106
TOBOCMAN, Irwin—190
TORIBIO Merino, Jose—81
TORO Hardy, Jose—178
TORRES, Gen. Juan Jose—49-50, 52, 56
TORRIJOS, Brig. Gen. Omar—104-5, 141-2, 145-7
TOURISM—20, 26, 63, 132, 137-8, 190, 193
TRADE Reform Act (U.S.)—3-6, 8-9, 64, 138
TRANSLINEAR, Inc. (U.S.)—193
TRANSPORTATION—19
TRINIDAD & Tobago—198-9
TRUCCO, Manuel—80
TRUDEAU, Pierre Elliott—105
TRUJILLO, Lopez—117
TURBAY Ayala, Julio Cesar—90

U

UEKI, Shigeaki—62
UGANDA—103
UGARTE Roman, Marta—80
UNAMUNO, Miguel—23, 25
UNEMPLOYMENT—37, 63, 83, 124, 131, 144, 177, 196-7
UNION of Soviet Socialist Republics (U.S.S.R.) 79-80, 84, 99-101, 104, 159-60, 169-70, 173, 176
UNITA—See NATIONAL Union for the Total Independence of Angola
UNITED Brands Co. (U.S.)—108, 143, 195
UNITED Fruit Co. (U.S.)—108, 143
UNITED Nations—11, 15-6, 38-9, 41, 43, 70-1, 74-5, 80, 100, 119, 125
UNITED Revolutionary Organizations (CORU)—109-11
UNITED STATES:
    Argentina—26, 40-1, 44-5. Arms sale—189-90
    Barbados—186. Brazil—7, 63-4. Bribery scandals—18, 132-3, 177-9, 188, 193, 195
    Chile—13-4, 77-9, 83-6. Colombia—7, 94. Congress—71, 83-5, 94, 129-31, 145-6, 161-5, 168, 187. Cuba—99-102, 105-7; Cuban exiles & terrorism—107-9, 182-4
    Defense, Department of—150-1, 158-9. Drugs & narcotics—21, 84-5, 135-7
    Economic aid & trade—3-9, 18-20, 63-4, 119-20, 150-1, 156
    FBI—183-4. Foreign investment developments—187-8, 193-4
    Guantanemo naval base—141
    Hijack pact—109-10. Human rights & torture—12-4, 38-41, 44-5, 70-1, 73-6, 80, 111, 135, 137, 149, 184
    Kennedy assassination—107-8
    Mexico—135, 137-8. Military aid—84, 150-1, 158-9
    Panama Canal dispute—1, 6, 141-8. Peru—7. Puerto Rican independence—161-5
    Refugees—194
    Securities & Exchange Commission—128. State, Department of—86, 152, 172, 183, 190-1
    Uruguay—168
    Venezuela—7, 175, 181-2
UNIVERSAL Federation of Christian Student Movements—170
UNIVERSITY of Chile—82
URREGO, Armando—18, 93-4
URRUTIA, Carlos—158

URUGUAY: Economy—17, 173. Foreign relations & trade—171, 173. Government & politics—167-9. Human rights & torture—39-41, 169-73

V

VACCA, Roberto—46
VADORA, Julio—172
VALE do Rio Doce, CIA. (Brazilian state steel firm)—132
VALENCIA, Abraham Varon—93
Van BENNEKOM, Pieter—114
VARGAS, Armando—126
VARGAS, Gen. Raul—82
VARGAS, Rene—116
VASCONEZ, Gen. Gustavo—113
VAZQUEZ Rana, Olegario—128
VEGH Villegas, Alejandro—169, 173
VELASCO, Belisario—72
VELASCO Alvarado, Juan—157
VELASCO Letelier, Velasco—76
VELASQUEZ, Ramon Ignacio—95, 177
VENADO Air Taxi (Colombian airlines)—95
VENEZUELA—69
    Canal zone dispute—145-6. Civil unrest & violence—175, 180-4.
    Colombia immigration—95, 175-6.
    Cuban exiles & terrorism—110
    Economy—3, 17, 177-9
    Foreign relations & trade—26, 119, 171, 175-6; U.S.—5, 19, 175; bribery scandals—18, 177-9
    Human rights violations—70-3, 180-1
    Nationalization—177-80
    Oil—176
    Population—95
VERA Serafin, Aldo—111
VESCO, Robert L.—187
VIASA (airlines)—179
VIDELA, Jorge Rafael—11, 23, 27, 31-2, 35, 37
VIERA Trejo, Bernardo—183
VILAS, Gen. Abdel—35, 37
VILLALON, Hector—27
VILLEGAS, Veha—167
VILLONE, Carlos—31, 35
VIOLA, Gen. Roberto—37
VIRGO, Robert—186
VOTTERO, Thomas—24

W

WALDHEIM, Kurt—125
WAQUIM, Gloria—28
WAQUIM, Norma—28

INDEX

WARREN Commission—107-8
WEEKS, Rev. James Martin—40-1, 44
WEIBEL, Jose—72
WEST Germany—84, 93
WHITECROSS, Cristiana—42
WHITECROSS, Richard—42
WHITFIELD, Chester Wallace—185
WILLIAMS, Eric—198-9
WILLIAMSON, Colin—197
WILLS, Frederick—191
WIRETAPPING—165-6
WOLFF, Rep. Lester L. (D, N.Y.)—21, 94, 135-6
WOODWARD, Robert F.—71
WORKERS' Power (Argentine guerrilla group)—42
WORLD Bank (International Bank for Reconstruction & Development)—52-3, 85, 153, 179

WORLD Council of Churches—4

Y

YPFB (Bolivian state oil company)—53
YUGOSLAVIA—106

Z

ZALAQUETT, Jose—10-1, 74
ZARLENCA, Dr. Jorge—30
ZENTENO Anaya, Joaquin—49
ZIMMERMAN, Augusto—158
ZINC—155
ZIONIST Resolution—126-7, 132, 138, 190
ZUBIA, Eduardo—172
ZUFRIATEGUI, Carlos—170

Facts on File Reference Books on Contemporary Issues

WESTERN HEMISPHERE

Argentina & Peron / 1970-75
Book chronicles the events of Juan Peron's brief second period as president. It records the maneuverings that resulted in his return to Argentina, his election, his policies, his death and his widow's elevation to the presidency. $8.95.

Chile & Allende
The election of Allende as Chile's president, the domestic and international developments of the following four years and the Marxist leader's downfall. It clarifies events in Chile as well as the political struggle between Left and Right throughout Latin America. $8.95.

Canada & the French
This book records the events of the 1960s and early 1970s, as Canada's two cultural communities confront each other over the issue of fair treatment for French Canadians. $10.95.

Latin America / 1976
The fifth annual volume in this Facts On File series records major economic and political events in Latin America and the Caribbean during 1976. $10.95. Back volumes available.

FOREIGN AFFAIRS AND INTERNATIONAL PROBLEMS

Kissinger & Detente
Steps that led to rapprochement with Moscow and Peking and the developments that followed. Charges that the detente is superficial—failing to deal with major problems and papering over underlying conflicts—are also covered in detail. $9.95.

Political Terrorism
Records the full story of such developments as the "Munich massacre" at the 1972 Olympics and the kidnapping of Patricia Hearst. It examines the activities of groups as diverse as al Fatah, the Weathermen, the Tupamaros and Canada's French separatists. $11.95.

World Food Crisis / 1970-75
Evidence for and against fears that the world's population will eventually exceed food supply. $8.95.

South Africa & Apartheid / 1944-74
The origin, development and effects of South Africa's racial policies are examined in detail. $9.95.

Energy Crisis/1969-75
Two-Volume Set
A complete and detailed survey tracing the development of the energy crisis. Volume 1 covers the discovery and exploitation of new petroleum fields, the price structure of energy resources, attempts to conserve dwindling reserves, experimental programs to develop new sources of energy, the Arab oil embargo, gasoline shortages and many other issues and developments.

The second volume studies the period following the Arab oil embargo of 1973. Volume 1, $10.95. Volume 2, $9.95. Two-Volume Set $18.95.

Portuguese Revolution/1974-76
The dissolution of the Portuguese empire, the overthrow of Portugal's civilian dictatorship and the contest between opposing forces following the 1974 revolt are covered in detail. $8.95.

South Vietnam/U.S.-Communist Confrontation in Southeast Asia/1961-73
7-Volume Set
A complete, unbiased, journalistic account of the U.S. involvement in the war in Indochina.
Complete 7-Volume Set $59.95

Israel & the Arabs/
Prelude to the Jewish State
A detailed, objective account of the creation of Israel. It covers the period from the end of World War II, when the survivors of the Nazi holocaust began to stream into Palestine, until Britain's Palestine mandate ended and the independent state of Israel was declared. $9.95.

Israel & the Arabs/The June 1967 War
A comprehensive review of the six-day war during which Israel defeated the Egyptian, Syrian and Jordanian armies to occupy Sinai, Golan and the West Bank. $9.95.

Israel & the Arabs/The October 1973 War
The indecisive but fierce fighting during the October 1973 war underscored the hazards for the combatants, the super-powers and the rest of the world of a continued armed confrontation in the Middle East. $8.95.
Complete 3-Volume Set/$24.95

GOVERNMENT AND POLITICS

The CIA & the Security Debate/1971-75 (Vol. 1)
The shadowy world of the CIA and other semi-secret federal agencies. Wiretapping, personal dossiers, IRS harassment of dissenters and military domestic spying are also covered in detail. $12.50

The CIA & the Security Debate/1975-76 (Vol. 2)

The Senate Report on the CIA, the Daniel Schorr affair, Attorney General Levi's attempts to investigate the FBI, CIA covert missions in Italy and Angola, the death of CIA station head Welch in Athens, President Ford's firing of Colby and reorganization of the CIA. $12.50.

Political Profiles Series
The Kennedy Years
The Johnson Years

Unique modern reference series based wholly on the biographical approach. For the first time, the biographies of more than 2500 of the most politically influential men and women of the postwar era will be available to readers in a systematic, convenient and permanent reference work.

Each profile is a rounded and readable portrait that gives shape and meaning to the public career of its subject, set against the major themes and events of a presidential administration.

The Kennedy Years, single volume $45.
The Johnson Years, single volume $45.
Set price for both books: $79.90.

Government & the Media in Conflict/1970-74

Chapters cover the Pentagon Papers case, the Nixon Administration's attacks on the media, the equal-time and fairness doctrines, judicial challenges to confidentiality and other major issues. Clothbound $11.50/Paperbound $4.50.

Watergate & the White House

This widely-acclaimed series offers an overall perspective on the Watergate story—from the break-in through the pardon.

Volume 1: June 1972-July 1973/$13.50
Volume 2: July-December 1973/$13.50
Volume 3: January-September 1974/$17.50
3-Volume Clothbound Set: $40.00
3-Volume Paperbound Set: $14.25

NEWS DICTIONARIES

News Dictionary/1976

The 13th edition in this annual series brings the key news stories of the year to your fingertips. Using its convenient alphabetical format, you can quickly research a news event as easily as looking up a word in Webster's. The 1976 News Dictionary is a complete, accurate and unbiased record of a dramatic year—its events, its personalities, and its history. Clothbound $11.95/Paperbound $6.95. Back volumes available.

All titles are clothbound unless otherwise specified. Prices subject to change without notice. Write for free catalog to:

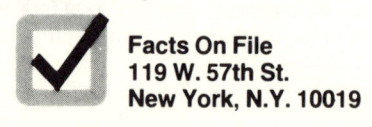

**Facts On File
119 W. 57th St.
New York, N.Y. 10019**